THE TRINITARIAN FAITH

The Niceno-Constantinopolitan Creed

WE
BELIEVE IN ONE GOD

the Father Almighty, Maker of heaven and earth, and of all things visible and invisible.

And in one Lord Jesus Christ, the only-begotten Son of God, begotten from his Father before all ages, Light from Light, true God from true God, begotten not made, of one substance with the Father, through whom all things were made: who for us men and for our salvation, came down from heaven, and was made flesh from the Holy Spirit and the Virgin Mary, and was made man, and was crucified for us under Pontius Pilate. He suffered and was buried, and the third day he rose again according to the Scriptures and ascended into heaven, and sits on the right hand of God the Father. And he shall come again in glory to judge both the living and the dead; his kingdom shall have no end.

And in the Holy Spirit, the Lord and Giver of life, who proceeds from the Father, who with the Father and the Son together is worshipped and glorified, who spoke by the prophets. And in one holy catholic and apostolic Church. We confess one baptism for the remission of sins: we look for the resurrection of the dead and the life of the world to come.

The Nicene Creed is the one fully ecumenically authorised Creed of Christendom. It was formulated by the Council of Nicaea in 325 A.D., definitively enlarged by the Council of Constantinople in 381 A.D., and confirmed by the Council of Chalcedon in 451 A.D.

The Icon of Saint Athanasius the Great by Ralles Kopsides of Athens was presented to me by A. J. Philippou in 1963.

THE TRINITARIAN FAITH

The Evangelical Theology of the
Ancient Catholic Church

THOMAS F. TORRANCE

T. & T. CLARK
EDINBURGH

Copyright © T. & T. Clark Ltd, 1988

Typeset by C. R. Barber & Partners (Highlands) Ltd,
Printed and bound in Great Britain by
Billing and Sons Limited, Worcester.

for

T. & T. CLARK LTD,
59 George Street, Edinburgh EH2 2LQ.

First printed 1988

British Library Cataloguing in Publication Data

Torrance, Thomas F. (Thomas Forsyth), 1913 –
  The Trinitarian faith.
  1. Nicene Creed – Expositions
  I. Title
  238′.142

ISBN 0 – 567 – 09483 – 9

To my sons
Thomas Spear Torrance
and
Iain Richard Torrance

Contents

Foreword

When I was invited by Dr James I. McCord, then President of Princeton Theological Seminary, to deliver the Warfield Lectures for 1981, it seemed right to devote them to the theology of the Nicene-Constantinopolitan Creed formulated sixteen hundred years earlier in 381 A.D. This Creed was developed in two stages, at the Council of Nicaea in 325 when the basic work was done, and at the Council of Constantinople in 381 when it was enlarged to cope with fuller understanding of evangelical issues clarified in the fifty years following Nicaea.

The principal themes I chose for these lectures were: the knowledge of God the Father, the Creator of heaven and earth and of all things visible and invisible, the Lord Jesus Christ his incarnate Son and his saving work for mankind, the Holy Spirit the Lord and Giver of Life who proceeds from the Father, and the One Holy Catholic and Apostolic Church. My intention was to offer an interpretation of them in the light of the Church fathers who had been most deeply involved in the elucidation of 'the evangelical and apostolic faith' during the fourth century, in the hope that it might form a useful hand-book for students. In the course of preparing it for publication I re-read the works of the great fathers for each chapter, finding that the book had to be rather larger than I had planned, both in order to do justice to their theology and to provide ample evidence for my attempt to offer a full and consistent presentation of it. There is some overlap in the material content of different chapters, together with repetition of argument and citation, which I found to be convenient as well as inevitable in an integrated presentation of successive themes, for in the coherent character of Nicene theology each doctrine is implicated in and deeply affects the others. The first and last chapters have been added, to present the general perspective of faith and devotion within which all

Nicene and Constantinopolitan theology must surely be understood, and to give definite expression to the trinitarian convictions of the Church that had been implicit in its faith from the beginning but became more and more explicit with the clarification of the doctrine of the Holy Spirit in the course of theological debate preceding and during the Council of Constantinople. The first chapter on 'Faith and Godliness' has been adapted from my contribution to the Festschrift for Archbishop Methodios of Thyateira and Great Britain, edited by Dr George D. Dragas, and presented in 1985.

Throughout this volume I have tried to let the patristic theologians concerned, almost entirely from the Greek East, speak for themselves, without the intrusion of material derived from later sources. I have deliberately refrained from discussing the interpretation of modern authors, while such references to their works as I have made are mostly of an incidental kind. It has been a principal concern of mine in each chapter to bring to light the inner theological connections which gave coherent structure to the classical theology of the ancient Catholic Church, particularly as it was brought to formulation during the fourth century. Problems arose within this development which had to do with significant differences in emphasis between the Athanasian and the Cappadocian traditions, but the general consensus that was reached at the Council of Constantinople in 381 A.D. has ever since provided the Church in East and West, Catholic and Evangelical alike, with its one authentically ecumenical Confession of Faith.

The Nicene-Constantinopolitan Creed was essentially the fruit of Eastern Catholic theology. It represents the work of the Greek fathers in reaching careful expression of crucial points in the Gospel where it had been seriously misunderstood and distorted under the influence of dualist ways of thought deriving from Hellenism and Hellenised Judaism. The central place accorded to Jesus Christ in the faith of the Church called for a clear answer to the question as to whether he was himself Lord and God or only a created intermediary between God and man. Where was the line of demarcation between God and the creature to be drawn, between God the Father and Jesus Christ, or between Jesus Christ the incarnate Son of God and the world?

That was the basic question faced by the Nicene fathers, and answered in their unqualified acknowledgment of the Deity of Jesus Christ as Lord and Saviour. But the same question was raised again after Nicaea in respect of the Holy Spirit. Is the Holy Spirit to be worshipped along with the Father and the Son as himself God, and having his being with the Son on the divine side of that absolute distinction between the Creator and the creature, or is he to be thought of in terms of the immanent forms of rationality in the created universe? The Nicene declaration of belief in the Holy Spirit was strengthened to make clear that he is the Lord and Giver of life and in no sense a creature.

The basic decision taken at Nicaea made it clear that the eternal relation between the Father and the Son in the Godhead was regarded in the Church as the supreme truth upon which everything else in the Gospel depends. Jesus Christ is himself the content of God's unique self-revelation to mankind. It is on the ground of what God has actually revealed of his own nature in him as his only begotten Son that everything else to be known of God and of his relation to the world and human beings is to be understood. It is only when we know God the Father in and through his Son who belongs to his own being as God that we may know him in any true and accurate way, that is, know God strictly in accordance with his divine nature. In order to know him in that way, however, we must enter into an intimate and saving relationship with him in Jesus Christ his incarnate Son, for it is only through reconciliation to God by the blood of Christ that we may draw near to him and have access to him. The Lord Jesus Christ, the crucified and risen Son of God, is the Way, the Truth and the Life, apart from whom no one has access to the Father. His incarnate reality has been made the supreme Principle of all God's ways and works within the order of creation and redemption alike, and the controlling Principle of all our understanding of them. Thus the very essence of the Gospel and the whole of the Christian Faith depend on the centrality and primacy of the relation in being and agency between Jesus Christ and God the Father.

Following upon the Council of Nicaea, it became clear through further controversy that the reality of the full humanity of Christ must be stressed as much as the reality of his Deity. If in Jesus Christ God did not really become one with us sinful men and women through taking our actual human nature upon himself, then all that Christ was and did on our behalf was finally empty of saving content. If in being made flesh the Son of God had not assumed a fully human soul and mind, as well as body, then we are unredeemed and unsaved in the rational essence and wholeness of our human being. However, if the incarnation did not mean that the Son of God came into man, in a dualist sort of way, but that he came among us *as man*, then it is as such in the integrity of his human as well as his divine nature that Jesus Christ is the one Mediator between God and man. In that event the historical human agency of Jesus belongs to the very heart of our salvation. Through identifying himself completely with us on our side of the relation between man and God, in order to act in our place, in our stead and on our behalf, Jesus Christ ministers not only the things of God to man but the things of man to God. The *vicarious humanity* of Christ thus became integral to the doctrine of the 'atoning exchange' effected by him and in him between God and man. Hence the Gospel of the reconciliation of man with God has to be understood not just in terms of God's mighty act of salvation upon our humanity, but in terms of its actualisation within the depths of our human existence in the perfecting and presenting in and through Jesus of our response in faith and obedience, in love and worship, to God the Father. For us to share in the worship of the Father through, with and in Jesus Christ, belongs to the essence of our reconciliation to God, and is of the very substance of the Gospel.

If this is the case, then the stress must also be laid on the teaching of the New Testament that it is in one Spirit as well as through the only begotton Son that we are given access to God the Father. It is only through the communion of the Holy Spirit, the Spirit of the Father and of the Son, that we may share in the saving, regenerating and sanctifying work in the life, death and resurrection of the Lord Jesus Christ, and thus share in his eternal offering of himself, and of us as redeemed and consecrated in him, to God the Father. However, if the Holy Spirit who unites us to Christ is no more than a creaturely being himself, and not fully and perfectly divine, then our participation in Christ and all he has done and continues to do for us, has no divine efficacy and is empty of any saving reality. Moreover, if the Spirit of the Father and of the Son is not divine then even the Deity of the Father and of the Son is called in question, and with it the validity of baptism in the name of the Father and of the Son and of the Holy Spirit and of our membership in the One Holy Catholic and Apostolic Church as the Body of Christ. Hence when movements of thought questioning the Deity of the Holy Spirit arose, the Church assembling once again in Ecumenical Council at Constantinople not only reinforced the Creed of Nicaea but wrote into it additional clauses in affirmation of belief in the Holy Spirit parallel to its declared belief in the Deity of Jesus Christ the incarnate Son of God.

It became indubitably clear to the Church in the fourth century that it is only when the Gospel is understood in this fully trinitarian way that we can really appreciate the New Testament teaching about Jesus Christ and the Holy Spirit, and appreciate the essential nature of salvation, prayer and worship. The Nicene-Constantinopolitan Creed was thus essentially trinitarian. The central hinge upon which the whole Confession of Faith turned was the declaration of the oneness in being between Jesus Christ and God the Father. In the Gospel God has revealed himself to us as Father, Son and Holy Spirit, but in such a way that we know that he is in himself what he is toward us in his saving acts in history, eternally Father, Son and Holy Spirit in his one divine being, and that what he is eternally in himself as Father, Son and Holy Spirit, he is in his activity toward us through the Son and in the Spirit. The general formula which the Nicene and post-Nicene fathers employed to speak of the Triune God and his one activity was *from the Father, through the Son and in the Holy Spirit*, in respect of God-manward relations; and *in the Spirit, through the Son and to the Father*, in respect of man-Godward relations. Since all this would fall to pieces in the faith of the Church if the divine nature of the Son and of the Spirit were brought into question, we can understand the determination of Church fathers at the Councils of Nicaea and Constantinople to clarify and secure the grounding of Christian belief in the indivisible relations of the Father, Son and Holy

Spirit in the Triunity of God.

It may be convenient for readers of this work if at this point some guide is offered to the contents of the chapters that follow.

In the first chapter an account is offered of the open-textured framework of faith and godliness which, together with the rule of truth inherited from the apostolic foundation of the Church, guided regular interpretation of the Holy Scriptures and fostered in its ministers and theologians a distinctive way of thinking and speaking about God in accordance with the nature of his revealing and saving acts in Jesus Christ. From the start the theology of the Church took the form, not of a set of abstract propositions, but of embodied truth in which the knowing and worshipping of God and the daily obedience of faith and life interpenetrated each other. The focus of attention is directed particularly to Irenaeus and Origen who in different ways left a decisive impact on the pre-Nicene Church. Irenaeus had made clear that it is only within the framework of the Faith entrusted to the Church and incorporated in the apostolic tradition as a rejuvenating deposit, that the Holy Scriptures may be faithfully interpreted and appropriated as the saving truth of the Gospel. Origen had laid great emphasis upon the need to think worthily and reverently of God, which required spiritual training in godliness in the ability to interpret the statements of the Old and New Testament Scriptures in the light of the truths to which they refer beyond themselves. That was the general matrix of faith and piety within which there took shape the theological intuition and godly judgment upon which the Nicene fathers relied in their epoch-making Confession of Faith.

The second and the third chapters are devoted to the doctrine of God, and to our knowledge of him as Father and Creator. The basic clue to the understanding of the Nicene approach is taken from Athanasius: 'It is more pious and more accurate to signify God from the Son and call him Father, than to name him from his works and call him Unoriginate'. To know God in any precise way we must know him in accordance with his nature, as he has revealed himself – that is, in Jesus Christ his incarnate Son in whom he has communicated not just something about himself but his very Self. Jesus Christ does not reveal the Father by being Father but by being Son of the Father, and it is through

Christ in the one Spirit whom he mediates that we are given access to God as he really is in himself. In contrast with Judaism and its stress on the unnameability of God, the Christian Faith is concerned with God as he has named himself in Jesus Christ, and incarnated in him his own Word, so that in Christ we know God as he is in his own inner being, as Father, Son and Holy Spirit. Jesus Christ is the *arche* (ἀρχή), the Origin or Principle, of all our knowledge of God, and of what he has done and continues to do in the universe, so that it is in terms of the relation of Jesus the incarnate Son to the Father, that we have to work out a Christian understanding of the creation. It is the Fatherhood of God, revealed in the Son, that determines how we are to understand God as Almighty Creator, and not the other way round. It was through thinking out the inner relation of the incarnation to the creation that early Christian theology so transformed the foundations of Greek philosophy, science and culture, that it laid the original basis on which the great enterprise of empirico-theoretical science now rests.

The fourth and fifth chapters are devoted to Christology and Soteriology. If the Father-Son relationship occupies a place of primacy and centrality in the Christian understanding of God and the world, and of the Gospel itself, everything depends on precisely how we understand the relation of Jesus Christ, the incarnate Son of God, to the Father. Is Jesus Christ 'of' God in the same way that the universe is 'of' God, as created by him and unceasingly dependent on him for its existence and continued being? Did the Son of God himself come into being through an act of the will of God or was he eternally in the being of God as Son of the Father, of the same being and nature as God, and therefore not like a creature which is of a different being and nature from God? The Nicene and Constantinopolitan fathers realised that if they allowed the dualist ways of thought in the prevailing culture to cut the bond of being between Christ and God the Father, then the whole substance and heart of the Christian Gospel would be lost. If what Christ does, for example, in forgiving our sins, is not what God does, then it is not finally valid. If God himself has not come to be one with us in the incarnation, then the love of God finally falls short of coming all the way to be one with us, and is not ultimately love.

If it was not God himself incarnate who suffered for us on the cross in making atonement, then the sacrifice of Christ has no ultimate and final validity, and we are still in our sins. If Jesus Christ and God are not of one and the same being, then we really do not know God, for he is some hidden inscrutable Deity behind the back of Jesus, of whom we can only be terrified – and then the final judgment of the world will be a judgment apart from and without respect to Jesus Christ and his forgiving love and atoning sacrifice. Cut the bond in being between Jesus Christ and God, and the Gospel message becomes an empty mockery. But if Jesus Christ is of one and the same being with God, then all that Jesus said and did on our behalf, has staggering significance for us and the whole creation. But in this case it is essential to realise that Jesus Christ the Son of God is also man, of one and the same being and nature as we are. If he is not really man, then the great bridge which God has thrown across the gulf between himself and us, has no foundation on our side of that gulf. Jesus Christ, to be Mediator in the proper sense, must be wholly and fully man as well as God. Hence the Creed stresses the stark reality and actuality of his humanity: it was for our sakes that God became man, for us and for our salvation, so that it is from a soteriological perspective that we must seek to understand the human agency and life of Jesus Christ. He came to take our place, in all our human, earthly life and activity, in order that we may have his place as God's beloved children, in all our human and earthly life and activity, sharing with Jesus in the communion of God's own life and love as Father, Son and Holy Spirit.

The sixth and seventh chapters are devoted to the doctrines of the Holy Spirit and of the one Church as the Body of Christ. Since it was the Word or Son of God, not the Father or the Spirit, who became incarnate, it is only through the Son that we have knowledge of the Spirit as well as knowledge of the Father. Thus our knowledge of the Spirit like our knowledge of the Father is taken from and controlled by our knowledge of the Son. As such the doctrine of the Spirit qualifies and completes the doctrine of the Father and the Son, and deepens it in our knowledge of the Holy Trinity. Following upon the Council of Nicaea it became widely evident that denial of the Deity of the

Son entailed denial of the Deity of the Spirit, so that the Nicene doctrine of the *homoousion* or *consubstantiality* of the Son called for a corresponding formulation of the doctrine of the Spirit, and that is what was given succinct credal expression at the Council of Constantinople. The doctrine of the Spirit was developed, however, not only from biblical statements or from doxological formulae, but from the essential structure of knowledge of God grounded in his own self-communication through the Son and in the unity of the Spirit. The confession of faith in the Holy Spirit emphasises the divine nature of the Spirit, and the fact that the presence of the Spirit is the presence of God in his own eternal being and reality as God. At the same time the presence of God in his mode of being as Spirit confronts us with the ineffability and sublime majesty of God, yet not in such a way that God overwhelms us by the presence of his being, for this is a presence of God that creates and sustains being and life, and acts upon us in a quiet and gentle self-effacing way which does not direct attention to himself but which reveals the Father in the Son and the Son in the Father. Through the incarnation and Pentecost the Holy Spirit comes to us from the inner communion of the Father, Son and Holy Spirit, creates union and communion between us and the Holy Trinity. In other words, the Spirit creates not only personal union but corporate communion between us and Christ and through Christ with the Holy Trinity, so that it is the Holy Spirit who creates and sustains the being and life of the Church, uniting the Church to Christ as his one Body. Regarded in this way, the doctrine of the Church is a function of the doctrine of the Spirit who proceeds from the Father through the Son, for it is in him and through the Son that we are brought near to God and are given to share in his divine life, light and love. Just as we have to regard the incarnation of the Son and Word of God as a movement of the saving love of God which penetrates into the ontological depths of our creaturely existence in order to redeem us, so we must regard the activity of the Holy Spirit as actualising our union and communion with God through Christ in the actual structure of our human, personal and social being. The Church as the Body of Christ is not to be regarded as merely a figurative expression, but as expressing an ontological reality within humanity, which affects the whole of the human race. The Church is thus the One, Holy, Catholic and Apostolic Church which took its rise from the pouring out of the Holy Spirit at Pentecost and took its shape from the foundation laid by Christ once for all upon his apostles, and as such reaches throughout all peoples and all ages to the consummation of Christ's Kingdom.

In the final chapter an attempt is made to draw together the various emphases within the Church as they reached a general consensus on the doctrine of the Holy Trinity as 'one Being, three Persons'. Attention is first given to Athanasius' conception of the Triunity of God as Trinity in Unity and Unity in Trinity. For him theology in its deepest sense as the knowledge and worship of God was identified with the doctrine of the Holy Trinity. The key to the Triunity of God he found in the Nicene *homoousion* (ὁμοούσιον) which pointed to eternal consubstantial relations within the Trinity and thus to the consubstantiality of the Trinity as a whole. It was he who developed the doctrine of completely interpenetrating or co-indwelling relations between the Father, the Son and the Holy Spirit, which was later called the doctrine of divine coinherence. This carried with it a revised conception of *ousia* (οὐσία) as being considered in its internal relations, and of *hypostasis* (ὑπόστασις) as being considered in its objective inter-relations. It was in that sense that he accepted the formula 'one Being, three Persons', which carried with it a doctrine of the *Monarchia* (Μοναρχία) as identical with the one indivisible being of the Holy Trinity. Attention is then given to the Cappadocian contribution to the doctrine of the Trinity, notably to the greater emphasis given by Basil to the distinguishing properties of the three divine Persons, and his attempt to preserve the unity of the Trinity by referring the particular modes of being of the Son and the Spirit to the Person of the Father, which operated with an abstract generic notion of God's being. The reservations of Gregory Nazianzen about the subordinationist implications of this approach led him to move back closer to Athanasius, but with a doctrine of eternally subsistent relations within the Holy Trinity which deepened and strengthened the Athanasian conception of the Triunity and Monarchy of God. While

Didymus, who stood closer to Basil, moved away from Nicene formulation, Epiphanius offered a powerful development of that Athanasian doctrine of the Trinity in Unity and the Unity in Trinity, or the consubstantial unity of three perfect co-equal enhypostatic Persons in the one indivisible being of the Godhead. It was this Athanasian and Epiphanian doctrine of God that provided the foundation on which the Nicene-Constantinopolitan understanding of the Holy Spirit and the Triunity of God was brought to firm theological expression.

I am very conscious of the great tradition in Patristic scholarship which I have enjoyed for many years, and of my indebtedness to those who have made the original texts so readily available. I have in mind the immense work of J. P. Migne, *Patrologia, Series Graeca et Series Latina*; *Die griechischen christlichen Schriftsteller der ersten drei Jahrhunderte* of the Berlin Academy; and not least the new *Library of Greek Fathers and Ecclesiastical Writers* still in process of being published in Athens which is very helpful. I have gratefully availed myself of translations in the *Ante-Nicene Christian Library*, *A Select Library of Nicene and Post-Nicene Fathers*, and C. R. B. Shapland, *The Letters of St Athanasius Concerning the Holy Spirit*, but have often revised or given a new rendering of passages cited.

I am more grateful than I can say for the friendship and hospitality of Dr James I. McCord extended to me and my wife over many years when he was President of Princeton Theological Seminary and more recently in his capacity as Chancellor of the Center of Theological Inquiry in Princeton. Once again I am happily indebted to my two sons, Dr Thomas S. Torrance of the University of Aberdeen, and the Rev Dr Iain R. Torrance, and his wife Morag, of The Queen's College, Birmingham, for generous help in the handling of computer software, and in the correction of proofs. I am also much indebted to my former student, the Very Rev Dr George D. Dragas of the University of Durham for additional assistance with the proofing of Greek citations.

Trinity, Edinburgh, 1987.

I

Faith and Godliness

Thus believes the Catholic Church: 'We believe ...'

The Council of Nicaea of 325 A.D. has a unique place in the history of the Christian Church as 'the Great and Holy Synod' or 'the Great Ecumenical Synod', to which all subsequent Ecumenical Councils looked back as their normative basis. The Creed framed by the fathers at Nicaea secured the apostolic and catholic faith against disrupting distortions of the Gospel in a decisive form that eventually commanded and unified the mind of the whole Church, grounding it unambiguously in the self-revelation of God the Father through Jesus Christ his Son and in one Spirit.[1] The essential connections of the Gospel and the inherent unity and structure of 'the faith which was once for all delivered to the saints'[2] were brought to light in such a simple and succinct way that what had taken place at Nicaea was afterwards regarded with awe as a work of the Holy Spirit, all the more astonishing in view of the troublesome diversity of opinion and contradictory credal formulae current at the time. As the century wore on, and the Church survived fierce heretical attacks that threatened the very substance of the evangelical message with which it had been entrusted, tradition increasingly honoured the Nicene Creed as 'an unalterable determination (*imperturbata constitutio*) of the Church', or a great

[1] Eph. 2:18.
[2] Jude 3.

13

irreversible event in the life of the Church,[3] second only to the one foundation which Christ himself had laid in the apostles and prophets,[4] but serving it, building on it, and in some sense sharing in its unrepeatable character. Gregory Nazianzen, who as the resident Archbishop presided over the opening session of the Council of Constantinople in 381, wrote to Cledonius, a presbyter of Nazianzus: 'We for our part never esteemed and can never esteem any doctrine preferable to the faith of the holy fathers who assembled at Nicaea to destroy the Arian Heresy. We adhere with God's help, and shall adhere, to this faith, supplementing gaps which they left concerning the Holy Spirit.'[5]

Gregory Nazianzen was also expressing the prevailing tradition when in his 'Oration on Athanasius the Great' he spoke of 'the Holy Synod of Nicaea, the gathering of the three hundred and eighteen chosen men', as 'united by the Holy Spirit'.[6] But he was also representative of many others in according to Athanasius the crucial role in the deliberations of the Council: 'Though not yet ranked among the bishops, he held first rank among the members of the Council, for preference was given to excellence as much as to office. As 'man of God and a mighty trumpet of truth' Athanasius 'both happily preserved the unity which belongs to the Godhead, and devoutly taught the Trinity which consists in personal relations, neither confounding the three Persons in the Unity, nor dividing the being among the three Persons, but remaining within the bounds of piety by avoiding excessive inclination or opposition to either side.'[7]

As Athanasius himself regarded the Council of Nicaea, however, the fathers of Nicaea did nothing new, but breathing the spirit of Scripture confessed 'the divine and apostolic faith'

---

[3]Hilary, *Con. Const.*, 27. See also Athanasius, *De syn.*, 9; *Ad Ant.*, 15; *Ad Afr.*, 10; *Ep.*, 55, 56; Basil, *Ep.*, 125.1; 127.2; 140.2; 159.1; 204.6; 251.4; Theodoret, *Hist. eccl.*, 2.15, 18.

[4]1 Cor. 3:10–11; Eph. 2:20.

[5]Gregory Naz., *Ep. ad Cled.*, 102.

[6]Gregory Naz., *Or.*, 21.14; *Ep. ad Cled.*, 102.1; Theodoret, *Hist. eccl.*, 2.15; Socrates, *Hist. eccl.*, 1.9; Eusebius, *Vita Const.*, 3.20.

[7]Gregory Naz., *Or.*, 21.13, 14; cf. also 19.33–35.

so accurately that many years later he could write to the bishops of Africa: 'The Word of the Lord which came through the Ecumenical Synod at Nicaea, abides for ever.'[8] By that he did not mean that any new revelation from God had been given to the bishops in Council at Nicaea, but only that they had been instrumental under God, in handing on in a true and faithful way the very Word of God which they themselves had received from the apostles' teaching in Holy Scripture regarding God the Father, the Son and the Holy Spirit. In fact for Athanasius apostolic tradition and the teaching given by the apostles in Holy Scripture were one and the same – there were no other written or unwritten traditions of truth, but only the one tradition comprised in the canonical Scriptures, and it was from those Scriptures and upon the truth they mediated that the true Faith of the Church was derived and was as such to be guarded and handed on again.[9] That was how he understood the work of the fathers at the Ecumenical Council. Thus, in his Synodical Letter to the Bishops of Africa he wrote 'concerning the sound faith which Christ gave us, the apostles proclaimed, and the fathers, who assembled at Nicaea from all over this world of ours, have handed down.'[10] When the traditional apostolic doctrine of the Holy Spirit had been questioned, he insisted that they must 'consider the very tradition, teaching and faith of the Catholic Church from the beginning, which the Lord gave, the apostles proclaimed and the fathers kept'; and speaking for himself he could say: 'In accordance with the apostolic faith delivered to us by tradition from the fathers, I have delivered the tradition, without inventing anything extraneous to it. What I learned, that I have inscribed in conformity with the Holy Scriptures.'[11] What was important was a devout, exact rendering of the Holy Scriptures and a faithful handling of the tradition.[12]

[8] Athanasius, *Ad Afr.*, 1f; cf. 4–6, 9–11; *De syn.*, 5f, 9, 43; *Ad Adel.*, 6; *Ad Ser.*, 1.28, 33; *Ep.* 55 & 56.
[9] Athanasius, *Ad Adel.*, 6; cf. *Ep.*, 2.6f; 39.1–7.
[10] Athanasius, *Ad Afr.*, 1.
[11] Athanasius, *Ad Ser.*, 1.28, 33.
[12] Athanasius, *De decr.*, 4f, 18ff, 31ff; *Con. Ar.*, 1.8, 10; 2.33f, 40; *De syn.*, 3, 6, 7, 33f, 39ff, 45f; *Ad Afr.*, 4ff; *Ep.*, 2.4–7, 59; *Ad Epict.*, 3; cf. also *Con. gent.*, 1; *De inc.*, 5.

Athanasius referred to the Nicene Creed fairly regularly as *The Faith Confessed by the Fathers at Nicaea*, according to the divine Scriptures and in the unimpaired tradition of the Church, which he claimed to be identical with 'the faith received from our Saviour through his apostles'. The drawing up of the Creed was essentially a *godly* or *devout* act of *faith* made by the whole Ecumenical Council 'as in the presence of God'.[13] There had been two reasons for convening the Council: to reach universal agreement regarding the day for celebrating Easter, and to pronounce on the Arian heresy which had been disturbing the harmony of the Church. However, as Athanasius pointed out, the kind of decision which the Council took in each case was very different. 'Concerning Easter they wrote: "It seemed good as follows", for it did then seem good that there should be general compliance; but about the faith they did not write, "It seemed good", but "Thus believes the Catholic Church"; and thereupon they confessed how they believed, in order to show that their own views were not novel, but apostolical; and what they wrote was no discovery of their own, but is the same as was taught by the apostles.'[14] Moreover, 'they expressed this teaching so exactly that people reading their words honestly cannot but be directed by them back to the devotion towards Christ (εἰς Χριστὸν εὐσέβειαν) announced in divine Scripture.'[15] That is to say, the Nicene Creed has to be understood as a *kerygmatic* formulation of the faith in the simple first principles of the Gospel, for the faith once for all delivered to the Church can be handed on only *by faith*, from faith to faith.[16] Athanasius evidently thought of the Nicene Council as fulfilling through its confession of faith, but in a very concise and ecumenically authoritative way, the kind of function which he had envisaged for his own pre-Nicene account of 'the capital point of the faith' (κεφάλαιον τῆς πίστεως), namely, the saving

---

[13] Athanasius, *Ap. con. Ar.*, 23f; *Ad Ep. Aeg.*, 5, 18, 20, 21; *De syn.*, 5; *Ad Ant.*, 3.5; *Ad Afr.*, 10f; *Ep.*, 51; 55; 56.1–4; 59.1; 61.5; 62.

[14] Athanasius, *De syn.*, 5; cf. 3f.

[15] Athanasius, *De syn.*, 6; cf. *De decr.*, 18–22; 31f.

[16] Athanasius, *Ad Ser.*, 1.17, 20; *De vita Ant.*, 16, 77–80, etc.

work of the incarnate Son of God,[17] in connection with the study of the Holy Scriptures and a deeper understanding of its message.[18]

An outstanding mark of the Nicene approach was its association of faith with 'piety' or 'godliness' (εὐσέβεια or θεοσέβεια), that is, with a mode of worship, behaviour and thought that was devout and worthy of God the Father, the Son and the Holy Spirit. This was a distinctively Christian way of life in which the seal of the Holy Trinity was indelibly stamped upon the mind (διάνοια or φρόνημα) of the Church. Godliness and theology, worship and faith, went inseparably together, with constant attention given to reverent interpretation of the Holy Scriptures, reverent use of the reason, and reverent ways of argument, in which there was no intrusion into the mystery of God or irreverent teaching about him. Even when theology was concerned with the inner trinitarian relations in God himself, the Church insisted on maintaining reserve and humility in its approach, conceptual formulation and language. All must be done before the face of divine majesty and glory, like the cherubim who cover their faces before the throne of God, in a holy way, appropriate to the transcendent holiness of God.

The Nicene interpretation of the apostolic message and the evangelical godliness of its confession of faith gave rise to a characteristic idiom which left an enduring mark upon the understanding of the Church. This became very evident at the Council of Constantinople in 381 at which the Nicene Creed was reaffirmed and finalised in the definitive form which made it the supreme Ecumenical Creed of Christendom. Nicene theology had not only gained an inner force and momentum of its own but had established itself in the evangelical foundations of the One Holy Catholic and Apostolic Church in such a way that it provided the basis on which Council after Council took its stand and completed its work in the centuries that followed, always with reference back 'to the Council of the three hundred and eighteen'.

[17] Athanasius, *De inc.*, 19.3; cf. *Exp. fidei*; *Con. Ar.*, 4.21; and Socrates, *Hist. eccl.*, 2.30.
[18] Athanasius, *De inc.*, 56.1.

Thus the Nicene Creed was regarded as a central and controlling factor in the on-going mission of the Church, to be treated both as an evangelical proclamation leading to faith in Christ and as an instructive formulation of the capital truths of the Gospel which could serve as an authoritative guide in reading and interpretation of the Holy Scriptures. In other words, in and through the Nicene Creed the Church was determined to defend and preserve the essential substance of the Faith committed to it as a sacred trust so that it could be transmitted in its evangelical integrity to others, and was thereby rendering an account to God of its stewardship in the mysteries of God.[19] That was the intention of the Church reflected in Athanasius' Letter to the Bishops of Africa: 'Let the Faith confessed by the fathers at Nicaea alone hold good among you ... in order that of us too the apostle may say: Now I praise you for remembering me in all things, and as I handed the traditions on to you, so do you hold them fast'.[20]

Under the rubric **We believe** the Catholic Church, meeting for the first time in Ecumenical Council at Nicaea in 325 A.D., made it clear that it was concerned to confess the fundamental truths of the Gospel calling for the commitment of faith, rather than laying down decrees (δόγματα) requiring compliance either like apostolic decisions[21] or like imperial edicts.[22] The Nicene fathers certainly offered some indication of how the terms they used were to be understood by referring to the 'boundaries' (ὁρισθέντα) of their confession of faith which could not be transgressed without lapses into heretical perversity or serious contradiction.[23] They also drew up a number of 'canons' or 'rules' to be observed in maintaining unity throughout the Church in its regular instruction and ministerial order.[24] However, these negative determinations

[19] I Cor. 4.1; Athanasius, *Ep. Enc.* I.
[20] I Cor. 11.12; Athanasius, *Ad Afr.*, 10.
[21] Cf. Acts 15.28f; 16.4.
[22] Cf. Luke, 2.1; Acts 17.7.
[23] Athanasius, *De decretis* – the traditional Latin title is a mistaken translation of ὁρισθέντα. Cf. *De syn.*, 5, and Hilary, *De Trin.*, 4.1–7.
[24] After the Council of Nicaea the term 'canon' tended to be used mainly with reference to ecclesiastical enactments or disciplinary decisions. Cf.

and formal rules were only appended to the credal statement and were not incorporated into the expression of the substance of the faith itself. Thus care was taken to preserve the character of the Nicene Creed as an evangelical declaration of saving faith which the Church found itself obliged to make under the constraint of divine truth mediated to it through the Holy Scriptures.

The primacy which the Nicene Council accorded to faith in this way is of immense significance. It represents the radical shift in people's understanding in the Church as they were grasped by the enlightening reality of the living God and were freed from imprisonment in the darkness of their own prejudices, baseless conjectures and fantasies, that is, a shift away from a centre of thinking in the in-turned human reason (ἐπίνοια) alienated from its intelligible ground in God, to a centre in God's revealing and reconciling activity in the incarnation of his Mind and Word (*Logos*) in Jesus Christ within the temporal and spatial structures of our creaturely world. That was the reason for the unshakeable confidence of the Church's faith in God, for it was caught up in the unswerving faithfulness and reliability of the love of God, which had laid hold upon it through 'the word of the truth of the Gospel',[25] and was steadfastly undergirded and supported by God himself. This primacy in the Nicene Creed accorded to faith reflects the settled patristic view of faith, not as a subjectively grounded but as an objectively grounded persuasion of the mind, supported beyond itself by the objective reality or ὑπόστασις of God's own being as he has made himself known to us in Jesus Christ. As Hilary expressed it, 'in faith a person takes his stand on the ground of God's own being (*in substantia dei*).'[26] That is how the Greek fathers regularly thought of scientific knowledge (ἐπιστήμη), as the standing or the establishment of the mind (διάνοια) upon objective reality and as certain or assured understanding. In biblical justification

---

Athanasius, *Ep. Enc.*, 1.6; *Ap. con. Ar.*, 25, 29, 31f; *Hist. Ar.*, 36, 51, where he refers to 'canons' derived from the apostles.
[25]Col. 1.5.
[26]Hilary, *De Trin.*, 1.18 – *in substantia* evidently refers to the ἐν τῇ ὑποστάσει of LXX Jer. 23.22; cf. 23.18.

for this view they frequently cited from the Septuagint, 'If you will not believe, you will not understand', or 'be established.'[27] They were thereby making the point that it is through faith that our minds are put in direct touch with reality independent of ourselves, for it is through faith that our minds assent to the inherent intelligibility of things, yield to their self-evidencing power, and are adapted to know them in their own nature (κατὰ φύσιν).[28] It is upon that kind of basic contact with reality that all sure knowledge rests and all genuine understanding is established, and upon it that we continue to rely in all further inquiry and all deepening of our understanding. While such a relation between faith and understanding applies to all scientific knowledge, it applies no less but all the more strictly to our knowledge of God who is the ultimate ground and source of all intelligibility and truth.[29] We do not seek to understand what we believe, Augustine used to say, but we believe that we may understand.[30]

It should now be evident that faith was not regarded in Nicene theology as some form of non-cognitive or non-conceptual relation to God, but was held to involve acts of recognition, apprehension and conception, of a very basic intuitive kind, in the responsible assent of the mind to truth inherent in God's self-revelation to mankind. Faith arises in us

[27]Is 7.9. Thus Irenaeus, *Dem.*, 3: 'And faith is produced by the truth; for faith rests on things that really are. For in things that are, as they are, we believe, and believing in things that are as they are, we keep firm confidence in them.' The translation, from the Armenian, is by J. Armitage Robinson, *St Irenaeus, The Demonstration of the Apostolic Preaching*, 1920, p. 72. Cf. also Clement of Alex., *Strom.*, 1.1; 2.2, 4; 4.21; Cyril of Jer., *Cat.*, 5.4, etc. The interpretation of Is. 9.9 in Greek plays upon the connection between ἐπιστήμη = standing on, and ὑπόστασις = being under, i.e. what is stood upon. See the explanation by Clement, *Strom.*, 4.21; and my discussion in *Oikonomia*, edit. by F. Christ, 1967, p. 224.

[28]See my *Theology in Reconciliation*, 1975, pp. 241f, 247ff, for an assessment of the use of *physis* (φύσις) in Alexandrian thought; and consult Archbishop Methodios Fouyas, *The Person of Jesus Christ in the Decisions of the Ecumenical Councils*, 1976, pp. 65ff.

[29]Cf. Hilary, *De Trin.*, especially books 1–4, for a remarkably perceptive account of theological epistemology.

[30]Augustine, *De Trin.*, 7.5; *In Jn. Ev.*, 27.9; 29.6; 40.9; *De lib. arb.*, 2.2.6; *De div. quaest.*, 48; *In Ps.*, 118, 18.3; *Ep.*, 120.1, 3, etc.

under the creative impact of the self-witness and self-interpretation of God in his Word, and in response to the claims of his divine reality upon us which we cannot reasonably or in good conscience resist.[31] It takes the form of listening obedience (ὑπακοὴ τῆς πίστεως)[32] to the address and call of God's Word, and the specific beliefs that are called forth from us like this entail at their heart a conceptual or epistemic consent (ἐπιστημονικὴ συγκατάθεσις) to divine truth and become interiorly locked into it.[33] It was indeed in just this way, Hilary pointed out, that faith and understanding were interlocked in the case of the apostles themselves when 'the truth which they heard for the first time clenched their certainty'.[34] When Hilary spoke of the apostles' confession that Christ is the Son of God as *the rock of faith* on which the Church was built,[35] he clearly understood it in an objective sense, for it is upon the truth of God confessed by the apostles, not upon their confession as such, that the Church is founded and on which it continues to rely in its own faith. It is to be granted, of course, that the apostolic confession of faith and their understanding of the truth are enshrined in the Holy Scriptures handed down to us from the apostles, so that in one sense it must be said that 'faith, and every part of it, is impressed on us by the evidence of the Gospels and the teaching of the apostles'.[36] In the ultimate analysis, however, we must learn from God himself what we are to think of him, for 'God cannot be apprehended except through himself.'[37] Our faith must repose upon the same truth which evoked the faith and understanding of the original apostles. This means that in our recourse to biblical statements we need to yield our minds to the direct constraint of the truth to which the

[31]Hilary, *De Trin.*, 1.18; 2.6f; 3.9f, 23; 4.14, 36; 5.20f; 6.13–16; 8.52.
[32]Rom. 1.5; 16.26.
[33]Cf. Clement Alex., *Strom.*, 2.2ff, 6, 11f; 8.3; and Augustine, *De spir. et litt.*, 21.54; 34.60.
[34]Hilary, *De Trin.*, 6.34; see also 4.6.14.
[35]Hilary, *De Trin.*, 6.36f; cf. 2.22f; 6.20f; and 'The Liturgy of St James', F. E. Brightman, *Liturgies of Eastern and Western Churches*, 1896, p. 54, where 'the catholic and apostolic Church' is likewise said to be founded upon 'the rock of faith'.
[36]Hilary, *De Trin.*, 2.22.
[37]Hilary, *De Trin.*, 5.20f.

Holy Scriptures bear witness independent of themselves. Biblical statements (*dicta*) are for their part to be interpreted in the light of the matters or realities (*res*) to which they refer and under the control of which they were made, and not the other way round, for they fulfil their divinely intended function when they mediate God's own self-witness and thus enable us to believe in God and think of him in the only way possible, in accordance with the way in which he actually presents himself to us.[38] Thus it becomes apparent that the primacy accorded to faith in our knowledge of God reflects the absolute priority of God over all human thought of him, and even over the human media which he has brought into the service of his self-revelation.[39]

Faith that arises in cognitive commitment to the compelling claims of God in Jesus Christ and is linked to the absolute priority of God over all our conceiving and speaking of him, is bound to manifest a two-fold character. On the one hand, faith appears determinate and bounded, under the control of the precise form God's truth has taken in the incarnation of his Word, but on the other hand, faith appears indeterminate and unbounded, through its correlation to the unbounded and immeasurable reality of God which transcends all finite comprehension. On the one hand, then, faith is characterised by a certainty of conviction which derives its force from the truth of God himself thrust upon it, but on the other hand, faith is characterised by an open, ever-expanding semantic focus which answers to the unfathomable mystery and inexhaustible nature of God.[40] That is evidently the double force of the **We believe** (πιστεύομεν) of the Nicene confession of faith in God, the Father, the Son and the Holy Spirit, which governs the way in which all its clauses are to be understood, namely, the *exclusiveness* and *open range* of belief.

In its commitment to one God the Father Almighty, the Nicene Creed is necessarily exclusive of belief in any other god

[38]Hilary, *De Trin.*, 4.14; 5.4, 7; 8.52.
[39]Hilary, *De Trin.*, 1.6, 16; 2.2ff, 12, 24ff, 52ff.
[40]Cf. Clement Alex., *Strom.*, 7.16: 'Knowledge of truth found among us Christians supplies, from what we already believe, faith for what has not yet been believed, faith which is, as it were, the substance of proof.'

than God the Father and of belief in any other revelation of this one God than his only begotten Son. This gives clear expression to the fundamental biblical asseveration that faith in the one God rules out the possibility of having any other gods and that faith in Jesus Christ as 'the Way, the Truth and the Life' excludes access to the Father by any other way than that provided by God himself in the incarnation of his Word in Jesus Christ, that is, in what Jesus Christ is in his own personal being. This would hardly be the case if faith were only subjectively grounded in some inner persuasion of the human mind, and not objectively grounded, as it is, in the universally binding reality of God embodied in Christ as his unique *self*-giving and *self*-communication to mankind as Lord and Saviour. In unconditional obedience to that normative divine revelation, Christian faith adopts an approach to God which sets aside any alternative approach, entails a judgment which excludes divergent belief, and endorses an affirmation of truth which thereby rejects other affirmations as false. The objective pole of the Church's faith is the truth of God which has seized hold of it in Christ and his Gospel and will not let it go, truth over which it has no control but truth which makes it free and establishes it in the love of God. Hence the Church cannot but confess its faith in God, before God, with an unreserved endorsement of belief in the truth of Christ and his Gospel, as the truth with which its very existence is bound up as the Church, the one Body of Christ, and as the saving grace of God which constitutes the very essence of its message and mission. That is surely what took place at the Council of Nicaea in the Ecumenical Confession of Faith promulgated by the fathers in the face of heretical denial of any ultimate oneness between God and his self-revelation in Jesus Christ. The Nicene Creed was a solemn corporate act of the Church in the presence of God, made with passionate commitment to the truth of divine revelation from the Father, through the Son and in the Holy Spirit, in the realisation that the very existence of the Christian Church and the validity of its evangelical message of divine salvation were at stake.

If there is no relation of oneness in being and agency between what God the Father is in himself and what he is toward us in the grace of the Lord Jesus Christ his Son, then the *kerygma* (κήρυγμα) of the Gospel is empty of saving content and the διδαχή of the apostles has no divine validity. But if the grace of the Lord Jesus Christ is the very grace of God himself, if in Jesus Christ the divine Gift and the Giver are one, then the Church has no option in fidelity to the Gospel but to commit itself to a positive affirmation of that grace which excludes any other possibility.[41] That was the critical issue which St Paul summoned the Galatian Church in the first century to face, namely, the threat to pervert the Gospel of Christ into 'another gospel' which was not a gospel, when he wrote: 'If anyone preaches to you a gospel contrary to that which you have received, let him be anathema.'[42] It was that apostolic example which the Nicene fathers followed in their own critical situation, when they appended a sentence to their confession anathematising those who taught that the Son of God was not eternally one with the Father but of 'a different hypostasis or being' from him, for the very substance of the catholic faith was thereby being denied.[43] Hence it came about that the Nicene Council expressed the fundamental beliefs which they found to be evangelically compelling in a Creed which has subsequently been universally acknowledged in the Church, and which by its intrinsic structure excludes alternative doctrine as arbitrary innovation in face of God's one self-revelation in Jesus Christ, i.e. as heretical deviation from the truth.[44]

There is another side to this picture, however, for while the Nicene Creed expresses what we are obliged to acknowledge within the general framework of the Church's commitment to the reality of God's self-revelation in Jesus Christ, it is all prefaced by *We believe* (πιστεύομεν). That is to say, everything that is affirmed in the Creed falls within the compass of faith pivoting upon the objective reality of God who infinitely transcends all that we can think or say about him. Precisely

[41] Athanasius, *Con. Ar.*, 4.12: 'Through the Son is given what is given; and there is nothing but the Father operates it through the Son; for thus grace is secure to him who receives it.'

[42] Gal. 1.9.

[43] Athanasius, *Ap. con. Ar.*, 49; *De decr.*, 2.5; *Ad Ep. Aeg.*, 2; *Ep.*, 2.6; Theodoret, *Hist. eccl.*, 1.3; 2.6; 5.10.

[44] Hilary, *De syn.*, 61–64.

because faith derives from and is grounded in the revelation of God in Jesus Christ which is identical with what God is eternally in his own being, it is *open* to whatever may yet be known through the Spirit of Christ who has been sent by the Father in the name of the Son to lead us into ever deeper understanding of the truth. By its very nature, then, Christian faith is locked into an inexhaustible depth of truth in God which always exceeds what we may grasp of its disclosure to us; but faith that is stretched out in this way indefinitely beyond itself is necessarily characterised by an *open range* in its focus (σκοπός) which cannot be foreshortened without being turned into something different.

The open range off faith was stressed by Athanasius and Hilary, as well as by other leading exponents of Nicene theology. Athanasius claimed that the more he pressed forward in seeking to apprehend God, the more he found knowledge of him outreaching his apprehension. He was unable to express in writing what he seemed to understand, and what he wrote fell far short even of the fleeting shadow of the truth in his mind.[45] The one fixed point, the object of faith, the scope of Holy Scripture, or of the truth in which we believe, is Jesus Christ himself. It is in and through God's unique self-revelation in him, that faith becomes firmly grounded in the truth of God's own being and provided with the normative control it needs in its correlation with what transcends the capacity of human comprehension.[46] It is faith of this kind that precedes and guides all theological inquiry and explanation, for it constitutes the sound cognitive base which gives force to all right argument.[47]

Hilary was no less emphatic about the fact that in faith we have to do with a way of apprehending God which does not confine him to the narrow limits of what we can conceive or express, but is constantly being expanded under the power of God to make himself known.[48] By its very nature, therefore, faith in God is characterised by a kind of 'infinity', for while

[45] Athanasius, *Ad mon.*, 1.1–3.
[46] Athanasius, *Con. Ar.*, 2.15; 3.28, 35, 58; cf. also my discussion of this in *Reality and Evangelical Theology*, 1982, pp. 106ff.
[47] Athanasius, *De vit. Ant.*, 77–80.
[48] Hilary, *De Trin.*, 1.7–16; 2.5–11; 3.1–6, 18–26.

God as a 'whole' eludes our comprehension, what he does allow us to apprehend of himself is inseparable from what he is as a 'whole' so that it breaks through the narrow confines of our grasp. This explains why in the very act of *apprehending* something of God, faith is bound to confess that it is incapable of *comprehending* him. Thus while God infinitely transcends the human mind he may nevertheless be known through a movement of faith in which it is opened toward the infinity and ineffability of God.[49] This means that through faith we are brought into contact with God in such a way that we are enabled to know more than we can bring into explicit forms of thought or speech, and that in and through faith theology is engaged in a fathomless inquiry, for the truth which we seek to know is so deep that we can never probe it to its end, let alone reduce our knowledge of it to adequate formulation.[50]

The epistemological implications of this open boundless range of faith were not lost to the Nicene theologians in their realisation that through faith theological inquiry is carried beyond the restricted scope of the ordinary reason defined by visible, tangible objects in created reality, and even beyond the explicit statements of Holy Scripture to the truth of God which they indicate independent of themselves. Thus the open range of faith gave rise to a perilous state of affairs in which the door appeared to be open to all manner of irrational and irreverent theorising.[51] For that very reason, however, the theologians of the Church cannot keep silence. With fear and trembling and in prayer to God, they must seek to express, as far as the slender resources of human language allow, the truth of God to which they are directed by Holy Scripture, if only to counter the damaging effect of an arbitrary and irreligious intrusion of creaturely modes of thought into the knowledge of God. That was precisely the situation in which the fathers of Nicaea found themselves when they felt forced to use the non-biblical term ὁμοούσιος in order to give clear and unambiguous expression to biblical and evangelical truth. Hilary had that critical event in mind in the following complaint. 'We are compelled by the

---

[49]Hilary, *De Trin.*, 1.8, 12; 2.5ff, 11.
[50]Hilary, *De syn.*, 65; *De Trin.*, 3.18; 10.53; 11.44–47; 12.24–37.
[51]Hilary, *De Trin.*, 2.1–5; 10.51–53.

error of heretics and blasphemers to do what is unlawful, to scale heights, to express things that are unutterable, to encroach on forbidden matters. And when we ought to fulfil the commandments through faith alone, adoring the Father, worshipping the Son together with him, rejoicing in the Holy Spirit, we are forced to stretch the feeble capacity of our language to give expression to indescribable realities. We are constrained by the error of others to err ourselves in the dangerous attempt to set forth in human speech what ought to be kept in the religious awe of our minds ... Their infidelity drags us into the dubious and dangerous position of having to make a definite statement beyond what heaven has prescribed about matters so sublime and so deeply hidden.'[52]

Quite evidently, affirmations of belief which we are obliged to make before God under the pressure of his divine revelation and its inherent truth, must remain open to whatever may yet be learned of God through that revelation. In so far as they are locked into that revelation and are controlled by it, they are put forward as articulating fundamental truth, even though they indicate far more than can be expressed at the time. Affirmations of faith of this kind have heuristic properties in virtue of which they prompt and guide further inquiry and deeper understanding. However, in virtue of their semantic reference away from themselves to the transcendent reality of the Holy Trinity which may be grasped only very impartially, they must be regarded as incomplete and inadequate in themselves and therefore as subject to revision in the light of deeper and fuller understanding of God's self-revelation. That is the profoundly objective yet open-textured character of the doctrinal statements asserted by the Council of Nicaea under the rubric **We believe.**

It is highly significant that, as Athanasius reported, 'The bishops who assembled at the Great Synod of Nicaea agreed, not without the will of God, that the decisions taken in one synod should be examined in another.'[53] That is to say, the Nicene fathers thereby gave synodal recognition to the point that by their intrinsic nature the affirmations of Nicaea indicated

[52]Hilary, *De Trin.*, 2.2, 5.
[53]Athanasius, *Ap. con. Ar.*, 22.

more than could be grasped at the time and therefore more than could be fully expressed and justified at the time. Although the canon of Nicaea to which Athanasius referred is not extant, it was certainly in accordance with it that subsequent Ecumenical Councils acted. After more than fifty years during which the Nicene Creed was subjected to detailed analysis, against and in support of it, it became so deeply and firmly established in the convictions of the Church that it was revised and finalised at the Council of Constantinople in 381 A.D. This in turn was reaffirmed at the Council of Ephesus in 431 A.D., when a canon was passed banning the use of any other Creed. However, it was evidently only at the Council of Chalcedon in 451 A.D. that complete ratification was formally given to the Nicene-Constantinopolitan Creed.[54]

Inextricably interwoven with faith, to which Nicene theology accorded primacy, there was another basic element which we must take into account, *godliness* (θεοσέβεια, εὐσέβεια), to which it also accorded primacy along with faith. Faith is itself an act of godliness in humble worship of God and adoring obedience to him, and godliness is a right relationship to God through faith which gives a distinctive slant to the mind and moulds life and thought in accordance with 'the word and truth of the Gospel'.[55] Godliness is thus an essential ingredient in the living tradition of the Church's believing commitment to God's incarnate self-revelation in Jesus Christ, and along with knowledge of the truth it belongs to the evangelical structure of 'the faith once for all delivered to the saints'. It is godliness of this kind that exercises a directive force in all 'sound doctrine', and that must be allowed to guide theological understanding particularly in the open range of faith where we are obliged to form concepts and make pronouncements about the truth beyond the explicit statements of Holy Scripture. It is right there, where the Scriptures bear upon the ineffable mystery of God which remains mystery even in the heart of his self-revelation, that we must be on our guard against irreverent and

---

[54]See Methodios Fouyas, *op. cit.*, pp. 45, 71f, 108f.
[55]Cf. G. Florovsky, *Bible, Church, Tradition: An Eastern Orthodox View*, 1972, on 'the scriptural mind' and 'the catholic mind', pp. 9ff, 57f.

impious intrusion into what God has kept secret in his own eternal being.

As found in Nicene theology εὐσέβεια referred to the orthodox understanding of truth embodied in the tradition of faith and worship that derived from the apostles. It is to be traced back to the Pastoral Epistles in the New Testament where 'godliness' was more or less a technical word for what had been called 'the Way' in the Acts of the Apostles,[56] the way of belief and worship characteristic of those who are committed to Christ and who have to suffer for it. The distinctive feature of godliness is that it is an embodiment of faith or a knowledge of the truth of the Gospel in a corresponding way of life and worship in the reverent service of God.[57] It is significant that considerable stress was laid upon the inherent interrelation between godliness, faith and truth, and thus upon 'teaching in accordance with godliness',[58] or upon 'sound doctrine',[59] in sharp reaction to the rise of rationalising and mythologising perversion of the Gospel.[60] Thus while godliness was held to be synonymous with belief and truth, ungodliness was held to be synonymous with unbelief and error. That was a contrast that set the pattern for the Church's struggle with heresy for the next three hundred years.

The passage that evidently governed the understanding of εὐσέβεια in the early Church was the Pauline correlation of the 'great mystery of godliness' with the incarnation. The apostle was writing to inform Timothy about 'how one ought to behave in the household of God, which is the Church of the living God, the pillar and ground of truth. Great indeed, we confess, is the mystery of godliness (τὸ τῆς εὐσεβείας μυστήριον): who was manifested in the flesh, justified in the Spirit, seen of angels, preached among the gentiles, believed on in the world, taken up in glory.'[61] There on the one hand, godliness was defined as penetrating into the inner mystery of

---

[56]Acts, 9.2; 19.9, 23; 22.4; 24.14, 22.
[57]1 Tim. 2.2; 3.16; 4.7, 8; 6.3, 5f; 2 Tim. 3.5; Tit. 1.1; 2 Pet. 1.3, 6; 3.11.
[58]1 Tim. 6.3; Tit. 1.1; cf. 2 Tim. 3.7.
[59]1 Tim. 6.3; 2 Tim. 1.13; 4.3; Tit. 1.9, 13; 2.1f.
[60]1 Tim. 1.4; 4.7; 6.3–6; 2 Tim. 4.4; Tit. 1.14; 2 Pet. 1.16.
[61]1 Tim. 3.15–16; e.g., Hilary, *De Trin.*, 11.9.

the faith, into the objective fact of the incarnate self-revelation of God, while, on the other hand, the Church was spoken of as supporting and upholding the truth of God. Expressed the other way round, the revealed truth of God is grounded in and built into human life and society as it is proclaimed and believed, known and taught by the Church in a way that promotes godliness. Thus the great mystery of godliness manifest in Jesus Christ and his saving grace became embodied in the Church as its godly counterpart, which corresponds to what St Paul elsewhere referred to as the great mystery concerning Christ and his Church, which is his Body.[62] The saving revelation of God in Jesus Christ and the faithful reception and understanding of it by the apostles were incorporated together in the foundation of the Church, so that in the economic purpose of God the truth as it is in Jesus was made accessible to people in history only through the apostolic preaching and teaching of the Gospel and only in living continuity with their godly tradition in the Church.

This is surely what was meant in the Pastoral Epistles by the deposit of faith (παραθήκη) entrusted to the Church, to be guarded, defended and transmitted in godliness to others.[63] In its primary sense the faith entrusted to the Church refers to the revealing and saving event of Jesus Christ in its self-interpretation and self-unfolding within the Church which he founded upon the apostles and prophets; but in its subsidiary sense it refers to the evangelical content of the apostolic message and tradition as it is mediated to us through the Scriptures of the New Testament and through participation in the mystery of godliness in the midst of the Church where Christ continues to make himself known and to be savingly at work through the enlightening power of his Spirit. It is only through reliance upon the apostolic witness and teaching, the subsidiary sense of the deposit of faith, and under the direction of its semantic reference to Jesus Christ as Lord and Saviour, that people throughout history are enabled to grasp and appropriate the

[62]Eph. 5.32.
[63]1 Tim. 6.20; 2 Tim. 1.12ff; 2.2, 4; 4.3; Tit. 1.9, 13; cf. also 2 Thess. 2.15; 3.6; Gal. 1.9; 2.2, 9; 1 Cor. 11.23; 15.3; 2 Cor. 11.3f; Rom. 6.17; 1 Tim. 4.6; Heb. 3.1; 4.14; 10.23.

doctrinal substance of the faith, which is what was primarily meant by the deposit. However, all that takes place only within the structured integration of truth, faith and godliness in the living tradition of the empirical Church as the Body of Christ or the earthly-historical form of his existence in the world.

If we are to appreciate the bearing and force of this biblical teaching upon Nicene theology, it will help us to consider what the early Church made of it in the period between the apostles and the Council of Nicaea, as reflected in the thought of Irenaeus and Origen.

Irenaeus worked with a powerful sense of the embodiment of the revealed truth of the Gospel in the apostolic foundation of the Church, and of the structured nature of the faith once for all delivered to the saints and mediated through the apostolic tradition. He made much of the deposit of faith which he thought of, not at least in the first place as a system of doctrinal statements, but as a body of objective evangelical truth which through the power of the Holy Spirit constantly rejuvenates the Church by renewing its bond with the creative source of its being in the Gospel, and structures its continuing life and mission in accordance with the image of Christ the incarnate Son of God and the pattern of divine truth embodied in him.[64] The Church of Jesus Christ is thus informed by a faith that is 'always one and the same', for it is grounded in the unchangeable reality of Christ and the once and for all revelation of God in him.[65]

God is utterly ineffable and incomprehensible to us, for his sublime greatness and majesty infinitely exceed the capacity of human beings to know and describe him as he is in his own nature. However, while retaining inviolate the mystery of his own being, God has chosen to make himself known to us through a movement of love and infinite condescension in which he has drawn near to us by becoming incarnate in Jesus Christ, thereby bringing himself within the range of human

[64]Irenaeus, *Adv. haer.* (edit. by Harvey, 1897), 3. *praef.*, 1–5, vol. 2, pp. 22ff; 3.38.1, pp. 131f; 4.40.2, p. 236. For this and what follows see, T. F. Torrance, 'The Deposit of Faith', *Scottish Journal of Theology*, 1983, vol. 36.1, pp. 1–28.

[65]Irenaeus, *Adv. haer.*, 1.3, vol. 1, p. 94; 3.1–4, vol. 2, pp. 1ff; 3.11.1, p. 47; 3.12.9, p. 62; 4.4ff, pp. 234ff; 5.20, pp. 377ff.

knowing.[66] Jesus Christ thus constitutes the bridge between God and man, between the invisible and the visible, the incomprehensible and the comprehensible, the immeasurable and the measurable. It is, then, in Jesus Christ, through 'union and communion' with him in love, and through sharing in the love of God incarnate in him, that we are enabled to know God in such a way that our knowledge of God is firm and sure, for it is anchored in the ultimate reality of God's own eternal being.[67] That would not be possible without the aid of the Spirit of God. But in and through the Lord Jesus Christ God has accustomed his Holy Spirit to dwell in human nature and at the same time has adapted human nature to receive the Holy Spirit, which enables us through the gift of the Holy Spirit to share in the relation of mutual knowing between the Father and the Son and thus in God's knowledge of himself.[68]

As Irenaeus understood it, communion with God through Christ in the Spirit, which arises out of the reconciling and healing assumption of our humanity that took place in the incarnation, necessarily takes a corporate form in the Church, for it is to the Church that God has entrusted the deposit of faith, to the Church that he has given his Holy Spirit, and in the Church that he has provided us with the ministry of the Gospel and all the other means through which the Spirit works. Thus he could claim that 'where the Church is, there is the Spirit of God, and where the Spirit of God is, there is the Church and every grace: but the Spirit is truth.'[69] While Irenaeus pointed to the Church as the location of well-grounded knowledge of the truth, and thought of the Church as structurally integrated with the truth embodied in it, he nevertheless laid the emphasis upon the objective self-revelation of God through Christ and in the

---

[66]Irenaeus, *Adv. haer.*, 2.15.4, vol. 1, pp. 282f; 2.39.1f, pp. 345f; 2.40–43, pp. 349–358; 3.38.1f, vol. 2, pp. 131f; 4.22.2, p. 178; 4.34.4, pp. 215–219.

[67]Irenaeus, *Adv. haer.*, 3.11f, vol. 2, pp. 43f; 3.17.6, p. 87f; 4.6, p. 153; 4.11.1–5, pp. 158–162; 4.34.1, 4–6, pp. 212, 215f; 4.6.1, p. 291; 5. *praef.*, 1–2, pp. 313ff; 5.27.2, pp. 398f.

[68]Irenaeus, *Adv. haer.*, 2.3.7, 1–4, vol. 1, pp. 342–344; 3.6.2, vol. 2, pp. 22f; 3.18.1, p. 92; 3.19.6, pp. 100f; 3.21.2, p. 107; 4.11.1–5, pp. 158–162; 4.34.5, 7, pp. 210, 218f.

[69]Irenaeus, *Adv. haer.*, 3.38, vol. 2, p. 132.

Spirit as the actual source of our knowledge of the truth.[70] His distinctive emphasis was very evident when, with reference to St Paul's word about the Church as 'the pillar and ground of truth'[71] he deliberately spoke of 'the Gospel and the Spirit of life' as 'the pillar and ground of the Church (στύλος δὲ καὶ στήριγμα ἐκκλησίας, τὸ εὐαγγέλιον καὶ πνεῦμα ζωῆς)'.[72] On the other hand, Irenaeus held that it is only within the framework of the faith entrusted to the Church and incorporated in the apostolic tradition that the Word of revelation in the Scriptures may be faithfully interpreted without lapsing into presumptuous and ungodly error, and Christ himself who is the treasure hidden in them may be truly known.[73]

For Irenaeus, then, knowledge of the truth of God or the truth of the Gospel is not given in an abstract or detached form but in a concrete embodied form in the Church, where it is to be grasped within the normative pattern of the faith imparted to it through the teaching of the apostles, and is therefore to be grasped only in unity and continuity with the faith, worship and godly life of all who are incorporated into Christ as members of his Body. He regarded the truth revealed through the Holy Scriptures as an organic structure, 'the body of truth', within which various truths, and correspondingly beliefs, may be distinguished but which form a coherent whole from which they cannot be separated, any more than the limbs of a living body can be severed from the body without dismemberment and destruction of the whole.[74] Nevertheless Irenaeus gave himself the important task of uncovering the intrinsic order embedded in the deposit of faith, and of bringing into clear focus the internal arrangement of 'the body of truth and the

[70]Irenaeus, *Adv. haer.*, 3.38.1–2, vol. 2, pp. 131f; 4.53.1f, pp. 261ff; 5.20.1, pp. 378ff.

[71]I Tim. 3.15.

[72]Irenaeus, *Adv. haer.*, 3.11.11, vol. 2, p. 47.

[73]Irenaeus, *Adv. haer.*, 1. *praef.*, vol. 1, pp. 1ff; 1.15, p. 67; 1.1.19–4.1, pp. 80–97; 2.7–9, pp. 271–274; 2.40–43, pp. 349–358; 3.1–5, vol. 2, pp. 1–20; 3.38, pp. 131–3; 4.40–42.1, pp. 234–238; 4.53–54, pp. 261–264; 5. *praef.*, pp. 313f; 5.20.1f, pp. 377ff.

[74]Irenaeus, *Adv. haer.*, 1.1.15, vol. 1, pp. 66f; 1.18, pp. 80ff; 2.40–45, pp. 347–358.

harmonious adaptation of its members', in line with the 'canon of truth' traditionally received in baptism,[75] as a guide in the interpretation of Holy Scripture, and thus to offer a clear demonstration of the apostolic *kerygma* in the face of heretical deviation and distortions.[76]

The work of Irenaeus in this respect clearly reflects the general activity of the Church in the second and third centuries in its attempt to clarify the doctrinal substance of the faith in the light of its own objectively grounded order, in the course of which there emerged explicit formulations of belief which were eventually to take the form of the early creeds.[77] From the way in which Irenaeus himself handled these incipient credal formulae, it seems clear that they were not doctrinal propositions connected together through a logico-deductive system of thought, but assertions of belief that are organised from beyond themselves by their common ground in the apostolic deposit of faith and ultimately by the self-revelation of God in Jesus Christ, the one incarnate truth of God from which all evangelical truths flow. Accordingly, they do not have their truth in themselves but in that supreme truth to which they refer and into which they are locked. While Irenaeus spoke of them as bound up with the 'canon of truth', he made it clear that the actual canon of truth or centre of reference is the truth itself.[78] These assertions of belief, however, were regarded as having regulative force in themselves in so far as they were rightly related to that truth and serve its supreme authority. All our theological knowledge is only 'in part', for there is much that belongs to God which we must reverently leave to him, since it would be ungodly even to think of intruding into it.[79] Hence it should be recognised that the credal formulations of what we

[75]Irenaeus, *Adv. haer.*, 1.1.14, vol. 1, p. 67; cf. 1.1.20, pp. 87ff; 1.3, pp. 93f; and Tertullian, *De virg. vel.*, 1.

[76]Irenaeus, *Adv. haer.*, 1.19f, vol. 1, pp. 80–90; 2.37–43, pp. 342–358; 3.12.11, vol. 2, p. 65; 3.38, pp. 131f; *Dem.*, 1–6.

[77]Irenaeus, *Adv. haer.*, 1.2, vol. 1, pp. 90f; 3.1f, 4, vol. 2, pp. 2ff, 25ff; 4.1, pp. 146ff; 4.53.1, pp. 261f; 5.20.1, pp. 377f; *Dem.*, 6.

[78]Irenaeus, *Adv. haer.*, 2.41, p. 349. The same point was made by Clement of Alexandria, when he spoke of 'cleaving to the truth by taking the canon of truth from the truth itself' – *Strom*, 7.16.

[79]Irenaeus, *Adv. haer.*, 2.15.3f, vol. 1, pp. 282f; 2.41ff, pp. 349–358.

may know of God, even under the control of what he has revealed to us, are not final but partial, not closed but open confessional statements which are revisable in the light of deeper and fuller understanding of the Gospel. Their importance lies not in 'the form of sound words' which they use, but in their service in bringing the mind of the Church under the compelling claims of divine truth, and in their guidance to the Church in its mission to guard and defend 'the evangelical and apostolic faith' entrusted to it, and to hand it on to others in accordance with 'the mystery of godliness'.

This account of the Irenaean contribution to the theological unfolding of the Church's confession of faith in the light of its implicit conceptual structure, requires to be complemented by some account of Origen's wide-ranging contribution to biblical and theological understanding which had a considerable impact upon thought in the Church leading up to the Council of Nicaea. Origen was a very learned biblical scholar unsurpassed in the early Church, but he was a theologian with an essentially speculative, though devout, mind, who felt compelled to carry his thinking beyond the literal content of biblical statements to the divine realities they signified. Although he held with Irenaeus that the controlling centre of reference in our knowledge of God is ultimately the truth itself as revealed in Jesus Christ, not in any human formulations of our knowledge of the truth,[80] unlike Irenaeus he worked with a dualist framework of thought, the Platonic or Philonic disjunction between the sensible world (αἰσθητὸς κόσμος) and the intelligible world (νοητὸς κόσμος).[81] The implications of that dualist way of thinking were very far-reaching: 'the invisible and incorporeal things in heaven are true, but the visible and corporeal things on earth are copies of true things, not true themselves.'[82] That outlook deeply affected Origen's understanding of the Holy Scriptures as providentially provided media within the sensible world through which the

---

[80]Origen, *De prin.*, *praef.*, 1.2, 6. Origen also spoke of Christ as αὐτοαλήθεια = self-subsistent truth, or the Truth himself, *In Jn.*, 6.6; cf. 1.27; 2.4; and *Con. Cel.* 8.12.

[81]See especially Origen, *In Jn.* 1.25–28 with 1.8.

[82]Origen, *In Cant.* 2; *Con. Cel.*, 7.31, 376.

divine *Logos* accommodated his communication to human weakness, wrapping up the mysteries of divine revelation in forms and figures that can be easily grasped, but only in order that through them he might lift up believing minds to a higher level where they may understand spiritual or divine realities in the intelligible world beyond.[83]

On the one hand, Origen held that through divine inspiration the human terms found in Holy Scripture are governed by the nature (φύσει) of the realities they signify, and are not just conventionally (θέσει) related to them. They are to be understood through an assent of rational faith to the compelling (*cataleptic*, καταληπτικός) claims of those realities upon the mind of the interpreter, but that means that he must engage in careful investigation to make sure that the assent of faith really does match, or set its 'seal' to, the truth.[84] On the other hand, he insisted that a spiritual interpretation of the Holy Scriptures, in accordance with the spiritual nature of those realities, must involve a passage in thought from a lower level of 'bodily' or literal sense to a higher level of spiritual, mystical meaning where the truth shines in its own self-evidencing intellectual light.[85] But that requires considerable spiritual training of the mind in theological insight (θεωρία), a kind of divine sense (αἴσθησις θεία), appropriate to knowledge of God.[86]

This combination of careful investigation and spiritual training was very characteristic of Origen. He was not unaware of the dangers it involved. It led him to distinguish between the 'bodily' or 'sensible' Gospel and the 'spiritual' or 'intellectual' Gospel, or the 'temporal' and the 'eternal' Gospel, which he held to correspond to the difference between the advent of the Saviour in his state of humiliation when he assumed the form of servant for our sakes, and the glorious advent of Christ in the

[83]Origen, *In Jn.* 1.7; *In Matt.*, 10.1; *In Deut.*, 1.21; *In Jer.*, 18.6; *Con. Cel.*, 4.71, etc.

[84]Origen, *Con. Cel.*, 1.2, 9f, 13, 24f, 42, 71; 3.23, 39, 42, 86; 4.2; 5.45; 6.27; 7.10; *De prin.*, 4.3.16.

[85]Origen, *De prin.*, 1.1.1f; 1.3.3; 2.2.2; 2.4.4; 2.5.2; 2.7.2; 2.11.2ff; 3.5.1; 3.12.4; 4.2.1ff, 15. Origen sometimes distinguished between three meanings – cf. 4.2.4.

[86]Origen, *Con. Cel.*, 1.48; 6.23; 7.34; *De prin.*, 1.1.9; 4.4.10; cf. LXX Prov. 2.5.

future, when the shadows of 'the temporal Gospel' will give way to the ultimate realities of 'the eternal Gospel'.[87] The implication of this was that the historical Christ was to be regarded as a time-conditioned form in which the eternal truth is mediated to fallen creatures, but that once the eternal truth is known the historical medium will be relativised.[88] This was evidently why Origen laid such stress upon allegorical exegesis and the cultivation of a spiritual 'feeling' for God which would enable the believer to penetrate through the husks and shadows of the historical revelation to the eternal, invisible realities of God that may be grasped only in a simple immediate way and cannot be expressed in human words.[89] This speculative outreach of the spiritual mind, beyond the realm of knowledge subject to the kind of criteria of truth with which Greek philosophy and science operated,[90] was undoubtedly dangerous. Nevertheless, Origen was fascinated with it, particularly since it was associated with the Old Testament men of God like Melchizedek the pioneer of heavenly worship, or Moses who spoke with God face to face, or with the experience of the disciples on the Mount of Transfiguration and with what St Paul wrote of his own exalted experiences, all of which pointed to the kind of sublime vision of God that may be opened up to 'the mystic and inexpressible insight'.[91]

There was another side to Origen's approach, however, which provided this 'theologising' (θεολογεῖν) with safeguards against a fanciful 'mythologising' (μυθολογεῖν), and with a normative frame of faith and devotion which could help to keep knowledge of God in the centre of the life and living tradition of 'the Great Church'. This had to do with the way in which he brought careful inquiry and training in godliness to bear upon each other. In line with the conception of scientific knowledge (ἐπιστήμη) which had long prevailed in Alexandria, that exact knowledge is in accordance with the nature (κατὰ φύσιν) of

---

[87]Origen, *In Jn.*, 1.8–10; 2.6; *De prin.*, 3.6.8; 4.2.6; 4.3.13.

[88]Cf. Origen, *In Matt.*, 10.14, where he committed himself to the expression 'beyond history'. See also *In Jn.*, 10.4, 18, 22; 20.3, 10, etc.

[89]Origen, *De prin.*, 4.3.15.

[90]Origen, *Con. Cel.*, 1.2; 8.32.

[91]Origen, *In Jn.*, 13.24; 32.25–29.

what is known, Origen concentrated on developing a way of knowing God which was strictly in accordance with the nature of God as he has revealed himself to us, that is, in a *godly* way; and he set himself to cultivate personal godliness in reliance upon the grace of Christ and the power of his Spirit, so that he could bring to knowledge of God an appropriately godly habit of mind. Hence **theologia,** which is properly the knowledge of the Holy Trinity, and **theosebeia** or **eusebeia** defined through Jesus Christ the Son of God incarnate, were regarded by Origen as mutually conditioning each other in the course of deepening theological inquiry.[92] The more truly God is known in accordance with his nature, the more godliness is advanced, and the more godliness is advanced the more likely we are to know God in a godly way that is worthy of his nature as God.[93] Generally speaking, then, 'the aim is to get as near the truth as possible and to shape our belief according to the rule of godliness.'[94] Thus *godliness* and *the rule of truth* became operational equivalents.

Behind everything lay Origen's immense respect for the Holy Scriptures and his 'priestly' devotion to the Word and Truth of God which they communicated.[95] As the inspired product of the Holy Spirit they have to be investigated and interpreted in accordance with their 'divine character' (θειότης), in a reverent and devout way, in the realisation that they have a 'superhuman' depth of meaning which does not admit of quick understanding.[96] By their very nature the Scriptures call for long study, meditation and prayer, and for hard labour.[97] This is just what Origen himself exhibited in his immense production of biblical commentaries, all of which bear impressive witness to conscientious treatment of the text in its linguistic detail and exact grammatical sense, and to prodigious research in the clarification of historical circumstances and

---

[92]Cf. Origen, *In Luc.*, 14.28.
[93]This was strongly emphasised by Origen in *Con. Cel.*, 3.8, 34, 60, 78; 5.33; 7.40, 49; 8.13, 75.
[94]Origen, *De prin.*, 1.5.4.
[95]Origen, *In Jn.*, 1.3.
[96]Origen, *De prin.*, 4.1.1f; 4.2.2.
[97]Origen, *Ep. ad Greg.*, 3; *Ep. ad Afr.*, 2–5.

background that might affect the meaning. But he also sought to bring to bear upon each book and each passage the whole world of biblical revelation and the whole tradition of Christian faith and understanding in the Church, so that as far as possible the Holy Scriptures might be understood out of themselves, in the light of the divine intention which they embodied and which they manifested in their inner coherence and continuity.[98]

Since the Scriptures are the result of the inspiration of the Holy Spirit by the will of the Father through Jesus Christ, and since the Word of God who speaks through all the Scriptures became incarnate in Jesus Christ, it is Jesus Christ himself who must constitute the controlling centre in all right interpretation of the Scriptures. To interpret the Scriptures, even the Gospels, in this way through 'the mind of Christ', is, Origen claimed, to keep 'the canon of the heavenly Church of Jesus Christ in accordance with the succession of the apostles'.[99] Jesus Christ himself defined for Christians what true godliness (θεοσέβεια, εὐσέβεια) is,[100] for he himself is 'the great mystery of godliness manifest in the flesh', who mediates in and through himself God's gracious condescension to us and our approach to God, both God's revelation to us and our knowledge and worship of God.[101] Hence in all investigation of the truth we must strive more and more to 'preserve in every way the attitude of godliness (τὸ εὐσεβές) towards God and his Christ',[102] while to be faithful to the mind of Christ in all our interpretation of the Holy Scriptures 'we must preserve the canon of godliness'.[103]

It is significant that for Origen godliness was defined not only

---

[98]Origen, *Con. Cel.*, 7.11; *De prin., praef.*; 4.2.4, 7–9; 4.3.5.

[99]Origen, *De prin.*, 4.2.3; cf. *praef.* 1–2; *In Jer.*, 3.22–4.

[100]Origen, *Con. Cel.*, 1.27; 3.60, 81; 5.33; 7.46; 8.20; *De prin.*, 4.1.2, 5; *In Jn.*, 28.23.

[101]Origen, *In Jn.*, 6.5f; *De prin.*, 4.1.2, 5; *Con. Cel.*, 2.4; 3.34, 81; 5.4; 8.13, 26, 59.

[102]Origen, *De prin.*, 3.1.17.

[103]Origen, *De prin.*, 1.5.4; 2 6.2; 3.1.17, 23; 3.5.3; 4.3.14; cf. *praef.* 2; 3.3.4; 4.2.2, 4; 4.3.15. The expression 'rule of piety' (*regula pietatis*) is that of Rufinus, the Latin translator of the *De principiis*. From his rendering of 3.1.17 it is evident that this did not always correspond to Origen's original text, but the term *pietas* = εὐσέβεια was not far from the mark. In his preface to the

by reference to Jesus Christ (κατὰ Ἰησοῦν Χριστόν) but through Jesus Christ (διὰ Ἰησοῦ Χριστοῦ), in respect of his unique relation to the Father as Son of God and God, and of his unique relation to us as our High Priest in whom and with whom and through whom we worship the Father.[104] By his atoning sacrifice he heals and cleanses us through his own divine power, so that we worship him as well as the Father, for he and the Father are one; but because he is one with us as well as with the Father, we may pray to him as our 'Mediator, High Priest and Paraclete', asking him to present our desires, petitions and intercessions, that ascend from us to him, to the Father, and thus we worship the Father in union with him and through him. As Son of God incarnate and High Priest Jesus Christ has shown mankind the pure way to worship God − that is what true godliness is in which our faith and understanding are confirmed in God.[105]

Undoubtedly what Origen wrote about Christ-centred and Christ-mediated worship of the Father reflected the prevailing mind of the Church in the living tradition of its faith and in its service for the salvation of mankind: reverential wonder in the knowledge of God, praise and thanksgiving for the saving acts of God in the death and resurrection of Jesus Christ, and godliness in words and deeds, were intimately and inseparably interwoven, as in the baptismal and eucharistic liturgy of the Church.[106] Hallowing the name of God, thinking and speaking appropriately of him, with the utmost respect for his self-revelation as Father, Son and Holy Spirit, were essential marks of the Christian mind and, as Origen believed, of the mind of the Church under the imprint left upon it by the apostles. Hence when Origen set about composing a work on the fundamental

---

translation of the third book, however, Rufinus appeared to equate 'the rule of piety' with 'the sound rule of the catholic faith', *GCS* edit. by P. Koetschau, 1913, *Origenes Werke*, vol. 5, p. 193.

[104]Origen, *Con. Cel.*, 3.34; 5.4; 7.46; 8.13; *De or.*, 10.2; 13.1; 15.1−4.

[105]Origen, *In Jn.*, 1.33, 35; 2.34; *Con. Cel.*, 3.34; 5.4; 7.41, 46, 49; 8.12f, 26, 75; *De prin.*, 1.3.4.

[106]Origen, *Con. Cel.*, 3.60; 5.4; 7.46; 8.57; 75; *De or.*, 14−16, 20, 31; *In Jn.*, 32.24; *In Mat.*, 11.14. See also Origen's *Dialogue with Herakleides*, SC, 67, ed. by J. Scherer, 1960, pp. 62, 64.

principles of the faith with a view to promoting order and harmony in the understanding of Christian doctrine, he first laid down 'a definite line and clear rule' to the effect that exposition of the faith must keep within the bounds of the unanimous teaching of the Church as it had been handed down from the apostles in the light of those doctrines which they considered to be absolutely necessary. However, in view of error and disagreement, Origen felt that he had to go further: to investigate 'the grounds of the statements made by the apostles' in their preaching of the faith of Christ in the hope of establishing the ultimate basis of Christian belief, and then to determine the rational interconnections of revealed truth so as to build a body of consistent Christian doctrine.[107] Throughout this undertaking, which was the first of its kind, Origen sought to apprehend the truth of God as faithfully as possible, and took care, especially in regard to 'the more difficult points', to allow his judgment to be guided and formed in accordance with the canon of godliness or the rule of piety. Only those theological conceptions which were felt to be worthy of God, formulated under the compelling claims of his transcendent being and nature as God, could be allowed.

Owing to the force of his philosophical presuppositions which were not sufficiently subjected to criticism in the face of his commitment to biblical revelation, Origen's speculative mind transgressed the rule of piety at a number of crucial points which brought his teaching into conflict with the mind of the Catholic Church. Nevertheless, Origen's combination of scientific investigation of the objective grounds of faith and his insistent deference to εὐσέβεια or θεοσέβεια in the knowledge of the Holy Trinity had an immense impact upon the Nicene and post-Nicene theologians. The great principle at work among them, to which of course many other factors contributed, was later known as: *lex orandi − lex credendi*.[108]

---

[107]Origen, *De prin.*, *praef.*, 2, 3, 10; cf. 1.4.4; 4.4.5.

[108]See Prosper of Aquitaine, *De gratia Dei et libero voluntatis arbitrio*, 8: *legem credendi lex statuat supplicandi*, MPL, 8, 209. lex orandi-lex credendi represents a telescoped form of Prosper of Aquitaine's thought, found in the *Ineffabilis Deus* of Pius IX, and the *Munificentissimus Deus* of Pius XII, *AAS*, 1947, pp. 540f.

Again and again in the history of the Church ideas about God born of a daring irreverence have been advanced which the Church has instinctively rejected out of a profound respect for the mystery and majesty of God which had been built into the fabric of faith through prayer and devotion. That was what happened at the critical juncture in its history brought about by the Arian heresy which called in question the unity of the Holy Trinity by asserting the creatureliness of the Son, thereby separating him from the being of the Father and introducing inconsistency into the Godhead. The bishops at Nicaea reacted in horror at the affront of this Arian 'ungodliness' or 'impiety' (ἀσέβεια) and advanced against it essentially 'godly argumentation' (ἀπόδειξις εὐσεβείας).[109] Athanasius told the bishops of Egypt that when he was writing down the ungodly and perverse statements of the Arians, he had to cleanse himself by thinking of the very opposite and holding fast to 'the mind of godliness' (τὴν τῆς εὐσεβείας διάνοιαν).[110] With reference to the fact that the Council of Nicaea had to use the non-scriptural term ὁμοούσιος to explain what was meant by the Scriptures in speaking of Christ as '**of** God' or '**from** God', Athanasius pointed out that it does not matter whether a person uses a non-scriptural term or not, so long a he has 'a godly mind' (εὐσεβῆ τὴν διάνοιαν), and that as a matter of fact the fathers of Nicaea, far from speaking irreverently of Christ, spoke reverently of him 'with an exalted mind and a Christ-loving godliness' (ὑψηλὴ διάνοια καὶ φιλόχριστος εὐσέβεια).[111]

When at a later period Arianising churchmen dared to make assertions about the creatureliness of the Holy Spirit, and presumed to subject to impertinent scrutiny the inner relations of the Holy Trinity where 'the cherubim spread their covering wings', Athanasius put forward counter arguments in the same Nicene way, governed by a Christ-centred godliness. The teaching that had been handed down was to be received through the hearing of faith and expounded not through

---

[109]Athanasius, *De decr.*, 1–3; cf. *Ep. Enc.*, 1, in which he spoke of 'godliness being persecuted by ungodliness' (εὐσέβεια ἀπὸ ἀσεβείας διώκεται).

[110]*Athanasius, Ad episc. Aeg.*, 13; cf. 4, 9, 12.

[111]Athanasius, *De syn.*, 39.

linguistic arguments but 'by a godly and reverent mode of reason' (εὐσεβεῖ λογισμῷ μετ᾽ εὐλαβείας).[112]

Athanasius used to insist that the obedience of faith gives rise to a lawful way of thinking and speaking of God in virtue of its being inwardly regulated by the worship of God. In every attempt to understand and give expression to the mysteries of the faith, what is needed is a reverent restraint and a disposition of mind attuned 'through constant prayer to God, godly knowing, and supplications offered not in some casual way but with the whole consent of the heart'. That would be an approach to God in which faith and godliness mutually condition each other in our knowing of him. 'For faith and godliness are connected and are sisters: he who believes in God is not cut off from godliness, and he who has godliness really believes.'[113]

The same principle, *lex orandi* – *lex credendi*, played an important role in Hilary's thought. As we have seen, he was rather troubled by the way in which heretics took advantage of the open range of faith to obtrude their own presumptuous ideas into knowledge of God, and by the need for orthodox theology in rebutting them to make definite pronouncements beyond the statements of Holy Scripture about matters that are ultimately inexpressible. In these circumstances, he held, we must rely upon the kind of apprehension of God that is implicit in faith expanded by worship, and the kind of worship into which we are initiated by God himself, as through the Son we are given access to the Father.[114] No matter how much we try to adapt our language to indicate the greatness of God, it falls immeasurably short of what God is in his eternal being and nature, but it may nevertheless be controlled and directed from below by the fundamental acts of worship which God calls forth from us through his self-revelation in the Gospel. Thus Hilary operated with a concept of faith structured in evangelical devotion, and with a concept of devotion expanded through faith in the inexhaustible reality of God. 'We must believe him,

---

[112]Athanasius, *Ad Ser.*, 1.17, 20; 4.4.
[113]Athanasius, *Ep.*, 11.9–11.
[114]Hilary, *De Trin.*, 5.18, 20.

apprehend him, worship him, and allow these acts of devotion to be the basic ways in which we speak of God.'[115]

By this approach Hilary did not mean that in shrinking in alarm before the transcendent majesty of God, we are to fall back entirely upon the silent veneration of the heart, but rather that we are to think of God only in such a way that we recognise that he infinitely exceeds the resources of human thought and speech. We must allow worship of God through the Son in whom the unfathomable mystery of the Father is disclosed, to govern all that we confess in faith or express in theological formulation.[116] Theological activity, as Hilary himself pursued it, must constantly be interlaced with prayer so that, in all our attempts to express that we believe and confess one God the Father and one Lord Jesus Christ in accordance with what we have been taught by prophets and apostles, God will grant us signification in language, light in understanding, reverence of statement, and fidelity to the truth.[117]

We have been probing deeply into the way in which the Nicene Creed is to be traced back to the state of affairs in the apostolic foundation of the Church in which saving faith in God the Father, Son and Holy Spirit, became once for all embodied in it, and also in the way in which that faith began to unfold its theological content in the direction of the Nicene Creed, under the control of the evangelical sub-structure of the apostolic tradition at work in the life, mission and worship of the early Catholic Church, evident in its interpretation of Holy Scripture and its expression of Christian doctrine. We have found in these centuries a continuing tradition characterised by a deep intertwining of faith and godliness, understanding and worship, under the creative impact of the primary evangelical convictions imprinted upon the mind of the Church in its commitment to God's self-revelation through the incarnate Son and in the Holy Spirit. Those convictions together with a Christ-centred disposition of mind continued to be generated and nourished in the on-going life and fellowship of the Church

[115]Hilary, *De Trin.*, 2.6f, 11.
[116]Hilary, *De Trin.*, 2.2, 5–8, 10–11.
[117]Hilary, *De Trin.*, 1.38.

through regular meditation upon the Holy Scriptures and participation in liturgical worship.

That constituted the matrix within which there took shape the theological intuition and godly judgment which were at work in the framing of more formal beliefs within the boundaries marked by the claims of Christ upon the obedience and service of the Church. Thus there emerged a general interpretative framework of life and godliness, and a particular framework of beliefs derived through and from holy baptism in which, as Athanasius expressed it, the whole substance of the trinitarian faith was loaded.[118] Under the normative functioning of that interpretative framework and of the rule of truth, but with continued recourse to divine revelation mediated in the Holy Scriptures, the Church's understanding and formulation of the truth of the Gospel expanded and deepened. Thus there was to be found in the pre-Nicene period of the Catholic Church a progressive penetration into the conceptual structure of the Christian Faith which, while increasing in comprehension and precision, took place within the scope of the premises of the Church's ultimate beliefs embodied in the apostolic deposit of faith.

It is significant that when explicit formulations of belief began to appear out of the integrated body of the apostolic faith they frequently included a clause on the Church which eventually came to be established in the mature form of the Apostles and the Nicene Creeds.[119] That would seem to represent the fact that even when formal creeds developed, they remained bound to the implicit structure of the faith embodied in the apostolic foundation of the Church, and would be seriously defective if they were abstracted from it. Thus the deepening integration between implicit and explicit belief, informal and formal acts of knowledge, was not forgotten but carried over into full-orbed confession of the catholic faith. While at the Council of Nicaea itself an explicit clause on the Church was not inserted in the Creed, clear and definite

---

[118]Athanasius, *Con. Ar.*, 4.21.

[119]See the *Der Balyzeh* papyrus, cited by J. N. D. Kelly, *Early Christian Creeds*, 1950, p. 89; or *Epistola Apostolorum, ibid.*, p. 82.

doctrinal formalisation of the faith was recognised as relying on what the Catholic Church had always believed and intuitively known to be true.[120] It was through that kind of explicit formalisation that the whole body of belief implicit in the apostolic tradition of the Church was reinforced and equipped with an institutional form that extended its regulative force in the life and mission of the Church. At the same time, as we have seen, the Nicene Creed as essentially a confession of faith before God was characterised by an open scope focussed indefinitely beyond the range of its explicit statements, for the truth that had laid hold of the Church, and which it felt bound to confess in Ecumenical Synod, reached back into the transcendent mystery of the Holy Trinity. By the same token, in being locked into that truth, the theological formalisations taken up in the Creed opened the door to deeper and fuller modes of understanding which could only be dimly appreciated, if at all, at the time. All that, however, reposed upon a 'knowledge of the truth according to godliness'[121] embodied in the Church's inheritance and yet transcending it, an instinctive sense of God imprinted upon the mind of the Church by divine revelation, and a divinely given insight into transcendent relations in God as Father, Son and Holy Spirit, who is more to be adored than expressed. Trinitarian worship and trinitarian faith thus provided the implicit controlling ground both for a faithful restructuring of the life of the Church and for a godly renewing of its understanding in the Mind of Christ.

---

[120]Cf. the anathema of Arian heretical ideas appended to the Creed in the name of 'the Catholic Church'.

[121]1 Tim. 6.3; 2 Tim. 1.13; 4.3; Tit. 1.9, 13; 2.1f.

2

Access to the Father

'We believe in one God the Father Almighty, Maker of heaven and earth, and of all things visible and invisible.'

When the Christian Church spread out from its centre in Judaea into the Mediterranean world its preaching and teaching of the Gospel came up against a radical dualism of body and mind that pervaded every aspect of Graeco-Roman civilisation, bifurcating human experience and affecting fundamental habits of mind in religion, philosophy and science alike. The Platonic separation (χωρισμός) between the sensible world (κόσμος αἰσθητός) and the intelligible world (κόσμος νοητός), hardened by Aristotle, governed the disjunction between action and reflection, event and idea, becoming and being, the material and the spiritual, the visible and the invisible, the temporal and the eternal, and was built by Ptolemy into a scientific cosmology that was to dominate European thought for more than a millennium. The combined effect of this all-pervading dualism was to shut God out of the world of empirical actuality in space and time.

When the Christian Gospel was proclaimed in that context, very quickly a sharp conflict emerged between Hellenistic and Hebraic patterns of thought, between a mythological way of thinking (μυθολογεῖν) from a centre in the human mind and a theological way of thinking (θεολογεῖν) from a centre in God. In particular, the biblical teaching about God's providential and saving activity in history, and the Christian message of incarnation and redemption in space and time, had to struggle

47

with the underlying assumptions of a dualist outlook upon God and the world in order to be heard aright and take root. That difficulty was made acute by an extraordinary combination of transcendentalist notions of God in Judaism and Hellenism. All Christians believed with Jews in the one God who is the Creator of heaven and earth, but the vast difference between the Creator and the creature tended to have the effect in some quarters of accentuating the dichotomous structure of Greek thought, whether Platonic, Aristotelian or Stoic. This was already evident in the influential teaching of Philo of Alexandria for whom God and the world were so far apart that he sought to correlate them through an intermediate realm of transcendental ideas. It was very apparent in the mythological systems of the Gnostic sects in which the dualism between God and the world had widened into a yawning chasm; and not least in the subtle dualism of the Arians who denied the true Deity of Jesus Christ and held that the Son of God, far from being eternal in nature, belonged to the creaturely side of the demarcation between God and the created universe.[1]

In its struggle with the prevailing dualist assumptions that distorted understanding of its message, the Church found it had to transform the very foundations of Graeco-Roman thought, and in so doing it laid the basis for a very different approach to the created universe and eventually for an empirical scientific account of its inherent rational order. Critical and reconstructive work of this kind called for strenuous intellectual activity in the Church during the first six centuries, which has left a permanent mark upon western civilisation, but it was subsidiary to its main missionary task in evangelising the world, disseminating among the nations the saving knowledge of God mediated through Jesus Christ his Son, and providing the people of God throughout history with an articulate grasp of the substance of the Faith. In accordance with the apostolic tradition the Church concentrated upon the primacy and centrality of the Father/Son relation which it found in the Gospel and high-lighted it in the Creed, for it was precisely on

---

[1] See Athanasius, *De syn.*, 46; *Ad episc. Aeg.*, 4ff. For fuller discussion of these issues consult *Theol. in Reconstr.*, 1965, Chapters 2 & 3.

and around that relation that everything else in the Gospel seemed to be built.

It is understandable, therefore, that when the upsurge of dichotomous ways of thinking in the Arian heresy threatened to undermine belief in the Deity of Christ, by cutting the essential bond between him and God, the Church took such care at the Council of Nicaea to put forward a precise and exact statement of the *oneness in being* between the incarnate Son and the Father, for that was the central issue upon which the whole Confession of Faith finally depended, not least faith in God the Father Almighty.[2] We shall give full attention to that statement in due course, but at this juncture, as we turn to the specific theme of this chapter, *Access to the Father*, we must presuppose its bearing upon the inner relation between the Son and the Father.

Let us take our cue from Athanasius: 'It would be more godly and true to signify God from the Son and call him Father, than to name God from his works alone and call him Unoriginate.'[3] In this statement Athanasius was reflecting the emphasis of the Council of Nicaea on the centrality of the Father/Son relation and its primacy over the Creator/creature relation. The latter is to be understood in the light of the former and not vice versa. He pointed out that to approach God as Father through the Son is a more devout and accurate way than to approach him through his works by tracing them back to him as their uncreated Source. Piety and truth (εὐσέβεια and ἀλήθεια), godliness and accuracy (θεοσέβεια and ἀκρίβεια), belong inseparably together in authentic knowledge of God through Jesus Christ his Son.[4] This combination of Christocentricity and theological precision was a highly distinctive feature of Nicene theology which we must constantly keep in mind.

The Nicene theologians contrasted these two approaches to God, from his Son and from his works, as from what God has

---

[2] Athanasius, *Ad Afr.*, 4–11; *Ad Jov.*, 1 etc.

[3] Athanasius, *Con. Ar.*, 1.34: Οὐκοῦν εὐσεβέστερον καὶ ἀληθὲς ἂν εἴη μᾶλλον τὸν Θεὸν ἐκ τοῦ Υἱοῦ σημαίνειν καὶ Πατέρα λέγειν, ἢ ἐκ μόνων τῶν ἔργων ὀνομάζειν καὶ λέγειν αὐτὸν ἀγένητον. Cf. 1.16, 33; *De decr.*, 31; Hilary, *De Trin.*, 1.17; 3.22; cf. 2.6–8.

[4] For Athanasius εὐσέβεια denoted 'orthodoxy', *De syn*, 3; *De decr.*, 1; *Con. Ar.*, 1.7, etc.; *Ep. Enc.*, 2; *Ad Afr.*, 2; *Ad Ant.*, 8, while ἀσέβεια, or δυσσέβεια, impiety, denoted 'heresy', *Con. Ar.*, 1.1ff, 37, 52f; 2.18; 3.10.55, etc.

begotten of his own nature and from what he has *made* out of nothing in complete difference from his nature. When we think and speak of God from the perspective of the Creator/creature relation, or the Unoriginate/originate relation, we can only think and speak of him in vague, general and negative terms, at the infinite distance of the creature from the Creator where we cannot know God as he is in himself or in accordance with his divine nature, but only in his absolute separation from us, as the eternal, unconditioned and indescribable.[5] In such an approach we can do no more than attempt to speak of God from his works which have come into being at his will through his Word, that is, from what is externally related to God, and which as such do not really tell us anything about who God is or what he is like in his own nature.[6] That line of approach, as both Athanasius and Hilary insisted, is entirely lacking in accuracy or precision (ἀκρίβεια). They differentiated themselves here sharply from the thesis of Basileides, the Gnostic of Alexandria, who taught, with reference to Plato's statement that God is beyond all being, that we cannot say anything about what God is, but can only say something about what he is not.[7] It was pointed out by Gregory Nazianzen, however, that if we cannot say anything positive about what God is, we really cannot say anything accurate about what he is not.[8]

According to the Nicene theologians it will not do to speak of God in empty negative conceptions for two further reasons. On the one hand, if we do not think of the Father in his relation to the Son, but only in contrast to what he is as Creator to the creatures, then we inevitably come to think of the Son himself as one of God's created works, and thus to think and speak of God in a way that is not personally grounded in God himself, but in an impersonal way far removed from what he is in himself.[9]

---

[5]Hilary, *De Trin.*, 2.6f.

[6]See Athanasius, *De decr.*, 13; *Con. Ar.*, 1.29; 2.22, etc.

[7]Athanasius, *De decr.*, 22; *De syn.*, 34. Athanasius could also cite this passage from Plato (*Republic*, VI, 509b) but emended it to say that God is 'beyond all created being' – *Con. gent.*, 2.2; 35.1; 40.2. Cf. Origen, *Con. Cel.*, 7.38; Gregory Naz., *Or.*, 30.18.

[8]Cf. Gregory Naz., *Or.*, 28.9; Athanasius, *Ad mon.*, 2; Basil, *Con. Eun.*, 1.10, and contrast John of Damascus, *De fide orth.*, I.4.

[9]Athanasius, *Con. Ar.* 1, 29–34; *De Syn.*, 35, 46–47.

Moreover, if we try to reach knowledge of God from some point outside of God, we cannot operate with any point *in God* by reference to which we can test or control our conceptions of him, but are inevitably flung back upon ourselves. Even if we relate God negatively to what we are in ourselves, we are nevertheless quite unable to escape using ourselves as some sort of measure for what we think and say of him. Thus in the last resort it is with reference to our private opinion (κατὰ τὸν ἴδιον νοῦν), and what we arbitrarily think up or devise (ἐπινοεῖν) from ourselves, that we form judgments about both the Son and the Father, which is precisely what the Arians were accused of doing.[10]

Any attempt to reach knowledge of God in that kind of way is self-willed and far from being devout (εὐσεβής), but neither is it scientific (ἐπιστημονική) or precise (ἀκριβής). In Alexandria particularly, a good deal of attention had been given to scientific inquiry and method which had influenced Christian thinkers like Clement, Anatolius and Athanasius.[11] Precise, scientific knowledge was held to result from inquiry strictly in accordance with the nature (κατὰ φύσιν) of the reality being investigated, that is, knowledge of it reached under the constraint of what it actually and essentially is in itself, and not according to arbitrary convention (κατὰ θέσιν). To know things in this way, strictly in accordance with their nature, is to know them in accordance with their truth or reality (κατ᾽ ἀλήθειαν) and thus to think and speak truly (ἀληθῶς) of them.[12] That is the only way to reach real, exact or scientific knowledge in any field of inquiry, through the faithful assent of the mind to the compelling or 'cataleptic' claims of reality upon it.

[10]Athanasius, *Con. Ar.*, 1.1f, 14f, 37, 52f; 2.18, 38; 3.10, 55; *De syn.*, 15. He charged Arians with thinking of God κατ᾽ ἐπίνοιαν, dreaming up conceptions of him with no ground in reality – *De sent. Dion.*, 2, 23f; *Ad episc.*, 12ff; *Con. Ar.*, 1.12; 2.37; 4.2f, 8f, 13; cf. *Con. Apol.*, 2.7.

[11]Consult my account of this in *Oikonomia. Heilsgeschichte als Thema der Theologie*, edit. by F. Christ, 1967, pp. 223–238; *Theol. in Reconcil.*, 1975, pp. 215ff, 239ff, 255ff.

[12]This Athanasian/scientific realism is very evident in *Con. Apol.*, 1.10, 13, 16f; 2.9. To think 'in accordance with nature' is contrasted with the fallacy of attempting to think 'beyond nature', 1.9; cf. 1.13, 17; 2.18f. See also *Ad Epict.*, 2.7; *De syn.*, 54.

This scientific approach, in which we know things only under the constraint of their distinctive nature, applies even more forcefully to the knowledge of God, for since there is no likeness between the eternal being of God and the being of created reality, God may be known only out of himself.[13] Thus if we are to have any true and precise scientific knowledge of God, we must allow his own nature, as he becomes revealed to us, to determine how we are to know him, how we are to think of him, and what we are to say of him. That is what happens when we approach God as Father through Jesus Christ his Son, for the Son is of one and the same nature and being (ὁμοφυής and ὁμοούσιος) as the Father. 'The fullness of the Father's Godhead is the being of the Son, and the Son is the whole God.'[14] He is God of God, the one way of access to God the Father. When we seek tó know God from his created works, on the other hand, we do not know him as Father, but only know of him as Maker, and are no better off than the Greeks.[15] But he who knows God as Father in and through his Son, the Word of God, also knows God as Creator, for it is through the Word that God has created all things.[16]

Two further remarks are called for. If we are really to have knowledge of God we must be given a point of access to him which is both in God himself and in our creaturely existence. That is precisely what we have in the incarnation, where God's self-revelation as Father takes place through his self-giving to us in Jesus Christ his Son. When God gives us access to knowledge of himself like that he does so within the conditions of space and time and therefore within the bounds of what we human beings may apprehend. At the same time the knowledge which God thus gives us of himself in his incarnate Son is from a centre in his own being, where all our human understanding and conceiving of him may be governed and tested in accordance with his

[13]Athanasius, *Con. Ar.*, 1.20; *Ad Ser.*, 1.9, 24; 2.5; cf. also *Con. gent.*, 9; *Con. Ar.*, 2.21, 41; *De decr.*, 11.

[14]Athanasius, *Con. Ar.*, 1.9; cf. 3.11.

[15]Cf. Plato, *Timaeus*, 28c, cited by Origen, *Con. Cel.*, 42.

[16]Athanasius, *Con. Ar.*, 1.33.

divine nature.[17] Thus when we approach God as Father through the Son, our knowledge of the Father in the Son is grounded in the very being of God and is determined by what he essentially is in his own nature. Since in Jesus Christ we are really enabled to know God in accordance with his own nature as Father and Son, we may know him in a way that is both godly and precise.

However, when we know the Father in this way, in and through Jesus Christ, we become aware that he infinitely exceeds all that we can think and say of him. The very God and Father, to whom we are given access though the Son, we know to be unlimited and inexhaustible in his divine reality. 'The infinite and boundless God cannot be made comprehensible by a few words of human speech.'[18] Hence, as Hilary expressed it, in faith we confess the truth that faith itself is not competent to comprehend him as its divine object.[19] It is in our actual *apprehending* of God, however, that we realise that we cannot *comprehend* him. We know much more than we can grasp or express; we feel or experience far more than can be put into thought or word.[20] We cannot embrace all that God is within our knowing of him, for he breaks through all our finite conceptions and definitions, but while God in his entirety eludes the grasp of our minds, Hilary argues, he nevertheless leaves something of himself within our grasp. It is, of course, not a part of God that we know, for God cannot be divided up in parts; rather do we know in part the whole God who exceeds what we can apprehend within the embrace of our human thought and speech. 'The perfect knowledge of God is so to know him that we are sure that we must not be ignorant of him, yet cannot describe him. We must believe, must apprehend, must worship; and such acts of devotion must stand in lieu of definition.'[21]

---

[17]Cf. Hilary: 'The very centre of a saving faith is the belief not merely in God, but in God as Father, and not merely in Christ, but in Christ as the Son of God, in him, not as a creature, but as God the Creator, born of God. *De Trin.*, 1.17; cf. 3.22; 5.20; 6.30.

[18]Hilary, *De syn.*, 62 & 69; cf. *De Trin.*, 2.5ff; 3.1ff; 4.2.

[19]Hilary, *De Trin.*, 2.6–11.

[20]Hilary, *De Trin.*, 2.6–7; cf. Athanasius, *Ad mon.*, 1ff; Gregory Nyss., *Or. cat.*, 3.

[21]Hilary, *De Trin.*, 2.7; cf. 2.6, 11; 3.1–5; 4.1ff; 11.44–49; *De syn.*, 69.

Here justice is done both to the ineffable and inexhaustible reality of God, and to accurate positive knowledge of him mediated in and through Jesus Christ. It is to know him in a way that is really proper to God, and thus in a godly way, worthy of him. But this is also to know God in a true and accurate way determined by his nature as it is manifested in the incarnate Son. It is only as our minds are open and adjusted to God in accordance with his revealed nature, and only as we respond to him in faith, obedience and worship, that we can think and speak of God with the kind of precision that is appropriate to his divine nature. Piety and precision, godliness and exactness belong together and condition one another, for knowledge of God arises and takes shape in our mind under the determination of his revealed nature, and is maintained in the experience of worship, prayer, holiness and godliness. Thus empirical and theoretical, religious and theological elements blend indivisibly together in theological understanding and formulation.[22]

Strictly speaking, as Irenaeus pointed out, only God can know himself so that it is only through God that God may be known. Since God alone exists within his own eternity and infinity, only he can know himself in a way that is strictly in accordance with who God is, proportionate to his being and commensurate with his nature as God. Hence if we are really to know God it can be only through sharing in some incredible way in the knowledge which God has of himself.[23] That is to say, we can know God only if he brings us into communion with him in the inner relations of his own being as Father, Son and Holy Spirit. This sharing in the knowledge that God has of himself was made possible through the incarnation of God's Son and his mediation of the Spirit of the Father and the Son. In the incarnation God communicated himself to us in Jesus Christ his beloved Son, not something about himself, but his very *Self*, and thereby made himself known to us according to his own divine nature as Father. And at Pentecost God poured out upon us his own Spirit who as the Spirit of the Father and the Son is

---

[22]See especially Athanasius, *Expositio fidei*, 1–4; and *In illud "Omnia mihi tradita"*, 1–6.

[23]Thus Irenaeus, *Adv. haer.*, 4.11.1–5, vol. 2, pp. 158–62. See 'The Deposit of Faith', *SJT*, vol. 36, 1983, No. 1, pp. 8ff.

the immediate presence of God to us in his own very being as God. In Jesus Christ God has embodied in our human existence the mutual knowledge which the Father and the Son have of one another and in the Holy Spirit he gives us communion in the mutual relation of the Father and the Son and thus makes us share in the knowledge which the Father and the Son have of one another. To express it the other way round, through Jesus Christ we are given access to the Father in one Spirit.[24]

It is not too much to say that this relation of the Son to the Father revealed in Jesus Christ provided Nicene theology with its central focus and basis, for the incarnation of the Son opened the way to knowing God in himself, as nothing else could have done. In Jesus Christ the Son of God took our human nature upon himself and made it his own so completely that he came among us *as man*; and by what he was *as man*, he revealed to us what he was and is *as God*. That is to say, without giving up his divine nature, he united himself to us in our human nature so completely, that by living out his divine life within our human life as a real human life he revealed something of the innermost secret of his own divine life as Son of the Father. But precisely in revealing to us his own nature as the Son, he revealed the nature of the Father, not just by word, teaching us what God is like, but by being what he was and is, the very Son of the Father incarnate in our human life. It was the overwhelming conviction of the Nicene Church that it is only with the incarnation of the Son that true knowledge of God has been brought within the range of our human understanding in a positive way, for it is only through sharing in the Son's knowledge of the Father that our thought and speech of God may really have God as their object and so have positive content. Through a movement of self-humbling or self-emptying for our sakes, God the Son condescended to share our creatureliness and littleness and ignorance, in order to lift us up in himself to communion with God and knowledge of him in accordance with what he really is in himself. 'To the Son only is he known, for no one knows the Father except the Son and he to whom the Son wills to reveal him, nor yet the Son except the

---

[24]Eph. 2.18.

Father. Each has perfect and complete knowledge of the Other. Therefore, since no one knows the Father except the Son, let our thoughts of the Father be at one with the thoughts of the Son, the only faithful witness who reveals him.'[25]

This focus upon the mutual knowledge of the Father and the Son as the ground of our knowledge of God was not held to detract in any way from the reality and work of the Holy Spirit, for it is only through the communion of the Spirit who is sent to us from the Father through the Son that we may actually partake of the relation of the Son to the Father and through him be given access to the Father himself. It is thus understandable that it was by reference to the inner relation of the Son to the Father in the centre of its faith that the Church formulated its understanding of everything else: creation, salvation, the Church, the resurrection of the dead and the life of the world to come.

In ourselves as contingent beings we are confined within the limited range of our creaturely consciousness and perception, but under the impact of God's self-revelation in Jesus Christ and the creative operation of his Holy Spirit our minds and capacities are opened and our thoughts are expanded far beyond their finite limits until they are made appropriate, in some measure at least, to their divine object.[26] It is the Holy Spirit who actualises the self-giving of God in Jesus Christ and so enables us to receive and apprehend what is beyond ourselves altogether, the self-knowledge of God himself incarnate among us in Christ. That is what is actualised in the faith and worship and obedient devotion of the Church to God's self-communication through the Son and in the Spirit. Hence, to cite Hilary again, 'God cannot be known except by devotion.'[27] That is to say, it is in and through the relation of intimate communion with God in Christ and through the Spirit in which we are engaged through faith, worship, meditation and adoration, that our human reason becomes adapted and adjusted to knowledge of God in accordance with his nature as Father, Son and Holy Spirit, and we are thereby initiated into accurate

[25]Hilary, *De Trin.*, 2.6; cf. 2.10, 20; and especially 5.20f.
[26]This was a favourite theme with Hilary, e.g. *De Trin.*, 1.18 or 7.41.
[27]Hilary, *De Trin.*, 22.44.

knowledge of him determined by what God really is in himself and as he manifests himself to us.

Before we proceed to examine more carefully what access to God the Father through the Son and in one Spirit means, let us note that by accuracy or precision in knowledge is not meant some narrow biblicist way of thinking and speaking about God. Accurate or precise knowledge of God is not gained by stringing together biblical statements but by allowing our thought to be informed and determined by the truth of God to which they direct us. To regard biblical statements as divine assertions does not mean that they are immediately intelligible, for they have to be interpreted in the light of the truth to which they refer, and in accordance with which our interpretations of them must be tested. Hence we have to think out for ourselves what they mean in the light of that reference.[28] This does not mean that we have to leave behind the guidance of the Holy Scriptures through which alone God's revelation is mediated to us, but that we refuse to be content with reproducing the mere letter of the biblical statements in our determination to rest our thinking and speaking upon the truth of God himself who addresses us through those biblical statements. This means that we have to decide what we ourselves say of the truth under the direction of the biblical statements, and how we are to formulate our statements in such a way that they are established as true through their adequacy to the truth itself. This involves what Athanasius called a 'freedom of religious discourse' on the basis of the Holy Scriptures when we pass beyond what they literally say to the truth of God which they convey, and seek to express that as accurately and precisely as we can.[29] And we dare not do that except in the most cautious and reverent way and with much prayer.[30]

As we have already noted, Nicene theologians like Athanasius and Hilary were very conscious of the difficult and dangerous position into which they had been put by having to make definite assertions beyond the explicit statements of the Holy Scriptures. It was only with trembling and prayer, they

[28] Thus Hilary, *De Trin.*, 3.1ff.
[29] Athanasius, *Con. Ar.*, 1.9.
[30] Athanasius, *Con. Ar.*, 1.25; *Ad Ser.*, 1.1; *Ad Epict.*, 13, etc.

claimed, that they could do so, but they felt compelled by the truth itself, which they met in the Holy Scriptures, to put into precise terms what they found they had to say in fidelity to the truth, and thereby to protect the Holy Scriptures from arbitrary interpretation and distortion.[31] Athanasius and Hilary were reflecting what had been done at the Council of Nicaea when the fathers sought to give accurate and exact expression to the heart and substance of the evangelical message as conveyed through the Holy Scriptures, and thus brought to light the underlying pattern of the truth of the Gospel in the light of which the Scriptures themselves become more intelligible to us.[32]

All Nicene theology was built up in the worshipping Church through biblical interpretation and meditation. Theologians and bishops searched through the Holy Scriptures, of the Old as well as the New Testament, and came to lay immense stress upon certain biblical texts which they regarded as key passages for the understanding of the Gospel. They distilled out of them the essential connections of the Gospel which gave coherent structure to their Christian faith, and forged them into an interpretative and theological instrument with which to clarify the mind of the Church and defend the deposit of faith entrusted to them through the apostles.[33] It will be sufficient for our purpose here to consider only several of these key passages.

Of quite fundamental importance for Nicene theology were the words of our Lord reported by St Luke and St Matthew: 'All things have been delivered to me by my Father; and no one knows who the Son is except the Father; and no one knows who the Father is except the Son and any one to whom the Son chooses to reveal him.'[34] Careful examination disclosed that the mutual relation of knowing between the Father and the Son, to which we have had to refer already, involved a mutual relation

[31]Athanasius, *De decr.*, 19ff; Hilary, *De Trin.*, 2.1–11.

[32]Athanasius, *De syn.*, 5ff; Hilary, *De syn.*, 62f, 88f.

[33]Athanasius, *De decr.*, 32; *Ad episc.*, 4; *Ad Jov.*, 1; *Ad Epict.*, 1. Cf. Cyril of Jer., *Cat.*, 5.12–13.

[34]Luke 10.22; Matthew 11.27. See especially Athanasius, *In ill. om.* Parallel passages from John, 10.15, 30, 38; 14.9, were also adduced by Athanasius, *Con. Ar.*, 3.3, 5f, 10, 16f; *De decr.*, 21, 31; *De syn.*, 45; *Ad episc.*, 9, 13 etc.

of *being* between them as well, and not only between the eternal
Son and the Father but between the incarnate Son and the
Father. This implies that we are given access to the closed circle
of divine knowing between the Father and the Son only
through cognitive union with Christ, that is only through an
interrelation of knowing and being between us and the
incarnate Son, although in our case this union is one of
participation through grace and not one of nature.

This stress on cognitive union with the incarnate Son of the
Father was greatly reinforced by Pauline teaching about
adoption and union with Christ and Johannine teaching about
mutual indwelling between us and Christ. For Nicene theology,
then, the mutual relation of knowing and being between the
Father and the Lord Jesus Christ constitutes the ontological
ground for our knowing of God, for in and through it our
knowledge of God the Father is objectively rooted in the eternal
being of God himself. Thus through union with Christ we are
given access to knowledge of God as he is in his own being.
Moreover, it is on the same ground that we know that the Holy
Spirit who comes to us from the Father through the Son, as the
Spirit of the Father and the Son, belongs to the one being of
God, for there is a mutual relation of knowing and being
between the Spirit and the Father and the Spirit and the Son, as
there is between the Son and the Father.[35] Thus the knowledge
of God the Father to which we are given access through the Son
and in the Spirit is a knowledge of God as he eternally is in
himself as Father, Son and Holy Spirit.[36] Christocentrism and
Theocentrism are thus coincident.

It must be noted that the Son reveals the Father not by being
Father but by being *Son*. It is precisely as the only begotten Son
that Jesus Christ is the place where we may meet and know the
Father, the Son incarnate who gives us access to the Father by
sharing with us his Sonship. In him the self-knowledge of God
has become incarnate in the two-way relation between the
Father in heaven and Jesus Christ on earth, into which we may

[35]See Gregory Naz., Or. 31.8–10; Basil, *De Sp. St.*, 18.47; Gregory Nyss.,
De Sp. St. adv. Maced., edit. by W. Jaeger, p. 98.
[36]Athanasius, *Ad Ser.*, 1.17; *Ad Jov.*, 4, etc.; Basil, *De Sp. St.* 18.47; Gregory
Naz., *Or.*, 6.13; 25.17.

be initiated through union with Christ. Thus the closed circle of knowing between the Father and the Son has been inserted into the realm of contingent reality where we human beings belong, intersecting our human knowledge of one another and of the world, in such a way that in Jesus Christ we may share in the very knowledge which God has of himself.

Knowledge of God the Father, then, and knowledge of God the Son are coincident. That is a very important. We do not know the Father first and then come to know the Son; nor do we know the Son first and then come to know the Father. If we begin with the conviction that Christ is God, we inevitably apply a preconceived idea of God to our understanding of Christ. But if we know Christ only as the Son of the Father, only as in and through him we know God, then our knowledge of Christ the Son and our knowledge of God the Father coincide. In this event any prior knowledge of God which we may claim to have is reconstructed through our sharing in the mutual knowing of the Father and the Son. It is in this light that we may understand why Jesus Christ did not immediately or openly proclaim himself to his disciples as the Son of God, for they could have interpreted that only in terms of their preconceptions of God. Instead, Christ chose to meet people in a humble anonymous way, deliberately holding back knowledge of himself, so that his self-revelation by word would take place only step by step with his self-revelation in act. Hence it was only as the disciples were initiated into the communion of Christ with the Father that they came to know who the Father is from the Son, and at the same time to know who the Son is from the Father. This is why Nicene theology found it had to reject both a docetic and an adoptionist or ebionite approach to the understanding of Christ, that is, both a 'a Christology from below', and a 'Christology from above', since our knowledge of Christ as the incarnate Son and our knowledge of God the Father interpenetrate each other, arise together and regulate each other. 'All who have God for their Father through faith, have him for Father through that same faith whereby they confess Jesus Christ is the Son of God.'[37]

---

[37]Hilary, *De Trin.*, 6.30. See also 1.17; 3.17 & 22; 5.20.

Another passage of prime importance for Nicene theology was taken from St Paul: 'Eye has not seen, nor ear heard, neither has it entered into the heart of man, the things that God has prepared for them who love him. But God has revealed them unto us by his Spirit, for the Spirit searches all things, even the very depths of God's own being. What man knows the things of a man except the spirit of man that is in him? Even so the things of God knows no one, except the Spirit of God.'[38] Theologically this is to be taken in conjunction with the passages already cited from the Gospels about the fact that entry into the exclusive knowledge of the Son by the Father and of the Father by the Son may be opened to us by the Son. That is what takes place when Jesus Christ gives us the Holy Spirit who is the Spirit of the Father and of the Son, and who comes to us from the inner being of the Triune God. As Jesus Christ was born of the Virgin Mary by the power of the Spirit, received the Spirit without measure in the human nature he took from us, offered himself to the Father through the eternal Spirit in atoning self-consecration on our behalf, so he now mediates to us the same Spirit who searches the depths of God's being, in order that we through the Spirit and in the Spirit may actually share in the self-knowledge of God.

It was because of this mutual relation between the agency of the incarnate Son and agency of the Holy Spirit, in the mediation of the Spirit by Christ and of Christ by the Spirit, that the Church found it had to go beyond what the fathers of Nicaea had said about the Son, supplementing it by corresponding statements about the Holy Spirit. It had become clear that the doctrine of the Son cannot be separated from the doctrine of the Holy Spirit any more, as we shall see, than the doctrine of the Spirit can be separated from the doctrine of the Son. Epistemologically, or even logically, the doctrine of the Son comes first because the Son is the Word or *Logos* of God become flesh. Nevertheless, since we may know God only through his Word, it is only through the same Word that we can have knowledge of the Spirit, as well as of the Father and the Son. On the other hand, we cannot understand the Word

---

[38] I Cor. 2.10.

except through sharing in the very Spirit through whom the Word was made flesh.

Attention must also be directed to the words of our Lord reported by St John: 'I am the way, the truth and the life: no one comes to the Father but by me.'[39] In their rejection of the divine nature of Christ the Arians had searched all through the Scriptures to find statements referring to the creaturely nature, and the lowly, servile status of the Son. They made great play with a text from the book of Proverbs which had long been applied to the divine *Logos*: 'The Lord created me a beginning of his ways for his works',[40] to show that the incarnate Son of God was a created intermediary. However, Athanasius and the Nicene theologians seized upon it and interpreted it in a *soteriological* sense, along with many passages from the New Testament, notably from the Epistle to the Hebrews, to show that the human nature of Jesus Christ, the incarnate Son of God, had indeed been created by God as the beginning (ἀρχή) of all his ways and works for our salvation. Thus, far from rejecting the creaturely, servile condition of Jesus, they insisted that out of his sheer grace the eternal Son of God had deliberately condescended to make our servile condition his own in order to redeem us.[41] What came out of this was an immense concentration by Nicene theology upon the *vicarious humanity* of the incarnate Son, which we shall discuss later. It was as such, they insisted, that Jesus Christ was the Way, the Truth and the Life, apart from whom no one can go to the Father.[42] And as such he is not only the Source or ἀρχή of all God's ways but the controlling Principle or ἀρχή by which all our knowledge of God is tested. Thus the downright humanity of Christ became the touchstone of genuine knowledge of God and authentic understanding of the Christian message. 'The Lord's humanity (κυριακὸς ἄνθρωπος) was created as "a beginning of ways" and he manifested it to us for our salvation. By it we have access to the Father, for he is the way which leads us back to the Father.

[39] John 14.6.

[40] Prov. 8.22 (LXX).

[41] See especially the long discussion of Prov. 8.22 in *Con. Ar.*, 2.18–82, but cf. also *Ad episc.*, 10.

[42] Cf. Basil, *De Sp. St.*, 8.17ff; 18.47.

And a way is a corporeal visible reality, such as is the Lord's humanity.'[43]

The Nicene focus of attention was thus directed upon the humanity in which the Son of God was born, crucified and died for us, rose again from the dead and was taken up into heaven – all that Christ became and did for our sakes and on our behalf, in mediating divine revelation and salvation to mankind. The soteriological understanding of the incarnate economy of the Son puts Jesus Christ into the very centre of our knowledge of God, but in such a way that he is made for us the one in whom we know God the Father. It is only as our knowledge of God conforms to Jesus Christ that it can be accurate and precise knowledge of God, for Jesus Christ the incarnate Son is the perfect and proportionate image of God, the one Form or *Eidos* (Εἶδος) of Godhead,[44] the 'exact seal', as Athanasius expressed it,[45] in whom the Father imparts to us knowledge of himself as he really is and as he has actually manifested himself. As the Son of God incarnate Jesus Christ is thus not only the image but the very reality of God in his self-communication to us, so that to meet and know him is to meet and know God the Father, for he is in the Father and the Father is in him.[46] As St Basil (or his brother Gregory) expressed it: 'All things that are the Father's are seen in the Son, and all things that are the Son's are the Father's; because the whole Son is in the Father and has all the Father in himself. Thus the Person (ὑπόστασις) of the Son becomes as it were Form and Face of the knowledge of the Father, and the Person (ὑπόστασις) of the Father is known in the Form of the Son.'[47] In the lapidary words of Athanasius, 'The Form of the Godhead of the Father is the *Being* of the Son.'[48]

Moreover it is in and through the humanity of Christ in all that he had done for us that the Holy Spirit is conveyed to us, so

[43] Athanasius, *Exp. fidei*, 4.

[44] Athanasius, *Con. Ar.*, 3.3, 6, 10, 15, 17; *De Syn.*, 2; *Ad episc.*, 10. Cf. Gregory Naz., *Or.*, 38.13f; Gregory Nyss., *Con. Eun.*, 3.2.8.

[45] Athanasius, *In ill. om.*, 5; cf. 3–4.

[46] Athanasius, *Con. Ar.*, 3.1.

[47] Gregory/Basil, *Ep.*, 38.8.

[48] Athanasius, *Con. Ar.*, 3.3 & 6.

that the Holy Spirit is given along with the incarnation of the Son a place of central significance in the structure of Christian theology. While the incarnate form of the Son provides our knowledge of God with its controlling and shaping principle, it is a knowledge mediated through the Son which we may have only through the activity of the Holy Spirit and as in the Spirit we participate in the Son and through him in God. The kind of Christocentricity that characterises the Nicene theology, therefore, is not one that detracts in any way from a Theocentricity, but rather serves what we might well call a 'Patrocentricity', and thus also gives unreserved place to the Spirit of the Father who is conveyed to us through the Son and on the ground of his saving and reconciling work. On the other hand, as Athanasius insisted so often,[49] we must not regard the doctrine of the Spirit as merely attached to the doctrine of God, for the Son and the Spirit are not additions to God, but belong to the eternal and essential being of God as God, the one Triune God who is in himself wholly Father, wholly Son and wholly Spirit, without division in the unity of his being. It is as one whole undivided God that he reveals himself to us as Father, Son and Holy Spirit.[50]

This 'evangelical and apostolic' doctrine of God who is revealed to us as Father through the Son and in the Spirit[51] was unfolded in its trinitarian structure and defended by Nicene theologians throughout the fourth century in the face of Judaism and Hellenism. They established firmly in the Church the catholic doctrine of the Trinity and Unity of God, preserving the Trinity from Judaising tendencies in a Sabellian contraction of the three Persons into an undifferentiated unity, and preserving the Unity from Hellenising tendencies in an Arian severance of the three Persons by a diversity of natures.[52] The fundamental significance of this distinctively Christian

---

[49]See especially, Athanasius, *Ad Ser.*, *passim*; and Basil, *De Sp. St.*, 13.30.
[50]Gregory Naz., *Or.*, 31.14.

[51]Thus Hilary, *De syn.*, 61. See also *De Trin.*, 1.37; 2.22; 4.1, 7; 5.35; 7.7; 8.4.
[52]Gregory Naz., *Or.*, 1.37; 18.16; 21.13, 34; 34.8; 38.15; 39.11; Basil, *Hom.*, 24.1–7; *De Sp. S.*, 30.77; *Hex.*, 9.6; *Ep.*, 189.2f; 210.3f; 265.2; Gregory Nyss., *Con. Eun.*, 1.18f; 3.8.2, 4; *Or. cat.*, Prol., 1, 3; *Ep.*, 2.

approach to knowledge of God the Father may be appreciated more fully in contrast with the approaches of Judaism and Hellenism.

(1) The contrast with Judaism

The Nicene doctrine of God was undoubtedly Hebraic in basic slant and character, clearly evident in its rejection of any conception of God so utterly transcendent that he cannot accommodate himself to natures other than his own, and does not interact with the world. But it is also evident in its stress upon the oneness and holiness of God who intervenes in history for the salvation of mankind, and upon the Word of God mediated through the biblical revelation of the Old Testament as well as of the New Testament. In its developed theological form it was a Hebraeo-Christian soteriological conception of God that prevailed, governed by the decisive fact that in Jesus Christ God himself personally intervenes in the world working out the salvation of mankind.[53] Jesus Christ is none other than God the eternal Word and Son revealing himself to us and acting directly on our behalf within our human existence and life. Hence the Nicene theologians argued that, with the incarnate presence (ἔνσαρκος παρουσία) of God among us, whatever is said and done by God is said and done exclusively *from the Person* (ἐκ προσώπου) of Christ.[54] Here the Old Testament concepts of the Face and Word of God[55] are so intensely personalised that to see and hear the Lord Jesus Christ is to see and hear God the Father himself face to face.

By drawing near to us in Jesus Christ who took our human nature upon himself and lived out his divine life within it as a human life, God has opened up to us knowledge of his innermost Self as a fullness of personal being and brought us into

[53]Thus Gregory Nyss.: 'the Deity effects salvation by a personal intervention.' *Or. Cat.*, 24. Cf. R. V. Sellers, *Two Ancient Christologies*, 1940, p. 66.

[54]This was a favourite expression of Athanasius, e.g. *De inc.* 3. See *Theol. in Reconcil.*, 245f, and R. V. Sellers, *op. cit.*, p. 46f.

[55]Gen. 32.30; Num. 6.25; 2 Chron. 7.14; Ps. 31.16, etc.

intimate personal communion with himself as Father, Son and Holy Spirit.[56] Let us recall once again the words of St Paul in Ephesians 2.18, which meant so much to the Nicene Church: 'For through him we both (i.e. Jews and Gentiles) have access by one Spirit to the Father.' Through his atoning reconciliation Christ Jesus has broken down the middle wall of partition separating Gentiles from Jews in drawing near to God in worship, thereby incorporating Gentiles into the community of divine revelation and salvation; but he has also opened a way through the veil between God and mankind, giving both Jews and Gentiles alike access into the immediate presence of God the Father.

For Judaism, on the other hand, God was held to be so utterly transcendent that he is ineffable and unnameable, quite unknowable in the undifferentiated oneness of his being, so that any claim to know him in himself was rejected with horror as impiety. There can be no knowledge of God in his internal relations, but only knowledge of him in his external relations – hence the desperate plight of a Judaism that becomes allied to some form of Hellenic dualism. Properly speaking, of course, historic Judaism was grounded in the unique self-revelation of God in covenant and dialogue with Israel, the people chosen to be the instrument of divine revelation to all mankind. Thus in ancient Israel God was known not in a detached, abstract way simply through a contrast between the Uncreated and the created, but in a positive, saving way through his Word and mighty acts as Creator, Lord and Redeemer. While mediators of divine revelation like Moses were said to speak with God 'face to face',[57] and prophets and psalmists clearly had moving intimate experiences of God, nevertheless before God's Word became flesh in the fullness of time the faithful were not brought into such a close personal relation with God that they came to know him directly in himself as he became known in Jesus Christ.

---

[56]It was in fact with the formulation of this distinctively Christian knowledge of the triune God that, as we shall see, the very concept of 'person', not found before, even in the Old Testament, emerged and became an all-important category in human thought.

[57]Exod. 33.11.

The Nicene theologians were not slow to appreciate the basic revolution in knowledge of God that had taken place in Jesus Christ, through whom as Mediator between God and man we who are far off from God are brought near and are actually given access to him. That is to say, with the incarnate παρουσία of his Son in Jesus Christ, God in himself is no longer closed to us, but has opened himself to our knowledge in his own being as Father, Son and Holy Spirit, for what he has revealed of himself to us through Christ and in the Spirit he *is in himself*. Hence we may now enter into personal communion with God without being limited by our creaturely incapacities or being obstructed by our alienation, because of what God in his love has done for us and our salvation in Jesus Christ and because of the gift of his Holy Spirit, the indwelling presence of God himself. Thus through Christ Jesus and in the Spirit whether we are Jews or Gentiles we may enter within the veil, and know God in the inner relations of his own sublime being as Father, Son and Holy Spirit.

To know God in this way does not mean that we can know *what* the being of God is,[58] but it does mean that we are given knowledge of God that is directly and objectively grounded in his eternal being. Epistemologically, that is what the doctrine of the Holy Trinity is about, and what the Nicene Creed is about: that we may really know God the Father Almighty in a positive way. It is at this fundamental point that Christianity differs from Judaism, for it means, quite astonishingly, that in some real measure we may have a conceptual grasp of God in his own internal relations. And yet at this point the Nicene theologians remained thoroughly Hebraic in their horror of presumption. Overwhelmed with awe and wonder, they were aware of treading upon holy ground where they must walk with the utmost reverence and humility, and impose upon themselves a disciplined reserve. If even the holy cherubim or seraphim cover their faces in the immediate presence of God,[59] how much more must human beings, for how can they look upon God, really know God as he is in himself, and live? Yet that is precisely what

[58] Athanasius, *Ad mon.*; cf. *De decr.*, 22; *De syn.*, 35.
[59] Athanasius, *Ad Ser.*, 1.17; cf. *In ill. om.*, 6.

the astonishing condescension (συγκατάβασις) of God in Jesus Christ has made possible, accurate but devout knowledge of God in accordance with his divine nature.

(2) The contrast with Hellenism

In his *History of Dogma* Adolph Harnack maintained that in the early centuries of the Christian Church there took place a radical Hellenising of Christianity, but he also showed that it was largely due to Athanasius that a complete Hellenising of Christianity was prevented.[60] It is certainly true that the Gospel was translated into Greek from the very start and it was largely in Greek thought-forms that the early Church gave public expression to its preaching and teaching. However, far from a radical Hellenisation having taken place something very different happened, for in making use of Greek thought-forms Christian theology radically transformed them in making them vehicles of fundamental doctrines and ideas quite alien to Hellenism. In fact, the mission of the Church had the effect of altering the basic ideas of classical Hellenism, as we have already seen, through its formulation of a distinctively Christian doctrine of God as one, as Creator of the universe out of nothing, and as triune in his eternal being, and not least through the doctrine of the incarnation as the personal and saving intervention of God himself in the affairs of mankind, together with the attendant conceptions of providence, judgment and resurrection. This was one of the most significant features of Nicene theology: not the Hellenising of Christianity but the Christianising of Hellenism, a feature for which the Church was peculiarly indebted to Athanasius.

In the next chapter we shall look into the far-reaching effect of the Nicene doctrine of God as the Almighty Creator of all things visible and invisible, but at this point let us restrict attention to three important differences between Nicene and Hellenic thought, in respect of the notions of *image* (εἰκών), *word* (λόγος) and *activity* (ἐνέργεια).

[60]A. von Harnack, *History of Dogma*, Eng. tr. 1897, vol. III, p. 194.

It was a characteristic of Hellenism that it gave primacy to the sense of sight over the other senses, and so developed an essentially *optical* model of thought.[61] This is evident in the fact that in Greek 'idea' (ἰδέα), 'form' (εἶδος), and 'theory' (θεωρία), as their derivations indicate, refer either to modes of seeing or to what is seen, and in the fact that words or names were regarded as imaging in a real or conventional way what they signify or represent. Add to this the Greek explanation of vision as taking place through a beam of light directed from the eye to the object, and it is understandable that in Hellenism the habit of thinking in images (εἰκόνες, εἴδωλα) projected by human beings beyond themselves in the form of myths, should have had such a predominant role in religion and philosophy alike.

The contrast between Christianity and Hellenism could hardly be greater than at this fundamental level, where biblical patterns of thought governed by the Word of God and the obedient hearing of faith (ὑπακοὴ τῆς πίστεως) conflict sharply with those of Greek religion and philosophy. The issue came to its head in the Arian controversy over the Father – Son relation at the heart of the Christian Gospel. Are the terms 'father' and 'son' to be understood as visual, sensual images taken from our human relations and then projected mythologically into God? In that event how can we avoid projecting creaturely gender into God, and thinking of him as grandfather as well as father, for the only kind of father we know is one who is son of another father? To think of God like that, in terms of the creaturely content of images projected out of ourselves, inevitably gives rise to anthropomorphic and polymorphic notions of deity and in fact to polytheism and idolatry.[62] However, if we think from a centre in God as he reveals himself to us through his Word incarnate in Jesus Christ, then we know him as Father in himself in an utterly unique and incomparable way which then becomes the controlling standard by reference to which all notions of creaturely fatherhood and sonship are to be understood. 'God

---

[61]Cf. Martin Buber, *Eclipse of God*, 1957, p. 40.

[62]Cf. the arguments of Athenagoras of Athens in the second century A.D. against the anthropocentric character of images, *Leg.*, 7–10, 15–18. See also Origen, *Con. Cel.*, 8.17–18; Eusebius of Caesarea, *Opera*, MPG 20, 1545–49; and cf. V. Weidlé, *The Baptism of Art*, Oxford, 1950.

does not make man his pattern, but rather, since God alone is properly and truly Father, we men are called fathers of our own children, for of him every fatherhood in heaven and earth is named.'[63] Unique Fatherhood and unique Sonship in God mutually define one another in an absolute and singular way. As Athanasius pithily expressed it in rejection of Arian anthropocentric mythologising: 'Just as we cannot ascribe a father to the Father, so we cannot ascribe a brother to the Son.'[64]

The fact that God has named himself to us as Father in and through Jesus Christ his incarnate Son means that we cannot and may not seek to have knowledge of God or express it in such a way as to by-pass his self-naming. Thus the terms 'father' and 'son' have not only been sanctioned by divine revelation but have been given a necessary function in our knowledge and experience of God. That is why we are baptised in the name of the Father and of the Son and of the Holy Spirit. The question that had to be clarified in Nicene theology was how the creaturely images latent in the notions of fatherhood and sonship, and indeed in all the human terms and concepts used in the Holy Scriptures, bear upon God.[65] Nowhere more than at this point does the Hebraic slant of Nicene theology appear, in the impact upon it of the Old Testament revelation of God with its uncompromising rejection, especially in the second commandment of the Decalogue, of all sensual pictorial imagery of God in heathen worship of the *Baalim* and *Astaroth*, the nature and sex deities of the old semitic world. The fundamental principle which the Church took over from this biblical tradition and incorporated steadily in its own reverent approach to God was that he utterly transcends all creaturely imagination. Hence in knowledge of God the Hellenic idea that

---

[63] Athanasius, *Con. Ar.*, 1.23, with reference to Eph. 3:15. See the preceding discussion, 1.21–22.

[64] Athanasius, *Ad Ser.*, 1.16. The Arians' mythological projection of human relations into Deity had the effect of sexising their notion of God, which in turn called for a form of demythologising! Thus also Gregory Naz., *Or.*, 31.7.

[65] See the epistemological analysis of the function of biblical analogies and images offered by Hilary, *De Trin.*, 2.1.18f; 2.6ff.

images are *mimetically* related to what they signify, was rejected and replaced by the Hebraic idea that all images properly used in speech and thought of God refer to him *without imaging* him.[66] As we shall see later when we come to the doctrine of the Holy Spirit and the Athanasian conception of the Spirit as 'the image of the Son', even the images employed in divine revelation bear upon God in an *imageless* way for he infinitely transcends their creaturely content. Thus Christian theology makes proper use of the terms 'Father' and 'Son' to speak of God as he is in himself, when it allows them to refer imagelessly to relations eternally inherent in God which are in their uncreated transcendent form the creative ground of what on our creaturely level of existence we are meant to understand by 'father'/'son' relations in human being.

This Hebraic approach was immensely reinforced by the Nicene doctrines of the incarnate Son and of the Holy Spirit. On the one hand, the fact that Jesus Christ is both the image and the reality of God in his own incarnate Person had the effect of excluding all other images or conceptions of God. Far from being the embodiment of what we human beings think of God, he is God's unique self-embodiment among us in human form. That is, the incarnation stands, not for the projection of the human into the divine, but for the projection of the divine into the human, and as such is the rock upon which all mythology is shattered.[67] On the other hand, as we shall see later, the fact that Nicene theologians paralleled the *homoousion* of the Son with the *homoousion* of the Spirit, in showing that what God the Father is toward us in the Son and in the Spirit he is antecedently and eternally in himself, had the effect of preventing believers from reading back into God the creaturely content in their notions of 'fatherhood' and 'sonship', and thus from thinking of the divine Fatherhood or Sonship in any material or sensual way. Moreover, the stress of Athanasius not only upon the fact that the Son is the sole Form (Εἶδος) of Godhead, but that the Spirit is the Image (Εἰκών) of the Son, made clear that God is to be thought of in an imageless way or in terms of imageless

---

[66]Gregory Naz., *Or.*, 28.12ff; 29.2; 31.7, 33, etc.
[67]Cf. F. W. Camfield, *Reformation Old and New*, 1947, p. 85.

relations.[68] The Father/Son relation is essentially a relation in the Spirit, and that does not allow us to read material images back into God. It was thus the central place given by Nicene theology to the doctrine of the Holy Spirit, as well as to the doctrine of the Son, that helped to cleanse the minds of the faithful from the Hellenic habit of thinking of God in mimetic, anthropocentric images.[69]

Instead of allowing itself to be Hellenised by the optical thinking endemic in the religion and philosophy of the Mediterranean world, Christian theology remained faithful to its Hebraic and biblical roots. But what of the impact of Hellenism upon Christianity in respect of the notions of 'word' (λόγος) and 'activity' (ἐνέργεια)? It is to Athanasius that we may turn once again for an answer, and specifically to his concepts of ἐνούσιος λόγος and ἐνούσιος ἐνέργεια, that is, of Word and activity intrinsic to the very being (οὐσία) of God as God.[70] Here we find that as Christian theology assumed form and developed within the milieu of Greek thought and speech there took place a far-reaching alteration in basic Hellenic ideas.

On the one hand, the Greek notion of *logos* (λόγος) was Christianised by being assimilated into the Old Testament notion of the Word of the Lord (דְּבַר־יְהוָה) and the New Testament notion of the Word, who was with God and was God, become flesh in Jesus Christ. In contrast to the Greek idea of the logos as an abstract cosmological principle, it was distinctive of Christian theology, that the Logos inheres in the very being of God (ἐνούσιος λόγος) and is identical with the Person of the Son. God is never without his Word (ἄλογος) for the Word and being of God are essentially and eternally one. The Word of God is not one thing and his being another, for

---

[68]Athanasius, *Con. Ar.*, 1.15; *De syn.*, 42 & 51; *Ad Ser.*, 1.24; Hilary, *De Trin.*, 7.37; 8.52; 10.6; Gregory Naz., *Or.*, 31.33; and cf. Cyril of Alexandria, *De Trin.*, 6, MPG 75.1089.

[69]Greek icons are not regarded as mimetic images but as images referring spiritually and imagelessly to what they signify in the communion of saints. This view of icons was clarified through the iconoclastic controversy. Cf. G. Florovsky, *Collected Works*, II, Belmont, 1974, pp. 101–119.

[70]For references to these Athanasian concepts see *Theol. in Reconcil.*, pp. 222f, 226ff, 235ff.

they coinhere mutually and indivisibly in one another. Hence far from being dumb in his inner being God is intrinsically eloquent, speaking being.[71] It was this ontological concept of the *Logos* of God that characterised the Christian understanding of divine revelation as embodying the objective self-communication of God in his Word, on the basis of which *theologia*, thinking of God from a controlling centre in his Word, was sharply differentiated from all *mythologia*, thinking of God from a centre in the human self and its fantasies.[72] At the same time, the general conception of the relation of *logos* to being in empirical realities was radically altered, as we shall see, through the doctrine of creation of the universe out of nothing, for it gave rise to the conviction that in creating all things through his Word God had endowed them with a contingent *logos* or intelligibility of their own. The radical change that this doctrine of the inherence of *logos* in being imported for Greek thought may be judged by the fact that in due course it opened up the way for the development of empirical science.

On the other hand, the Greek notion of *energeia* (ἐνέργεια) was also Christianised under the transforming impact of the biblical conception of the creative and providential activity of the living God. In contrast, especially to the Aristotelian view of God who is characterised by an 'activity of immobility' (ἐνέργεια ἀκινησίας) and who moves the world only as 'the object of the world's desire' (κινεῖ ὡς ἐρώμενον),[73] the Athanasian view of God was one in which activity and movement were regarded as intrinsic to his very being as God (ἐνούσιος ἐνέργεια). God is never without his activity (ἐνέργεια), for his activity and his being are essentially and eternally one. The act of God is not one thing, and his being another, for they coinhere mutually and indivisibly in one another. Hence far from God being inactive in his inner being, it belongs to the essential and eternal nature of his being to move

[71]Cf. Hilary: 'The Word is a reality, not a sound, a being, not a speech, God, not a nonentity.' *De Trin.*, 2.15.

[72]Cf. Plato's discussion of what happens in the absence of a 'divine logos' from beyond ourselves, *Phaedo*, 85 c.

[73]Cf. Aristotle, *Eth. Nic.*, 7, 1154b; *Met.*, 1072b.

and energise and act. It was this dynamic conception of God that marked so distinctively the Christian understanding of the incarnation as the personal embodiment in space and time of God's providential and redemptive interaction with mankind. Thus the Nicene theologians thought of Jesus Christ as one with God the Father in *act* as well as in *being*, for he incarnated the *active presence* of God himself in human history, and constituted in all he was and did the free outgoing movement of the divine being in condescension and love toward mankind. This saving *philanthropia* (φιλανθρωπία) – Athanasius' favourite word for God's active love toward us – was the very antithesis of the Aristotelian *eros* (ἔρως), the immanent desire for itself by which the unmoved Mover timelessly affects the world. Whereas with the Aristotelian conception of this inertial relation of God to the cosmos, there could be no idea of any creation of being out of nothing or of any beginning of time, the Judaeo-Christian conception of the living and acting God established the doctrine of the creation of all things out of nothing, and laid the foundation for a very different conception of motion in created reality as well.

It should now be clear, even from these twin conceptions of ἐνούσιος λόγος and ἐνούσιος ἐνέργεια, that while the Nicene theologians made considerable use of Greek terms and ideas in articulating the conceptual content of the Christian Faith, they reshaped them in a very basic way under the creative impact of the Holy Scriptures. *Being, word,* and *act* in patristic theology came to mean something very different from what they meant in Platonic, Aristotelian or Stoic thought: they are in fact radically 'un-Greek'. Thus far from Nicene theology resulting from a Hellenisation of Biblical Christianity, it represents a recasting of familiar Hellenic thought-forms in order to make them worthy vehicles of the Gospel, and enable the Church to clarify and give consistent expression to the trinitarian structure inherent in evangelical knowledge of God the Father to whom we have access through the Son and in one Spirit. It was above all in their service to the understanding and adoration of the Holy Trinity in the Church that the thought-forms appropriated from Greek culture received their indelible Christian stamp. It was thus that godliness and accuracy, worship and precision, were allied inseparably together in the theological activity of the Church fathers and theologians who gave Christendom the Nicene–Constantinopolitan Creed.

3

The Almighty Creator

'One God the Father Almighty, Maker of heaven and earth and of all things visible and invisible.'

In its confession of belief in *one God the Father Almighty, the Maker*, the Nicene Council deliberately gave primacy to the concept of the Fatherhood of God, for knowledge of God as Creator is taken from knowledge of God as Father, and not the other way round. As we have seen, however, knowledge of the Father is derived from Jesus Christ his Son who is of the same being as the Father, for in him the Father has revealed himself to us as he is in his own essential nature. This is why Athanasius, in that key statement of his which we have allowed to guide us, insisted that 'it would be more godly and true to signify God from the Son and call him Father, than to name him from his works and call him Unoriginate (ἀγένητον)'.[1] It follows from this, however, that our understanding of God as Creator must likewise be taken from the Son, for it is through the Son and Word who is eternally in God and proper to his essential nature that God is the Creator and Maker of everything. 'He who calls God Father, signifies him from the Son, being well aware that, since there is a Son, it is of necessity through the Son that all things that have come into being were created. When they call him Unoriginate, they name him only from his works, and do not know the Son any more than the Greeks. But he who calls him Father, names him from his Word and, knowing the

[1] Athanasius, *Con. Ar.*, 1.34.

Word, acknowledges him to be the Maker of all, and understands that through him all things have come into being.'[2] Thus for Athanasius the concept of God as Creator is wholly governed by the coinherent relation between the Father and the Son and the inseparable activity in which they are engaged. Since the Father is never without the Son, any more than the Son is ever without the Father, all that the Father does is done in and through the Son and all that the Son does is identical with what the Father does. The same must be said of the relation between God and his Word, for since God is never without his Word, as the Word is never without God, everything that is created is created by God, through his Word, by his Word and in his Word.[3] Of paramount importance, of course, for Athanasius and all the Nicene theologians were the first chapters of St John's Gospel and of the Epistles to the Colossians and the Hebrews, in which a Christ-centred and Word-centred doctrine of creation was presented.

It was with precisely the same stress upon the Fatherhood of God, and access to God the Father through God the Son, that Hilary interpreted the Nicene doctrine of God as Creator. 'Remember', he wrote, 'that the revelation is not of the Father manifested as God but of God manifested as the Father.'[4] 'The very centre of saving faith is belief not merely in God, but in God as Father; not merely in Christ but in Christ as the Son of God; in him not as a creature, but as God the Creator, born of God.'[5] 'It is to the Father that all existence owes its origin. In Christ and through Christ he is the Source of all.'[6] For Hilary, then, it is understanding of the Fatherhood of God, mediated in and through the Person and Work of Jesus Christ, his beloved Son, that governs all that is truly thought and said of God as the Creator. 'God can never be anything but love or anything but the Father: and he who loves, does not envy; he who is Father, is wholly and entirely Father.'[7]

[2]Athanasius, *Con. Ar.*, 1.33; *De decr.*, 30–31.
[3]Athanasius, *Con. Ar.*, 2.31ff. And cf. *De decr.*, 7, 11f.
[4]Hilary, *De Trin.*, 3.22.
[5]Hilary, *De Trin.*, 1.17.
[6]Hilary, *De Trin.*, 2.6.
[7]Hilary, *De Trin.*, 9.61.

It is within this perspective of the primacy and centrality of the Father/Son relation, and of the fact that we have access to the Father only through the Son, the Word made flesh, that we may now offer an account of the Nicene doctrine of God as Almighty Creator. We cannot understand the almightiness or creatorship of God in terms of abstract possibilities and vague generalities – from what we imagine God is not, or from examining what God has brought into being in complete difference from himself. As we have just recalled, it is only in the light of God's self-revelation and self-giving to us in Jesus Christ his Son, the incarnate Offspring of his own divine nature, and not from his works, that we can have any real understanding of *who* God is, and come to know him, as far as we may, in accordance with his own nature as Father. It is only on the same ground and in the same way that we may know God in his almightiness as Creator of heaven and earth and of all things visible and invisible, that is, when we know him directly at work in Jesus Christ to whom all power in heaven and earth has been committed by the Father.[8] Owing to the unity of nature between the Father and the Son, there is also a unity of activity between them: what the Father does the Son does, and the works of the Son are to be regarded as works of the Father.[9] Thus our understanding of God's omnipotent sovereignty and of his creative activity must be strictly controlled from within the centre of actual knowledge of God in Jesus Christ as Father, his Father uniquely and our Father through him. There we learn that *it is as the Father Almighty that God is Almighty Creator*.

Throughout the early Church the *Father* was understood in a two-fold but indivisible way, as the one being (μία οὐσία) of the Godhead, and as the Father of the Son, whose Person (ὑπόστασις) is distinct from the Person of the Son and from the Person of the Spirit – although, of course, the one being of God is known to us only through the Son and in the Spirit.[10] God the

---

[8] At the Council of Constantinople the words 'of heaven and earth' were transferred to the Creed at this point from the Nicene statement about the Son.

[9] Hilary, *De Trin.*, 7.17, with reference to John 5.17–22. Cf. *De Trin.*, 8.4.

[10] See Gregory Nyss., *De Trin.*, *Opera*, edit. by W. Jaeger, 3.1, pp. 1ff; *non sint tres Dei*, 3.1, pp. 35–57. It was upon the double meaning of 'Father' that Eunomius traded his heretical ideas, *Con Eun.*, 1.36ff.

Father, precisely as Father = Godhead, is the one supreme almighty being, uncreated, self-sufficient, all-perfect, who is the transcendent Fount (πηγή), Source (ἀρχή) and Author (αἴτιος) of all other being.[11] It may even be said that in the fullest sense he alone is *being*, for all other beings are beings only in a derived sense, as his creatures.[12] God is this ultimate Source or Fountain of being, however, only as he is eternally Father (αἴτιος) of the Son and as such is the Fount of being intrinsically in his very nature as God.[13] To name God *Father* is not to name some quality in God, but 'to signify his very being'.[14] This is not to imply that God is the Fount of created beings in the same way as he is the Fount of the eternal Son, but to say that if he is not the Father who has eternally generated the Son from his own being (ἐκ τῆς οὐσίας), he cannot be essentially generative (γεννητικός) or fruitful (καρπογόνος) in his own being,[15] or therefore be regarded as intrinsically a Source of being or indeed as the Source of any being at all, for he would be no more than a mere Maker and Shaper of being.[16] It is because God *is* inherently productive and creative in his very being as God, that he is Creator. This is why Athanasius insisted that those who deny that the almighty God is Father cannot believe in him as Creator. 'If God is without Offspring (ἄγονος), then he is without work (ἀνενέργητος); for the Son is his Offspring through whom he works.'[17]

It was a fundamental principle of Athanasius that since the whole being of the Son is proper to the Father's being, and they are one in the propriety and peculiarity of nature and in the identity of the one Godhead, *whatever is said of the Father is said of*

---

[11]Athanasius, *Con. Ar.*, 2.54; 3.1; 4.3; *De decr.*, 16; *De syn.*, 46; *Ad Ant.*, 5.

[12]See Athenagoras, *Leg.*, 4.2; 15.1, where created being in relation to God as the only uncreated being is described as 'non-being'. Cf. Origen, *Con. Cel.*, 7.42f; *De prin.*, 1.1; Athanasius, *Con. gent.*, 2, 35, 40; *De inc.*, 17.

[13]Athanasius, *De syn.*, 46ff.

[14]Athanasius, *De decr.*, 22; cf. *De syn.*, 34; and *Ad Afr.*, 8.

[15]Athanasius, *De decr.*, 15; *Con. Ar.*, 1.14; 2.2, 33; 3.66; cf. 1.14, 19; *Ad Ser.*, 2.2.

[16]Cf. here G. Florovsky, 'The Concept of Creation in Saint Athanasius', *Studia Patristica*, Vol. IV, 1962, pp. 45f.

[17]Athanasius, *Con. Ar.*, 4.4; cf. 2.41; 3.11f.

the Son, except 'Father'.[18] If 'the Son has all that is the Father's' and indeed 'is the Father's All', if the Son is 'whole and complete God' (ὅλος καὶ πλήρης θεός), then in a real sense he too must be Origin or Principle (ἀρχή) of being along with the Father.[19] There cannot, of course, be two or three Sources or Origins any more than there can be two or three Fathers or Supreme Beings.[20] The Father, the Son and the Holy Spirit are indivisibly One, eternally coinhering in one another as the Blessed and Holy Trinity, but with 'one Godhead and one Principle' (μία Θεότης καὶ μία ἀρχή).[21] That is to say, it is the *triune God*, the undivided Trinity, who is the one only ultimate Principle or ἀρχή of all things. Expressed otherwise, the one being of God is whole and complete not in the Father alone but in the Son and in the Holy Spirit as much as in the Godhead. Each is the whole God (ὅλος Θεός) and wholly all that God eternally is as God.[22] It is in this sense that we are to understand the distinction and oneness in the creative activity of the Father and the Son, and never of one without the other, for what the Father does is in the Son and what the Son does is in the Father. 'While having given all things to the Son the Father still has them in the Son, and while the Son has them, still the Father has them; for the Godhead of the Son is the Godhead of the Father, and so the Father in the Son effectuates his providential ordering (πρόνοιαν) of all things.'[23] In fact 'there is nothing but the Father operates it through the Son.'[24]

It is precisely as *Father*, then, that God is the one supreme almighty being, who is the Fount (πηγή) of all being. He the eternal Father, with the eternal Son and the eternal Spirit who are consubstantial and co-equal with himself, is the transcendent

[18]Athanasius, *Con. Ar.*, 3.3–6; *De syn.*, 49. For the same principle see Gregory Nyss., *Con. Eun.*, 1.38 and 42, ed. Jaeger, I, pp. 196f and 222f; *Con. Eun.*, 3.4, II, p. 260; *Antir.*, 6 and 7, II, pp. 330f and 337.

[19]Athanasius, *Con. Ar.*, 3.6; 4.1.

[20]Athanasius, *Con. Ar.*, 3.15; 4.1–3; *Ad Ser.*, 1.28.

[21]Athanasius, *Ad Ant.*, 5; 6–11; *Con. Ar.*, 2.33; 3.1f, 15; *Ad Afr.*, 11; *In ill. om.*, 5; *Exp. fidei*, 1–4.

[22]Athanasius, *De decr.*, 16ff., 22f; *Ad episc.*, 17f; *Con. Ar.*, 1.16.28; 2.33; 3.1ff; *Ad Afr.*, 4f; cf. also *Exp. fidei*, 1f; *In ill. om.*, 6.

[23]Athanasius, *Con. Ar.*, 3.36.

[24]Athanasius, *Con. Ar.*, 3.12.

Origin (ἀρχή) of all created things, visible and invisible alike, whose transitory natures are utterly different from his own. It is exclusively as almighty Father, the unlimited and ineffable Cause (αἰτία) of all that is, that God is to be recognised as the almighty Creator.[25] 'We believe in one unbegotten God, Father Almighty, Maker of all things both visible and invisible, who has his being from himself.'[26] This conviction was given memorable expression by Hilary.

'It is the Father to whom all existence owes its origin. In Christ and through Christ he is the Source of all. In contrast to all else he is self-existent. He does not draw his being from without, but possesses it from himself and in himself. He is infinite, for nothing contains him and he contains all things; he is eternally unconditioned by space, for he is illimitable; eternally anterior to time, for time is his creation. Let imagination range to what you may suppose is God's utmost limit, and you will find him present there; strain as you will there is always a further horizon towards which to strain. Infinity is his property, just as the power of making such effort is yours. Words will fail you, but his being will not be circumscribed. Or again, turn back the pages of history, and you will find him ever present; should numbers fail to express the antiquity to which you have penetrated, yet God's eternity is not diminished. Gird up your intellect to comprehend him as a whole; he eludes you. God, as a whole, has left something within your grasp, but this something is inextricably involved in his entirety. Thus you have missed the whole, since it is only a part that remains in your hands; nay, not even a part, for you are dealing with a whole which you have failed to divide. For a part implies division, a whole is undivided, and God is everywhere and wholly present wherever he is. Reason, therefore, cannot cope with him, since no point of contemplation can be found outside himself and since eternity is eternally his. This is a true statement of the mystery of the unfathomable nature which is expressed by the name *Father*: God invisible, ineffable, infinite. Let us confess by our silence that words cannot describe him; let sense admit that

[25] Athanasius, *De decr.*, 11.
[26] Athanasius, *Exp. fidei*, 1.

it is foiled in the attempt to apprehend and reason in the effort to define. Yet he has, as we said, in *Father* a name to indicate his nature: he is a Father unconditioned. He does not, as men do, receive the power of paternity from an external source. He is unbegotten, everlasting, inherently eternal. To the Son only is he known, for "no one knows the Father save the Son and he to whom the Son wills to reveal him", nor yet the Son save the Father. Each has perfect and complete knowledge of the other. Therefore, since "no one knows the Father save the Son", let our thoughts of the Father be at one with the thoughts of the Son, the only faithful witness who reveals him to us.'[27]

This is a very instructive passage, for while Hilary shows that the almighty God made known to us through the Son infinitely transcends all that we can ever conceive or express, he nevertheless insists that everything we actually think and say of God must be constrained and controlled within the bounds of the revelation of the Father in and through the incarnate Son.[28] This is a revelation of God's almightiness that conflicts with the ideas of limitless arbitrary power which we generate out of our this worldly experiences, make infinite, and attribute to God, for the divine power manifest in Jesus Christ is of an altogether different kind. It is not in terms of what *we* think God *can do*, but in terms of what God *has done and continues to do* in Jesus Christ that we may understand something of what divine almightiness really is.[29] What overwhelmed Hilary, perhaps above all else in this respect, was the utterly astonishing power of God manifested in his condescension to become incarnate within the frame of poor creaturely humanity, and in his self-abasing life on earth in the lowliness of the flesh from the wailing infant in the cradle to the weakness of the man on the cross. That God Almighty should become so little, poor and helpless, all for our sake, while remaining who he eternally is as God, was an act of indescribable majesty and power beyond anything that unaided human reason could grasp.[30] Quite clearly, Christology and

---

[27]Hilary, *De Trin.*, 2.6.
[28]See Hilary's discussion of this in *De Trin.*, 1.13–19.
[29]Hilary, *De Trin.*, 3.1–5; cf. 1.12; 2.33.
[30]Hilary, *De Trin.* 2.24–27; 3.20; 9.4–14; *Com. in Ps.* 53(54).3.

Soteriology have and must have critical significance for our understanding of God as almighty and of his distinctive activity in creation and redemption.

Athanasius brought this Nicene teaching to its sharpest focus in his account of Christ as the incarnate correlate of the ἀρχή that God is in his triune being. 'The humanity of the Lord' (ὁ κυριακὸς ἄνθρωπος) which he took from the Virgin Mary is the economic form which the divine ἀρχή has taken in the condescension of the Son and Word of God personally to enter the creation and actualise within it the providential activity (πρόνοια) of God the Father Almighty.[31] In justification of their view that the Son or Logos of God, while the divine agent in creation, was essentially a creature, the Arians had appealed to the Septuagint rendering of Proverbs 8.22: 'The Lord created me a beginning (ἀρχήν) of his ways for his works.'[32] Instead of rejecting it, Athanasius interpreted it to mean that in his human nature Jesus Christ had been created by God as the Beginning and Archetype of all God's providential and redemptive operations toward us. He took great care first to establish the fact that far from being a creature the incarnate Son was very God of very God, by whom all creatures have been brought into being from nothing and in whom they all consist and hold together.[33] Then he went on to show that the Son had deliberately become man, 'in the form of a servant', in order to carry out God's saving and renewing work on our behalf.[34] In linking it together with the uncreated *arche* (ἀρχή) which God is in his transcendent being, Athanasius clearly regarded the created *arche* (ἀρχή) which Christ constituted in our human being both as the Beginning of a new beginning within the creation and as the fundamental Principle or archetypal Pattern of God's gracious provision for his creation.[35] As the *arche* in this empirical or economic form in space and time of all God's ways for us, the incarnate Son has a two-fold vicarious function

[31] Athanasius, *Exp. fidei*, 1 and 4.
[32] Prov. 8.22 (LXX) reads: Κύριος ἔκτισέν με ἀρχὴν ὁδῶν αὐτοῦ εἰς ἔργα αὐτοῦ.
[33] Athanasius, *Con. Ar.*, 2.18–43.
[34] Athanasius, *Con. Ar.*, 2.44–82.
[35] Cf. also Athanasius, *De decr.*, 13f.

to fulfil. On the one hand, he is the actual *Way* which God's saving economy has taken among us in this world, and the one *Way* which leads us back to the Father. We shall give full attention to this later in the chapters that follow on the doctrines of the Person and Work of Christ, but at this juncture our concern is to focus attention on the fact that as the divine *arche* in this creaturely economic form, Jesus Christ is the Head of all creation, the one Source and controlling Principle with reference to whom we are to understand all the ways and works of God.

What does this *Christocentric* approach have to tell us of God as almighty Creator?

(1) God was not always Creator

We noted earlier that while God the Father is the Fount of all being, he is not the Fount of created beings in the same way as he is the Fount of the Son. The Son is eternally begotten of the Father within the one being of God, as God of God, while created beings are not begotten of God but made by him out of nothing and as such are external to God. The Son is begotten of God's nature and is without beginning (ἄναρχος) like the Father and without any interval between him and the Father, for he is one and the same being and nature as the Father. Creatures, on the other hand, are freely brought into being from non-being by the will of God and have an absolute beginning, for they are utterly different in being and nature from God. The crucial point here is the distinction between the generation of the Son by the nature (φύσει) of God, and the creation of the world by the will (βουλήσει/θελήσει) of God.[36] It became increasingly clear in the early decades of the fourth century that, unless a clear distinction of this kind could be drawn, the Church would finally lapse back into paganism.

That was the pressing issue that lay at the root of the problems facing the Nicene fathers. The disturbing ideas that irrupted in

[36]See the Epistle of Alexander, Athanasius' predecessor, recorded by Theodoret, *Hist. eccl.*, 1.3; the overture of the Council of Antioch to the Council of Nicaea, J. N. D. Kelly, *Early Christian Creeds*, pp. 150, 209f; and Athanasius, *Con. Ar.*, 3.59–62.

the teaching of Arius ran back to Origen's blurring of the difference between the internal and external relations of God, that is, between the eternal generation of the Son within the one being of God and the creation of the cosmos by the eternal Son or Word of God.[37] Origen was unable to think of God as *Pantokrator* (Παντοκράτωρ) or the Almighty except in a necessary eternal conjunction with all things (τὰ πάντα). Thus for Origen the creation had to be regarded as concomitant with the being of God and as eternally coexisting with him.[38] This failure to give clear-cut ontological priority to the Father/Son relation in God over the Creator/cosmos relation, was aggravated by the fact that Origen was critical of the idea that the Son was begotten 'of the being of the Father' (ἐκ τῆς οὐσίας τοῦ Πατρός), and appeared to think of the generation of the Son and the creation of the cosmos as both due to the will of the Father.[39]

Two basic problems had to be resolved. First, Origen's monistic view of the eternity of the world had the effect both of undermining the transcendence of God over the creation, for it made external relations necessary for God, and of undermining the unique historical reality of the incarnation, for it implied that historical events are ultimately no more than transitory symbolic representations of 'the eternal Gospel'. Second, Arius' dualistic view of God's relations with the world had the effect of severing the bond of being between the incarnate Son and God the Father upon which the very substance of the Gospel depended, and of including the Son among the works of God brought into being by his creative will. Thus Arius restricted human knowledge of God to his external relations with the creation. Hence for him God was primarily Creator and not Father, and it was only as Creator that he was Father, and not the other way round.

Once again it was to Athanasius above all that the Church

---

[37]This has been clearly shown by G. Florovsky, 'The Concept of Creation in Saint Athanasius', *op. cit.*, pp. 39ff; see also 'Creation and Creaturehood', *Collected Works*, Vol. III, pp. 47ff.

[38]Origen, *De prin.*, 1.2f, 10. See the fragment of *De rebus creatis* by Methodios of Olympus, preserved by Photius, *Bibliotheca*, c. 235.

[39]Origen, *De prin.*, 1.2, 6; 4.4, 1; *In Jn.*, 20.18.

was indebted for the clarification of its apostolic and evangelical faith. On the one hand, he rejected the notion of the eternity of the world and its necessity for God, by showing that according to the nature of things that have come into existence they have no likeness in being to their Maker but are external to him (ἔξωθεν αὐτοῦ) and depend for their existence on his grace and will.[40] On the other hand, he rejected the Arian disjunction between the being of the Son and the being of the Father, and confirmed the Nicene *homoousion* in showing that the Son belongs to the divine side of the Creator/creature relation.[41] We shall have to take up this second point later, but meantime our concern is with the decisive rejection of the notion of an eternal coexistence of the world with God.

The crucial issue was forced sharply upon the Church in the claim that 'God is always Maker', since the power to create did not accrue to him subsequently.[42] Here, as Florovsky has pointed out,[43] the Arians had recourse to Origen's argument but drew from it a very different conclusion. Since all God's works were eternal, what would be wrong, they asked, in saying that they did not exist before they were generated? That is to say, the Arians wanted to equate the kind of 'eternity' attributed to creatures brought into existence by the will of God with the kind of 'eternity' they attributed to the Son in the light of their notorious statement that 'there was once when he was not'.[44] Athanasius argued in reply that there was no likeness between a son and a created thing which might equate the function of a father and of a maker, for there is a vast disparity between a created thing brought into being from nothing by the will of God as a 'work external to his nature', and the Son who is 'the proper offspring of the being of God' and is internal to his nature. Compared to the Son, therefore, who is as eternal

---

[40]Athanasius, *Con. Ar.*, 1.20.

[41]Athanasius, *De syn.*, 45.

[42]Cited by Athanasius, *Con. Ar.*, 1.29: ἀεὶ ποιητής ἐστιν ὁ Θεός.

[43]G. Florovsky, 'Creation in Saint Athanasius', *op. cit.*, p. 50f, an essay to which I am much indebted.

[44]See Athanasius, *Con. Ar.*, 1.5: ἦν ποτε, ὅτε οὐκ ἦν. See also *De syn.*, 15; the letter of Arius to Eusebius, Theodoret, *Hist. eccl.*, 1.4; and Epiphanius, *Haer.*, 69.6.

as God the Father is, created things (things made, not begotten) do not eternally coexist with God.[45]

As we have already seen, Athanasius showed that in virtue of his intrinsic and eternal Fatherhood, God always had the power to create, and did actually create because he was and is the Father of the Son. God *is*, and always is, *Father*, but to create something out of nothing utterly different from himself is an *act* of his will and freely follows from what he eternally and intrinsically is. Hence, 'for God to create is secondary, and to beget is primary'.[46] In answer to the question why God, though always with the power to make, does not always make, Athanasius pointed to the fact that owing to their intrinsic nature created things could not have existed eternally, for they were created out of nothing. 'How can things which did not exist before they were brought into being be coeternal with God?'[47] God's decision to create things outside of himself had in view what was good for their existence and stability. Athanasius also pointed to the incarnation, for though God was able, even from the beginning in the time of Adam or Noah or Moses, to send his own Word, nevertheless he did not send him until the consummation of the ages, for he saw that to be good for the whole creation. It was the same with created things themselves: God made them when he willed to do so, and as it was good for them.[48] It is only in the light of what God has done in creation and redemption and revealed of his eternal purpose that we may speak of him in this way.

The truth of the matter, then, is that *while God was always Father, he was not always Creator or Maker*. This is not to say that the creation was not in the Mind of God before he actually brought it into being, but that he brought it into being by a definite act of his will and thereby gave it a beginning. Quite clearly words like 'was', 'before', 'when' and 'beginning' are time-related, and present us with problems when we speak of God, for the time-relations they imply may not be read back

---

[45] Athanasius, *Con. Ar.*, 1.29.
[46] Athanasius, *Con. Ar.*, 2.2.
[47] Athanasius, *Con. Ar.*, 1.29; 2.2.
[48] Athanasius, *Con. Ar.*, 1.29.

into God.[49] These terms have one sense when used of God when they are governed by the unique nature of God, and another sense when used of creatures in accordance with their transitory natures.[50] Thus when the Scriptures tell us that 'in the beginning God created' we must understand 'beginning' in a two-fold way: with reference to the creating act of God, and with reference to what he has created or his works (ἔργα). Hence Athanasius could say that 'while the works have a beginning in being made, their beginning precedes their coming to be'.[51] Behind the beginning of creation there is an absolute or transcendent beginning by God who is himself eternally without beginning.[52] This is what makes the creation of the world out of nothing so utterly baffling and astonishing. It is not only that something absolutely new has begun to be, new even for God who created it by his Word and gave it a contingent reality and integrity outwith himself, but that in some incomprehensible way, to cite Athanasius again, 'the Word himself *became* the Maker of the things that have a beginning'.[53] God was always Father, not always Creator, but now he is Creator as well as Father. It is in similar terms that we may speak of the eternal Son who *became* Man. The Son was always Son of God, but now he is Man as well as God. 'He was not man previously, but he became man for our sake.'[54]

Here let us pause to reflect upon the way in which Athanasius bracketed together the creation and the incarnation in showing that in both of them we have to do with new decisive acts willed by God. If God was not always Creator, the creation of the universe as reality 'external to God' was something new in the eternal Life of God. If the Son or Word of God by whom he created all things was not always incarnate, but became man in

---

[49]Athanasius, *Con. Ar.*, 1.2, 11, 13.

[50]Athanasius, *Con. Ar.*, 1.11; 2.3.

[51]Athanasius, *Con. Ar.*, 2.57.

[52]See especially, Basil, *Hex.*, 5–6, for a shrewd discussion of this point.

[53]Athanasius, *ibid.*

[54]Athanasius, *In ill. om.*, 3. There was, of course, no change in the essence of God, *Con. Ar.*, 1.62–64; 2.8f; 2.12ff; 4.15. See Hilary, *De Trin.*, 11.16; and cf. Gregory Naz.: 'He did not change what he was, but assumed what he was not.' *Or.*, 39.13.

the fullness of time, then God's communication of *himself* to us in Jesus Christ who is of one and the same being and nature as the Father, is something new to the eternal being of God. Thus the incarnation and creation together, the latter interpreted in the light of the former, have quite breath-taking implications for our understanding of the nature of God. They tell us that he is free to do what he had never done before, and free to be other than he was eternally: to be the Almighty Creator, and even to become incarnate as a creature within his creation, while remaining eternally the God that he is.

This doctrine of the absolute origin of the creation, the idea that something entirely new took place, new even for God, was undoubtedly offensive to the Greek mind, but it was powerfully reinforced by the doctrine of the incarnation. Together creation and incarnation conflicted sharply with Greek philosophical categories of the necessity, immobility and impassivity of God. Here, however, we come to the highly distinctive feature of the doctrine of creation, its radicalisation through the revelation that it was by the eternal Son or Word of God who became man in Jesus Christ that God the Father Almighty was the Maker of heaven and earth and of all things visible and invisible, and that it is in Jesus Christ that the whole creation is ordered and held together.

(2) God does not will to exist for himself alone

We have been considering the point that God was always Father, but not always Creator. However, we must be careful, as Gregory Nazianzen warned, not to understand 'God always was' in a time-related way. 'God always was and always is; or rather, God always *is*. For was and will be are fragments of our time, and are of changeable nature, but he *is* eternal being.'[55] The point at issue is that God is who he is in himself, entirely unconditioned by any reality other than himself, and thus totally independent of his creation and infinitely exalted over all time and space. As Hilary expressed it: 'The Father to whom all

[55]Gregory Naz., *Or.*, 38.7 and 45.3.

existence owes its origin . . . in contrast to all else is self-existent. He does not draw his being from without, but possesses it from himself and in himself. He is infinite, for nothing contains him and he contains all things; he is eternally unconditioned by space, for he is illimitable; eternally anterior to time, for time is his creation.'[56] In himself, then, God is transcendently free and in need of nothing beyond himself, for he is the Creator and Lord of all other being.

While God is Creator in virtue of his being eternally Father, with us the reverse is the case, for God has become our Father, not by nature but by grace, after he had become our Creator.[57] Nevertheless, he is truly known by us within the creation only in accordance with what he is eternally, intrinsically and antecedently in himself as Father, and indeed as Father, Son and Holy Spirit, apart from the creation.[58] There is, therefore, no necessary relation between God and the created cosmos, as if God needed relation to what is not himself in order to be what he eternally is in himself as God the Father Almighty.[59] That is why, as we have already noted, Nicene theology would have nothing to do with the idea that God was always Creator as well as Father, although it held that his creative activity flows from his eternal nature as Father of the eternal Son. It is thus from the free ground of God's own eternal being as Father Almighty that we may properly speak of the creation and of God's continuing interaction with it.

In himself, as Hilary used to say, God is not 'solitary',[60] for as Father, Son and Holy Spirit he is an eternal communion of love and personal being in himself. Earlier Irenaeus had argued that although God is wholly self-sufficient in the inner fellowship of his being, God does not will to exist for himself alone, but has freely and spontaneously brought a world into existence out of

[56]Hilary, *De Trin.*, 2.6.

[57]Athanasius, *Con. Ar.*, 2.59ff.

[58]This was early noted by Athenagoras, *Leg.*, 8–10, 13, 16.24; *De res.*, 12–14.

[59]Gregory Thaumaturgos, *In Origenem*, 8; Athanasius, *De decr.*, 22; *De syn.*, 34; Hilary, *De Trin.*, 2.6ff; 9.72; 11.44ff.

[60]Hilary, *De syn.*, 37; *De Trin.*, 4.21; 6.12, 19; 7.3, 8, 39; 8.52. He already sensed the danger that was to result from an Aristotelian idea of God allied to an Arian conception of his Fatherhood – cf. the monotonous solitariness of the Allah of Islam.

non-existence to which he has given an integrity of its own and in which he has planted rational creaturely beings upon whom he may bestow his bounty and with whom he may share his divine communion of love and personal being. Although he is utterly transcendent he does not hold himself aloof from his creation, but is freely present and at work within it, intervening personally and providentially in the events of the world and in the affairs of his human creatures.[61]

Irenaeus had directed attention to the teaching of Plato who, in answer to the question *why* the Maker produced the world in the first place, had pointed to the ungrudging goodness of God who instead of keeping his goodness to himself framed the world in order that it might reflect his own goodness and order.[62] With Plato's words evidently in mind, Athanasius also gave as the reason for the existence of the world the fact that God, the Source of all goodness and excellence, does not grudge existence to anything he has made. However, like Irenaeus, he gave this idea a Christian interpretation by stressing that God created all things *out of nothing* and wishes them to exist as objects of the loving-kindness (φιλανθρωπία) which he has now manifested to the world in Jesus Christ, in whom the very Word, by whom they have been brought into being and are upheld in substantive existence, has become incarnate. Far from grudging the creation existence and reality beyond himself, God freely brought it into being out of his sheer liberality, in order to lavish his love upon it.[63]

This Christocentric approach to the mystery of creation was central to all Nicene theology. It was from the standpoint of God's incarnate condescension and self-revelation in Jesus Christ his beloved Son, the Word through whom all things were made, that Nicene theologians contemplated the baffling origin of the universe as a substantive reality external to God. Its creation out of nothing and continued existence were understood to derive from and to be grounded in the limitless

---

[61]Irenaeus, *Adv. haer.*, 2.47.2, vol. 1, pp. 367f; 2.56.1f, p. 382f; 4.25.1f, vol 2, pp. 184f; 4.34.1f, pp. 212ff; 4.63.1f, pp. 294ff; *Dem.*, 3ff, 11f.

[62]Irenaeus, *Adv. haer.*, 3. *Praef.* and 41, vol. 2, pp. 1ff; 4.25.1f, pp. 184ff; 4.63.1, p. 294f; Plato, *Timaeus, 29e–30b. Cf.* Philo, *De migr. Abr.*, 32.

[63]Athanasius, *Con. gent.*, 41; *De inc.*, 3; cf. *Con. Ar.*, 2.29.

love of God, the love which God eternally is as Father, Son and Holy Spirit and which he wishes to share with his creation.[64] Creation like redemption was a sheer act of God's inexplicable grace exhibited in his incarnate Son who was 'created a beginning of God's ways for his works' – it was in him and through his saving activity that the hidden reason for creation was to be traced.[65] No attempt was made to answer the question *how* the universe was created out of nothing (ἐκ τοῦ μὴ ὄντος). It was sufficient to follow the teaching of the Scripture in believing that 'all things come from God (ἐκ τοῦ θεοῦ)'.[66] However, that 'genesis from God' (γένεσις ἐκ θεοῦ), as Gregory Nyssen expressed it, is to be understood, not as an emanation from God's being, but as the product of his will and the activity of his love.[67] Thus the love of God became a primary principle (ἀρχή, in both senses of the word) in all Christian thought of the creation.

How then are we to think of the relation of God to the universe? It is neither a necessary relation, nor an arbitrary relation. God was *free* to create the universe, but he was also free not to create it.[68] The universe did not come into being just by itself, or accidentally (κατὰ συμβεβηκός), as the product of irrational, random chance.[69] The fact that the universe was created by God through his eternal *Word* or *Wisdom* means that it was neither conceived nor brought into being 'without reason', but on the contrary was an intelligible product of the divine Mind.[70] That is why, as Athanasius argued, the created

---

[64]Basil, *Hex.*, 1.2; Gregory Nyss., *Or. cat.*, 5; *De an. et res.*, MPG 46.9Bff; Gregory Naz., *Or.*, 38.9; 45.5. See also Athenagoras, *De res.*, 12–13.

[65]Athanasius, *De inc.*, 1.1ff; *Con. Ar.*, 2.14, 44–65; 3.43, 67; 4.33.

[66]1 Cor. 11.12.

[67]Gregory Nyss., *De op. hom.*, 23f; *De an. et res.*, MPG 46.94–125; *Or. cat.*, 5 – ἐκ θεοῦ refers creation to its *terminus a quo*. Cf. Evagrius' reference to creation as τὴν ἀπὸ τοῦ μὴ ὄντος εἰς τὸ εἶναι παραγωγήν, Evagrius/Basil, Ep., 8. 11.

[68]1 Clement 27.4; Tatian, *Or.*, 7.3; Aristides, *Apol.*, 13; Athanasius, *Con. Ar.*, 2.31; Gregory Naz., *Or.*, 29.6.

[69]Athenagoras, *Leg.*, 6–9, 16, 20, 22, 25; *De res.*, 12–13; Basil, *Hex.*, 1.5–7; Gregory Nyss., *Con. Eun.*, 1.20.

[70]Theophilus, *Ad Aut.*, 1.7; 11.4, 10, 13; Athenagoras, *Leg.*, 10, 13–16; Irenaeus, *Adv. haer*, 2.2.1ff, vol. 1, pp. 254ff; 2.8f, pp. 271ff; 2.47.2, p. 367f; 3.41, vol. 2, p. 135f; 4.25.1f, pp. 184f; 4.83.1, p. 295; 5.3.2, p. 326; 5.18.1f, pp. 372ff; Basil, *Hex.*, 1.5–10; 2.2; 4.6; 5.5.

universe is not sufficient when considered in itself, apart from the Son or Word, to make God known to us, but is rightly contemplated in and through the *Logos* who framed it, gave it its rational order, and in whom it holds consistently together.[71]

On the other hand, the universe did not come into existence through any inner compulsion in God's being.[72] No, the universe flowed freely from and is unceasingly grounded in the eternal love that God is. Although in his complete self-sufficiency God has no need of the universe, he nevertheless freely created it out of his love and grace, so that the universe must be regarded as having an ultimate rational ground in the beneficent nature and love of God. It was the manifestation of that divine love in Jesus Christ, the Logos, Mind or Reason of God made flesh, which made theologians realise that the universe has a transcendent reason for its being, grounded beyond itself in the love of the Father and the Son and the Holy Spirit. Hence they sought to understand God the Creator and his work in the light of his undivided activity as Father, Son and Holy Spirit, one God *from* whom and *through* whom and *in* whom are all things.[73] Thus Athanasius declared: 'The Father creates all things through the Word in the Spirit.'[74] And Gregory Nazianzen insisted: 'When I say God, I mean Father, Son and Holy Spirit.'[75]

Now this implied that we must really think of the universe as brought into being from the Father, through the Son and in the Holy Spirit in such a way that it constitutes, as it were, what, in our own day, Karl Barth has called a 'temporal analogue, taking place outside of God, of that event in God himself by which God is Father of the Son' or, otherwise expressed, a 'created correspondence' to the Holy Trinity.[76] And that is indeed what

---

[71]Athanasius, *De inc.*, *passim*; *Con. Ar.*, 1.11–12 – a comment on Romans 1.19f.

[72]See again Athanasius, *Con. Ar.*, 3.59–62.

[73]2 Cor. 8.6 and Romans 11.36. See Irenaeus, *Adv. haer.*, 4.34.1f, vol. 2, pp. 212ff; *Dem.*, 3; Hilary, *De Trin.*, 8.36f; Gregory Naz., *Or.*, 39.12; Basil, *De Sp. St.*, 4.6 – and the whole discussion from 4 to 16 of God's triune activity in creation.

[74]Athanasius, *Ad Ser.*, 3.5.

[75]Gregory Naz., *Or.*, 38.8 and 45.4.

[76]Karl Barth, *Dogmatics in Outline*, p. 52; *Church Dogmatics*, III.1, pp. 13ff.

we find again and again in the works of the Nicene and post-Nicene theologians, as in the reference of Gregory Thaumaturgus to 'the sacred economy of the universe'.[77] It was Irenaeus particularly who spelled out the biblical teaching about the universe as the good creation of God who unceasingly maintains and harmoniously disposes it in covenanted relations with himself, whereby it reflects his glory and constitutes the sphere of his loving purpose for mankind.[78] Athanasius on his part made considerable use of musical terms such as harmony and symphony to speak of the wonderful unity and symmetry of the created order which proclaim and celebrate God as its Lord and Creator.[79]

With the realisation that in the incarnation the Creator had himself become a creature and that in the coming of the Holy Spirit God himself was personally and creatively present throughout his creation, upholding its being and order and exercising immediate providential care over all events within it, Christian theologians were convinced that the whole universe of space and time had been set upon a new basis.[80] They felt bound to regard the created order, renewed and sanctified in Christ in this way, as intended by God to be a creaturely correlate of the fellowship, communion and faithfulness which are manifested in God himself, for it is grounded in God's own steadfastness and depends for its continued existence on the constant presence of his Spirit.[81] The whole *raison d'être* of the universe lies in the fact that God will not be alone, that he will not be without us, but has freely and purposely created the universe and bound it to himself as the sphere where he may

[77]Gregory Thaum., *In Origenem*, 8.

[78]Irenaeus, *Adv. haer.*, 2.2.3f, vol. 1, pp. 255f; 2.37.1f, pp. 342f; 2.43.2f, pp. 356f; 2.47.2, p. 367f; 3.11.2ff, pp. 35ff; 3.12.14f, vol. 2, pp. 66ff; 4.6, p. 152; 4.18–19, pp. 168–172; 4.27.3–30, pp. 189–200; 4.34.1ff, pp. 212ff; 5.18.1f, pp. 372ff. This idea is not to be confused with a Gnostic myth of divine archetypes, *Adv. haer.*, 2.7.1ff, pp. 270ff, etc.

[79]Athanasius, *Con. gent.*, 34ff. Cf. *Con. Ar.*, 2.20: 'The whole earth hymns the Creator.'

[80]Irenaeus, *Adv. haer.*, 3.11.2, vol.2, p. 35.

[81]See also Athenagoras, *Leg.*, 4.2; 6.2; 10.2–5; 12.3; 18.2; and Theophilus, *Ad Aut.*, 1.4, 7; 11.13.

ungrudgingly pour out his love, and where we may enjoy communion with him.

(3) The universe was created by God out of nothing

Hitherto our attention has been focused mainly upon God as the Creator of the universe, but now we must give closer consideration to the nature of creation itself, and in particular to the difficult concept of *creatio ex nihilo*. That God created the universe in matter and form out of nothing, giving it an absolute beginning in existence and time is essentially a Judaeo-Christian idea rooted in the teaching of the Old Testament that God 'created the heaven and the earth, the sea and all that is in them',[82] which found strong echoes in the New Testament.[83] In the influential opening sentence of the book of Genesis, 'In the beginning God created the heaven and the earth', the concept of creation out of nothing was not mentioned in so many words, but in Jewish exegesis it was taken to be implied.[84] The Hebrew term used to speak of God's act in *creating* heaven and earth was, not *asah* (עָשָׂה) which was regularly employed to speak of the work of man as well as of God in *making*, causing or effecting things, but the distinctive *bara* (בָּרָא) which was reserved exclusively for what God does, in bringing about something utterly new that had not happened before and could not have happened otherwise,[85] and was never used to speak of what God does with already existing matter.[86] That is to say, in contrast to עָשָׂה (make), בָּרָא (create) refers to the unique aboriginal act of God through his commanding Word in bringing into being what did not previously exist and giving it

[82]Exod. 20.11; cf. Gen. 1.1; Ps. 146.6; 148.4f; Is. 45.7; Amos 4.13; Prov. 8.24; Neh. 9.6; Jonah 1.9, etc.

[83]Acts 4.24; 14.15; Rom. 4.17; Rev. 10.6; 14.7; John 1.1f; Col. 1.1f; Heb. 1.1f. Cf. also Acts 17.28; Rom. 11.36; 2 Cor. 8.6; Eph. 4.5; Heb. 2.10.

[84]*E.g.*, Philo, *De spec. leg.*, 4.187; *De op. mundi*, 26, 28, and 31; cf. Justin Martyr, *Dial.*, 5.

[85]Cf. Exod. 34.10; Num. 16.30, etc.

[86]See Basil, *Hex.*, 1.7, where the distinction between God's 'creating' and his 'making' was clearly drawn. Cf. Athanasius, *Con. Ar.*, 2.21f, 27, 31, 57ff.

reality and stability before him. 'He spoke and it came to be, he commanded and it stood forth.'[87]

The first recorded testimony in Jewish writings explicitly mentioning creation out of nothing is attributed to a Maccabean mother: 'I beseech you, my son, lift up your eyes to the heaven and the earth, and see everything in them, and recognise that God made them of things that were not, and that mankind came into being in the same way.'[88] By New Testament times belief in God's creation of the universe out of nothing was already established and taken for granted, but the earliest explicit statement concerning it in Christian literature is found only at the end of the first century in *The Shepherd* of Hermas, in a passage that had a considerable impact upon the development of Christian thought. 'First of all believe that God is one, who created all things and arranged them and brought them into existence out of the non-existent; and he bounds all things but he alone is unbounded.'[89] It seems clear that belief in God's creation of all things out of nothing had already become a recognised article in the 'rule of faith'.[90]

The bare idea of *creatio ex nihilo* had evidently been raised a number of times in the history of Greek thought, as we learn from people as different as Aristotle,[91] Plutarch,[92] Diogenes Laertius,[93] and Sextus Empiricus,[94] but only to be rejected as impossible and self-contradictory.[95] Early Christian thinkers,

---

[87]Ps. 33.9; cf. Ps. 119.91f; also Ecclus. 43.36; Wisd. 16.24ff.

[88]2 Macc. 7.28, cited by Origen, *De prin.*, 2.1.5 and *In Jn.*, 1.18; and Hilary, *De Trin.*, 4.16; cf. Basil, *Ep.*, 6.2. And see also Jubilees 12.4.

[89]Hermas, *Mand.* 1.1 (linked by Origen with 2 Macc. 7.28, *De prin.*, 2.1.5). See also *Vis.*, 1.1.6 and 2 Clement, 1.8.

[90]Compare *Mand.*, 1.1 with Irenaeus, *Adv. haer.*, 1.15.1 and 4.34.2, vol. 1, p. 188f and vol. 2, p. 213f; *Dem.*, 4–6; Origen, *De prin.*, praef., 3f; 3.3; and Tertullian, *De praescr. haer.*, 13.

[91]Aristotle, *De coelo*, 1.10, 279f; 3.1, 298; cf. *Met.*, 10.1075b; also Pseudo—Aristotle, cited by A. Ehrhardt, in 'Creatio ex nihilo', *Studia Theologica*, IV, 1950, p. 24.

[92]Plutarch, *De an. procr.*, 5.

[93]Diogenes Laertius, *Vitae*, 9.4.

[94]Sextus Empiricus, *Adv. Math.*, 1.53 and 60; cf. 7.66f.

[95]Cf. the Epistle of Epicurus cited by Diog. Laert., 10.38. On the notion of an absolute beginning in Greek thought see A. Ehrhardt, *The Beginning. A*

however, like Theophilus of Antioch,[96] Athenagoras of Athens,[97] Aristides,[98] and Tatian,[99] seized upon the idea that the universe was created in both matter and form out of nothing as absolutely basic to belief in the one and only God. It is highly significant, however, that their real starting-point for the doctrine of creation, as Athenagoras in particular made clear,[100] was the mighty act of God in raising Jesus Christ from the dead, for it was there that the absolute power of God over life and death, over all being and non-being, was uniquely exhibited. This emphasis was entirely in line with the New Testament witness, and it set the stamp upon the development of a Christ-centred doctrine of creation in the pre-Nicene Church.[101]

Early in the fourth century, however, there appeared a serious weakness in current conceptions of creation due to a confusion between the eternal generation of the Son of God and the creative act of God in bringing the universe into existence. That is the basic problem we have been considering with the help of Athanasius who drew a clear distinction between the absolute being of God and the existence of the world wholly dependent on his creative Word and Will, and thereby disentangled for the Church the twisted lines of thought between the ontological and cosmological dimensions in Origenist and Arian ideas about God, Christ and the world. That had the effect of clarifying Christian understanding of God as Father and as Creator in the light of the relation of the incarnate Son to the Father, as we have seen, but the fact that in Jesus Christ God the Creator himself had become a creature within his creation in order to redeem the world, forced theology to probe more deeply into the traditional concept of creation out of nothing and the nature of created existence.

Study in the Greek Philosophical Concept of Creation from Anaximander to St John, 1968.

[96]Theophilus, *Ad Aut.*, 1.4; 1.8; 2.4; 11.4; 11.10; 11.13.

[97]Athenagoras, *Leg.*, 4.1f, 7–8.

[98]Aristides, *Apol.*, 1.4f, 13.

[99]Tatian, *Or.*, 4f, 7.

[100]Athenagoras, *De res.*, 3–5.

[101]Thus, for example, Origen, *De prin., praef.*, 4; Irenaeus, *Adv. haer.*, 3.4.1, vol. 2, p. 15f; cf. 3.17.6, p. 87; *Apost. Const.*, 5.7; 7.33; 8.12.

It was Athanasius who more than any other perceived what the real issues were, and led the way in clarifying the *contingent* nature and status of created reality and its God-given creaturely order. Hence once again we shall take our cue from him, yet not without help from other early Church theologians, in drawing out the profound implications of the incarnation of the Word for a Christian understanding of the contingence, intelligibility and freedom of God's creation.

(a) The contingence of the creation

In his earliest work, *Contra Gentes*, Athanasius had already singled out the basic question posed by the incarnation as to the relation of the one and only begotten Word of God, who is unchanging, unlimited and not composite in his being and nature, to things created out of nothing which are changing, limited and composite in their existence and nature. The answer to that question, however, he found in the incarnation itself, for it was the wonderful union of the Word with created things that showed that the nature of things created out of nothing, when considered in themselves, is not only weak and mortal but fleeting or in a state of flux, and subject to dissolution even so far as its own laws are concerned. However, when created nature is considered in the perspective of the ungrudging goodness and loving-kindness of God, it is found to be maintained in being by the creating and ordering activity of the Word of God, and thus preserved by divine grace from lapsing back into nothing. It is indeed, as St Paul taught, through and in Christ that all things visible and invisible consist.[102]

These ideas were followed up by Athanasius in the *De Incarnatione*, with explicit reference to the first verse of the book of Genesis, 'In the beginning God created the heaven and the earth', and to the teaching of the Epistle to the Hebrews 11.1: 'By faith we understand that the worlds have been framed by the Word of God, so that what is seen has been made out of the things which do not appear', which he interpreted in line with

---

[102]Athanasius, *Con. gent.*, 41 – the reference is to Col. 1.15–18.

the passage cited above from *The Shepherd* of Hermas.[103] Athanasius was quite clear about the fact that the creation of the universe out of nothing does not mean that God created the universe out of some 'stuff' called 'nothing', but that what he created was not created out of anything. It does mean, however, that the creation depends for its very existence upon the will and kindness of God, and has no stability at all apart from that freely imparted to it by the continuous presence and activity of the Word of God. This was wholly in accord with the teaching of Irenaeus that the substance of all created things is to be attributed to the power and will of God, for they are grounded beyond themselves in his Word.[104]

Athanasius clearly had some trouble in finding the right language with which to describe the elusive nature of created things, for while they were endowed by God with a reality of their own, their continuing existence was suspended, as it were, over the abyss of nothingness out of which they had been brought by the grace of God. He used the word ῥευστός[105] to speak of the fleeting, evanescent, intrinsically unstable nature of creaturely events (γενητά, τυγχάνοντα) which are nevertheless sustained as creaturely realities through the divine presence of the Word.[106] He borrowed from Greek thought the terms συμβεβηκός[107] and ἐνδεχόμενος,[108] to express the fact that creaturely events were not necessary, but rejected the idea that they were merely accidental or that they had come about just by chance.[109] Taken together this account of the nature of created realities approximates closely to what we have come to speak of as 'contingent'.[110] Indeed that is surely what Athanasius

---

[103] Athanasius, *De inc.*, 3. Cf. *De decr.*, 18, where a similar statement is made.

[104] Irenaeus, *Adv. haer.*, 1.15, ovl. 1, p. 188f; 2.1; p. 251; 2.10.2, p. 274f; 2.47.2, p. 367f; 3.8.3, vol. 2, p. 29f; Athanasius, *Con. Ar.*, 2.24; 2.31; *Ep.*, 11.4.

[105] Athanasius, *Con. gent.*, 41; *De decr.*, 11; *Con. Ar.*, 1.23 and 28. Cf Basil, *Con. Eun.*, 2.23; Gregory Naz., *Or.*, 28.22.

[106] Cf. Athanasius, *Con. gent.*, 39 and 41; *De decr.*, 11, etc.

[107] Athanasius, *De decr.*, 22; *Con. Ar.*, 1.20; 1.36; 4.2; cf. 3.65. See also Gregory Nyss., *Con. Eun.*, 1.26.

[108] Athanasius, *Con. Ar.*, 1.51; 3.62; *In Ps.*, 88.36–37.

[109] Athanasius, *De inc.*, 2; cf. *De decr.*, 19; *De syn.*, 35.

[110] In modern Greek ἐνδεχόμενος is now used for 'contingent', which is rather appropriate since ἐνδέχεται is the Greek equivalent of the Latin *contingit*.

intended, for under the impact of the incarnation upon the Christian mind a quite new concept was being born which could not be construed in terms of traditional secular modes of thought.

In Greek philosophy or science the 'contingent' was identified with what is merely accidental, that is, as the antithesis of what is necessary or logical, and was thus regarded as lacking any kind of rational order, as no more than transient appearance defective of reality. It was quite unthinkable and impossible, a surd which could not be included in rational discourse or scientific explanation, and was in fact a form of evil. Hence due to the paradigms of classical Greek thought, there was an in-built resistance to the Christian concept of the contingence of nature.[111]

Admittedly contingence is not an easy concept. As we have seen, creation of the universe out of nothing means that it has been brought freely into being as something utterly distinct from God, while having a reality of its own and therefore a measure of genuine independence – that is what contingence implied. This way of thinking was both radicalised and reinforced by the doctrine of the incarnation of God the Creator within his creation. On the one hand it rested upon an absolute distinction between uncreated and created being, but on the other hand it affirmed the full reality of material existence and events even for God. The difficulty in the concept of contingence lay in the fact that the independence given by God to the creation is itself dependent upon God. God has made nature in such a way that it operates with a certain measure of autonomy: it brings forth its fruit and its own kind of itself – 'automatically', as the New Testament once expressed it.[112] That implies that whenever we seek to explore and understand nature we may do so only by examining nature as it actually is in itself, and by discovering its own operations and inherent structures or laws. And yet the very reality of this independence of nature is itself dependent, or contingent, upon God. It is this elusive interlocking of dependence and independence that

[111]See John Philoponos, *De aetern. mundi con. Proclum*, 9.11–13; *In physica, apud* Simplicius, *Comm. in Artist. Gr.*, vol. 10, p. 189.

[112]Mark 4.28.

makes contingence so difficult for us to grasp and express. The universe is not self-supporting or self-explaining as though it had an interior principle of its own, but neither is it mere appearance for it is ontologically grounded beyond itself on God who has given it an authentic reality and lawfulness of its own which he unceasingly sustains through the presence of his Creator Word and Spirit. If he were to withdraw that presence from the creation it would vanish into nothing.[113] Thus in the last resort the inherent meaning and truth of the universe lie beyond its own limits in God who loves it, sustains it, and undergirds it by his own divine reality. In a real sense, then, the universe may be thought of as 'in God', embraced within the power and presence of the Creator Word and Spirit.

The doctrine of the incarnation played a further role in the patristic doctrine of creation, for it disclosed that the world was in such a precarious state that God the Son had to unite it to himself in order to save it. This was a major theme in Athanasius' early work *On the Incarnation of the Word*, in which he had particularly in mind the contingent nature of human beings. This was defined with reference, on the one hand, to their inherent deficiency in existence (τὸ μὴ εἶναι ποτέ), but, on the other hand, to their being called into existence (εἰς τὸ εἶναι) by the presence and loving kindness (παρουσίᾳ καὶ φιλανθρωπίᾳ) of the Word. Brought into existence out of non-existence by the grace of God, they naturally waste away into non-existence when they turn away from God and fall under the condemnation of death. The incarnation of the Word within that contingent existence, however, revealed that human creatures had become infected with a deep-seated corruption (φθορά), beyond the corruptibility of their natural contingence, which worked for their utter dissolution.[114] This was not just the kind of natural corruption that all beings with finite origins and finite ends have in respect of their perishability or mortality, but the corruption of evil that has divine judgment stacked against it and which cannot be overcome except through the

---

[113]Aristides, *Ad Aut.*, 1.7; Basil, *Hex.*, 3.1f; 4.1f; 5.1f; 8.1; *De Sp. St.*, 16.37–38; 19.49.
[114]Athanasius, *De inc.*, 4ff.

atoning and redeeming activity of God himself.[115]

The restoration of God's creation was the reason for the incarnation of the eternal Son and Word of God in Jesus Christ. By taking our frail, contingent nature upon himself who is the one source and origin of all creaturely being, he transferred our origin into himself, in order to secure our being from final dissolution into nothingness, but at the same time he took upon himself our alienated and corrupt nature, including the curse of sin, in order to redeem us and renew our being in himself. That is to say, Christian theology recognised that the contingence of creation was corrupted by an inherent being-destroying (*meonic*) tendency that had to be overcome if the creation were to be saved and directed toward the end for which it had been designed by its Creator. However, by transferring our contingent existence into himself, in whom, as we shall discuss later, divine and human, uncreated and created, realities and natures are indissolubly united, Jesus Christ has secured its origin and end in his own eternal being. Regarded in this way, the incarnation is to be understood as completing the work of creation and of consummating its contingent relation to God. Thus in a certain sense the creation is to be thought of as proleptically conditioned by redemption.[116]

(b) The intelligibility of the creation

If the idea of the contingence of the creation was difficult for the Greek mind, that of created or *contingent intelligibility* was even more difficult, yet that is precisely what the Christian doctrine of the creation of the universe out of nothing involved. It was contingent precisely in its immanent rational order which, far from being self-explanatory, was grounded beyond itself in the transcendent intelligibility of its Creator. Hence the Church confessed in its Creed that God created the heaven as well as the earth, all things invisible as well as visible, intelligible as well as sensible. It was not only the matter of the universe that God brought into existence with its creation, but its rational form

[115]Athanasius, *De inc.*, 3–10.

[116]See Athanasius, *Con. Ar.*, 2.65–72, 74ff, 77; 3.33, 38; 4.33; cf. *Con. gent.*, 40ff; *De inc.*, 2ff & 44f.

and order. Even the human mind or soul has been created out of nothing.[117] If in the incarnation it was the Creator *Logos* of God, the one eternal uncreated *Autologos* (Αὐτολόγος) or Self-Word, who became flesh in Jesus Christ, then all the *logoi* (λόγοι) or rational forms pervading the universe were thereby revealed to be created. Just as there is an absolute distinction between the uncreated being of God and created being, so there is an absolute distinction between the uncreated rationality of God and the created rationality of the world, between uncreated light and created light, whether physical or mental. As such, however, creaturely rationality, or creaturely light, derives from God himself and is what it is through a created participation in his uncreated rationality and light, and thus far from being overwhelmed by it, it is upheld by God in its contingent reality.[118]

It is hardly surprising, then, that Athanasius had to reject the Greek dualism between the intelligible and sensible realms, with the notions of the divine *logos* as an immanent cosmological principle and of 'seminal reasons' (λόγοι σπερματικοί), or eternal rational forms embedded in nature, that often went with it.[119] He put forward in its place the biblical distinction between Creator and creation, with the claim that all the rational order in the universe was to be traced back to its creative source in the Word of God, for it is through that same Word incarnate in Jesus Christ that the whole universe has been endowed with its wonderful creaturely intelligibility and continues to be sustained by him in that condition.[120] Due to the all-embracing disposing and integrating activity of the divine *Logos*, a single rational order pervades all created existence contingent upon the transcendent rationality of God, the Lord of creation who is beyond all created being.[121]

[117]Basil, *Hex.*, 2.1ff; Gregory Nyss., *Con. Eun.*, 1.22; *De op. hom.*, 23, 29, 39; *De an. et res.*, MPG 46.30B, 105B, 124B, 125C.

[118]Basil, *Hex.*, 6.1ff.

[119]Athanasius, *Con. gent.*, 35ff; 40ff; 44 & 46; *De decr.*, 11; *Exp. fidei*, 1; cf. *Con. Ar.*, 3.16.

[120]Athanasius, *Con. Ar.*, 2.2, 24, 31f, etc.; cf. Gregory Nyss., *De op. hom.*, 23f.

[121]This was the underlying theme of both the *Con. gent.* and the *De inc.*, but see especially *Con. gent.*, 29ff, 34ff, 38ff, 40ff, 44, 46. Cf. *Con. Ar.*, 2.28, 41.

Let us approach this from the fact that in creating the universe out of nothing, God created time and space along with it. These ideas are usually attributed to Augustine, but they are found in Greek theology as early as the second century, while it was in Alexandria well before the time of Augustine that they saw their full development.[122] With the doctrine of the incarnation, which meant that the Lord became man and did not come into man, as Athanasius expressed it,[123] Christians found themselves in sharp conflict with the container notions of space and time which in various forms, Platonic, Aristotelian and Stoic, had long prevailed in Greek philosophy and science. The actuality and reality of the incarnate *parousia* of God in space and time forced the Church fathers to develop *relational* conceptions of space and time which could be applied variationally: to God in one way in accordance with his transcendent nature, and to creaturely beings in another way in accordance with their contingent natures. Thus they sought to express the fact that within the created order of this world there are spatio-temporal structures which are open to the creative and ordering activity of God, and came up with quite new conceptions of natural law of an open-textured kind which broke free from the necessitarian or deterministic notions that had prevailed in Greece.[124] In line with their understanding of the creation, they thought of natural laws as the orderly sequences and enduring structures in nature that arise under the commanding voice of the Creator.[125] That is to say, the laws of nature were regarded as dependent on the Word of God as their source and ground. They are essentially contingent forms of order which are only finally intelligible as they point beyond themselves to a transcendent ground of rationality in the *Logos* of God the Creator, for it is upon that ground that their reliability and constancy repose.[126]

[122]Refer to my discussion of this in *Space, Time and Incarnation, 1969*; and in 'The Relation of the Incarnation to Space', my contribution to the Festschrift for Georges Florovsky, *The Ecumenical World of Orthodox Civilization*, Vol. III, 1974, pp. 42–70.

[123]Athanasius, *Con. Ar.*, 3.30; cf. *Ad Ant.*, 7.

[124]Athanasius, *Con. gent.*, 11f, 26, 28, 32, 39, 41.

[125]Basil, *Hex.*, 4.2ff; 5.1f, 5; 8.5; 9.1ff; Gregory Nyss., *Con. Eun*, 1.26.

[126]Basil, *Hex.*, 1.8–10; 3.1ff; 9.2ff. This view of the constancy of nature was

(c) The freedom of the creation

The full concept of the contingence of the creation carries with it the idea that God is related to the universe, neither arbitrarily nor necessarily, but through the freedom of his grace and will, when out of sheer love he created the universe and grounded it in his own transcendent Logos or Rationality.[127] By the same token the sheer contingency of the created order upon the will of God carries with it the notion of a contingent freedom fully dependent on God's freedom. He does not grudge his creation a genuine freedom any more than he grudges it a reality distinct from himself, but on the contrary grants it to share in an appropriate way in his own freedom. As we have already noted, God was absolutely free both to create and not to create the universe, which means that the universe might not have come into existence at all. There was no necessity in God to create anything, and, if it pleased him, the creation might even cease to exist, for there is no necessity for it eternally to exist.[128] The unique interlocking of dependence and independence in the notion of contingence must be viewed from the side of God as well as from the side of the creature. Hence, as Georges Florovsky used to point out, we have to think in terms of a 'double contingency': in the free creative act of God who need not have done what he did, and in what he actually brought into being which need not have happened as it did or even have happened at all.[129] This does not mean, of course, that God's free sovereign act of creation was irrational or arbitrary in any way, for the creation (and everything in it) has its divine reason.[130]

reinforced by John Philoponos in the sixth century in his *De opificio mundi*, 3.4; and in his lost *Contra Aristotelem*, fragments of which are preserved by Simplicius, *Comm. in Arist. Gr.*, vol. 10, pp. 329ff.

[127]See especially Athanasius, *Con. Ar.*, 1.20; 2.2; 2.24f; 3.60ff. Cf. his insistence that Jesus Christ himself is the will of God, *Con. Ar.*, 2.31; 3.63; and Gregory Nazianzen's distinction between 'the person who wills' and 'the act of willing', *Or.* 29.6.

[128]Athanasius, *Con. Ar.*, 1.20; 2.24, 29f.

[129]Georges Florovsky, 'The Concept of Creation in Saint Athanasius', *Studia Patristica*, 1962, p. 37; *Collected Works*, Vol. II, pp. 48f, 57ff.

[130]Basil, *Hex.*, 5.4; Athanasius, *Con. Ar.*, 2.31.

This Christian belief in the freedom of the universe was quite new to the ancient world which was dominated by ideas of the essential unchangeability of nature and the eternity of the world, due to a cosmological synthesis of nature with Deity.[131] That was what lay behind notions of the implacable nature of the wheel of destiny, reflected in the classical literature of Greece and Rome, but also of the equation of necessity and rationality found throughout their philosophy and science. Early Church apologists like Athenagoras of Athens were not slow to show how the Christian outlook upon God and the creation had the effect of breaking the oppressive link in people's minds between God and an all-controlling impersonal fate, and liberating them from the superstitious hold of astrology and divination.[132]

How did this conception of the freedom of the universe, or the freedom of nature, arise? Undoubtedly it came from the new outlook upon the world and its history generated by the Gospel message that in the incarnation of his Word in Jesus Christ the Creator himself had come to redeem and liberate mankind from the bonds of sin and guilt, corruption and death.[133] This redemption and liberation, however, apply to the whole creation for Christ is the Head of the whole creation, its Origin and its End. Through him all things were created; they consist in him; and through him they are reconciled to God. Thus in Jesus Christ God has established and secured a new relation between the creation and himself in which the creation is given a freedom grounded in the transcendent and unlimited freedom of God.

This view of the redemption and renewal of the whole creation in Christ was far stronger in Greek than in Latin patristic thought. This was due, on the one hand, to the profound interrelation between the doctrines of incarnation, atonement and creation in Alexandrian and Cappadocian

[131]Origen, *Con. Cel.*, 5.7; Basil, *Hex.*, 1.3; cf. particularly the Stoic view of nature, J. von Arnim, *Stoicorum veterum Fragmenta*, Vol. II, 1027; Cicero, *De natura deorum*, II. 22, 57, etc. Rejection of the eternity and unchangeability of the world was the main theme of the works of John Philoponos, *De aeternitate mundi contra Proclum* and *Contra Aristotelem*.

[132]Athenagoras, *Leg.*, 6.3–4; 20.3; 22.12; 25.2; *De res.*, 19.1–3. The same theme is found in the *Con. gent.*, and *De inc.*, of Athanasius.

[133]Athanasius, *Con. Ar.*, 1.48f; 2.14, 56, 61ff, 67–69, 70–72; *Ad Ant.*, 7.

theology, and, on the other hand, to the damaging dualism between the intelligible and sensible realms retained in Augustinian theology. In the East the fact that there had become incarnate in Jesus Christ none other than the Creator, the ultimate Ground and Source of all being, order and rationality, who had himself penetrated into our death and triumphed over it in the resurrection, was held to mean that the whole universe is ontologically bound to the incarnate and risen Jesus, and therefore that the whole universe is brought to share in the freedom of the Creator. Just as it had its beginning in him, so through redemption, sanctification and renewal it will have its consummation in him.

Let us pause to consider what this freedom of the creation means. As the freedom of a contingent universe it is essentially a contingent and therefore a limited freedom. It is no less free because it is limited. Unlimited freedom of a contingent universe would be a contradiction in terms. But the fact that the freedom of the created universe is contingent, means that it is limited only by that transcendent Freedom in God which is its very ground precisely as contingent freedom. And so here again we have the peculiar interlocking of dependence and independence we found in the fundamental concept of contingence. However, if the universe is correlated to the unlimited and inexhaustible freedom of God, if it is continuously open to his creative power, then the freedom of the creation must mirror the freedom of God, and be unlimited and inexhaustible in its own way and on its own creaturely level. In other words, owing to its contingent relation to God, there are unlimited, and inexhaustible possibilities in the created universe. That is an essential ingredient in the basic concept of contingence. It is because the universe is characterised by contingence of this elusive, indeterminate kind, that we are unable to make any scientific discoveries about the universe merely through logico-deductive or necessitarian modes of thought. Due to its measure of real independence, given and supported by God, we may bring to light the secrets of nature only through experiments in which we put our questions to nature and let nature tell us about itself, without imposing upon it the presuppositions hidden in our questions.

Some of the Church fathers were already aware of this, and were therefore unwilling to impose logically derived or abstractive patterns of thought upon nature.[134] It cannot be said that they were ready at that stage to develop anything like an adequate doctrine of nature. What they did see was that in its correlation to the freedom of God nature must be regarded as incomplete in itself.[135] Precisely as such, however, it is endowed with an openness, spontaneity and freedom which will always take us by surprise. All God's ways and works in nature have such a surprising quality that they defy any anticipation on our part. And yet within this freedom of nature, as in a transcendent way in the freedom of God, there is an astonishing constancy and reliability. The one thinker in the early Church who, as far as I know, really grasped and applied this truth in any significant way, was John Philoponos of Alexandria, in his persistent rejection of Platonic and Aristotelian notions of the eternity of the world, and in his rather remarkable physics of light.[136] He thought of the created light of the Universe as a created reflection of the uncreated light of God, and as contingently correlated to its constancy and invariance. It is surely in a similar way that we must think of the relation between the created freedom of the universe and the uncreated freedom of God.

It is in and through the incarnate self-revelation of God in Jesus Christ that we may discern something of this combination between freedom and constancy, spontaneity and reliability, unpredictability and order. Everything hinges, however, upon what we understand of the love, constancy and faithfulness of Jesus Christ as Lord and Saviour, and whether what he reveals of the nature of God is really true of God the Father Almighty, Creator of heaven and earth and all things visible and invisible, in his own essential nature. Is there a relation of absolute fidelity between the self-manifestation of God in the incarnation and what he is in his own eternal being? If there is such a relation of utter fidelity and constancy, then Jesus Christ in his redeeming love and liberating grace is the divine pledge for our

---

[134]E.g., Basil, *Hex.*, 3.8.

[135]Thus Basil, *Hex.*, 2.1f.

[136]John Philoponos, *De op. mundi*, 2.1ff, which was evidently influenced by Basil's discussion in *Hexaemeron*, 6.1ff; *De aetern. mundi con. Proclum*, 1.6–8, etc.

understanding of the freedom, integrity and reliability of the creation even in its physical order and behaviour.[137]

It may not be very easy for us today to appreciate the immense importance of this discovery for the early Church. They had to struggle to acquire a coherent picture of the universe as endowed with a rational orderliness of its own, one that was neither arbitrary nor necessary, but while genuinely contingent – in that it might not have come into being at all, and might have been quite other than it actually is – was nevertheless stable, reliable, and constant, open to the providential disposition of the Creator in the fulfilment of his purpose of love. All that was an unpacking in the light of the Christian Gospel of what the Old Testament had spoken of as the 'goodness' of the creation as it came from the hand of God, namely, its integrity and reality. Christians did succeed, however, in bringing together the concepts of contingency and constancy, flexibility and reliability, as essential features of created reality – which we have come to call 'nature'. That was not at all easy for people whose outlook was governed by the ultimate identification of God and nature (*deus sive natura*). The idea that this actual empirical universe, the world of sensible, physical existence, has an integrity and reliability of its own, was quite foreign to classical civilisation. This radically new outlook upon the world had deep roots, as we have seen, in the Judaic tradition, but it was the integrity and constancy of the love of God in Jesus Christ that was the decisive factor in Christian understanding and appreciation of the universe that God had made. Thus in the last analysis the doctrine of creation hinges upon the *homoousion*, that is, upon whether it was through Jesus Christ who is of one substance with the Father that 'all things were made', as the Nicene Creed laid down. This is the great issue to which we come in the next chapter.

---

[137]Cf. the statement of Aristides that God has established everything on his own steadfastness (ἀσφάλεια), *Ad Aut.*, 1.4. See Athanasius, *Con. Ar.*, 1.9, 35ff, 51f; 2.6–10; 3.36; *De decr.*, 14; cf. *De syn.*, 27.12; *Con. Apol.*, 1.12, 15.

4

God of God, Light of Light

'And in one Lord Jesus Christ, the only begotten Son of God, begotten from his Father before all ages, Light from Light, true God from true God, begotten not made, of one being with the Father, through whom all things were made.'

In the second chapter we were concerned with the Father/Son relation. It is exclusively from within that relation that we are given access to know God as he is in himself, for it is only in the Son, the one only begotten Son, the one Word of God incarnate, that God has revealed himself to us so that we may know him strictly in accordance with his divine nature. And here we found that godliness and precision, theology and science, go together, in a realist approach to God's self-revelation to us in Jesus Christ within time and space and in the radical change of mind it calls forth from us.

In the third chapter we discussed the fact that it is only from within the Father/Son relation that we are to understand the creation as the work of God the Father. God the Creator is to be understood in terms of God the Father, and not the other way round, for it is in and through the Son that all things were created. What the Father does, the Son does, and what the Son does, the Father does. Both the almighty Creatorship of God and the nature of the creation are therefore to be understood from the perspective of Jesus Christ. Thus the Christian doctrine of creation and its radicalisation of contingency rest on the doctrine of the incarnation. It is as we think out together the doctrines of the incarnation and the creation that we find the whole structure of our understanding of God, Christ and the world being transformed.

Everything depends, then, on the relation and the nature of the relation that obtains between Jesus Christ the incarnate Son and God the Father. In this chapter we turn to ask: How are we to think of that relation between the Son and the Father? What does the Gospel mean when it tells us that Jesus Christ was sent *by* God, was *from* God, and that he is *of* God the Father? What are we, then, to think of Jesus Christ himself in his revelation of the Father, for everything evidently hinges upon it? That is the question to which these clauses in the Nicene-Constantinopolitan Creed offer an answer.[1] Given the priority of the Father/Son relation over the Creator/creature relation, how are we to understand the relation of the Son to the Father in an accurate and precise way, that is in such a way as to exclude the ambiguities and errors which in the fourth century seemed to threaten the very heart and substance of the Christian faith?

These problems in the fourth century were undoubtedly thrown up by the sharp dualism between the sensible and intelligible realms which we noted at the outset of the second chapter, and by the way in which that dualism affected the contrast between Hebraic and Hellenistic patterns of thought within the Church as soon as it expanded beyond its original base in Jerusalem and Judaea and put down roots within Graeco-Roman culture. Very soon conflicting attempts were made to interpret the mystery of Jesus Christ, operating not only from contrasting Hebraic and Hellenistic starting-points but from the sharp antithesis between God and the empirical world in the prevailing framework of knowledge. Thus there arose the so-called 'ebionite' and 'docetic' types of Christology which had the effect in different ways of breaking up the wholeness of the New Testament presentation of Jesus Christ as God and man by separating the divine Christ from the man Jesus. Before we go further we must probe a little into those deviations, for they represent earlier forms of the problems that confronted the Church in the fourth century.

[1] The words 'God of God', or 'God from God', in the original Nicene Creed were omitted in its Constantinopolitan form as redundant.

Ebionite Christology derived from an early community of Jewish converts to Christianity who were styled 'the poor' (*ebionim*, אֶבְיוֹנִים).[2] They accounted for the mystery of Christ as Jesus the man elected to special divine sonship through the descent upon him of the Holy Spirit at his baptism. They did not think of him as begotten of the Father, but as created. Far from being God become man, he was rather like a prophet indwelt by God. Hence they rejected any idea of an internal relation of being between him and the Father in favour of an external moral relation in virtue of which he fulfilled his messianic vocation as Christ. Through an approach from below upwards, ebionite Christology sought to explain *how* God was in Jesus Christ in such a way as to give full value to his unique place within Christian faith, and yet in such a way as not to compromise the absolute oneness and transcendence of God. However, Jesus Christ was placed quite definitely on the creaturely side of the radical difference between God and the creation, and as such could not be regarded as embodying in his own person the real presence or saving activity of God himself among men. It was not Jesus Christ, therefore, who was the focus of faith, but only 'the heavenly Father' to whom he directed mankind in his teaching. Since the ebionites considered God to be related to the world only in a tangential way, he remained for them essentially the hidden, unknowable God of Judaism who does not give human beings access to any knowledge of himself as he is in his own eternal being. To be successful in offering the world a real message of divine revelation and redemption, this ebionite approach to Jesus Christ had in some way to present him as divine, but that meant cutting itself loose from its starting point in the humanity of Christ.

Docetic Christology took its name from spiritualistic sects which held that the body of Christ the incarnate Son of God was

[2]See Justin Martyr, *Dial. c. Tryph.*, 47–48, Irenaeus, *adv. haer.*, 1.22.1, vol. 1, pp. 212f; 3.11.10, vol. 2, p. 45; 3.15.1f, pp. 78f; 4.52.1f, pp. 259f; 5.1.3, pp. 316f; Hippolytus, *Ref. haer.*, 7.34f; 9.13ff; Origen, *De prin.*, 4.1.22; *Con. Cel.*, 2.1; 5.61, 65; Minucius Felix, *Dial. Oct.*, 36; Tertullian, *De praescr.*, 33; Eusebius, *Hist. eccl.*, 3.27; 4.22; Hilary, *De Trin.*, 1.26; 2.4; 7.3, 7; 8.40; *De syn.*, 38f, 50; Epiphanius, *Haer.*, 29f; Jerome, *Ep.*, 112, 13. Cf. Ignatius, *Philad.*, 8; *Magn.*, 8ff.

not real but only seemed to be.[3] Warnings against docetism were already given in the New Testament,[4] but it was among the gnostics of the second and third centuries that it became rampant. Through an approach from above downwards, docetic Christology sought to explain on a dualist basis *how* God became man in Jesus Christ in such a way as to give full weight to his divine reality, and yet in such a way as not to compromise his eternal immutability and impassibility through union with the flesh. The effect of this was to treat the human nature and suffering of Christ as unreal and thus to idealise the Gospel message and to undermine the objective and historical reality of Christ. The incarnation of the Word could thus be no more than the instrument in the hands of God for the introduction of divine truth into the world, but which was bound to come to an end when that purpose was fulfilled. On the other hand, this ideal Christ presented by docetism was inevitably understood and interpreted under the control of preconceived notions reached apart from the Gospel. Thus in the process of commending the Christian message docetic Christology regularly cut itself off from its starting point in the Divinity of Christ, and tended to transmute itself into human speculations or mythological constructs projected into God from below. For a docetic Christology the Divinity of Christ was finally no more than a divinised human idea.

Quite clearly a strange dialectic was at work in ebionite and docetic Christologies, for owing to the cognate dualisms they each presupposed, an antithesis between Creator and creature and between divine idea and physical event, they tended inevitably to pass over into each other.[5] However, the fact that each could end up on the other side of the gulf between God and

---

[3]Ignatius, *Eph.*, 7.18–20; *Trall.*, 9; *Smyrn.*, 1–3, 5, 7; *Magn.*, 11; Justin, *De res.*, 2; Irenaeus, *Adv. haer.*, 1.16.2, vol. 1, p. 193f; 3.17.5f, vol. 2, pp. 86ff; 4.55.2ff, p. 266ff; 5.1.2, pp. 315f; Hippolytus, *Ref. haer.*, 8.8–11; 10.16; Clement Alex., *Strom.*, 7.17; Eusebius, *Hist. eccl.*, 6.12; Theodoret, *Haer.*, 5.12; *Ep.*, 82. See also Tertullian, *De carne Christi, passim.*

[4]1 John 2.22; 4.2f; 2 John 7.

[5]Athanasius was evidently aware of this dialectic, but reckoned that the Nicene Creed was a bulwark against them all – cf. *Con. Ar.*, 1.8; 2.12, 14; *De decr.*, 12, 32; *De syn.*, 45; *Ad. Afr.*, 11. See also Evagrius/Basil, *Ep.*, 8.3; and Basil, *Ep.*, 125.1.

man where the other had begun, showed that neither had really started from the fundamental datum of the Gospel: that in Jesus Christ, who was born of Mary and suffered under Pontius Pilate, God himself has come to be with us and reveal himself to us, and that in the one Person of Jesus Christ God and man are inseparably united for us and our salvation. The New Testament did not present Jesus Christ in contrast to God or alongside of God, or argue from one to the other, as in ebionite and docetic Christologies, but presented him in the undivided wholeness of his divine-human reality as God become man.[6] It is as such that Jesus Christ is Lord and Saviour, the immediate object of faith, the only begotten Son of God apart from whom there is no way to knowledge of the Father. If Jesus Christ were not God, he would not reveal God to us for only through God may we know God; and if he were not man, he would not be our Saviour for only as one with us would God be savingly at work within our actual human existence. As Origen claimed, belief in Jesus Christ as God become man, as himself at once God and man, belonged to the biblical teaching handed down from the very beginning of the Church.[7] Moreover, as R. V. Sellers pointed out, in connection with the teaching of Origen's disciples on the unity of Christ's Person: 'seemingly, they would all attribute the actions and sayings of Jesus Christ, without distinction, to the incarnate Logos himself – to the one Person that is at once God and man.'[8] Athanasius was often to repeat the claim advanced by Origen that this had been the tradition, teaching and faith of the Catholic Church from the very beginning. Thus he claimed (in an important passage to which we refer again) that at Nicaea the fathers 'wrote not what seemed good to them but what the Catholic Church believed. Hence they confessed how they had come to believe, in order to

[6]Cf. the Athanasian stress on Christ as 'whole man and God together (ὅλον αὐτὸν ἄνθρωπόν τε καὶ Θεὸν ὁμοῦ)', *Con. Ar.*, 4.35, which was at once anti-docetic and anti-ebionite. Thus also *Con. Ar.*, 3.41: 'He was true God in the flesh, and true flesh in the Word.'

[7]Origen, *De prin.*, 1. *praef.*; 1.2.1ff; 2.6.2f, etc. Cf. Ignatius; 'There is one Physician, of flesh and of Spirit, generate and ingenerate, God in man, true life in death, of Mary and of God, first passible and then impassible, Jesus Christ our Lord.' *Eph.*, 7.2 – cited by Athanasius, *De syn.*, 46.

[8]R. V. Sellers, *Two Ancient Christologies*, 1940, p. 29.

show that their own opinions were not novel but apostolical, and that what they wrote down was no invention of their own, but the same as was taught by the apostles.'9

That Jesus Christ *is* God's Son or Word, and that God's Son or Word *is* Jesus Christ, was the central evangelical truth which the Council of Nicaea reaffirmed, and had to reaffirm, in order to cope with Arianism and Sabellianism, and other heretical successors of ebionite and docetic Christologies, threatening the integrity of the Church's faith. The Church refused to weaken or compromise faith in Jesus Christ as God and man in one Person, for if he was not really God then there was no divine reality in anything he said or did, and if he was not really man then what God did in him had no saving relevance for human beings. The issue was well summed up by Athanasius in the following statement regarding the divine and human activity of the incarnate Word. 'In recognising what is proper to each, and in seeing and understanding that both these things are done by One, we are right in our faith and shall never go astray. But if someone, looking at what is done divinely by the Word, were to deny the body, or, looking at the properties of the body, were to deny the coming of the Word in the flesh, or, from what is human, think poorly of the Word, such a person, mixing water and wine like a Jewish vintner, will count the Cross a scandal, or like a Greek consider preaching to be folly. That is what happened to God's enemies, the Arians. In looking at the human properties of the Saviour they considered him to be a creature. Hence in looking at the divine works of the Word they ought to deny the birth of his body and number themselves with the Manichees.'10 Faith in Jesus Christ as God become man for us and our salvation requires emphatic belief equally in his Deity, for it is God himself who has become man in him, and in his humanity, for in Jesus Christ it is our human nature that God has made his own. Arianism, on the other hand, so confused truth and error that it sinned against both essential poles of evangelical

9Athanasius, *De syn.*, 5; see *De decr.*, 5; *Ad Ser.*, 1.28; *Ad Afr.*, 1; *Fest. Ep.*, 2.4–7, etc. Cf. also Alexander of Alexandria, *Ep.*, 1.12–13; Theodoret, *Hist. eccl.*, 1.3.

10Athanasius, *Con. Ar.*, 3.35. The biblical allusions are to Is. 1.22 (LXX); and 1 John 4.3.

belief, and was particularly damaging to the saving message of the Gospel for it was guilty of ebionite and docetic error at the same time.

The controversial teaching of Arius, as Alexander, the Patriarch of Alexandria, soon realised,[11] made it indubitably clear that the decisive issue for saving faith was the nature of the relation between Jesus Christ the incarnate Son and God the Father. How, then, must the Church think of that relation? What does the Gospel mean when it brackets Jesus Christ together with God in all his decisive acts of revelation and salvation? And what must be said about the nature of that relation in order to safeguard from misunderstanding and distortion all that it stands for in the Gospel? It was in answer to such questions that the Nicene fathers formulated their confession of faith: 'And in one Lord Jesus Christ, the Son of God, begotten from the Father, only-begotten, that is, from the being of the Father, God from God, Light from Light, true God from true God, begotten not made, of one being with the Father (ὁμοούσιος τῷ Πατρί), through whom all things were made . . .' Moreover they attached to the Creed a canon to the effect that the Catholic Church anathematises 'those who say "There was when he was not", and "Before being begotten he was not", and that "He came into existence out of nothing"; or who allege that the Son of God is of a different ὑπόστασις or οὐσία, or that he is created, or changeable or alterable.' All these statements of the Nicene Council were subjected to severe testing in face of prolonged criticism in the fourth century, which served to deepen and confirm the convictions of the Church, with the result that they were fully ratified by the following Council at Constantinople and given their final form as: 'And in one Lord Jesus Christ, the only begotten Son of God, begotten from his Father before all ages, Light from Light, true God from true God, begotten not made, of one being with the Father, through whom all things were made . . .' The changes

[11] See the epistles of Alexander preserved by Theodoret, *Hist. eccl.*, 1.3; and by Athanasius, *De decr.*, 35; Socrates, *Hist. eccl.*, 1.6; Gelasius, *Hist. eccl.*, 2.3. Consult Vlasios Pheidas, 'Alexander of Alexandria and his two Encyclical Epistles', in 'Αντίδωρον Πνευματικόν, Athens, 1981. Cf. the earlier teaching of Dionysius of Alexandria discussed by Athanasius, *De sent. Dion.*

made in these clauses at Constantinople evidently had little real significance beyond a tidying up through dropping unnecessary repetition.[12]

By beginning the second article of belief with 'one Lord Jesus Christ' the Nicene fathers related him directly to 'one God the Father Almighty' in the first article, thereby indicating that in Jesus Christ and God the Father they were referring to one and the same being. Thus they gave expression to the actual content of the New Testament presentation of Christ in which faith in Christ perfectly coincided with faith in God. To have faith in one Lord Jesus Christ is to have faith in one God the Father, and to acknowledge him as God equally with the Father. This unique relation of Christ to the Father within the oneness of God was then spelled out by the phrases 'the only begotten Son of God, begotten from his Father before all ages . . . begotten not made'. The terms 'Son' and 'Father' point to a distinction within the one being of God, for the Son is Son and not Father and the Father is Father and not Son.[13] But as there is only one Lord and one God, so there is only one Son of God who is eternally Son of the Father as the Father is eternally Father of the Son, for there is no interval of time or of any other kind between them. The import of these phrases was then gathered up in concentrated form by the emphatic 'of one being with the Father' (ὁμοούσιος τῷ Πατρί),[14] to express the oneness in being between the incarnate Son and God the Father, with the addition of the words 'through whom all things were made', to make quite explicit the identification of the Son with the Creator.[15]

In framing the Creed in these terms, of course, the Nicene

---

[12]Cf. the creed cited by Epiphanius shortly before the Council of Constantinople, *Anc.*, 120.

[13]This distinction involved rejection of the Sabellian notion of a 'Son-Father' (υἱοπάτωρ) – Athanasius, *De syn.*, 16; cf. *De sent. Dion.*, 5ff; *Con. Ar.*, 3.4, 36; 4.1ff; *Ad Ant.*, 3–6, 11; *Con. Ar.*, 4.2.

[14]'The word ὁμοούσιος is a compound adjective deriving from ὁμοῦ (meaning 'together', 'in solidarity') and οὐσία (being).' Archbishop Methodios, 'The Homoousion', *The Incarnation. Ecumenical Studies in the Nicene-Constantinopolitan Creed*, 1981, p. 6 (ed. by T. F. Torrance).

[15]Athanasius, *De decr.*, 7, 18f; *De syn.*, 12, 35; *Con. Ar.*, 1.9ff; *Ad Afr.*, 4–9; *Ad Ser.*, 2.2–5.

Council clearly had the 'impiety' of Arius in view.[16] He had
taught that owing to its utterly unique, eternal and transcendent
nature, the being of the one God is unknowable,
undifferentiated and incommunicable, which necessarily ruled
out of consideration the idea of a Son or Word as another being
(οὐσία or ὑπόστασις) who is eternally of the same nature as
God himself, for that would mean that God's being is divisible
and even plural.[17] That there might be another being beside the
Father, the unoriginated source of all reality, was only
conceivable to Arius if it were brought into existence out of
nothing. Hence he taught that the Son or Word of God is not
from the Father but was created out of nothing through an act
of his will and, although he was adopted by God as a Son, he is in
no sense proper to the being of God, equal to him, or for that
matter of the same being (ὁμοούσιος). On the contrary, like all
things created out of nothing he is altogether alien and different
from the being and propriety of the Father.[18] It follows from
this that the Father is ineffable and quite incomprehensible to the
Son or Word, so that the Son or Word cannot have or mediate
any authentic knowledge of God, for he can know and
understand only what is 'in proportion to his own measure' as a
creature.[19] Moreover, Arius held that the Logos 'is a creature,
but not as one of the creatures; a work, but not as one of the
works, an offspring, but not as one of the offsprings'.[20] That is
to say, as the created intermediary between God and man, the
Logos was regarded as neither properly divine nor properly
creaturely.[21] According to Epiphanius and Theodoret, Arius
had a defective conception of the humanity of Jesus, evident in

---

[16]Athanasius, *Ad episc.*, 13; *De decr.*, 1f; *De syn.*, 3; *Con. Ar.*, 1.7; Basil, *Ep.*,
52.2, etc.

[17]See the citations from Arius' *Thalia* in Athanasius, *De syn.*, 15–16; *Con.
Ar.*, 1.5ff; *De decr.*, 16; *Ad episc.*, 12; Arius' letters to Alexander, in Athanasius,
De syn., 16, and to Eusebius, in Epiphanius, *Haer.*, 69.6. Cf. also the first
Encyclical of Alexander on the Arian heresy, Theodoret, *Hist. eccl.*, 1.3; and
Socrates, *Hist. eccl.*, 1.6.

[18]Athanasius, *Con. Ar.*, 1.5–6; *De syn.*, 15.

[19]Athanasius, *ibid.*, and cf. also *Ad episc.*, 12.

[20]See Athanasius, *Con. Ar.*, 2.19, and *De syn.*, 16, for this citation from
Arius' letter to Alexander.

[21]Athanasius, *Con. Ar.*, 2.24–26, 30; *De decr.*, 8, 24.

his idea that in the incarnation the Logos assumed a body without a human or rational soul, and replaced the soul with itself.[22]

It is not surprising that the Nicene fathers considered Arianism as the most dangerous heresy, for it struck at the very roots of the Church's faith by calling in question the divine reality of Christ's revelation and saving activity, not to speak of their human actuality. They reacted by affirming in unmistakable terms their belief that as the only begotten Son of God, the Lord Jesus Christ is the offspring of the very being of God, and not created, true God from true God, of one and the same being with the Father.[23] The crucial point in the debates of the Council was over how the biblical expressions *by*, *from*, and *of* God, applied to the incarnate Son, were to be understood. Were they to be understood to mean, as the Arians claimed, that he is the Son of the Father only by an act of his will, by grace? Or did they mean that he is Son of the Father from his very being (ἐκ τῆς οὐσίας), that is, from his essential reality and nature as God? If he is from the very being of God, as the Nicenes held, then 'what is of the being of the Father is entirely the Son', for the Father and the Son are each 'proper' (ἴδιος) to the other. Thus the Father/Son relation falls within the one being of God, the Father and the Son inhering and coexisting eternally, wholly and perfectly in one another. God is Father precisely as he is eternally the Father of the Son, and the Son is God of God precisely as he is eternally Son of the Father. There is perfect and eternal mutuality between the Father and the Son, without any 'interval' in being, time or knowledge between them.[24] In Gregory of Nazianzen's expressions, the Son is begotten of the

---

[22]Epiphanius, *Anc.*, 33; Theodoret, *Haer.*, 5.11. Cf. Eustathius, *De an. adv. Ar.*, *MPG*, 18.689B; Athanasius, *Ad Ant.*, 7; Gregory Naz., *Ep.*, 101, *MPG*, 37, 134A; Gregory Nyss., *Con. Eun.*, 2.124, Jaeger, II, p. 365; Athanasius, *Con. Apol.*, 1.15; 2.3, 17; Theodoret, *Ep.*, 103. See also the evidence adduced by V. Pheidas from the Colluthian schism, Τὸ Κολλουθιανὸν Σχίσμα καὶ Ἀρχαὶ τοῦ Ἀρειανισμοῦ, 1973.

[23]See the interpretation of these Nicene clauses by Athanasius, *De decr.*, 6ff; *Con. Ar.*, 1.9ff; *De syn.*, 41ff.

[24]Athanasius, *Con. Ar.*, 1.1–29, 34; 2.22ff, 33; 3.1ff; 65f; 4.1ff; *De syn.*, 41–54; *De decr.*, 24, 27; Basil, *Ep.*, 52.2; Hilary, *De syn.*, 25.

Father 'timelessly', 'causelessly', and 'unoriginately' (ἀχρόνως, ἀναιτίως, ἀνάρχως).[25] For Athanasius and the Nicene fathers the generation of the Son is something that exceeds and transcends the conceptions of men.[26] It is not to be imagined as having taken place at some 'moment' or by 'an act of will' in God, as Arius and Eusebius evidently did,[27] but as an ineffable relation between Father and Son eternally subsisting in God. 'God, in that he ever is, is ever Father of the Son'.[28]

It was recognised by Athanasius and the Nicene fathers that they could not but make use of human images and analogies in seeking to express their understanding of the relation of the Son to the Father, for that is how divine revelation has been mediated to us, in and through human language. Taken by themselves these images and analogies are unsatisfactory and so they may not be pressed,[29] but they are nevertheless employed by divine revelation with an admirable exactness in being made to point beyond their creaturely content to what God discloses of his own inner divine relations.[30] This means that we must interpret the images and analogies according to the sense given them by the Scriptures and within the whole scope and framework of the biblical narrative and message.[31] It was in this way, according to Athanasius, that the fathers of Nicaea

[25]Gregory Naz., *Or.*, 30.11 & 19; cf. 29.3f; 31.14.

[26]E.g. Basil, *Ep.*, 52.3: 'The mode of divine begetting is ineffable and inconceivable by human thought.' Also *Con. Eun.*, 2.16 & 24; Gregory Naz., *Or.*, 29.8.

[27]Cf. C. Stead, *Divine Substance*, 1977, pp. 26 & 229.

[28]Athanasius, *De decr.*, 12; cf. 20. Also *Ad Episc.*, 2; 'The Son is continuously coeternal with the Father.' This understanding of Fatherhood and Sonship as eternally subsisting relations in the Godhead was strongly upheld by Gregory Nazianzen, also in respect of the Holy Spirit, in his 'Theological Orations', *Or.*, 29.16 & 20; 31.9. Cf. Basil, (or his brother) on 'a certain communion indissoluble and continuous' between Father, Son and Holy Spirit – *Ep.*, 38.4; and Gregory Nyss., *Con. Eun.*, 1.33; 8.5; 9.2; *Or. cat.*, 1.

[29]Athanasius, *In ill. om.*, 3; 'One must use a poor analogy taken from tangible and familiar objects to put our thought into words, for it is presumptuous to intrude into the incomprehensible nature.'

[30]Athanasius, *In ill. om.*, 3–5. For Athanasius' concept of biblical images and analogies as παραδείγματα see *De decr.*, 12; *Con. Ar.*, 1.20; 2.30; 3.3, 10; *De syn.*, 42; *Ad Ser.*, 1.19f, etc.; refer to *Theol. in Reconstr.*, pp. 31ff.

[31]See further my account of the hermeneutics of Athanasius, *Reality and Evangelical Theology*, 1982, pp. 100ff.

brought the biblical image or paradigm of light (φῶς) and radiance (ἀπαύγασμα) to help them elucidate the relation of Christ as Son and Word to God the Father.[32] This had the effect of preventing any projection into God of the creaturely or corporeal ingredient in the terms 'father', 'son', 'offspring', 'generation', 'word', etc., but it also had the effect of making clear that as light is never without its radiance, so the Father is never without his Son or without his Word.[33] Moreover, just as light and radiance are one and are not alien to one another, so the Father and the Son are one and are not alien to one another but are of one and the same being. And just as God is eternal light, so the Son of God as eternal radiance of God is himself eternally light without beginning and without end.[34] It was then on biblical ground, Athanasius claimed, that they could 'speak confidently of Christ as the true and natural Son of the Father who is proper to his being (ἴδιος τῆς οὐσίας αὐτοῦ), and as himself true God and of one being (ὁμοούσιος) with the true Father. For 'he is the express image of the Father's ὑπόστασις', and light of light, and true power and image of the being of the Father.'[35] Thus the words 'God of God, Light of Light, true God of true God', were specifically inserted into the Creed at Nicaea in order to clarify and define the unique nature of the relation of the incarnate Son to the Father.[36]

This was clearly not an easy task for the fathers, for as Athanasius tells us in several of his works,[37] the Nicene Council had a hard struggle to reach its final formulation of the crucial clauses. Several stages were involved. At first, when the Arians agreed to the formula that the Son is 'of God' or 'from God', as in 'Light from Light', the Nicene fathers insisted on defining the 'of God' or 'from God' as 'from the being of the Father' (ἐκ τῆς οὐσίας τοῦ Πατρός), thereby qualifying the analogies in the light of each other and of the objective relations within God to

[32] Athanasius, *De decr.*, 21–24.

[33] Athanasius, *Con. Ar.*, 1.24; *De decr.*, 27; *In sent. Dion.*, 25.

[34] Athanasius, *De decr.*, 24; *Con. Ar.*, 1.13, 25; 2.33; *Ad episc. Aeg.*, 13; *Ad Afr.*, 8.

[35] Athanasius, *Con. Ar.*, 1.9, with reference to Hebrews 1.3.

[36] Consult the illuminating discussion of Jaroslav Pelikan, *The Light of the World. A Basic Image in Early Christian Thought*, 1962, pp. 55ff.

[37] Athanasius, *De syn.*, 33ff, 46; *De decr.*, 19ff; *Ad Afr.*, 5f.

which they pointed beyond themselves. This meant that the Son
is proper (ἴδιος) to the very being or substance of God, and is *of*
God the Father, as creatures are not: he is *God of God*. But when
the Arians and Eusebians, to their astonishment, seemed to agree
to the phrase 'from the being of God' or 'from the being of the
Father', they realised that they were going to interpret it in a
sense in which it might be applied to human beings who are
created not only as 'children of God' but in 'the image and glory
of God'. The Council then decided to cut away all ambiguity
and remove any possibility for misunderstanding by inserting
the crucial expression 'of one being with the Father' (ὁμοούσιος
τῷ Πατρί), which meant that the Son and the Father are equally
God within the one being of God.[38] At the same time they
added a rider repudiating the idea that the Son is 'from some
other ὑπόστασις or οὐσία', thereby condemning both Sabellian
and Arian heresies which were apt to run into each other.[39]
Thus they rejected any idea that the Son is from a being other
than God, or that he is Son of God only through partaking of
God, and stated quite definitely and unambiguously that the
Son is of the very being of God and is God in precisely the same
sense in which the Father is God, for he is uniquely and
completely one with him.[40] He is in union with the Father, the
eternal 'I Am' of the Godhead.[41]

In order to offset the term *homoousios* (ὁμοούσιος) it was
argued by some people at the Nicene Council and afterwards
that the term *homoiousios* (ὁμοιούσιος) might be employed; that
would mean that the Son has only a 'likeness in being' to the

---

[38] Athanasius, *De syn.*, 41.

[39] See Basil's explanation of this, *Ep.*, 125.1, in which he claimed that the
Nicene terms ὑπόστασις and οὐσία were not just identical, for had they
expressed one and same meaning there would have been no need for both.
Basil, himself, however, was to develop the distinction between them by
arguing that 'οὐσία has the same relation to ὑπόστασις as the common to the
particular', *Ep.*, 214. See also *Ep.*, 236.6; Gregory/Basil, *Ep.*, 38.1ff, etc. Cf.
Athanasius, *Con. Ar.*, 3.65; 4.33; *Ad Afr.*, 4ff & 8.

[40] Athanasius, *De syn.*, 48–54; *Ad Afr.*, 8–9.

[41] Athanasius, *Con. Ar.*, 1.11ff, 34, 46ff, 60; 2.12, 14, 18, 20, 53f, 56, 59, 61,
82; 3.1f, 5f, 9, 19, 22, 24f, 27, 33; 4.4; *De decr.*, 22, 30; *De syn.*, 34, 48f; *Ad Afr.*, 4;
Ad Ser., 1.28; 2.2; *In Ill. om.*, 4. See also Gregory Naz., *Or.*, 30.18,

Father.[42] Actually Athanasius himself could sometimes speak of the Son as 'like the Father', although with reservations,[43] but finally declined to do so, even when the notion of likeness was reinforced by the idea of exact and essential image, for likeness applies to habits and qualities and not to being, and in any case it implies an element of unlikeness.[44] It became clear to the Nicene theologians that the expression 'like the Father' was not theologically adequate even when qualified by 'altogether' or 'essentially', for it still left room for misinterpretation. A proper understanding of *homoiousios* (ὁμοιούσιος) would have to imply *homoousios* (ὁμοούσιος).[45] Hence it is understandable that the Nicene Council adopted the latter.[46] The Son is then thought of as the Offspring of the Father by nature (φύσει), who is proper to, and identical with, the very being of God the Father, of one nature (ὁμοφυής) with the Father who begot him eternally in himself. He does not just partake of the Father, but is essentially and wholly one with the Father in being and reality.[47] 'The fullness of the Godhead *is* the being of the Son, and the Son *is* whole God.'[48]

Because *homoousios* (ὁμοούσιος) was a non-biblical and relatively new term, however, it had to be interpreted, as Hilary pointed out, with scrupulous care.[49] That is what the Nicene

[42]Athanasius, *De decr.*, 20; *De syn.*, 8, 26, 29 (the Arian creeds); 37f, 41, 46, 50 52f. Cf. Theodoret, *Hist. eccl.*, 1.3.

[43]Athanasius, *Con. Ar.*, 1.20f, 26, 40; 2.17f, 22, 34; 3.11, 20, 26, 67; *Ad episc.*, 17; *Ad Afr.*, 7; cf. *Exp. fidei*, 1.

[44]Athanasius, *De syn.*, 41 & 53; *De decr.*, 20; cf. Evagrius/Basil, *Ep.*, 8.3.

[45]Athanasius, *Con. Ar.*, 1.21, 26, 40; 2.17f, 22, 33; 3.10f, 14, 26, 67; *De Syn.*, 26, 38, 41. 47–54; *De decr.*, 20, 23; *Ad episc.*, 17; Hilary, *De syn.*, 89; Evagrius/Basil, *Ep.*, 8.3; 9.3. Cf. Epiphanius, *Haer.*, 73.22; and Cyril of Jerusalem, *Cat.*, 4.7; 11.4, 18.

[46]Cf. the stance taken by Basil of Ancyra, Athanasius, *De Syn.*, 41; Epiphanius, *Haer.*, 73.22.

[47]According to Athanasius, this relation of 'wholeness' between the Son and the Father was also implied by the analogy of light and radiance, *Con. Ar.*, 2.33, 35; cf. *De inc.*, 17; *Con. Ar.*, 3.6. The analogy was also found to imply the coinherence of the Son and the Father, *De decr.*, 25.

[48]Athanasius, *Con. Ar.*, 3.3 Cf. *Ad. Ser.*, 1.16 and *Exp. fidei*, 1, where the Son is said to be 'wholly from the whole' (ὅλος ἐξ ὅλου).

[49]Hilary, *De syn.*, 70, 91.

theologians undertook to do after the meeting of the Council.[50]
It steadily became clear that ὁμοούσιος used in this way as a
technical theological term meant 'of one and the same being and
nature'. As such it was reckoned to be an accurate and precise
declaration of Christian belief in the face of the Arian heresy.[51]

The lead was undoubtedly given by Athanasius who
perceived that by expressing the equality of the Son with the
Father, ὁμοούσιος carried with it, as was right, the meaning that
the Son is identical in being with the Father and of one nature
(ὁμοφυής) with him. Thus properly understood the Nicene
ὁμοούσιος τῷ Πατρί means 'of identically the same being as the
Father'. It is the self-same God who is revealed to us as the Son
and the Father – the incarnate Son *is* the very same being as God
the Father.[52] No statement about this could be stronger than
that of Athanasius when he argued that 'the whole being of the
Son is proper to the being of the Father', and that 'the being of
the Son is the fullness of the Father's Godhead'.[53] The Son and
the Father are so essentially and completely one and the same
God that – a phrase Athanasius reiterated – the Son is everything
that the Father is, except 'Father'.[54] This being the case, any
detraction from the Son cannot but be a detraction from the
Father, for to deny the divine nature of the Son is to deny that
God is eternally and intrinsically Father, and to deny the divine
reality of the Word is to say that in himself God is essentially
wordless and wisdomless (ἄλογος, ἄσοφος).[55] As Jesus himself
taught, he who honours the Son, honours the Father, but he
who does not honour the Son, does not honour the Father who
sent him. The incarnate Son has all the prerogatives of God,
except Fatherhood.[56]

Homoousios (ὁμοούσιος), however, has another important

[50]Hilary, *De Trin.*, 4.4–7; *De syn.*, 84.

[51]Cf. Archbishop Methodios, 'The Homoousion', *op. cit.*, pp. 1–15.

[52]Athanasius, *De syn.*, 49–54; *Ad Afr.*, 8.

[53]Athanasius, *Con. Ar.*, 3.3, 6; 4.1ff.

[54]See Athanasius, *Con. Ar.*, 3.4; *De syn.*, 49; *Ad Afr.*, 8, etc. Thus also the
Cappadocian theologians, e.g., Gregory Naz., *Or.*, 30.11.

[55]Athanasius, *Con. Ar.*, 1.8, 14ff, 18ff, 24f; 2.2, 32f; 3.42, 61ff; 4.2f, 14; *De
decr.*, 15, 26; *De sent. Dion.*, 16, 23; *Ad Ser.*, 2.2.

[56]Athanasius, *Con. Ar.*, 1.8, 15ff, 33; 2.24f, 32; 3.4ff, 35f, 44; *Ad episc.*, 17; *Ad
Afr.*, 8; *Ad Ser.*, 1.30; 3.2; 4.6.

nuance. If the Son is eternally begotten of the Father *within* the being of the Godhead, then as well as expressing the oneness between the Son and the Father, ὁμοούσιος expresses the distinction between them that obtains within that oneness. 'For nothing can be ὁμοούσιος with itself, but one thing is ὁμοούσιος with another.'[57] As we have seen, it implies that while the Father and the Son are the same being they are eternally distinct for the Father is unchangeably the Father and not the Son and the Son is unchangeably the Son and not the Father. The *homoousion* was thus a bulwark against Sabellianism and Arianism, against unitarianism and polytheism, alike.[58] This internal reference of ὁμοούσιος to eternal distinctions within the one being of the Godhead, will come before us later when we consider its application by Athanasius to the Holy Spirit, which enabled him and the other theologians in the fourth century to clarify the Church's understanding of the Holy Trinity.[59]

Two years before the Council of Constantinople Epiphanius described the oneness in being between the incarnate Son and the Father, which lay at the heart of the Nicene Creed, as 'the bond of faith' (σύνδεσμος τῆς πίστεως).[60] That is certainly what it has proved to be in the Church: in guiding the faithful in their interpretation of the Holy Scriptures, in clarifying and securing their grasp of evangelical truth, and in enabling them to discern the inner coherent structure of Christian doctrine. It is, I believe, through considering the *homoousion* in this range of its significance that we may appreciate more fully the central Christological thrust of the Nicene–Constantinopolitan Creed.

(1) The hermeneutical significance of the *homoousion*

It was in the Nicene era that the clarification of the canon of

---

[57]Basil, *Ep.*, 52.3 A distinction is already implied, of course, in the derivation of the compound word ὁμοούσιος from ὁμοῦ and οὐσία.

[58]Athanasius, *De decr.*, 23; *Con. Ar.*, 3.4; 4.2; *De syn.*, 34, 45; Basil, *Ep.*, 52.1ff; Epiphanius, *Anc.*, 6.4; *Haer.*, 65.8; 69.72; 76.7.

[59]Cf. Athanasius, *Ad Ser.*, 1.27; 3.2; and *Ad Jov.*, 4; *Ad Ant.*, 6; *Con. Apol.*, 1.9.

[60]Epiphanius, *Anc.*, 6.4; cf. *Haer.*, 69, 70; Ambrose, *De fide*, 3.15.

truth (or the rule of faith)[61] through the unfolding of its kerygmatic content in trinitarian formulation, and the recognition of the canon of Holy Scripture as the embodiment of divine revelation mediated through the apostles and prophets, came to fruition.[62] That was not an accident, for the elucidation of the apostolic deposit of faith in the defence of the Gospel against erroneous teaching, and the differentiation of the apostolic tradition from all other tradition, were deeply interconnected. There was constant interplay between the canon of truth and the canon of Holy Scripture. Only those Scriptures were accepted as mediating divine revelation which were in accord with the canon of truth embodied in the apostolic deposit of faith, and only that tradition of faith was accepted as authentically apostolic which was in accord with the teaching of the accepted Scriptures. In that process, however, the primacy accorded to the apostolic tradition over all other tradition carried with it the primacy of the apostolic Scriptures. The full acknowledgement of the Holy Scriptures took place only as the inner structure and harmony of the Holy Scriptures were found to be essentially the same as the inner structure and harmony embedded in the deposit of faith.

That is clearly what we find emerging at 'the Great Synod' where 'they of Nicaea', as Athanasius expressed it, 'breathed the spirit of Scripture'.[63] On the one hand, they were concerned with the faithful determination of the fundamental sense of the Holy Scriptures in their many statements about the relation of the Lord Jesus Christ to the Father through penetrating into the inner substance of the Gospel; but on the other hand, they were

---

[61] Recall that for Irenaeus 'the kerygma of the truth' and 'the canon of the truth', were equivalent, *Adv. haer.*, 1.20, vol. 1, p. 87f; 1.15, pp. 188f; 2.8.1, p. 272; 2.40f, pp. 347ff; 3.1–5, vol. 2, pp. 2–20; 3.11.7, pp. 41; 3.12.6f, pp. 58ff; 3.15.1, p. 79; 3.38.1f, pp. 131f; 4.57.2ff, pp. 273ff; 5. Pref., p. 313f; 5.20.1f, pp. 377ff; and *Dem.*, 1–6. Recall also Origen's conception of 'the canon of godliness' which enables the Church to interpret the Scriptures in accordance with 'the mind of Christ' – *De prin.*, praef. 1–2; 1.5.4; 2.6.2; 3.1.17, 23; 3.3.4; 3.5.3; 4.2.2f; 4.3.14f. This must be distinguished from Tertullian's rather legalist notion of *regula fidei*, *De praescr. her.*, 13f, 20–28, 31f; *Adv. Prax.*, 2; *De virg. vel.*, 1; *De an.*, 2.; *de spect.*, 4.

[62] Cf. again my essay 'The Deposit of Faith', *SJT*, 1983, vol. 36.1, pp. 1–28.

[63] Athanasius, *Ad Afr.*, 4.

concerned to give precise formulation to coherent belief in Jesus Christ as the incarnate Son of God by bringing to light the true nature of his relation to God the Father, in the course of which they found themselves compelled by biblical revelation to confess their belief in the unqualified Deity of Christ as God of God, of one being with the Father. Thus through their exegetical and theological activity the Nicene fathers came up with the all-important ὁμοούσιος τῷ Πατρί which brought to decisive expression the ontological substructure upon which the evangelical message of the New Testament about Jesus Christ rested and in terms of which its various writings could be integrated in accordance with their saving import.

By clarifying the inner structure of the Gospel through subordinating its mind to the meaning (διάνοια) of the Holy Scriptures and the apostolic mind (φρόνημα), indeed the Mind (νοῦς) of Christ, which they enshrined, and by giving that structure authoritative expression in the Creed, the Nicene Council had the effect of establishing in a hitherto unprecedented way the primacy of the Holy Scriptures in the mind of the Catholic Church.[64] Certainly the Gospels and the Pauline Epistles had already been accepted informally along with the Old Testament as of canonical authority, but it was only after the Nicene Council that exact determination of the canon of Holy Scripture was made. It is hardly surprising, then, that Athanasius, to whom above all the *homoousion* owed its firm establishment in the mind of the Church, should be the one to whom we are indebted for the first definite account of 'the books included in the canon, handed down and accredited as divine'. 'These', he declared, 'are fountains of salvation, so that he who thirsts may take his fill from the living words in them. In these alone is proclaimed the doctrine of godliness. Let no man add to these, neither let him take anything from them.'[65]

It is apparent from the reports given to us of the proceedings at the Council of Nicaea that the *homoousion* was in the first

---

[64] It was rightly pointed out by Alfred Robertson that the conception of a general council as the supreme expression of the Church's mind did not give rise to Nicaea, but *vice versa* – Introduction to *St Athanasius: Select Works and Letters*, pp. xvii and lxxv.

[65] Athanasius, *Fest. Ep.* (of 367), 39.1–7; cf. Eusebius, *Hist. eccl.*, 4.26.14.

instance an exegetical and clarificatory expression, shaped within the believing worship of the Church, and forged under the impact of God's self-revelation in Jesus Christ, to help the Church grasp the meaning (διάνοια) and truth (ἀλήθεια) of biblical images, statements and conceptions. Thus Athanasius tells us that, faced with the slippery way the Arians cited and interpreted the Scriptures, the fathers of Nicaea subjected passage after passage from the Scriptures, from the Old Testament as well as the New, to careful comparative scrutiny, with strict attention to the scope, time, place, person and matter in question, and the distinctive biblical way of speaking, in order to elucidate their true and right sense and to collect from them as honestly as possible the exact meaning of what was being conveyed.[66] They rejected the crude materialist and mythologising ideas thrust upon the Scriptures by the Arians as fundamentally unbiblical and irreligious.[67] However, they found themselves reluctantly compelled to have recourse to non-biblical terms and phrases such as οὐσία and ὁμοούσιος in order to express more decisively the religious force (δύναμις) and meaning (διάνοια) of biblical statements about the indivisible unity of Jesus Christ with the Father. When charged with going beyond the Scriptures in this way, they agreed that ways of making the truth known taken from the Scriptures, rather than from other sources, were more accurate, but they were nevertheless forced by the craftiness of irreligious invention and corrupt interpretation to forge new terms in order to preserve the truth and sovereign principle of their faith and safeguard it from misunderstanding.[68] The all-important point, as Athanasius argued, was not the actual words or the

---

[66]Athanasius, *Con. Ar.*, 1.55; 2.44; 3.28ff; *De decr.*, 10f, 14, 19–22; *De syn.*, 38–45; *Ad Afr.*, 4–9; *Ad Ser.*, 2.8. Cf. also *Ep. Euseb.*, 5 – appended to the *De decr.*

[67]Athanasius, *De decr.*, 24; *Ad episc.*, 4, 9, 12f; *De syn.*, 39, 42, 45; *Con. Ar.*, 1.1, 8ff, 15, 37, 53; 2.1ff, 33, 72; 3.18f, etc.

[68]Athanasius, *De decr.*, 18f, 32; Hilary, *De syn.*, 88, 91. In any case, Athanasius pointed out, the non-biblical terms used were actually taken from earlier fathers, *De decr.*, 18, 25; *De syn.*, 43; cf. 33ff. See C. Stead's examination of the use of οὐσία and ὁμοούσιος before the Council of Nicaea, *op. cit.*, pp. 199–232.

terms used in the Scriptures but the *meaning* which they convey and the *realities* to which they refer.[69]

It was a general rule with Athanasius that terms are to be understood in one sense when used of human beings and in another sense when used of God, for God and human beings are utterly different. Thus when the same terms are used of God and man they must be interpreted differently in accordance with the nature of the beings to which they refer.[70] The linguistic and conceptual change that took place under the language-moulding power of the Gospel was expressed by Athanasius in laying it down as a basic hermeneutic principle: 'Terms (λέξεις) do not detract from his (God's) nature; rather does his nature draw those terms to itself and transform them. For terms are not prior to beings (οὐσίαι), but beings are first and terms come second.'[71] This hermeneutical principle, however, governs not only our understanding of biblical terms and expressions, but those we bring to the Scriptures in our interpretation and elucidation of them. Thus technical terms like *ousia* and *homoousios* applied to God in the Council of Nicaea were not employed with the sense commonly given them in Greek textbooks, but only with the new meaning given them under the transforming impact of God's self-revelation in Jesus Christ.[72]

Regarded in this light the Nicene ὁμοούσιος τῷ Πατρί was a *heremeneutical* as well as a *theological* instrument. It was certainly a strict theological statement arising out of the examination of biblical statements, derived by following through the ostensive reference of biblical forms of speech, and giving compressed expression in exact and equivalent language, not so much to the

[69] Athanasius, *De decr.*, 18, 21; *De syn.*, 39, 41, 45; *Con. Ar.*, 2.3; *Ad Afr.*, 9; *Ad episc.*, 4, 8; cf. *Ad Ant.*, 8.

[70] Athanasius, *De decr.*, 10f. This applies, for example, to 'create' and 'make' – *De decr.*, 11; *De syn.*, 51. Cf. Hilary, *De syn.*, 17; Basil, *Con. Eun.*, 2.23; Gregory Naz., *Or.*, 20.9. See further my essay 'The Hermeneutics of St Athanasius', *Ekklesiastikos Pharos*, vol. 52, 1970, pp. 446–468; 89–106; 237–49; vol. 53, 1971, pp. 133–149.

[71] Athanasius, *Con. Ar.*, 2.3. Cf. also Gregory Naz., *Or.*, 42.16; Gregory Nyss., *Con. Eun.*, 1.37, and Hilary, *De Trin.*, 4.14.

[72] In view of this variable use of terms, found even in the Scriptures, Athanasius declared that attention should be given to the fact that 'each council has a sufficient reason for its own language' – *De syn.*, 45.

biblical words themselves as to the meaning or reality they were designed to convey or indicate.[73] Once established, however, as an interpretative instrument of thought, the *homoousion* served as a further guide to the understanding of the Holy Scriptures, yet always in subordination to the inspired teaching of the apostles, and as a cardinal point of belief by reference to which the on-going instruction of the faithful could be given steady and authoritative guidance. It is when the Church is engaged in this kind of theological interpretation, Athanasius claimed, that it keeps its feet upon the apostolic foundation and is able to hand on to the next generation the true teaching as it had received it from the previous generation without perverting it.[74]

When the concept of the *homoousion* had been adopted in this way, it carried further the profound reconstruction in basic concepts of Greek thought which we noted in an earlier chapter. The meanings of οὐσία and ὑπόστασις, λόγος and ἐνέργεια, underwent a radical change through the use to which they were put in the hermeneutical and theological activity of the Church. They have to be understood in the light of the evangelical message to which they were adapted and through which they were reminted, that is, in light of the fact that in Jesus Christ God who is the creative Source of all being has become man, one with us, in such a way as to give us access through the Son and in the Spirit to the Father as he is in himself. The ὁμοούσιος τῷ Πατρί was revolutionary and decisive: it expressed the fact that what God is 'toward us' and 'in the midst of us' in and through the Word made flesh, he really is **in himself;** that he is in the **internal relations** of his transcendent being the very same Father, Son and Holy Spirit that he is in his revealing and saving activity in time and space toward mankind.[75]

In precise theological usage *ousia* (οὐσία) now refers to being not simply as that which is but to what it is in respect of its internal reality, while *hypostasis* (ὑπόστασις) refers to being not just in its independent subsistence but in its objective otherness. As Prestige expressed it, *ousia* denotes being in its 'inward

---

[73] Athanasius, *De decr.*, 10f, 20–24; *Con. Ar.*, 1.20, 55ff; 3.19ff.
[74] Athanasius, *De decr.*, 4.
[75] Athanasius, *Con. Ar.*, 2.11; 3.1ff; *Ad Ser.*, 1.14–17, 20f, 30f; 2.2; 3.1f; 4.6.

reference', while *hypostasis* denotes being in its 'outward reference'.[76] It must also be noted that in theological usage these terms have an essentially personal meaning which they do not have in classical Greek. The term *homoousios* (ὁμοούσιος), then, refers to immanent personal relations in the Godhead. Within the one being of God, Father, Son, and Holy Spirit, who are each distinct (ἄλλος) from one another, are all consubstantial, yet in relation to one another they are *hypostatic* (ὑποστατός, ὑποστατικός) or *enhypostatic* (ἐνυπόστατος, ἐνυποστατικός). The consubstantiality of the Son and the consubstantiality of the Spirit refer, then, to their substantive identity with God the Father, to their unity and equality with him within the one indivisible being or οὐσία of God. It was thus that the trinitarian formula 'one Being, three Persons' (μία οὐσία, τρεῖς ὑποστάσεις) came to be accepted as a satisfactory way of speaking of the Triunity of God.[77]

Here we must recall the conceptual change that came over theological understanding of the being of God implied in the Athanasian expressions *enousios logos* (ἐνούσιος λόγος) and *enousios energeia* (ἐνούσιος ἐνέργεια), which we have already had occasion to note. If God is in himself what he is in the Person and activity of his incarnate Word and Son, then the being or *ousia* (οὐσία) of God must be understood in a very un-Greek way. Applied to God ἐνούσιος λόγος and ἐνούσιος ἐνέργεια express the fact that the being of God is not intrinsically empty of word or activity, not mute or static, but is essentially eloquent and dynamic. God's being is to be understood as speaking being, for his being and his Word inhere in one another. His very being is Word, and his very Word is being. Likewise God's being is essentially dynamic, for his being and his activity inhere in one another. His being is his act-in-his-being and his act is his being-in-his-act. While it was under the impact of God's revealing and saving activity in Jesus Christ that the Nicene *homoousion* was

---

[76]G. L. Prestige, *Fathers and Heretics*, 1954, p. 88; *God in Patristic Thought*, pp. 168f, 188ff. See also, T. F. Torrance, *Theology in Reconciliation*, 1975, pp. 243ff; and Methodios Fouyas, *The Person of Jesus Christ in the Decisions of the Ecumenical Councils*, 1976, pp. 65ff.

[77]Athanasius, *Ad Ant.*, 5–6.

forged, its adoption and use immediately deepened and reinforced the distinctively Christian doctrine of God.

(2) The evangelical significance of the *homoousion*

It should now be clear that the debates and decisions at Nicaea were not primarily metaphysical, although metaphysical and epistemological issues were involved. The main point, the oneness between Jesus Christ and God in being, word and act, had to do essentially with the integrity of the Gospel message. And it was on that issue that the basic decision had to be taken and was in fact taken. The primary intention of the Councils at Nicaea and Constantinople in formulating and reaffirming the *homoousion*, therefore, was to be faithful to the Gospel with which the Church had been entrusted, and to provide an authoritative confession of faith that enshrines at its heart the supreme evangelical truth by which the Church stands or falls. Far from imposing an alien Hellenism on the Gospel,[78] the terms οὐσία and ὁμοούσιος were adapted to allow the evangelical witness and teaching of the New Testament to come across without distortion through an alien framework of thought. As such the *homoousion* proved to be a primary movement of thought from an incipiently conceptual to a fully conceptual act of understanding which the godly mind could not but take under the compelling claims of the truth as it is in Jesus. It was the hinge upon which the whole Nicene Creed turned, and has remained the cardinal concept to which the Church has kept returning in theological renovation of its mind in the understanding and proclamation of the Gospel. It is the bearing of the *homoousion* upon the evangelical message of the New Testament that is all-important for us. In the last analysis, it is by that test that it must be judged and through it that its significance will be disclosed.

The evangelical significance of the *homoousion* may be thrown into sharp relief by posing the question: *What would be implied if there were no oneness in being between Jesus Christ and God*

---

[78]Athanasius, *De syn.*, 51.

the Father? If there were no oneness in agency as well as being between Christ and God, what would that mean for our understanding of Christ as Lord and Saviour, and what would happen to the import of the Gospel message of the saving love of God? And what would all that mean for our knowledge of God himself? The answer to that question ought to make clear to us what really is at stake here, and whether we are concerned with the Gospel of God's saving grace or not.

In the first place, then, what would be implied if there were no oneness in **being** between the incarnate Son and God the Father?

The primary and all-embracing significance of the *homoousion* was its categorical assertion that Jesus Christ is *God*, and that as God he shares equally with the Father in the one being of the Godhead. As the only begotten Son of the Father he is the embodiment of the whole being of God and his exclusive self-revelation as the Word made flesh. However, if Jesus Christ is not God, as Arius frankly declared, he must be regarded as having been created out of nothing, and therefore as being external to God, altogether different from his being and foreign to him. It follows from this, as again Arius did not hesitate to assert, that God is utterly unknowable, for no creaturely being, however exalted, can mediate any authentic knowledge of him.

That is to say, if a line of utter distinction is drawn between the being of the incarnate Son and the being of the Father,[79] it cannot be held that there is any oneness between what the Gospel presents as the revelation of God and God himself. If what God is in himself and what he is in the Lord Jesus Christ were not the same, there would be no identity between God and the content of his revelation and no access for mankind to the Father through the Son and in the Spirit. Hence we would be left completely in the dark about God. God would be for us no more than an absolute blank, of which we can neither think nor speak. As Athanasius expressed it, if the Son were divided from the Father, or the Word were not eternally inherent in God, then the being of God would be quite irrational (ἄλογος) – a light that does not shine (μὴ φωτίζων), an infertile desert

[79]Cf. Athanasius, *De syn.*, 45.

(ἔρημος), a dry fountain or just an empty pit (λάκκος).[80] The plain fact is, as Basil insisted, that if the Son were only a creature, mankind would be without any revelation of God whatsoever.[81] In that case the Church would be left with no more than some kind of human self-understanding projected into God from a centre in itself and passed off as 'revelation'. As Athanasius frequently pointed out, that was the kind of 'revelation' heretics trafficked in, something they devised (κατ' ἐπίνοιαν) in accordance with their subjective fantasies, rather than something which they received from beyond themselves and thought out (κατὰ διάνοιαν) in accordance with the objective truth of God. If it is not with God himself in his own being that we have to do in revelation, then it is not with *theologia* (θεολογία) but *mythologia* (μυθολογία), not with theology but mythology, that we are concerned. Moreover, if Christ is detached from God, then he himself is no longer central to the substance of the Gospel, but is only a transient variable representation of God, a detached symbolic image and no more. And inevitably, as Arius claimed, there would be 'many words', and even 'myriads' of conceptions of God.[82]

What kind of God would we have, then, if Jesus Christ were not the *self*-revelation or *self*-communication of God, if God were not inherently and eternally in his own being what the Gospel tells us he is in Jesus Christ? Would 'God' then not be someone who does not care to reveal himself to us? Would it not mean that God has not condescended to impart himself to us in Jesus Christ, and that his love has stopped short of becoming one with us? It would surely mean that there is no ontological, and therefore no epistemological, connection between the love of Jesus and the love of God – in fact there would be no revelation of the love of God but, on the contrary, something that rather mocks us, for while God is said to manifest his love to us in Jesus, he is not actually that love in himself.

For the Nicene fathers these ideas and their consequences

[80]Athanasius, *Con. Ar.*, 1.19; 2.2, 14, *De decr.*, 15. Cf. G. D. Dragas, *Athanasiana*, vol. 1, 1980, p. 54.

[81]Basil, *Con. Eun.*, 1.18ff.

[82]See the citations from Arius' *Thalia*, in Athanasius, *De syn.*, 15; *De decr.*, 16; *Ad episc.*, 14, 16.

were in flagrant contradiction to the Gospel message, that to believe in the Lord Jesus Christ is to believe in God himself. Hence they inserted the ὁμοούσιος τῷ Πατρί in the Creed in order to affirm the supreme truth that in the incarnation God has revealed *himself* to us, and that God is completely identical with his self-revelation in Jesus Christ. Everything depends upon the unity in being and act and word between Jesus Christ the only begotten Son and God the Father. If the ὁμοούσιος τῷ Πατρί were not true, the Gospel would lack the very foundation in the self-revelation or self-communication of God in Jesus Christ which it needs in order to be Gospel. As we have seen, however, the ὁμοούσιος τῷ Πατρί expresses the identity between the 'I am' of the Lord Jesus Christ and the 'I am' of God the Father Almighty, for the Son of God in his incarnate Person is the place where we may know the Father as he is in himself, and know him accurately and truly in accordance with his own divine nature. The *homoousion* asserts that God *is* eternally in himself what he *is* in Jesus Christ, and, therefore, that there is no dark unknown God behind the back of Jesus Christ, but only he who is made known to us in Jesus Christ. 'The knowledge of the Father through the Son and of the Son from the Father is one and the same.'[83] Thus Basil, echoing Athanasius, wrote: 'All things that are in the Father are beheld in the Son, and all things that are the Son's are the Father's; because the whole Son is in the Father and has all that the Father has in himself. Thus the Person of the Son becomes as it were the Form and Face of the knowledge of the Father, and the Person of the Father is known in the Form of the Son.'[84]

Before we go further let us note, in anticipation of the discussion in the following chapter, that the *homoousion* applies to the relation between the *incarnate* Son and God the Father. That is to say, it grounds the reality of our Lord's *humanity*, and of all that was revealed and done for our sakes by Jesus, in an indivisible union with the eternal being of God. We have already noted the significance of the fact that the incarnate Son, 'the Lord's humanity' or 'the dominical man', as Athanasius

[83]Athanasius, *Con. Ar.*, 2.82.
[84]Basil, *Ep.*, 28.8. Cf. Athanasius, *Con. Ar.*, 2.18, 22; 3.3f.

expressed it, is to be regarded as the *arche* (ἀρχή) of God's ways for us.[85] This had a crucial epistemological bearing upon Christian understanding of God in accordance with who he is and what he has revealed to us of himself in his own nature. We shall return to this when we draw out the far-reaching implications of the vicarious life and work of the incarnate Son. Meantime, however, let it be sufficient to note that the significance of the *homoousion* is lodged in the relation of Christ in the reality and integrity of his humanity to his reality and integrity as the eternal Son of the Father. It is the wholeness of Christ's humanity that we have to keep in mind here – that is, the completely human, spatio-temporal being of Jesus who is our brother, flesh of our flesh and blood of our blood.[86] It is precisely as the incarnate Son shares with the Father his eternal being and nature, that he also shares with us our contingent and mortal being and nature. The utterly astonishing thing proclaimed in the Gospel is that God himself came among us precisely as man.[87] It is as such that God meets us, reveals himself to us, and acts on our behalf, as he who fully shares with us in the wholeness of our human being, nature, and condition, in body, mind, and soul.[88]

This was one of the primary truths of the Gospel evaded by the Arians, in their determination to keep God at an infinite distance from human being. They held the strange idea that since creatures could not endure the absolute presence and hand of God, God first created the Logos and then through the Logos as his agent brought the rest of the creation into existence.[89] The

[85]Athanasius, *Exp. fidei*, 1 & 4; *De decr.*, 13f; *Ad episc.*, 17; *Con. Ar.*, 2.18–67, etc.

[86]Athanasius, *Ad Epict.*, 2–9; *Con. Ar.*, 4.30–36.

[87]Athanasius, *Con. Ar.*, 3.30. Cf. Epiphanius, *Haer.*, 77.29: 'The self-same was God and man, not as if he dwelt in a man, but that he himself became man wholly.'

[88]The two treatises *Contra Apollinarem* present powerful arguments for the full reality of the humanity of Christ in effecting salvation of the whole man. See the recent work of G. D. Dragas, *St Athanasius Contra Apollinarem*, 1985, for a full discussion of the Athanasian Christology and soteriology of these treatises.

[89]Athanasius was quick to ask how, in that case, the Logos himself could endure the absolute presence and hand of God, if he too, according to the Arians, was a creature. *De decr.*, 7ff.

Logos was thus regarded as occupying the status and role of a created intermediary between God and the world. On hearing these statements the fathers of Nicaea began to hold their ears, and unanimously acted to exclude the Arian heresy in the most categorical way – that was the negative purpose of the ὁμοούσιος τῷ Πατρί.[90] In the face of schismatic notions of that kind 'which rent the coat of Christ', 'the seamless garment of God', by 'dividing the indivisible Son from the Father', the *homoousion* had the effect of rejecting dualist modes of thought and securing the wholeness and reality of Christ's human nature, upon which the wholeness and reality of our salvation depend.[91] This is particularly important for our understanding of the consubstantiality of the incarnate Son with God the Father, as we shall see, for it binds creation and redemption together in such a way that the creation is anchored in the love of God himself as its ultimate ground. Not to agree to the ontic oneness between Christ and God has the effect of rejecting this essentially Christian outlook upon God, creation, and redemption. Everything finally depends, then, upon the genuineness and actuality of the humanity of the incarnate Son in his oneness in being with God the Father.

In the second place, what would be implied if there were no oneness in *act* between the incarnate Son and God the Father? The ὁμοούσιος τῷ Πατρί clearly asserted, not only that there is no division between the being of the Son and the being of the Father, but that there is no division between the acts of the Son and the acts of God. As Jesus said in the Gospel, 'My Father works hitherto and I work', thereby identifying his activity with that of God the Creator.[92] 'He who made us through his Word made all things small and great. It is not for us to divide the creation, and say this is the Father's and this is the Son's, for they are of one God, who uses his proper Word as his hand, and creates all things in him . . . "There is one God, from whom are all things; and one Lord Jesus Christ, through whom are all

---

[90] Athanasius, *Ad episc.*, 13.

[91] Athanasius, *Ep. fest.*, 4.4; 5.6; 10.9; *Ad Adel.*, 2ff.

[92] John, 5.17, cited frequently by Nicene theologians – e.g. Athanasius, *In ill. om.*, 1; *Ad episc.*, 17; *Con. Ar.*, 2.21f, 29, etc.

things." '[93] However, if a sharp line of demarcation is drawn between the Son and the Father, that would differentiate absolutely the activity of the Son from the activity of the Father, for it would degrade the Son's activity to that of a creature.[94] If Jesus Christ is not himself God, then there is no final authority or validity for anything he said or did for human beings. If he were not divine, he could not act divinely, and if he were not Creator, he would not be able to save and recreate humanity.[95] 'No creature can ever be saved by a creature'.[96]

Thus in answer to our test question, it must be said that if the actions of Jesus Christ are cut off from the actions of God the Father Almighty, Creator of heaven and earth and all things visible and invisible, then the bottom falls out of the Gospel. If what Christ has done for us is not the work of God become man, but only of a man who as a reward for his service to other human beings has been designated 'Son of God', then he does not embody for mankind the saving grace (χάρις) of God, and is utterly incapable of divine activity (θεοποίησις).[97] On the other hand, if Jesus Christ cannot be divided in being and act from God the Father, then he constitutes in being and act in his incarnate presence or saving economy the creative self-giving of God to mankind.[98] Thus just as the ὁμοούσιος τῷ Πατρί asserts that God himself is the content of his revelation in Jesus Christ, so it also asserts that God himself is the content of his saving grace in Jesus Christ.[99] In Jesus Christ the Giver of grace and the Gift of grace are one and the same, for in him and through him it is none other than God himself who is savingly and creatively at work for us and our salvation.[100]

The distinctive term that Greek patristic theology came to

[93] Athanasius, *De decr.*, 7, & 1 Cor. 8.6 – see further *De decr.*, 19ff; *Con. Ar.*, 1.19; 2.31; 3.4, 39; *De syn.*, 35, etc.

[94] Athanasius, *De syn.*, 46.

[95] Athanasius, *Con. Ar.*, 2.21ff, 29, 31, 56ff; *Ad Max.*, 3f.

[96] Athanasius, *Ad Adel.*, 8.

[97] Athanasius, *Con. Ar.*, 1.6, 38–39, 42–43.

[98] Athanasius, *De decr.*, 1, 25; *Con. Ar.*, 2.6, 9f; 45, 51f, 75f; *Ad Ant.*, 7.

[99] 'One and the same grace is from the Father in the Son, as the light of the sun and of the radiance is one, and as the sun's illumination is effected through the radiance.' Athanasius, *Con. Ar.*, 3.11; cf. also 3.13.

[100] Athanasius, *De decr.*, 14; *Con. Ar.*, 1.16, 39f, 50; 3.12f.

use to express this consubstantial self-giving of God to mankind
through Christ and in his Spirit was θέωσις.[101] He is not divine
because he participates in God, for he is himself fully and wholly
God, of one and the same being with the Father. In virtue of his
divine reality and presence incarnate within mankind he acts
upon people in an utterly divine and creative way, making them
partake of himself through grace and thus partake of God.
Θεοποίησις or θέωσις, then, was used to describe the unique act
of God incarnate in Jesus Christ, but act which inheres in his
divine being and is inseparable from it: it is his being-in-act or
his act-in-being. Jesus Christ *is* in his incarnate Person the
unique act of God whereby we are saved and made new, but in
the nature of the case we are not saved or renewed by the
activity of Christ without being united to him and partaking of
him. In developing their concept of θεοποίησις the Nicene
theologians took their cue from the statement of our Lord that
the Scripture 'called them gods (θεοί) to whom the Word of
God came'.[102] They understood this to refer to those who,
while created, become partakers of the Word through his
creative impact upon them. Christ alone is *Theos* (Θεός), true
God of true God, he alone is properly (κυρίως) Son of the
Father, but through his divine activity (θεοποίησις) we are
adopted and made sons of God in him, and in that respect, as
those who through union with Christ receive the grace and
light of his Spirit, are said to be *theoi* (θεοί).[103]

In its application of the *homoousion* to the incarnate Son and
Word of God, Nicene theology rejected entirely the idea that he

---

[101] While the word θέωσις is not found in the writings of Athanasius, it does
seem to express what lay behind his use of the verb θεοποιέω – cf. *De inc.*. 54;
'He became man that we might be made divine' (αὐτὸς γὰρ ἐνηνθρώπησεν, ἵνα
ἡμεῖς θεοποιηθῶμεν).

[102] John, 10.35 – see Athanasius, *Con. Ar.*, 1.39; *Ad Afr.*, 7. This concept of
θεοποίησις was also reinforced by that of enlightenment (φωτισμός), for since
Christ is God of God and Light of Light, not just a witness to the Light but the
real Light, his enlightening of us is necessarily a divine and deifying activity.
See *De decr.*, 23f; *Con. Ar.*, 1.43; 2.41; 3.3ff, 125; 4.18; *Ad Ser.*, 1.19f, 30, etc.

[103] Athanasius, *Con. Ar.*, 1.9, 16, 37–43, 46–50; 2.47, 53, 59, 63–70, 74,
76–78; 3.17, 19–25, 34, 39–40, 53; 4.33–36. See also *De decr.*, 14; *De syn.*, 51; *Ad
Adel.*, 4; *Ad Ser.*, 1.24.

is a created intermediary. Rather is he to be understood as Mediator in the full sense as he who is God and man in one Person. In him God himself in his own eternal being has condescended to become man, in order to give *himself* and reveal *himself*, and not just something of himself, to mankind. Likewise in its application of the *homoousion* to the gift of grace, Nicene theology rejected entirely the idea that grace is a created medium between God and man. Rather is grace to be regarded as the self-giving of God to us in his *incarnate* Son in whom the Gift and the Giver are indivisibly one.[104] 'Through the Son is given what is given; and there is nothing but the Father operates it through the Son; for thus is grace secure to him who receives it.'[105] In such a mode of giving governed by the oneness of the Father and the Son, grace cannot be regarded as a detachable and transferable divine quality which may inhere in or be possessed by the human being to whom it is given in virtue of which he is somehow 'deified' or 'divinised'.[106]

The grace of the Lord Jesus Christ is to be understood in the same way as the Holy Spirit who is 'the Lord and Giver of life', as the Nicene–Constantinopolitan Creed expressed it. This point was constantly emphasised by Athanasius, not least in his letters to Serapion. 'The Holy Spirit is always the same, and does not belong to those who partake, but all things partake of him.'[107] So it is with grace, for grace is the self-gift of God in Jesus Christ, which, or rather who, cannot be separated or detached from him in any way, for he is of one and the same

---

[104]Thus in a comment on Philippians 2.9–10, Athanasius wrote: 'For as Christ died and was exalted a man, so as man he is said to take what as God he ever had, that the grace thus given (ἡ τοιαύτη δοθεῖσα χάρις) might come to us. For the Word did not suffer loss in taking a body in order that he should seek to receive grace, but rather he even deified (ἐθεοποίησεν) what he put on, and more than that graciously gave (ἐχαρίσατο) it to mankind.' *Con. Ar.*, 1.42. Cf. 2.69; 3.39–40.

[105]Athanasius, *Con. Ar.*, 3.12.

[106]It is unfortunate that θέωσις or θεοποίησις, with reference to 2 Peter 1.4 (θείας κοινωνοὶ φύσεως), is often misunderstood in this debased sense of grace – an idea that Athanasius clearly rejected, *Con. Ar.*, 2.17ff, 24f. For Athanasius' use of 2 Peter 1.4, see *Ad Adel.*, 4, with reference to the fact that in becoming man the Son of God transferred our 'erring generation' (πλανηθεῖσαν γέννησιν) into himself that we might be a 'holy race'.

[107]Athanasius, *Ad Ser.*, 1.27.

being as God the Giver.[108] This self-giving of God in grace is no more divisible than the one being and activity of the Holy Trinity. 'The Holy and blessed Triad is indivisible and one in himself. When mention is made of the Father, there is included also his Word, and the Spirit who is in the Son. If the Son is named, the Father is in the Son, and the Spirit is not outside the Word. For there is *one* grace from the Father fulfilled through the Son and in the Holy Spirit.'[109] 'This grace and gift that is given is given in the Triad, from the Father through the Son and in the Holy Spirit. As the grace given is from the Father through the Son, so we can have no communion in the gift except in the Holy Spirit. For it is when we partake of him that we have the love of the Father and the grace of the Son and the communion of the Spirit himself.'[110]

The evangelical significance of the *homoousion* is very apparent in its direct bearing upon the saving acts of Jesus Christ, in healing, forgiving, reconciling and redeeming lost humanity, for it asserted in the strongest way that they are all done out of a relation of unbroken oneness and communion between Jesus Christ and God the Father. The cognate significance of *theopoiesis* (θεοποίησις), however, lies in its stress upon the oneness in agency as well as in being between the Son and the Father, thereby identifying the saving acts of Jesus Christ in the Gospel as the downright acts of God himself 'for us and our salvation'. It thus throws into sharp focus the divine finality and validity of those saving acts, by insisting in the most uncompromising way that they are the kind of acts which *only* God the Father Almighty, Creator of heaven and earth and of all things visible and invisible, can do.

Unless this is the case – this is what the Nicene fathers saw so clearly – the saving essence goes out of the Gospel. What would be the value, for example, of his word of forgiveness to a sinner, if the Lord Jesus were only a creature, for it is only God who can

---

[108]Athanasius, *Con. Ar.*, 2.18; 3.11ff, 24–25, 39f; 4.6f.

[109]Athanasius, *Ad Ser.*, 1.14; cf. 3.5: 'The Spirit is not outside the Word, but, being in the Word, through him is in God. And so the spiritual gifts (τὰ χαρίσματα) are given in the Triad . . . For the Father himself through the Word in the Spirit works and gives all things.'

[110]Athanasius, *Ad Ser.*, 1.30.

forgive sins, really forgive in such a way that he undoes sin and recreates the being of the sinner? Unless Jesus' words and acts of forgiving love are completely backed up by the sheer being and reality of God, they do not finally amount to anything.

What about the passion and sacrifice of Christ in which, as our Lord claimed, he gave himself for the redemption of mankind? What would be the message of the Cross if Christ and God were ultimately divided there, Christ only a creature on earth, and God infinitely removed in the exaltation of his divine being? How could the great reconciling exchange have taken place unless it was God himself who in his infinite loving-kindness had come in Jesus Christ to make our nature, our sin and our death his own, in order to save us? That is the question to which Athanasius addressed himself in his long exegetical arguments with the Arians, in which he showed that in Jesus Christ God the eternal Son had taken on himself 'the form of a servant' precisely in order to constitute himself both Priest and Sacrifice in his saving operation on our behalf.[111] Nicene theology had no doubt about the fact that unless the death of Christ on the Cross was the vicarious act of God himself in order to effect atoning reconciliation in the ontological depths of our creaturely existence, then what took place on the Cross would have been in vain. Only if God himself were directly and immediately engaged in the passion of Christ could it be the vicarious means of redeeming and liberating the creation. 'God crucified'! That is what Gregory Nazianzen in an Easter oration once declaimed as a 'miracle'. 'We needed an incarnate God, a God put to death, that we might live. We were put to death together with him, that we might be cleansed; we rose again with him, because we were put to death with him; we were glorified with him, because we rose again with him'[112] Atoning reconciliation would be utterly empty of content, had not God the incarnate Son, true God from true God, suffered and died for us on the Cross.

And what about the ultimate destiny of mankind, the day when the Lord Jesus Christ will come again to judge the living

[111]Athanasius, *Con. Ar.*, 1.41ff, 59ff; 2.7ff, 68ff, 75f; 3.31ff, 56f; 4.6f; and see especially the Athanasian *Con. Apol.*, I & II.

[112]Gregory Naz., *Or.*, 45.28f; cf. also *ibid.*, 22.

and the dead? How are we to think of that if Jesus Christ is not after all Light from Light, true God from true God, but is no more than a transient being who passes away with the rest of the creation? In that event, Jesus Christ would not in the last analysis go bail for our future, and all we could look forward to at the end would be some utterly unknown, arbitrary Deity who bears no relation to Jesus Christ or all he stood for. But what if Jesus Christ is God become man who has taken on himself the judgment of the world, and as such is the Mediator between God and man, and if it is through him that God will judge all men at the Last Day?[113] That is precisely what the Nicene Creed asserts. Quite clearly the *homoousion* makes an immense difference to our understanding of the divine judgment, for it asserts that there is no interval or gap of any kind between Jesus Christ and God the Judge of all the earth. The judgment of Jesus and the judgment of God are one and the same. Even in the final judgment God the Father and the incarnate Son are perfectly one in being and agency. This is partly why the Creed insists that Christ's Kingdom shall have no end, for the incarnation does not finally vanish away but remains on into eternity.[114]

As the great Church fathers were forced to think carefully through the implications of the ὁμοούσιος τῷ Πατρί they found that it expressed much more than had evidently been realised at the time it was formulated and inserted into the Creed. It soon became clear that it was the main point of Christian orthodoxy or godliness, and to reject it, as Gregory Nyssen claimed, 'is nothing short of a plain denial of the message of salvation'.[115] But there was more to it than that. They were overwhelmed with astonishment and awe at the significance of the **internal** relation of the incarnate Son to the one being of the living God, and what it meant for the whole life of Jesus which had to be regarded as embraced within the coinherent relations of the Holy Trinity. What the Son of God became in Jesus Christ, experienced, said, and undertook for us and our salvation, is

---

[113]Athanasius, *Con. gent.*, 47; *De inc.*, 20f, 56; *In ill. om.*, 2; *Con. Ar.*, 1.59f; 2.14, 31, 69, 76; 4.6f; *Con. Apol.*, 1.11; cf. *De inc. et con. Ar.*, 22; and *Serm. maj. de fid.*, 26.

[114]See Athanasius, *Con. Ar.*, 1.42f.

[115]Gregory Nyss, *Con. Eun.*, 1.15; cf. 2.12.

grounded in God and has been assumed into God as his very own. The most breath-taking aspect of all this was that the man Jesus, Son of Mary, who lived a fully human life among us as one of us, is none other than God himself come to us as man, and for ever belongs to the innermost being and life of the Godhead.[116] No wonder that the Church fathers fought desperately to maintain the integrity of this Gospel as it broke in upon the mind of the Church so forcefully at Nicaea, evoking from the faithful wonder and praise in the conviction that what had happened through the Council was truly of God.

In the Nicene formulation of the *homoousion* something absolutely fundamental took place in the mind of the early Church. It was a decisive step in deeper understanding of the Gospel, taken in the continuity of the apostolic tradition, upon which the Church, in obedience to God's saving revelation in Jesus Christ, could not go back. It was an irreversible event in the history of Christian theology. The significance of what happened may be indicated by reference to what we do with a jig-saw puzzle. We assemble the scattered pieces together, fitting them appropriately to each other until the pattern they conjointly make comes to view. If we then break it all up and throw the pieces back into disorder, we may have little difficulty in fitting them all together again, but it will be impossible for us to do that without recalling the picture we reached the first time. Something irreversible would have taken place in our mind and memory, which could not but influence all subsequent attempts to recover the coherent pattern made by the different pieces.

An ineraseable event of that kind happened in the mind and memory of the Church at the Council of Nicaea in 325 A.D. It was a turning-point of far-reaching significance, with conceptual irreversibility. When the conception of the oneness in being between the incarnate Son and the Father was formed and given explicit expression in the clause ὁμοούσιος τῷ Πατρί, a giant step forward was taken in grasping the inner ontological coherence of the Gospel as it had been mediated through the

---

[116]See especially Athanasius, *Con. Ar.*, 1.46; 2.69–76; 3.1–6, 30–35; 4.1ff. 33–36; *Ad Epict.*, 5–9.

apostolic Scriptures. Once that insight had been reached, the Church could not go back upon it, because the evangelical substance of the faith, with its distinctively Christian doctrine of God, had been secured in its mind and understanding in a permanent way. 'The Word of God which came through the Ecumenical Synod at Nicaea abides for ever.'[117]

In this chapter we have been considering the supreme importance of the *homoousion* in its expression of the oneness in being between Jesus Christ and the Father. We have been concerned to bring home to ourselves the evangelical fact that what God is in Jesus Christ in all his relations of revelation and salvation toward us, he really is in himself, for in Jesus Christ it is God in his own being who has come among us. But there is an obverse to that truth. The *homoousion* holds not simply between the eternal Son and the Father, but, as we have already noted, between Jesus, the incarnate Son, and the Father. And so we must go on to examine what it implies from the side of Christ's humanity. That was a question which arose within the Church soon after the Council of Nicaea, as we can see from Athanasius' *Epistle to Epictetus*. What of the humanity of the Lord Jesus, if we are to give the *homoousion* this central place in our faith and thought? Unquestionably, it is of Jesus in the wholeness and integrity of his human being and nature that we must say ὁμοούσιος τῷ Πατρί. As the one Mediator between God and man, he must be as fully man of man as he is God of God. We shall discuss this question in the following chapter, but in the nature of the case it is a question that must be answered from within a soteriological perspective. That was, in fact, just how it had been raised by Alexander, the Patriarch of Alexandria, and was then taken up and expounded so convincingly by Athanasius, his successor in the Patriarchal Chair.

---

[117]Athanasius, *Ad Afr.*, 2.

5

The Incarnate Saviour

'Who for us men and our salvation, came down from heaven, and was made flesh from the Holy Spirit and the Virgin Mary, and was made man and was crucified for us under Pontius Pilate. He suffered and was buried, and the third day he rose again according to the Scriptures and ascended into heaven, and sits on the right hand of God the Father. And he shall come again in glory to judge both the living and the dead; his kingdom shall have no end.'

We have been considering the fact that the great conviction expressed in the Church's confession of the oneness of the Son with the Father arose out of the evangelical and doxological approach of the Nicene fathers. They found they had to make explicit, in exact and accurate ways, the relation of the Son in being and act to the Father, in order to conserve the very essence of the Gospel of God's saving and redeeming work in Jesus Christ. But the consubstantial or homoousial relation of the Son to the Father was asserted to be between the *incarnate* Son, Jesus Christ, and the Father. Both ends of the *homoousion*, the divine and the human, had to be secured. Everything would be emptied of evangelical and saving import if Jesus Christ were not fully, completely, entirely *man*, as well as *God*. It was to make this indubitably clear that clauses and expressions were added to the original Creed of Nicaea relating to the humanity of the Son. However, when we turn to consider the clauses of the Creed that speak of the incarnation we find that they are dominated by a *soteriological* concern, 'for us men and for our salvation'.[1] The basic approach of these Church fathers at Nicaea and Constantinople was that of the worship of redeemed sinners who rejoiced in the message of the Gospel and who, like St Paul, believed in Christ as *God and Saviour*.

At the beginning of his work on the Nicene Council Athanasius pointed to the fact that when people were confronted with the mighty acts of Christ in healing the sick, making the lame walk, opening the eyes of the blind, and even raising the dead, together with his forgiving of sin, the Jews insisted on asking questions about his authority, demanding a sign from him, complaining about his behaviour on the Sabbath Day, and asking 'Why do you, as a man, make yourself equal to God?'[2] What they ought to have asked, Athanasius wrote, is 'Why have you, being *God*, become man?'[3] It is only in the light of the primary fact that God himself is directly present and active in him that the saving significance of Jesus in his forgiveness of people's sins is to be understood. It was characteristic of Athanasius that he should refer everything in Jesus Christ back to God the Father, and then from the Father seek to understand the import of the incarnate activity of the Son. If Christ were separate from the Father, if what he did on our behalf were not directly the act of God himself, then everything he was and did would be of no ultimate significance to us, for it would mean that God himself is utterly indifferent to the desperate plight of mankind. On the contrary, the supreme truth that lies behind everything else in the Gospel and gives it its decisive import and redemptive power is the love of God the Father for mankind – the divine *philanthropia* manifested in the astonishing event in which God the Son became man, not 'man' in some ideal or abstract sense, but actual historical man.[4]

[1] See the Epistle of Alexander on the Arian controversy, preserved by Theodoret, *Hist. eccl.*, I.3; and his homily *De anima et corpore deque passione Domini*, *MPG*, 18, 585–604.

[2] John 10.33.

[3] Athanasius, *De decr.*, 1; cf. *Con. Ar.*, 1.39f; *Con. Apol.*, 2.7. This was evidently indebted to Alexander of Alexandria, *De an. et cor.*, 5 & 7. It was surely to this Athanasian question διατὶ σὺ θεὸς ὢν ἄνθρωπος γέγονας; that the Anselmian *Cur Deus homo?* must be traced.

[4] Cf. Athanasius *De inc.*, 1 & 12; *Con. Ar.*, 1.62–4, etc.

Worshipping the goodness of the Father and amazement at the saving economy of the Son belong inseparably together.[5]

There can be no doubt that for Athanasius this oneness between the direct act of God the Father and the incarnate work of the Son, 'for us men and our salvation', was the primary theme which he sought to think out, as we can see all through his various works from the *De Incarnatione*, written before Nicaea, to the *Contra Arianos* written in the years after Nicaea, and the *Ad Epictetum* written toward the end of his life. His whole approach to the Father/Son relation, to the doctrine of God as almighty Creator, and to the doctrine of the Son in his consubstantial relation to the Father, was *soteriologically* orientated. We find the same strong soteriological slant in the extant works of the Patriarch Alexander, in whose household in Alexandria Athanasius had been educated, whom Athanasius accompanied to Nicaea, and whom he succeeded in the Patriarchal See in Alexandria. Thus from the perspective of Alexander and Athanasius alone one can discern something of the depth of the soteriological emphasis that pervaded Nicene theology. The Saviour came, Athanasius repeatedly insisted, *not for his own sake but for our sake and for our salvation*.[6] The concepts of 'the economy of the incarnation' (ἡ τῆς ἐνανθρωπήσεως οἰκονομία), 'the economic condescension' (ἡ οἰκονομικὴ συγκατάβασις) of God the Son, or of 'the advent in the flesh' (ἡ παρουσία ἔνσαρκος), 'the divine and loving condescension and becoming man' (ἡ θεία καὶ φιλάνθρωπος συγκατάβασίς τε καὶ ἐνανθρώπησις) etc., that is, of God's loving assumption of our actual human nature and condition in space and time, all for our sake, were quite dominant in his thought.

This provides us, I believe, with the major premise of all that must be said about the Nicene-Constantinopolitan doctrine of the saving work of Christ: while everything pivots upon the downright act of God himself in Christ, that act of God takes the concrete form of the actual historical man Jesus. As St Paul had expressed it: 'God our Saviour desires all men to be saved and to come to the knowledge of the truth. For there is one God, and

---

[5] Athanasius, *De decr.*, 1.
[6] E.g., Athanasius *Con. Ar.*, 2.55.

there is one Mediator between God and men, the man Christ
Jesus, who gave himself a ransom for all.'[7] For Athanasius this
meant that the mediation of Christ involved a twofold
movement, from God to man and from man to God, and that
both divine and human activity in Christ must be regarded as
issuing from one Person.[8] Here we see again the soteriological
significance of the Nicene *homoousion*: If Jesus Christ the
incarnate Son is not true God from true God, then we are not
saved, for it is only God who can save; but if Jesus Christ is not
truly man, then salvation does not touch our human existence
and condition.[9] The message of the Gospel, however, is that
Jesus Christ embodies in his human actuality the personal
presence and activity of God. In him God has really become
man, become what we are, and so lives and acts, God though he
is, 'as man for us' (ὡς ἄνθρωπος ὑπὲρ ἡμῶν). *Only God can save,
but he saves precisely as man* – Jesus Christ is God's act, God acting
personally and immediately as man in and through him, and
thus at once in a divine and in a human manner (θεϊκῶς and
ἀνθρωπίνως).[10] With this basic Nicene principle in mind, we
shall consider first the significance of the incarnation and the
incarnate Mediator, and then the import of the atoning
mediation, reconciliation and redemption accomplished by
Christ on our behalf and for our sakes.

The Incarnation

Let us begin by recalling the point discussed in the second
chapter that the incarnation is to be understood as *God really
become man*. Jesus Christ is not just man participating in God but
is himself essential Deity (οὐσιώδης Θεότης).[11] The Word of

[7] I Tim. 2.4–6. Cf. the stress of Augustine on *Mediator inquantum homo* –
Conf., 10.68; *In Jn. ev.*, 82.4; *De Trin.*, 4.14, 19.

[8] Athanasius, *Con. Ar.*, 2.7ff, 16, 31, 71; 3.31f, 35, 38ff; 4.3ff; *Ad Ser.*, 2.7; cf.
Gregory Nyss., *Con. Eun.*, 3.4.14, Jaeger, 2, p. 139; Hilary, *De Trin.*, 9.3, 14;
11.20.

[9] Athanasius, *Ad Epict.*, 5–9.

[10] Athanasius, *Con. Ar.*, 3.32, 34f, 38ff, 46, 48, 57f; *Ad Ant.*, 7, etc.

[11] See again the discussion by Athanasius in *De syn.*, 51.

God did not just descend upon Jesus as upon one of the prophets, for in him 'the Lord became man and did not just come into man'. That is to say, in Jesus Christ God came to dwell among us *as himself man*.[12] The Johannine statement that 'the Word became flesh' must be understood to mean 'became man', but 'became man' is to be understood in such a way as not to give place to a dualist conception of man, for, as we shall see, it is the whole man who is body of his soul and soul of his body, not a body without soul or mind, that is meant.[13]

This was decisive, for it was a way of understanding the incarnation as an act of *God himself* in which he really became man, and took the whole nature of man upon himself. In the fullness of his Deity he became man in the undiminished reality of human and creaturely being, without of course ceasing to be God the Son.[14] The incarnation was not the bringing into being of a created intermediary between God and man, but the incarnating of God in such a way that in Jesus Christ he is both God and man in the fullest and most proper sense. The incarnation is to be understood, then, as a real becoming on the part of God, in which God comes *as man* and acts *as man*, all for our sake – from beginning to end God the Son acts among us in a human way (ἀνθρωπίνως),[15] 'within the measures of our humanity', as Cyril of Alexandria expressed it.[16] This understanding of Jesus Christ, as, not God *in man*, but God *as man*, implies a rejection of the idea that the humanity of Christ was merely instrumental in the hands of God,[17] but it also implies, therefore, that the human life and activity of Christ

---

[12]Athanasius, *Con. Ar.*, 3.30ff; *Ad Ant.*, 7; *Ad Epict.*, 2; *Ad Max.*, 2, etc.; and see Cyril of Alexandria, *Dial.*, 1, *MPG*, 75, 681A–C; *De rect. fid.*, *MPG*, 76, 1228C. Cf. *Theol. in Reconcil.*, pp. 156f, 227f.

[13]Athanasius, *De inc.*, 15; *Con. Ar.*, 2.53f; 3.20, 30–35, 53; *Ad Epict.*, 7f; *Ad Ant.*, 7; *Ad Ser.*, 2.7ff.

[14]Basil, *Ep.*, 261.2–3; Hilary *De Trin.*, 9.14f.

[15]Athanasius, *Con. Ar.*, 1.41, 45; 2.35, 52, 71; 3.26ff, 31ff, 35, 37ff, 40, 43ff, 48, 51ff, 57f, 63; 4.6ff, etc.

[16]Cyril of Alexandria, *Ep. ad Nest.*, *MPG*, 77.3, 116BC; *Adv. Nest.*, *MPG*, 76.1, 17B; 20D; 21AB; 28C; 35A, etc.; or *Quod unus sit Christus*, *MPG*, 75, 1257A; 1272B; 1277C, etc. For further references see *Theol. in Reconcil.*, pp. 163ff.

[17]This is very evident in the way that Athanasius in his later writings spoke

must be understood from beginning to end in a thoroughly personal and *vicarious* way. This is a point of quite crucial importance which we shall have to consider more fully later.

The incarnation, far from being some sort of docetic epiphany of God the Son in the flesh, involves the full reality and integrity of human and creaturely being in space and time. The immediate focus is undoubtedly centred on the *human agency* of the incarnate Son within the essential conditions of actual historical human existence, and therefore on the undiminished actuality of the whole historical Jesus Christ who was born of the Virgin Mary, suffered under Pontius Pilate, was crucified and buried, and rose again from the dead.[18]

It was when this stress on the wholeness and reality of the human nature, being and agency of the incarnate Son was challenged, and heretically dualist notions began to creep back, that Athanasius wrote the highly important letter to Epictetus of Corinth, in which he defended the truth of the birth and descent of Jesus from the seed of David, and yet the unimpaired relation of this historical Jesus to the eternal Son, for while he was physically born of Mary, born of earth, he was not changed into flesh. His conception and birth of the Virgin Mary, apart from a human father, did not alter the fact that the birth of Jesus was truly of the flesh just like that of all other human beings.[19] Questions had also been raised which troubled the Church for some decades through Apollinaris of Laodicea.[20] Apollinaris taught that the Son or Word of God became man in such a way that 'in place of the inward man within us there is a heavenly mind in Christ (ἀντὶ τοῦ ἔσωθεν ἐν ἡμῖν ἀνθρώπου νοῦς ἐπουράνιος ἐν Χριστῷ) ... he took that which is without mind

---

of Christ's body as his own personal instrument (ὄργανον), in effecting the restoration and sanctification of our nature in himself – e.g. *De inc.*, 2.30; 3.31, 35, 53. Cf. also *Con. Apol.*, 1.2, 15; Gregory Naz., *Ep.*, 102.

[18]Cf. Athanasius, *Con. Ar.*, 2.70; 4.35; *Ad Epict.*, 7.

[19]Athanasius, *Ad Epict.*, 2ff, 7f; cf. *Ad Max.*, 3; *Con. Ar.*, 2.70.

[20]See especially *Con. Apol.*, 1 & 2, which are of Athanasian provenance and probably of Athanasian authorship. The theory that they were not written by Athanasius has now been subjected to a convincing critical examination by George D. Dragas, *St Athanasius Contra Apollinarem*, Athens, 1985.

(τὸ ἀνόητον) that he might himself be mind in it (ἵν' αὐτὸς ᾖ νοῦς ἐν αὐτῷ).'[21]

It is to be noted that the defence of the complete reality and integrity of the historical humanity of Christ by Nicene theologians was offered mainly on *soteriological grounds*. It was the *whole man* that the Son of God came to redeem by becoming man himself and effecting our salvation in and through the very humanity he appropriated from us – if the humanity of Christ were in any way deficient, all that he is said to have done in offering himself in sacrifice 'for our sakes', 'on our behalf' and 'in our place' would be quite meaningless. As Athanasius wrote to Epictetus, 'The Saviour having in very truth become man, the salvation of the whole man was brought about . . . Truly our salvation is no myth, and does not extend to the body only – the whole man, body and soul, has truly received salvation in the Word himself.'[22] He wrote in similar terms to the Antiochenes: 'The body possessed by the Saviour did not lack soul or sense or mind, for it was impossible when the Lord became man that his body should be without mind; nor was the salvation effected in the Word himself only of the body but also of the soul.'[23] Thus the whole life of Christ is understood as a continuous vicarious sacrifice and oblation which, as such, is indivisible, for everything he assumed from us is organically united in his one Person and work as Saviour and Mediator. The teaching given here in face of the critical questions that arose after the Council of Nicaea was in fact but an extension of what he had first put forward in his early work *On the incarnation of the Word*, as well as in his debates with the Arians: the redemption of the whole man through the incarnation, and the redemption of the whole man effected in it by way of Christ's vicarious sacrifice for sin and his victory in death and resurrection over corruption and death.[24]

[21]Cited by Athanasius in *Con. Apol.*, 1.2. The extant fragments of Apollinaris have been compiled by Hans Lietzmann, *Apollinaris von Laodicea und seiner Schule, Texte und Untersuchungen*, 1904. See also *Theol. in Reconcil.*, pp. 143–150.

[22]Athanasius, *Ad Epict.*, 7.

[23]Athanasius, *Ad Ant.*, 7.

[24]Cf. Athanasius, *De inc.*, 4–10; *Con. Ar.*, 1.60ff; 2.7ff; 3.30ff; 4.6f. See also the citations from Athanasius by Theodoret, *Dial.*, 2, *MPG*, 83.177f.

In his incarnation the Son of God took on himself not only the form of man but the form of a *servant* – for his incarnation was an act of utter self-abasement and humiliation in which he assumed our abject servile condition, our state under the slavery of sin, in order to act for us and on our behalf from within our actual existence. It must be noted, however, as Basil insisted, that the Pauline expression 'form of a servant' should be taken to mean, not some 'likeness' or 'resemblance' assumed by Christ in his incarnation, but the actual form of existence which he took over from 'the lump of Adam' – it was a 'real incarnation'.[25] The Nicene theologians could never suppress their utter astonishment at the incredible act of condescension on the part of God in the stark *reality* of the incarnation. Thus Gregory Nyssen exclaimed: 'Why did the divine being descend to such humiliation? Our faith staggers at the thought that God, the infinite, inconceivable and ineffable reality, who transcends all glory and majesty, should be clothed with the defiled nature of man, so that his sublime activities are abased through being united with what is so degraded.'[26] The Pauline concept of *kenosis* (κένωσις) was not interpreted in any metaphysical way as involving a contraction, diminution or self-limitation of God's infinite being, but in terms of his self-abnegating love in the inexpressible mystery of the *tapeinosis* (ταπείνωσις), impoverishment or abasement, which he freely took upon himself in what he became and did in Christ entirely for our sake.[27]

The Arians, before the Council of Nicaea[28] and afterwards,[29] had made a point of searching the Scriptures for every possible passage or text indicating the creatureliness, human weakness, the mortality of Christ, his subordinate and servile condition,

---

[25] Basil, *Ep.*, 261.2f.

[26] Gregory Nyss., *Or. cat.*, 14.

[27] Gregory Naz., *Or.*, 1.23; 30.5f; Hilary, *De Trin.*, 9.3–14; 10.7–15; 11.15ff.

[28] Cf. Alexander of Alexandria: 'For they, retaining in their memory all that they can collect concerning his passion, his abasement, his κένωσις, and what they call his poverty, and in short all those things to which the Saviour submitted as Saviour for our sakes, bring them forward to refute his eternal existence and Godhead.' In Theodoret, *Hist. eccl;.*, 1.3.

[29] Athanasius, *Con. Ar.*, 1.8ff, but especially 37–64.

which were stressed in contrast to the transcendent Godhead of the Father. Instead of rejecting these passages, however, Athanasius seized upon them and emphasised them in order to show that it was deliberately in this servile condition that the eternal Son came among us, became one of us and one with us, precisely in order to be *our* Saviour.[30] Here we find closely allied, and knit into each other, the notions of the *servant* and of the *priest* – the teaching of St Paul and that of the Epistle to the Hebrews (which was held to be Pauline) were integrated. The servant form of Christ was discerned to be essential to his priestly oneness with us in virtue of which he could act on our behalf, in our place, and in our stead, before God the Father. As we shall see, this involved an understanding of Christ in which his Person and his act, what he was and what he did, were completely one, for he was himself both the one offered and the one who offered for mankind.[31] This view of the mediatorial and priestly nature of Christ's Person and work, in the unity of his divine and human agency, in virtue of which 'he might minister the things of God to us and of us to God',[32] also had the effect of making the whole event of our redemption one which is properly to be understood within the context of worship.[33] Hence it is not surprising that an essential element in redemption was reckoned by the Nicene and post-Nicene fathers to be redemption from 'false worship'.[34]

The Atonement

On this incarnational basis let us now consider what atonement or mediation and redemption mean.

[30] Athanasius, *Con. Ar.*, 1.49; 3.38.

[31] Athanasius, *Con. Ar.*, 1.64; 2.2, 7ff, 31ff, 56; 2.69ff; 3.22ff, 26ff, 31ff, 37ff, 45ff, 51ff, 58; 4.6ff.

[32] Athanasius, *Con. Ar.*, 4.6; also 2.7ff, 16, 31, 71; 3.31f, 38f; 43ff. For an earlier insistence on this two-fold activity of God, see Irenaeus, *Adv. haer.*, 3.19.6, vol. 2, p. 100f; 4.34.5 & 7, pp. 215f, 218f; 5.17.1, p. 369.

[33] Cf. the attention given to Christ's high-priestly redemption of mankind in the following passages: *Con. Ar.*, 1.41f, 59–60, 64; 2.7–9, 14, 55, 68–70, 75f; 3.31–35, 56–57; 4.6–7.

[34] Athanasius, *Con. Ar.*, 2.14. See my essay 'The Mind of Christ in Worship: the Problem of Apollinarianism in the Liturgy', *Theol. in Reconcil.*, ch. 4, pp. 139–214.

Here we must remind ourselves right away that the Father/Son relation subsists eternally within the being and life of God. This means that we cannot but think of the incarnation of the Son as *falling within the being and life of God* – although, as we have had occasion to note, the incarnation must be regarded as something 'new' even for God, for the Son was not eternally man any more than the Father was eternally Creator. Moreover, since Jesus Christ is himself God and man in one Person, and all his divine and human acts issue from his one Person, the atoning mediation and redemption which he wrought for us, fall *within* his own being and life as the one Mediator between God and man.[35] That is to say, the work of atoning salvation does *not* take place *outside* of Christ, as something external to him, but takes place *within* him, *within* the incarnate constitution of his Person as Mediator.[36]

The general parameters for this understanding of incarnational redemption had already been worked out by Athanasius in his early work *On the Incarnation* in which he argued for the divine validity and universal range of the saving work of Christ as the Word of God become man. In his incarnation he who by nature is internal to the being of God has embodied the creative source and ground of all human being in himself as man. As the Head of creation, in whom all things consist, he is the only one who really can act on behalf of all and save them. When he took our human nature upon himself, and in complete somatic solidarity with us offered himself up to death in atoning sacrifice for man, he acted instead of all (ἀντὶ πάντων) and on behalf of all (ὑπὲρ πάντων). Thus the redemptive work of Christ was fully representative and truly universal in its range. Its vicarious efficacy has its force through the union of his divine Person as Creator and Lord with us in our creaturely being, whereby he lays hold of us in himself and acts for us from out of the inner depths of his coexistence with us and our existence in him, delivering us from the sentence of death

---

[35] See again Athanasius, *Con. Ar.*, 2.7ff; 3.35ff; *Ad Ser.*, 2.7.
[36] Athanasius, *De inc.*, 9; *Con. Ar.*, 1.41, 46–49; 2.47, 53, 56, 67; 3.22ff, 31ff, 53, 61f; 4.33; *Ad Ant.*, 7; *Ad Epict.*, 7.

upon us, and from the corruption and perdition that have overtaken us.[37]

This way of connecting redemption with the incarnation has sometimes been decried as the 'physical theory' of redemption, with the implication that it is merely through the physical union of the divine Logos with decaying humanity that the salvation of the human race is brought about. In this connection reference is regularly made to the Athanasian statement: 'He became man that we might be made divine.'[38] To put it simply like that, however, as if the incarnation by itself effects man's redemption, is a serious misrepresentation, for it overlooks the fact that as the incarnate Logos Christ acts *personally* on our behalf, and that he does that from within the ontological depths of our human existence which he has penetrated and gathered up in himself. This was already made clear particularly by Irenaeus in his application of St Paul's conceptions of 'recapitulation' and 'economy' to the redemptive restoration of humanity through the obedient life and sacrifice of the incarnate Son. While this was presented within the framework of the fulfilment of God's covenant purpose in the union and communion with God actualised in Christ, the focus of faith was centred on Christ himself as the Saviour whose Person and work are inseparably integrated.[39] The intense personalisation of salvation in the theology of Irenaeus is strikingly evident in his identification of the knowledge of salvation with 'the knowledge of the Son of God who is called and really is *Salvation* and *Saviour* and *Saving Act*'.[40] That is to say, as Saviour Christ embodies the act and fact of our salvation in his own Person.

It was in this tradition that Athanasius presented his early account of incarnational redemption in which he linked so

[37] Athanasius, *De inc.*, 7–10. See the discerning exposition of these chapters by G. D. Dragas, *op. cit.*, pp. 228–242.

[38] Athanasius, *De inc.*, 54.3.

[39] Irenaeus, *Adv. haer.*, 1.2.1, vol. 1, p. 90f; 2.32.2, p. 330f; 3.11.1f, vol. 2, p. 35f; 3.11.10, p. 47f; especially 3.17.6–3.24.2, pp. 87–133; 4.11.2, p. 159; 4.18.1, pp. 168f; 4.24.4f, pp. 215f; 4.62–63.2, pp. 292ff; 5.1.1ff, pp. 314ff; 5.2.1ff, pp. 317ff; 5.14.2ff, pp. 360ff; 5.16.1–17.1, pp. 368ff; 5.19.1f, pp. 375f; 5.21.1f, pp. 380f; 5.23.2, p. 387f; *Dem.*, 31ff.

[40] Irenaeus, *Adv. haer.*, 3.11, 2, vol. 2, p. 36; *agnitio salutis erat agnitio Filii Dei, qui et Salus, et Salvator, et Salutare vere et dicitur et est.* Cf. 3.19.3, p. 97f.

closely together the *personal* and the *ontological*. Through his incarnation the Son of God has made himself one with us as we are, and indeed made himself what we are, thereby not only making our nature his own but taking on himself our lost condition subject to condemnation and death, all in order that he might substitute himself in our place, discharge our debt, and offer himself in atoning sacrifice to God on our behalf. Since sin and its judgment have affected the actual nature of death as we experience it, Christ has made our death and fate his own, thereby taking on himself the penalty due to all in death, destroying the power of sin and its stronghold in death, and thus redeeming or rescuing us from its dominion. No explanation was offered *why* atonement should take this form beyond the requirement to make restitution and reparation which had to be regarded as wholly fitting and reasonable.[41] The crucial point to be noted here is that the traditional biblical language about atonement was used of what takes place within the incarnate being of the Son of God and in his ontological solidarity with mankind.

It was within the parameters of this profound interlocking of creation and redemption, of incarnation and atonement, that Nicene theology continued to expound and deepen its grasp of the Gospel of the saving grace of God in Jesus Christ with which the Church had been entrusted by the apostles.[42] In the course of that development the soteriological implications of the Nicene *homoousion*, and in particular of the oneness in act as well as in being between the Lord Jesus Christ and God the Father, were worked out more fully through persistent exegetical activity in the face of Hellenising and Judaising distortions of the Gospel. As a result Nicene theology considerably deepened the Church's understanding of the personal self-offering of Christ in terms of his vicarious obedience and the inner relation between his Person and work. The prolonged debates of Athanasius with Arians and semi-Arians, and of the Cappadocians with Eunomians and Apollinarians, were of great importance in this

---

[41]Athanasius, *De inc.*, 1-7, 20, 26.
[42]Compare the discussion of Athanasius in *Con. Ar.*, 2.67-70 with his presentation in *De inc.*, 7-10.

respect. At the same time they brought to light the basic issues in the doctrine of atoning mediation and redemption, but with the realisation that the mystery of the incarnate assumption of our humanity in Christ and of his mediatorship reaches out beyond all forms of theological expression.[43] As we probe into these issues, however, we shall find that they form a more coherent doctrinal pattern than is usually claimed.

(1) As we have seen, it became very clear to the Church during the Arian controversy that the dualist habits of thought that lay behind the Arian heresy inevitably disrupted any unitary approach to the Person of Christ or any coherent understanding of the Gospel of salvation. Moreover, if Jesus Christ were not the incarnation of the only begotten Son who is eternally in God, then he would constitute no more than a created and temporal centre ontologically external to God. In that event all relations between Jesus Christ and God could be construed only in *external moral* terms without any unifying centre in the Person of Christ who as God and man is the one Mediator between God and man. That is to say, the atoning sacrifice of Christ would then be understood only in terms of some kind of superficial socio-moral or judicial transaction between God and mankind which does not penetrate into the ontological depths of human being or bear savingly upon the distorted and corrupt condition of man's actual human existence. Everything is different, however, if Jesus Christ really is the only begotten Son of the Father who is eternally in God and as such has come into our human being and united our human nature with his own. Then atoning reconciliation must be understood as having taken place within the personal being of Jesus Christ as the one Mediator between God and man, and thus within the ontological roots and actual condition of the human and creaturely existence which he assumed in order to save. In this event atonement is not an act of God done *ab extra* upon man, but an act of God become man, done *ab intra*, in his stead and on his behalf; it is an act of God as man, translated into human actuality and made to issue out of the depths of man's

---

[43]See especially Hilary, *De Trin.*, 11.20.

being and life toward God.[44] This point was later well put by
Cyril of Alexandria. 'If the Word did not suffer for us humanly,
he did not accomplish our redemption divinely ... if Christ
who suffered for us was mere man (ψιλὸς ἄνθρωπος) and only
the organ (ὄργανον) of Deity, we have not really been
redeemed.'[45] As an act of reconciling at-onement, it is
simultaneously an act from God to man and an act from man to
God.[46]

'The salvation not of the body only but of the soul was
worked out *in the Logos himself*.'[47] This approach to an
understanding of the atonement embedded in Nicene theology
was of the greatest importance. On the one hand, the refusal to
let dualist forms of thought determine the meaning of the
atonement, allowed the incarnation and the atonement to be
thought together in terms of their intrinsic coherence in the
divine-human Person of the Mediator — the incarnation was
seen to be essentially redemptive and redemption was seen to be
inherently incarnational or ontological. Union with God in and
through Jesus Christ who is of one and the same being with God
belongs to the inner heart of the atonement. The theological
effect of this was to provide the Nicene Church with a unifying
centre for its understanding of the saving work of Christ, apart

[44]It is surely in this way that the saving import of the virgin birth of Jesus is
to be understood, for while it was a pure act of divine grace, it was an act made
to issue out of true human flesh — Athanasius, *Con. Ar.*, 2.70; 3.56; *Ad Epict.*,
4–8; cf. *De vit. Ant.*, 67. Note that while in these passages Athanasius could
speak of holy Mary as 'ever-virgin' and 'God-bearer', he could also insist that
she was 'our sister in that we are all from Adam'. See also *Con. Ar.*, 3.29;
Epiphanius, *Haer.*, 78.5; Didymus, *De Trin.*, 1.27.

[45]Cyril of Alex., *Ep. ad mon. Aeg.*, 25–26.

[46]This was the emphatic teaching of Irenaeus, *Adv. haer.*, 3.19.6, vol. 2,
pp. 100f; of Athanasius, *Con. Ar.*, 1.38–44; and of Gregory Naz., *Or.*, 30.14.
Augustine represents much the same teaching in the West, *Conf.*, 10.68; *Serm.*,
293.7; *In Jn. ev.*, 82.4. For 'real atonement', not as direct deed of God 'over
man's head', but as God's act in man and from the side of man, and as issuing
forth from man's life and offered to God, consult the illuminating essay by
F. W. Camfield, 'The Idea of Substitution in the Doctrine of Atonement',
SJT, vol. I, 1948, pp. 282–293.

[47]Athanasius, *Ad Ant.*, 7: οὐδὲ σώματος μόνου, ἀλλὰ καὶ ψυχῆς ἐν αὐτῷ τῷ
Λόγῳ σωτηρία γέγονεν.

from which interpretation of the various aspects of his death in terms of external relations could not but break up into different 'theories of the atonement' – which unfortunately is what has regularly happened in Western theology.

On the other hand, the understanding of the atonement in terms of the inner ontological relations between Christ and God and between Christ and mankind, implies that the very basis for a merely moral or legal account of atonement is itself part of the actual state of affairs between man and God that needs to be set right. The moral relations that obtain in our fallen world have to do with the gap between what we *are* and what we *ought* to be, but it is that very gap that needs to be healed, for even what we call 'good', in fulfilment of what we ought to do, needs to be cleansed by the blood of Christ. Within the moral order as it stands, as Gregory Nyssen saw,[48] it would be irresponsible and immoral for one person to take the place of another, for no one can represent another from within his moral responsibility, and no one can therefore be a responsible substitute for another from within his guilt. The inexplicable fact that God in Christ has actually taken our place, tells us that the whole moral order itself as we know it in this world needed to be redeemed and set on a new basis, but that is what the justifying act of God in the sacrifice of Christ was about. Thus while, in St Paul's phrases, Christ subjected himself 'under the law' to redeem those who are 'under the law', nevertheless his act of grace in justifying us freely through redemption was 'apart from law'.[49] Such is the utterly radical nature of the atoning mediation perfected in Christ, which is to be grasped, as far as it may, not in the light of abstract moral principle, but only in the light of what he has actually done in penetrating into the dark depths of our twisted human existence and restoring us to union and communion with God in and through himself. In this interlocking of incarnation and atonement, and indeed of creation and redemption, there took place what might be called 'a soteriological suspension of ethics' in order to reground the whole moral order in God himself.[50] This helps us to

[48]Gregory Nyss., *Or. cat.*, 22.
[49]Gal. 4.3f; Rom. 3.20f.
[50]I have in mind here what Kierkegaard spoke of as the 'teleological

understand why the main stress by Western theologians on forensic transactional accounts of the death of Christ was rather foreign to Greek patristic theology – not that it excluded forensic elements, as we shall see, but that they were held within a doctrine of atonement set at a deeper level.

(2) A realist approach to the fact that in Jesus Christ God the Son has united himself with us in our actual existence, combined with the view that atonement takes place within the incarnate life and being of the Mediator, led Nicene theology to give full place to the teaching of St Paul about the way in which God in Christ has substituted himself for us in making our sin and death his own that we may partake of his divine life and righteousness. In order to reconcile us to himself and set us free, 'God sent his own Son in the concrete likeness of sinful flesh (ἐν ὁμοιώματι σαρκὸς ἁμαρτίας), and as a sacrifice for sin, condemned sin in the flesh', and so 'made him who knew no sin to be made sin on our behalf, that we might become the righteousness of God in him'.[51]

Thus Athanasius could say that 'the whole Christ became a curse for us', for in taking upon himself the form of a servant, the Lord transferred to himself fallen Adamic humanity which he took from the Virgin Mary, that is, our perverted, corrupt, degenerate, diseased human nature enslaved to sin and subject to death under the condemnation of God.[52] However, far from sinning himself or being contaminated by what he appropriated from us, Christ triumphed over the forces of evil entrenched in our human existence, bringing his own holiness, his own perfect obedience, to bear upon it in such a way as to condemn sin in the flesh and to deliver us from its power.[53] As Hilary expressed it:

---

suspension of ethics' in the transition from a merely moral to a religious situation before God – *Fear and Trembling* (Eng. tr. by Robert Payne), pp. 75ff.

[51]Rom. 8.3; 2 Cor. 5.21. See Athanasius, *Con. Ar.*, 1.43, 51, 60; 2.47, 55, 66, 69; 3.31ff; *Ad Adel.*, 4; *In Ps.*, 21.31; *Con. Apol.*, 1.7; and cf. *De vit. Ant.*, 7; and also Irenaeus, *Adv. haer.*, 3.21.2, vol. 2, p. 107; and Eusebius of Caesarea, *Dem. ev.*, 1.10; 10.1.

[52]Athanasius, *Con. Ar.*, 1, 43, 51, 60; 2.14, 47, 55, 66, 69; 3.31ff; *Ad Adel.*, 4; *In Ps.*, 50.12; and *ap.* Theodoret, *Dial.* 2, MPG.83.177.

[53]Cf. *Con. Apol.*, 2.6: 'If sinlessness had not been seen in the nature which had sinned, how could sin have been condemned in the flesh, when that flesh

'For God took upon himself the flesh in which we have sinned that by wearing our flesh he might forgive sins; a flesh which he shares with us by wearing it not by sinning in it.'[54]

Moreover, what Christ united to himself in this way he redeemed and saved, for from beginning to end, from his birth of the Virgin Mary to his resurrection from the empty tomb, the whole incarnational assumption of our human nature was at the same time a reconciling, healing, sanctifying and recreating activity.[55] In making himself one with us he both took what is ours and imparted to us what is his. In his great compassion he did not reject union with our nature, fallen though it was as the result of sin, but gathered it up in himself in order to purify it and quicken it in his own sinless life-giving life. In the stark words of Gregory Nyssen, 'Although Christ took our filth upon himself, nevertheless he is not himself defiled by the pollution, but in his own self he cleanses the filth, for it says, the light shone in the darkness, but the darkness did not overpower it.'[56] No one used stronger language than Gregory Nazianzen in reinforcing St Paul's teaching about Christ being made a curse and sin on our behalf. 'Just as he was called a curse for the sake of our salvation, who cancels my curse, and was called sin, who takes away the sin of the world, and instead of the old Adam is made a new Adam – in the same way he makes my rebellion his own as Head of the whole Body. As long, therefore as I am disobedient and rebellious by the denial of God and by my passions, Christ also is called disobedient on my account.

---

had no capacity for action, and the Godhead knew not sin?' Cf. T. A. Smail, *Reflected Glory. The Spirit in Christ and in Christians*, 1975, p. 67f.

[54]Hilary, *De Trin.*, 1.13. However, Hilary had a habit of qualifying what he said in this connection which appears to leave his conception of God's self-identification with sinful humanity somewhat ambiguous – see *De Trin.*, 10.47f; 11.16f.

[55]Athanasius pointed out that it was from the virgin birth of Jesus that 'the beginning of our new creation took place', *Con. Ar.*, 2.70. Cf. Irenaeus, *Adv. haer.*, 3.32.1, vol. 2, pp. 123f; *Dem.*, 37f.

[56]Gregory Nyss., *Adv. Apol.*, 26, Jaeger, vol. 3.1, p. 171. Thus also his *Ep. adv. Apol.*: 'Although he was made sin and a curse because of us, and took our weaknesses upon himself, yet he did not leave the sin and the curse and the weakness enveloping him unhealed ... Whatever is weak in our nature and subject to death was united with his Deity and became what the Deity is.'

But when all things have been subjected to him, then he himself will have fulfilled his subjection, bringing me whom he has saved to God.'[57]

While recognising that God's atoning self-identification with us in our sinful humanity is ultimately beyond human comprehension, the leading Nicene theologians felt that they had to express their conviction that it was in Christ himself and not in some external way that the Saviour bore our infirmities and sins and the whole inheritance of judgment that lay against us, for otherwise we would have no part in his saving, healing and sanctifying activity.[58] At the same time they found they had to emphasise, especially after the rise of the Apollinarian controversy, that it was 'the whole man, body and soul', and not some truncated humanity that the Son of God had assumed, for otherwise there could be no salvation of man in the completeness and integrity of his human being. As Athanasius expressed it: 'The Saviour having in very truth become man, the salvation of the *whole man* was brought about ... Truly our salvation is not merely apparent, nor does it extend to the body only, but the whole body and soul alike, has truly obtained salvation in the Word himself.'[59] This was held to include the redeeming and sanctifying in Christ of the mind and affections of 'the inward man', for they have been appropriated and renewed in the self-sanctification of Christ for our sakes.[60]

This soteriological principle, that only what the incarnate Son has taken up from us into himself is saved, had been earlier enunciated by Origen,[61] but now reinforced by Athanasius, it

[57]Gregory Naz., *Or.*, 30.5.

[58]Cf. *Con. Ar.*, 1.41, 49; 2.47, 53, 56, 67–70, 74ff; 3.22ff, 53, 56f; 4.33.

[59]Athanasius, *Ad Epict.*, 7; see also *Ad Ant.*, 7; *Con. Ar.*, 2.36; 3.22; 4.35; *Con. Apol.*, 1.5, 14f. For the same emphasis on the whole man see Irenaeus, *Adv. haer.*, 5.6.1, vol. 2, p. 333f; 5.9.1, p. 342; 5.20.1, p. 378; Hilary, *De Trin.*, 10.15, 19, 21, 59; Epiphanius, *Haer.*, 77.29.

[60]Athanasius, *De inc.*, 15; *Con. Ar.*, 1.41–50; 2.14, 53, 56; 3.27f, 30–35, 38f, 43f, 52f; 4.6; *Ad Epict.*, 7; *Ad Ant.*, 7, 11; *Ad Ser.*, 1.6, 9; 2.9; *ap.* Theodoret, *Dial.*, 2, *MPG*, 83.177; see also *Con. Apol.*, 1 & 2, *passim*, especially 1.5, 13–19; 2.1, 6, 10, 13, 16ff.

[61]Origen, *Dialektos*, 7: 'The whole man would not have been redeemed if he had not assumed the whole man (εἰ μὴ ὅλον τὸν ἄνθρωπον ἀνειλήφει).' *SC*, 67, p. 70. Cf. Irenaeus, *Adv. haer.*, 5.9.1, vol 2, pp. 341f.

was given a central place in the teaching of the Cappadocian theologians. 'If Christ had not come in our flesh,' Basil argued, 'he could not have slain sin in the flesh and restored and reunited to God the humanity which fell in Adam and became alienated from God.'[62] It was Gregory Nazianzen who provided the principle with its most epigrammatic expression in a trenchant refutation of Apollinarian denial that Christ had a human soul or mind. 'The unassumed is the unhealed (τὸ γὰρ ἀπρόσληπτον, ἀθεράπευτον); but what is united to God is saved. If only half Adam fell, then what Christ assumes and saves may be half also; but if the whole of his nature fell, it must be united to the whole nature of him who was begotten, and so be saved as a whole.'[63] Much the same argument for the salvation of 'the whole man, not just half a man' was put forward by Gregory Nyssen against the Arian ideas of Eunomius. 'He who came for this cause, that he might seek and save that which was lost (i.e. what the shepherd in the parable calls the sheep), both finds that which is lost, and carries home on his shoulder the whole sheep, not just the fleece, that he might make the man of God complete, united to God in body and soul. And thus he who was in all points tempted as we are yet without sin, left no part of our nature which he did not take up into himself.'[64]

The emphasis here is undoubtedly on the redemption of the human mind, for it is in the inner man, in his rational human soul, that man has fallen and become enslaved to sin. It is in the mind, not just in the flesh, as both Athanasius and Apollinaris had insisted, that sin is entrenched, but whereas this led Apollinaris to put forward a notion of incarnation in which the human mind was not assumed, Athanasius found it all the more

---

[62]Basil, *Ep.*, 261.2. For Western views of this see Marius Victorinus, *Adv. Arium*, 3.3: *Assumptus ergo homo totus, et assumptus et liberatus est*; and Damasus, *Ep.*, 2: *Quod si unique imperfectus homo susceptus est, imperfectum Dei munus est, imperfecta nostra salus; quia non totus homo salvatus. Et ubi erit illud dictum Domini, Venit filius hominis salvare quod perierat totum? id est, in anima et in corpore, in sensu atque in tota substantia suae naturae. Si ergo totus homo perierat, necesse fuit ut id quod perierat, salvaretur* – with reference to Matt. 18.11. Also Ambrose, *Ep.*, 261.2: 'The very purpose for which he came was to save the whole man. If he had not redeemed the whole man, he would have failed.'

[63]Gregory Naz., *Ep.*, 101; cf. *Or.*, 1.23; 22.13.

[64]Gregory Nyss., *Antir. con. Eun.*, Jaeger, 2, p. 386.

important to stress that it is in our very mind that we need to be redeemed, otherwise redemption would be empty of saving significance or relevance for us. That is the teaching about the redemption of the whole man in the whole Christ which is so powerfully reflected in the two books *Contra Apollinarem*. 'It was impossible to pay one thing as a ransom in exchange for a different thing; on the contrary, he gave body for body and soul for soul and complete existence for the whole man. This is the reconciling exchange of Christ.'[65] This is precisely the point that Gregory Nazianzen found so necessary to stress in the vicarious work of Christ within and on behalf of man's 'intellectual existence' which was subject to condemnation. 'In order that he might destroy that condemnation by sanctifying like by like, then, as he needed flesh for the sake of flesh which had incurred condemnation, and soul for the sake of soul, so too he needed *mind* for the sake of mind, which not only fell in Adam but was the first to be affected... That which transgressed was that which stood most in need of salvation; and that which needed salvation was that which he took upon him. Therefore mind was taken upon him.'[66] This Athanasian and Cappadocian conception of the rational nature of man as assumed and redeemed in Christ was considerably reinforced by Cyril of Alexandria under the rubric of the same soteriological principle, '*what has not been taken up, has not been saved* (ὃ γὰρ μὴ προσείληπται, οὐδὲ σέσωσται)'.[67]

We shall consider below the significance of the 'reconciling exchange' which lay at the heart of the Nicene doctrine of salvation, but at this juncture two important implications of the redemption of our alienated mind that took place in Christ should be noted.

In the first place, it means that the healing and reconciling of the human mind must include the saving effect of God's self-revelation to man mediated in and through Jesus Christ. Redemption through the Son is redemption through the *Logos*.

---

[65]Athanasius, *Con. Apol.*, 1.17.

[66]Gregory Naz., *Ep.*, 101; cf. also *Or.*, 1.13; 30.21.

[67]Cyril of Alex., *In Jn.*, MPG 74, 89CD. For my account of Cyril's teaching in this respect see *Theol. in Reconcil.*, pp. 156–185.

This is very evident in the Athanasian conception of the incarnation of the *Logos*, whereby man recovers the true knowledge of God in Christ, and the image of God is restored in him.[68] This is tied up, as we have seen, with the doctrine of 'deification' (θεοποίησις) understood in accordance with the teaching of Jesus that 'he called them gods to whom the Word of God came'.[69] Thus redemption through Christ and knowledge of Christ as the incarnate *Logos*, redemption and knowledge (ἀπολύτρωσις and γνῶσις), regeneration and illumination (παλιγγενεσία and φωτισμός), were closely interconnected in Greek patristic thought, not least in early Alexandrian theology.[70] An unbalanced stress upon *gnosis* (γνῶσις), particularly when detached from the incarnation and the saving Person and work of Christ, could easily give rise to serious distortion of the Gospel as in the Gnostic movement.[71] Nevertheless, since knowledge of the truth of God in Christ, and the vision of God in and through him, bring light and life, freedom and salvation, the prophetic office of Christ cannot be separated from his priestly office, so that the teaching of Jesus handed down to us in the Gospels cannot but be regarded as an essential ingredient in his saving work. On the other hand, there is no mediation to us of saving and life-giving knowledge of God apart from 'union and communion' with him through the incarnation of his Son.[72]

In the second place, the redemption of man's estranged and rebellious mind in Christ, means that atoning reconciliation had to be regarded as including the whole of our Lord's incarnate

---

[68] Athanasius, *De inc.*, 11–16.

[69] Ps. 83.2, LXX – Athanasius, *Con. Ar.*, 1.39; *Ad Afr.*, 7.

[70] See, for example, Clement, *Paed.*, 11; *Protr.*, 11; or *Strom.*, 6.15. Clement could make effective use of traditional biblical teaching about Christ giving himself as a ransom in the new covenant, but he transmuted simple faith in Christ as Redeemer into a spiritualistic *gnosis* – cf. *Quis dives salvetur?*, 23, 34, 37; *Paed.*, 3, 12, 37, 39; *Strom.*, 2.15.64; 4.7; 5.1.2f; 5.1.1ff.; 5.10.70; 5.26.1ff.; *In Jn.*, 5.6.

[71] Cf. Irenaeus' discussion of the Gnostic idea that '*gnosis* is the redemption of the inner man' (ὥστε εἶναι τὴν γνῶσιν ἀπολύτρωσιν τοῦ ἔνδον ἀνθρώπου), *Adv. haer.*, 1.14.3, vol. 1, p. 185f.

[72] Cf. Irenaeus, *Adv. haer.*, 4.11.1–5, vol. 2, pp. 158–162; 4.34.1–12, pp. 212–225; 5, *praef.* & 1.1–2, pp. 313–7.

life from his cradle to his grave in which, as one of us and one with us, he shared all our experiences, overcoming our disobedience through his obedience and sanctifying every stage of human life, and thereby vivified and restored our humanity to communion with God.[73] He sanctified himself for our sakes that we might be sanctified in him.[74] This was expounded by the Nicene theologians in terms of our Lord's vicarious obedience in the form of a servant[75] and his priestly self-offering to the Father in life as well as in death in our place, with reference to the teaching of the Epistle to the Hebrews.[76] We may turn here once again to Gregory Nazianzen's account of the vicarious life of the incarnate Son. He pointed out how in his cry of dereliction on the Cross, 'My God, my God, why hast thou forsaken me?', 'Christ was in his own Person representing us, for we were the forsaken and despised before, but now by the sufferings of him who could not suffer, we were taken up and saved. Similarly he makes his own our folly and our transgressions.' Then Gregory declared: 'The same consideration applies to the passages, "he learned obedience by the things he suffered", and his "strong crying and tears", and his "entreaties" and his "being heard" and his "godliness",[77] all of which he wonderfully wrought out, like a drama whose plot was devised on our behalf ... In the character of the form of a servant, he condescends to his fellow servants and servants, and assumes a form that is not his own, bearing all me and mine in himself, so that in himself he may consume the bad, as fire does wax, or as the sun does the mist of the earth, and that I may partake of what is his through being conjoined to him.'[78] That is to say, the priestly self-consecration and self-offering of Christ throughout the whole of his earthly life are to be regarded as belonging to the innermost essence of the atoning mediation he fulfilled between God and mankind. Reconciliation through

---

[73]Irenaeus, *Adv. haer.*, 2.33, vol. 1, p. 330; 3.18.1–3, vol. 2, pp. 92ff; 3.19.5f, p. 99ff.
[74]Cf. Hilary, *De Trin.*, 11.18ff.
[75]Athanasius, *Con. Ar.*, 1.37–52.
[76]Athanasius, *Con. Ar.*, 1.53–62; 2.1–10.
[77]Hebrews, 5.8f.
[78]Gregory Naz., *Or.*, 30.5–6; cf. *Or.*, 2.23ff.

the life of Christ and reconciliation through the passion of Christ interpenetrate each other.

(3) We have been considering the fact that, according to Nicene theology, the redeeming and reconciling activity of Christ on our behalf takes place within his incarnate constitution and earthly life as the Mediator between God and man. This is clearly to be understood in terms of what we call 'representation and substitution'. That is particularly evident in the habit Athanasius had of combining several prepositions (ἀντί, ὑπέρ, διά, περί), as though none was sufficient of itself, to help him express the range and depth of the vicarious work of Christ 'for us', 'for our sake', 'for our salvation', 'on our behalf', 'in our place', 'in our stead', 'for our need', and so on.[79] When we ask what the precise nature of this vicarious activity of Christ was, we find Nicene theologians regularly falling back upon familiar biblical and liturgical terms like ransom, sacrifice, propitiation, expiation, reconciliation, to describe it, but always with a deep sense of awe before the inexpressible mystery of atonement through the blood of Christ. They used these terms, however, as we have indicated, to refer, not to any external transaction between God and mankind carried out by Christ, but to what took place within the union of divine and human natures in the incarnate Son of God. Regarded in this way, the various aspects of atoning mediation they represent reveal a coherent pattern governed by an underlying unity in the Person and work of Christ. That is a pattern, however, which inevitably disappears whenever they are torn away from their biblical roots and their unifying ground in the incarnational assumption of sinful humanity, and are then interpreted along the lines of dualist and external relations. How are we to understand that unifying ground?

Undoubtedly it was our Lord's own interpretation of his passion, perpetuated in the eucharistic liturgy, that constantly nourished the early Church's understanding of atonement.[80]

---

[79]See Athanasius, *De inc.*, 8ff, 20f, 25, 31, 36, 43; *Con. Ar.*, 1.41ff, 46ff; 2.7ff, 44ff; 51ff, 69ff; 3.30ff, etc.

[80]Cf. the eucharistic prayer in the Der-Balyzeh papyrus, J. Beckmann, *Quellen zur Geschichte des christlichen Gottesdienstes*, 1956, pp. 8ff; and the

We recall particularly the words that Jesus spoke to his disciples toward the end of their last journey up to Jerusalem, and at the institution of the Holy Supper on the night in which he was handed over, for in them he gave his supreme revelation of the meaning of his life and death, and provided the Church with a permanent centre of reference to which it could return in proclaiming his death until he returned. 'The Son of Man came not to be served but to serve, and to give his life a ransom for many (καὶ δοῦναι τὴν ψυχὴν αὐτοῦ λύτρον ἀντὶ πολλῶν).'[81] 'This is my blood of the covenant which is shed for many (τοῦτό ἐστιν τὸ αἷμα μου τῆς διαθήκης τὸ ἐκχυννόμενον ὑπὲρ πολλῶν).'[82]

The first of these words speaks more about the actual event of redemption, while the second speaks specifically of the means of redemption and the mode of atonement in the shedding of the blood of Christ, with direct relation to the covenant will of God for his people. When interpreted in the light of Jesus' other statements about the salvation or redemption of human life and of their obvious Old Testament allusions, the general meaning is quite clear. No one can provide for himself or for another a means of salvation which will be accepted in exchange for his life or soul. But this is precisely what Jesus claims to do: to give his *life* as a sacrificial propitiation or ransom (λύτρον), thereby giving an interpretation of his life and death in terms both of cultic atonement and of the suffering servant. Jesus declares that he has come as the servant to mediate God's covenant with his people and offer his life in an act of sacrifice that will emancipate the lives of many (i.e. of all, as St Paul interpreted it). It was his whole life, and above all that life poured out in the supreme sacrifice of death on the Cross, that made atonement for sin, and constituted the price of redemption for mankind.

There can be no doubt that the New Testament conception of redemption (ἀπολύτρωσις) and of the price of redemption or

---

Liturgies of St James and St Mark, F. E. Brightman, *Liturgies Eastern and Western*, vol. 1, pp. 31ff, 113ff.

[81] Mark 10.45; Matt. 20.28; and cf. Mark 8.55f; Matt. 16.25f; Luke 9.24f; Job 33.24 & 28; Ps. 49.8f.

[82] Mark 14.24; Matt. 26.28; Luke 22.20; cf. 1 Tim. 2.6; Tit. 2.14; Exod. 24.8; Is. 42.6; 49.8; 53.10ff; 55.3; Jer. 31.31ff.

ransom (λύτρον), thus rooted in the self-interpretation of Jesus himself, became quite central. But what precisely is to be understood by these terms? For an answer we have to turn to the theological dictionary employed by the writers of the New Testament, namely, the Septuagint. There we find, as modern research has shown, that behind this conception of redemption there are three basic Hebrew terms which, with their cognates, are used to speak of different but profoundly interrelated aspects of divine redemption: *pdh* (פדה), *kpr* (כפר), *g'l* (גאל).[83]

Pdh (פדה) with its cognates speaks of redemption as a mighty act of God bringing deliverance from oppression, as in the redemption of Israel out of Egypt and the house of bondage, and from the power of death. It refers very significantly to a redemption at once out of the oppression of evil and out of the judgment of God upon it, but with emphasis upon the cost of redemption through the substitutionary offering of a life for a life, and also upon the dramatic nature of the redeeming act as a sheer intervention on the part of God in human affairs. It is essentially an act of redemption from unlawful thraldom which strips it of its vaunted right and usurped authority, bringing them to nothing, so that the impossible idea of a ransom being paid to evil does not and could not arise. *Kpr* (כפר) with its cognates has to do with the expiatory form of the act of redemption, the sacrifice by which the barrier of sin and guilt between God and man is done away and propitiation is effected between them. This is primarily a cultic concept of redemption, but one in which God is always the subject and never the object of the reconciling or atoning act, for even when it is liturgically carried out through a priest, it is only by way of witness to the fact that it is God himself who by his own judicial and merciful act makes atonement and blots out sin. Atonement is here understood as involving both judgment upon the wrong through the offering of an equivalent, or of life for life, and

---

[83]See J. J. Stamm, *Erlösen und Vergeben im Alten Testament. Eine begriffsgeschichtliche Untersuchung*, 1940; and the articles by O. Procksch and H. Büchsel in G. Kittel, *Theological Dictionary of the New Testament*, vol. IV, 1942, pp. 328–356; and also my essay on 'The Understanding of Redemption in the Early Church', tr. into Swedish by L. G. Rignel, *Svensk Teologisk Kvartalskrift*, 1959, pp. 73–100.

restoration to favour and holiness before God. *G'l* (גאל) with its cognates refers to a concept of redemption out of destitution or bondage or forfeited rights undertaken by the advocacy of someone who is related to the person in need through kinship or some other bond of affinity or covenant love. In this type of redemption the focus is on the nature of the redeemer, the person of the *go'el* (גֹּאֵל), who claims the cause of the one in need as his own, and stands in for him since he cannot redeem himself. In the Old Testament this remarkable conception of redemption is also applied to God who acts on Israel's behalf in virtue of his special relation with Israel through election and covenant. It is on the ground of this bond and because of the blood of the covenant forging it that God takes the cause of his people upon himself as their kinsman–advocate, justifying them in the face of accusation and making sure their redemption in himself, and thus delivers them out of bondage into the freedom of their inheritance in communion with himself.

It is evident that in the teaching of the Old Testament all of these major conceptions of redemption overlap with each another and modify each within the unique relations of God with his people, whether they are applied to communities or individuals. This differentiates them sharply from secular conceptions of redemption. It is particularly significant that all three concepts are used to speak of the redemption of Israel out of Egypt in the Passover and the Exodus, which constitutes the paradigm instance of divine redemption. They are also used, however, in Deutero-Isaiah in association with the promise given to Israel of a new Exodus when the Holy One of Israel will redeem God's people through his anointed servant who mediates the covenant and is afflicted with the judgments of God as he bears the iniquities of his people and makes his soul an offering for sin, pouring it out unto death in intercession for the transgressors. No identification of the servant with the divine *Go'el* was actually made, and could not have been made for that would have implied that God had become incarnate within the existence of his people, had actually taken their sin on himself and made expiation for it in atoning self-sacrifice in order to redeem their life. It remained for the New Testament to make that identification in the incarnate Son of God, but in doing that it gathered up this whole conception of redemption and reinterpreted it in terms of what the Son of God had actually become and had actually done in the flesh. Like the Old Testament, the New Testament nowhere makes systematic use of these three conceptions of redemption. But they are all taken for granted and are found woven together in the apostolic understanding and presentation of the vicarious life and death of Christ in ways that seeped into the mind of the early Church and moulded its preaching and teaching about the priestly ministry of Christ in the form of a servant and the atoning sacrifice which he offered in and through himself for all mankind. Judging by the soteriological pattern generally found in the liturgies of the early centuries, it seems clear that it was at the celebration of the Eucharist that the Church regularly adjusted its doctrine of redemption in accordance with the supreme truth with which the Lord had invested his own self-offering when he inaugurated the new covenant in his body and blood in fulfilment of what had been written of him in the Old Testament Scriptures.

In several early homilies on the *Pascha* or Christian Passover, notably by Melito of Sardis[84] and Hippolytus of Rome,[85] the Exodus account of the passover sacrifice and the redemption of Israel is used as a frame within which to expound the saving work of Christ. The events recorded in the Exodus are transposed into terms of the advent of the Son of God in the flesh and the physical reality of his saving passion on the Cross. All the major Old Testament conceptions of redemption show through, but they are Christologically reinterpreted, for the shadowy prefigurements of redemption under the old covenant have now given way to the final truth of redemption through the sacrifice of Christ in the new covenant.

For the theological development of this rich biblical conception of redemption we have to turn to Irenaeus. With

---

[84]See the editions of Campbell Bonner, *The Homily on the Passion*, 1940, and by Stuart G. Hall, *On Pascha*, 1979. Cf. also the *De anima et corpore deque passione Domini* of Alexander of Alexandria which is indebted to Melito – *MPG*, 18.585–604.

[85]Pierre Nautin, *Une Homelié Inspirée du Traité sur la Pâque d'Hippolyte*, vol. 1 of *Homélies Pascales*, *SC*, 27., 1950.

him it was the *g'l* mode of redemption that was most pervasive for it supplied the general frame within which the other two modes of redemption had their powerful significance. The emphasis was clearly upon the Person of Christ as the Redeemer who through his incarnational union with the human race, and on the ground of the covenant bond which it actualises in kinship and friendship, reconciles us to God and brings us into union and communion with him. Here it was the *ontological* aspect of atonement that was uppermost, as in the doctrine of saving recapitulation of our human nature in Christ and its restoration through his vicarious obedience.[86] It was within this union of Christ with us, and in and through what he is in himself as Mediator between God and man, that Irenaeus thought of the *pdh* mode of redemption as operating, but not by any violent or unjust means.[87] As he interpreted it, redemption was the mighty and victorious intervention of God on our behalf, rescuing us from the tyranny of Satan and delivering us from the thraldom of evil and death, but it took place through the blood of Christ in atoning expiation of guilt and in the reconciliation and justification of the sinner. The mighty hand of God was the holiness of Jesus Christ, his obedience unto the death of the Cross. While the stress here was on the *dramatic* aspect of atonement in the victory of Christ over the devil and all the hostile powers of darkness, no secular concept of redemption (λύτρον) as ransom or compensation paid to the devil was involved.[88] Interpenetrating both these aspects of redemption was the *kpr* concept of atoning propitiation through the self-sacrifice and self-oblation of Christ, who intercedes for us, substitutes himself for us, taking upon himself the judgment of our sin, and offering reparation in our place. He is both the Priest and the Victim, the Servant and Lamb of God, through whose blood sin and guilt are expiated and the barrier

[86]Irenaeus, *Adv. haer.*, 3.11.1, vol. 2, p. 35; 3.19.6, p. 100f; 4.24.2ff, pp. 212ff; 4.27.3–28.1, pp. 190ff; 5.1.1ff, pp. 314ff; 5.14.1ff, pp. 360ff; 5.17.1ff, pp. 369ff; 5.21.1ff, pp. 380ff.

[87]Cf. *Ad Diognetum*, 7.4; 9.4.

[88]Irenaeus, *Adv. haer.*, 3.8.2f, vol. 2, p. 28f; 3.17.4; p. 85; 3.19, 5f, pp. 100f; 3.32.2, p. 125; 3.36.1, p. 129; 4.67.2, pp. 302f; 5.1.1ff, pp. 312ff; 5.2.1f, pp. 319ff; 5.21.1ff, pp. 380ff.

of enmity between man and God is removed. In this concept of redemption forensic and cultic factors are inseparably intertwined, while its central focus is on the *intercessory mode* of the atoning act and the restoration to fellowship with God which it brings about.[89]

Quite clearly none of these aspects of redemption stands alone; they all overlap and contribute essentially to one another. Hence justice could not be done to this rich complex of conceptions in the biblical theology of Irenaeus if any one of these aspects of redemption were to be isolated and made the major basis of a doctrine of atonement, for that would involve serious dislocation of their structure within the incarnate constitution of the Mediator. It has been shown that the incipient credal formulations found emerging in Irenaeus' interpretation of the truth of the Gospel and his unfolding of the trinitarian pattern implict in the deposit of faith, contributed to the content and structure of the Nicene confession of the faith.[90] Likewise, I believe, it is this wholeness which we find in the biblical understanding of atoning redemption in the theology of Irenaeus that lies at the root of the doctrine of atonement shared by the leading Nicene theologians. We must not forget, however, that it was the celebration of the Paschal Mystery of Christ at the Eucharist throughout the Church which continued to nurture and integrate their understanding of atonement as it had that of Irenaeus. Here is a revealing passage from an Easter message of Athanasius about 'the true glory of the Redeemer'. 'This is the Lord who is seen in the Father and in whom the Father also is seen. Although he was the true Son of the Father, he became at last incarnate for our sakes, that he might offer himself to the Father in our stead, and redeem us through his oblation and sacrifice. This is he who once brought his people out of Egypt, but who afterwards has redeemed all of us, nay, the whole race of men, from death, and rescued them from the grave. This is he who of old was sacrificed as a Lamb (for it was

---

[89]Irenaeus, *Adv. haer.*, 3.5.3, vol., p. 20; 3.17.9f, pp. 90f; 4.10.1, pp. 156f; 4.17, pp. 166f; 4.34.2, p. 214; 5.1.1ff, pp. 314ff; 5.2.1f, pp. 319ff; 5.14.2ff, pp. 361ff; 5.17.1f, pp. 369f.

[90]See Oscar Cullmann, *The Earliest Christian Confessions*, tr. by J. K. S. Reid, and my essay, 'The Deposit of Faith', *SJT*, vol. 36, 1983, pp. 1–28.

under the figure of a lamb that he was designated) but who was afterwards slain for us, "for Christ our Passover has been sacrificed" '.[91]

When we take a fresh look at the teaching of Athanasius from this perspective we find that he had a rich and full doctrine of the atonement in which all the various aspects of redemption, the dramatic, the priestly and the ontological, were never separated but were held together. The overall pattern was supplied by the concept of incarnational redemption through the appropriation and healing of corrupt human nature, but that was understood almost exclusively from the perspective of the saving and priestly work of Christ. Thus even in the *De incarnatione*, while the general framework of redemption was that of deliverance from the power of death under the threat of the law and the judgment of God and of the universal victory of Christ over all the forces of evil, at the heart of everything primary place was given to the offering (προσφορά) and sacrifice (θυσία) of Christ as a substitute (ἀντίψυχος) and a ransom (λύτρον) in place of all and on behalf of all.[92] 'He it is who is the life of all, and who offered his own body to death like a sheep as a substitute for the salvation of all (ὑπὲρ τῆς πάντων σωτηρίας ἀντίψυχον).'[93] What was envisaged there was the infinite cost of redemption in the expiatory sacrifice of Christ before the holy will of God. Athanasius was fond of citing the following passage from the Scripture: 'Since the children are partakers in flesh and blood, he also himself in like manner partook of the same; that through death he might bring to nought him that had the power of death, that is the devil; and might deliver all them who through fear of death were all their lifetime subject to bondage.'[94] There is not the slightest trace here of Origen's notion of ransom to the devil, for the very idea that the powers of darkness have any inherent right over man to which deference is to be paid was

[91]Athanasius, *Fest. Ep.*, Easter A.D. 338, 10.10 – 1 Cor. 5.7; also *Ep.*, 14.7. Cf. Origen, *In Jn.*, 28.25.

[92]Athanasius, *De inc.*, 9f, 16, 20ff, 25, 31.

[93]Athanasius, *De inc.*, 37; cf. 9.

[94]Hebrews 2.14f; Athanasius, *De inc.*, 10, 20; *De decr.*, 14; *Con. Ar.*, 2.9, 55; *Ep.*, 2.7; 16.7; *Ad Adel.*, 7.

quite impossible for Athanasius.[95] The interpretative tradition
followed was that of the Irenaean emphasis upon the fact that
divine redemption through the death of Christ takes place in
perfect justice and without stratagem, for it is impossible to
think of redemption as a divine act apart from a complete
vindication of God's righteousness and his uncompromising
rejection and judgment of all evil.[96]

The emphasis of Athanasius upon the vicarious sacrifice of
Christ in virtue of his kinship with us continued to have a central
place in the development of his thought, not least in the *Contra
Arianos* which reflects his careful and detailed examination of
the biblical foundations on which Nicene soteriology rested.
Here in line with his understanding of atoning reconciliation
taking place within the incarnate constitution of the Mediator,
we find a concentration upon Christ who as Servant-Son and
High Priest *offers himself* in propitiatory sacrifice to God in our
stead and on our behalf (ἀνθ' ἡμῶν καὶ ὑπὲρ ἡμῶν). It is the
combination of Christ's incarnate sonship with his priestly office
that is particularly noteworthy.[97] The overall framework of the
vicarious humiliation and exaltation, death and resurrection is
maintained, but within it the central act of atonement is
described principally in terms of the self-abasement and self-
sacrifice of Christ as the means of redemption from sin. As our
High Priest Christ cleanses us from our sins in his own blood,
and presents us in and through his own ascension to the Father in
whose presence he now appears on our behalf. While Christ has
offered himself once and for all through death to the Father his is
a faithful sacrifice which remains and does not come to an end.[98]

In none of the other theologians in the Nicene tradition, until
we come to Cyril of Alexandria, do we have a doctrine of
atonement as rich and full as that of Athanasius. Nevertheless,
the centrality he gave to the substitutionary sacrifice of Christ

[95]Origen, *In Matt.*, 16.8; cf. *In. Rom.*, 2.13; 3.8, 24; 4.11 but cf. also *In Lev.*,
9.10 & *In Jn.*, 28.14.
[96]Thus also Adamantius, *De recta fide*, 1.27; and Gregory Naz., *Or.*, 45.22;
39.13; *Carm. theol.*, 10.65f.
[97]*Con. Ar.*, 1.41., 59f, 64; 2.7ff, 14, 55, 68ff, 75f; 3.31–35, 56f; 4.6f; *De decr.*,
14.
[98]*Con. Ar.*, 1.41; 2.7–10; cf. *Ad Epict.*, 5f; *Ad Adel.*, 4ff; *Ad Max.*, 3f.

offered to the Father in redemption from sin and in reparation of man's indebtedness is clearly reflected in their writings. This is evident not least in their interpretations of the death of Christ with reference to the Old Testament conceptions of redemption through the offering of life for life, to the Mosaic ordinances for propitiatory sacrifice well pleasing to God, and to the suffering servant led as a lamb to the slaughter.[99] It is also very evident, however, in the emphasis laid upon the fact that Christ is at once High Priest and Sacrifice, 'the Offerer and the Offering' (ὁ προσφέρων καὶ προσφερόμενος), the expression used by Basil in his Liturgy and incorporated into the Byzantine rite.[100] Augustine's memorable statement clearly represents the ruling idea in the teaching of the Church in the East as well as the West: 'Since in sacrifice four things are to be considered, to whom it is offered, by whom, what and for whom, the same one true Mediator, reconciling us to God by the sacrifice of peace, remains one with him to whom he offered, made himself one with those for whom he offered, is himself one as Offerer and Offering.'[101]

It was certainly Gregory Nazianzen who stood closest to Athanasius in this respect, as in his understanding of the redemptive kinship between man and God effected by the incarnation within which the atonement was accomplished. While Christ is *homoousios* (ὁμοούσιος) with the Father he has come in the form of a servant to bear in himself all our evil and bear it away, crucifying our sins with himself.[102] As such, Gregory claimed, 'he *is* redemption in that he sets us free from the captivity of sin, offering himself as a ransom in our places (λύτρον ἑαυτὸν ἀντιδιδοὺς ἡμῶν), the cleansing sacrifice for the world.'[103] 'He is both Victim and Priest', 'the Lamb offered and

---

[99]Thus Eusebius of Caesarea, *Dem ev.*, 1.3, 10; 4.12; 8.2; 10.1; cf. the expositions of Origen, *In Lev.*, 9.10; 14.4; *In Num.*, 24.1; *In Jn.*, 6.53; *In Rom.*, 3.24. See also Augustine, *In Ps.*, 39.12.

[100]F. E. Brightman, *op. cit.*, vol. 1, *The Eastern Liturgies*, pp. 318, 378, etc.; Chrysostom, *In Heb.*, 6.20; 9.25f. For characteristic reference in the liturgical tradition to the priestly office of Christ, see *Apostolic Constitutions*, 2.4.25, 26; 5.5.6; 6.3.11; 6.6.30; 7.1.38; 7.4.47; 8.2.12; 8.5.46.

[101]Augustine, *De Trin.*, 4.14.19.

[102]Gregory Naz., *Or.*, 4.5f; 38.16.

[103]Gregory Naz., *Or.*, 30.20.

the offering Priest.'[104] Gregory appealed to the same identity between the Person and work of Christ in his indignant rejection of the shameful notion that 'the precious blood of our God and High Priest and Sacrifice' should be paid as ransom or something given in exchange (λύτρον or ἀντάλλαγμα) to the evil one.[105]

Under the constraint of the Epistle to the Hebrews and the celebration of the eucharist, Gregory Nyssen spoke in similar terms of the oneness in Christ of Offerer and Offering, the Mediator between God and man who is at once High Priest and Paschal Sacrifice, provided in the overflowing love of God for the redemption of mankind.[106] This teaching was presented, however, within an incarnational framework in which insufficient attention was given to the gravity of guilt, which modified its significance. Since in his view 'sin is nothing else than alienation from God', the redemptive import of the incarnation was apparently limited to the activity of Christ in purifying the whole man, body and soul, rescuing him from the curse of sin and healing the inner disruption of his being.[107] While Gregory regarded the salvation of mankind as an act of personal intervention on the part of God, he seems to have had a deficient sense of the moral requirements of God's nature and therefore of the piacular character of atonement. This helps to explain how he could commit himself to such a morally repugnant concept as ransom to the devil.[108] However, this utterly unbiblical conception was so decisively refuted by Gregory Nazianzen, that it never entered into the main stream of the Church's teaching, in spite of its popular appeal over a

[104]Gregory Naz., *Carm.*, 2; cf. 10; *Or.*, 30.21; 38.16.

[105]Gregory Naz., *Or.*, 45.22; cf. 39.13; and *Carm.*, 10.

[106]Gregory Nyss., *De perf. Christ.*, MPG, 46.264A; *De occ. Dom.*, MPG, 46.1165B–D; *Con. Eun.*, 2.4, Jaeger, vol. 2, p. 140.

[107]Gregory Nyss., *Or. cat.*, 16, 24f, 27f; *Con. Eun.*, 2.12f, Jaeger, 2, pp. 373–386. Cf. 3.10.10: 'He who knew no sin was made sin for us and in order to free us from the curse, he made our enmity against God his own slaying it in himself, as the apostle expressed it (the enmity was sin), and becoming what we are he reunited humanity to God through himself.' Jaeger, 2, p. 293f.

[108]Gregory Nyss., *Or. cat.*, 22–26; cf. Basil, *In Ps.*, 7.2; 48.3f.

long period in the West.[109] It was doubtless the liturgical tradition and the biblical expositions of Chrysostom and Cyril of Alexandria that helped to relegate this mythological theory of redemption to the periphery of the Church's tradition.

(4) We must now give attention to a bridge concept between what we have been considering in this chapter and what follows: the 'wonderful exchange' embedded in the incarnation. This was the redemptive translation of man *from* one state *into* another brought about by Christ who in his self-abnegating love took our place that we might have his place, becoming what we are that we might become what he is. 'You know the grace of our Lord Jesus Christ, that though he was rich yet for your sakes he became poor that you through his poverty might become rich.'[110] As Irenaeus expressed it, 'Out of his measureless love our Lord Jesus Christ has become what we are in order to make us what he is himself.'[111]

Theological expression was early given to this redemptive translation as the 'exchange' (ἀνταλλαγή) effected between God and sinful humanity described by the New Testament term for 'reconciliation' (καταλλαγή), thereby bringing out its profound import as 'atoning exchange'. Thus the unknown author of the epistle to Diognetus spoke of 'the sweet exchange' (γλυκεῖα ἀνταλλαγή) whereby God in his kindness and love 'took our sin upon himself, gave up his own Son as ransom (λύτρον) for us, the holy for the wicked, the innocent for the guilty, the just for the unjust, the incorruptible for the corruptible, the immortal

---

[109]Contrast Augustine, for whom the expiatory and propitiatory elements in the atonement made the idea of compensation to the devil unthinkable – *De Trin.*, 4.14.17; *De Civ. Dei*, 10.22; *Enchir.*, 41.

[110]2 Cor. 8.9.

[111]Irenaeus, *Adv. haer.*, 5. *praef.*, vol. 2, p. 314. Cf. John Calvin: 'This is the wonderful exchange (*mirifica commutatio*) which out of his boundless kindness he has entered into with us: by becoming Son of Man with us he has made us sons of God with him; by his descent to earth he has prepared our ascent to heaven; by taking on himself our mortality he has bestowed on us his own immortality; by taking on himself our weakness he has made us strong with his strength; by receiving our poverty into himself he has transferred to us his riches; by taking upon himself the burden of the iniquities with which we are weighed down, he has clothed us with his righteousness.' *Inst.*, 4.17.2; also 4.17.3 & 42. Cf. Luther, *Tr. de lib. christ.*, *WA*, 7, p. 25f.

for the mortal.'[112] At the same time this concept of atoning exchange was linked to that of 'sacrificial exchange' (ἀντάλλαγμα) which brought out further its substitutionary significance. As Origen expressed it: 'A man cannot give anything in exchange (ἀντάλλαγμα) for his own life, but God has given an exchange (ἀντάλλαγμα) for the life of us all, the precious blood of Jesus Christ.'[113] Thus also Athanasius: 'It was not possible to give one thing as ransom in exchange (ἀντιδοῦναι λύτρον) for another thing, but he gave body for body, and soul for soul, and a perfect existence for the whole man: this is Christ's exchange (τὸ ἀντάλλαγμα τοῦ Χριστοῦ).'[114]

It is, then, upon this concept of atoning exchange as its inner hinge that the whole doctrine of incarnational redemption through the descent (κατάβασις) and ascent (ἀνάβασις), the death and resurrection, the humiliation and exaltation, of the Son of God rests.[115] It lies at the heart of the Nicene theological orientation in which the death and resurrection of Christ were never treated in isolation from each other, and in which therefore redemption was thought of as taking place through the resurrection and ascension as well as the death of Christ, not just from death, bondage and judgment, but into new life, freedom and blessedness in God.[116]

Here let Gregory Nazianzen speak for Nicene theology. 'Let us become like Christ, since Christ became like us. Let us become divine for his sake, since he for ours became man. He assumed the worst that he might give us the better; he became poor that we through his poverty might be rich; he took upon himself the form of a servant that we might receive back our liberty; he came down that we might be exalted; he was tempted that we might conquer; he was dishonoured that he might glorify us; he ascended that he might draw us to himself,

---

[112]*Ad Diog.*, 9.2.

[113]Origen, *In Matt.*, 12.28, with reference to Matt. 16.26; Mark 8.27; Is. 43.3f; 1 Pet. 1.18f; 1 Cor. 6.20. Cf. Irenaeus, *Adv. haer.*, 5.1.1, vol. 2, p. 315.

[114]Athanasius, *Con. Apol.*, 1.17.

[115]Cf. Irenaeus, *Adv. haer.*, 3.6.2, vol. 2, p. 22f; 3.19.2, p. 95f, etc.

[116]See, for example, Athanasius, *Con. Ar.*, 1.41–45. This inseparability in the early Church's thought of the death and resurrection of Christ was expressed in the use of the word *pascha* (πάσχα) to refer both to Christ's passion and to his resurrection.

who were lying low in the fall of sin. Let us give all, offer all, to him who gave himself a ransom and reconciliation for us.'[117]

This atoning exchange, then, embraces the whole relationship between Christ and ourselves: between his obedience and our disobedience, his holiness and our sin, his life and our death, his strength and our weakness, his grace and our poverty, his light and our darkness, his wisdom and our ignorance, his joy and our misery, his peace and our dispeace, his immortality and our mortality, and so on. But all this is worked out within the saving economy of the incarnation, and in the ontological depths of the humanity which he made his own, and therefore reaches its appointed end and fulfilment through his transforming consecration of us in himself and through his exaltation of us as one body with himself into the immediate presence of the Father. Through this saving interchange between Christ and ourselves we have a window open to all the creative, redemptive and sanctifying purposes of God which reach far beyond the subject of this chapter, but it will be helpful for what is to follow in the succeeding chapters if we now reflect on several of the implications of this interchange.

(a) First we must remind ourselves of the boundless significance of what took place in Jesus Christ – if God did not spare his own Son but delivered him up for us all, as St Paul wrote to the Romans, the gifts of his love that flow to us freely with Christ are quite unlimited.[118] The benefits of God's free gift of Jesus Christ to mankind are as inexhaustible as his love. Clement of Alexandria had this in mind when he pointed out that, when out of his great love God gave himself as a ransom in establishing the new covenant and laid down his own life for every one of us, he offered a life which, not only exceeds what was called for, but has a value that outweighs the whole universe.[119] This concept of the transcendent worth of the

---

[117]Gregory Naz., *Or.*, 1.5. See also Athanasius, *Con. Ar.*, 1.41; 4.6–7; *De decr.*, 14; *Ad. Epict.*, 6; *Ad Adel.*, 4. But cf. Gregory Nyss., *Or. cat.*, 24, where he strangely misuses the concept of 'exchange' (ἀντάλλαγμα) in his theory of a ransom paid to Satan.

[118]Romans 8.32.

[119]Clement of Alex., *Quis div. salv.*, 31; cf. 27, 36–39.

sacrifice of Christ and its universal range was taken up by Basil of Caesarea,[120] John Chrysostom,[121] and Cyril of Jerusalem.[122] It was Cyril of Alexandria, however, who argued most powerfully for the infinite worth of Christ's sacrifice. He picked up the language of Clement and in stronger terms reinforced the claim that the death of Christ was much more than offering an equivalent for the redemption of man, because Christ himself was of infinite worth.[123] While Athanasius did not speak specifically of the infinite value of Christ's sacrifice, he did insist on the universal range of the vicarious work of Christ in incarnation and redemption, which was due to the fact that it was not just a man who suffered and died for us but the Lord as man, not just the life of a man that was offered to save us but the life of God as man. As we have seen, he never tired of asserting that what Christ accomplished on our behalf and in our place, whether in bearing the whole burden of the divine judgment on sin or in freely bestowing upon mankind the immeasurable grace of God, applied to *all* without any qualification.[124] In spite of this, there is no suggestion in the thought of Athanasius of the kind of 'universalism' advocated by Origen[125] or by Gregory Nyssen.[126]

In the profound interaction between incarnation and atonement in Jesus, the blessed exchange it involved between the divine-human life of Jesus and mankind has the effect of finalising and sealing the ontological relations between every man and Jesus Christ. Thus 'our resurrection', as Athanasius once expressed it, 'is stored up in the Cross.'[127] Through his

---

[120]Basil, *In Ps.*, 48.3.

[121]Chrysostom, *In Rom.*, 5.17; 'For Christ has paid down far more than the death we owe, yes, as much more as the boundless ocean exceeds a tiny drop of water.' But cf. *In Heb.*, 9.28, where Chrysostom claimed that while Christ's death was 'equivalent to the death of all', 'he did not bear the sins of all men, for they were not willing'!

[122]Cyril of Jer., *Cat.*, 13.2–4, 33.

[123]Cyril of Alex., *De inc. Dom.*, 27; *De rect. fid.*, 2.7; *In Jn.*, 1.29; 3.16.

[124]Athanasius, *De inc.*, 7–10, 16, 20ff, 25, 37f; *Con. Ar.*, 1.41, 49, 60; 2.7, 9, 13f, 53, 70; 3.20, 31ff, 39; 4.36; *Ad. Adel.*, 4–8; *Ep.*, 10.10.

[125]Origen, *De prin.*, 1.6.

[126]Gregory Nyss., *Or. cat.*, 26.

[127]Athanasius, *Con. Ar.*, 1.43.

penetration into the perverted structures of human existence he reversed the process of corruption and more than made good what had been destroyed, for he has now anchored human nature in his own crucified and risen being, freely giving it participation in the fullness of God's grace and blessing embodied in him. Since he is the eternal Word of God by whom and through whom all things that are made are made, and in whom the whole universe of visible and invisible realities coheres and hangs together, and since in him divine and human natures are inseparably united, then the secret of every man, whether he believes or not, is bound up with Jesus for it is in him that human contingent existence has been grounded and secured.[128]

It is precisely in Jesus, therefore, who was born of the Virgin Mary, crucified for us under Pontius Pilate and rose again in space and time, that we are to think of the whole human race, and indeed of the whole creation, as in a profound sense already redeemed, resurrected, and consecrated for the glory and worship of God. How could it be otherwise when he who became incarnate in him is the very one through whom all worlds, all ages, were made? At the same time this means, of course, that the stress upon the cross and resurrection which involves all creation, carries with it the fulfilment of salvation throughout all space and time, and thus reaches forward to the consummation of all things, in the return of Christ to make all things new, to judge the quick and the dead, and to manifest the new creation. And so, as the Creed insists, the kingdom of Jesus Christ shall have no end. The incarnation, crucifixion and resurrection of Christ, are not a transient episode but a saving fact which has been perfected once and for all, and now endures for all eternity within the one divine–human being of the Mediator.

If the saving act of God in Christ were something external to Christ, something merely between Christ and us or between Christ and the world, then when completed it would be over and done with. But if the soteriological exchange takes place within the constitution of the incarnate Person of the Mediator,

---

[128]Athanasius, *Con. Ar.*, 1.41; 2.22, 31, 69f; 3.33.

then it is as eternal as Jesus Christ himself, the eternal Son. That is the staggering truth of the Gospel that so overwhelmed the early Church which they sought to express in their doctrine of *theopoiesis* (θεοποίησις) which we shall consider again below: the fact that through the kinship which the Son of God has established with us in the incarnation, our creaturely evanescent existence is as securely anchored in the very being and life of God as Jesus Christ himself. Such is the blessed end of the atoning exchange effected in the death, resurrection and ascension of Jesus Christ. Since he has been taken up into God, in him our humanity, in spite of its temporal changeable nature, is given a place in God, and is thus grounded in his eternal unchangeable reality.

(b) The second implication of the atoning exchange that we must consider is the redemption of suffering. To understand this, it is best to approach it from the fact that when the Son of God became incarnate in Jesus Christ, he did not cease to be God, and when he became man within the conditions of our limited existence in space and time, he did not leave the throne of the universe.[129] We must also bear in mind the point we discussed above that when the holy Son of God took our sinful humanity upon himself, he did it in such a way that instead of sinning himself he brought his holiness to bear upon it so that it might be sanctified in him. He was made sin for us that we might be made the righteousness of God in him.

It is along this line, I believe, that we must approach the question of *impassibility*, for here too the atoning exchange applies with its redemptive reversal of human suffering in Christ. How are we to understand the passion of the incarnate Son of God, when he offered *himself* and not just his body in vicarious sacrifice for the sins of mankind? What does the suffering of Christ really mean for what he was and is in his own *Person* as the one Mediator between God and man? There is

[129]Clement, *Strom.*, 2.2; Origen, *De prin.*, 1.1; Athanasius, *De inc.*, 8, 16ff, 41ff; *De decr.*, 14; *Con. Ar.*, 1.23; 2.26; 3.1ff, 22f; 4.36; Hilary, *De Trin.*, 2.25; 10.16; Gregory Nyss., *Or. cat.*, 10; Gregory Naz., *Or.*, 28.7ff; 3.19, etc. Consult my essay, 'The Relation of the Incarnation to Space in Nicene Theology', Andrew Blane (Editor), *The Ecumenical World of Orthodox Civilisation*, vol. III, 1974, pp. 43–70.

certainly a sense in which we must think of God as impassible (ἀπαθής), for he is not subject to the passions that characterise human and creaturely existence, but that is not to say that he is not afflicted in all the afflictions of his people or that he is untouched by their sufferings.[130] If we think of the atonement as taking place within the incarnate constitution of the Mediator who is God and man in one Person, then, as Athanasius argued against the Arians, we cannot think of the sufferings of Christ as external to the Person of the Logos. It is the very same Person who suffered and who saved us, not just man but the Lord as man; both his divine and his human acts are acts of one and the same Person.[131]

The point is this. In Jesus Christ God himself has penetrated into our passion, our hurt, our violence, our condition under divine judgment, even into our utter dereliction, 'My God, my God, why hast thou forsaken me?', but in such a profoundly vicarious way that in the very heart of it all, he brought his eternal *serenity* or ἀπάθεια to bear redemptively upon our passion.[132] Thus we may say of God in Christ that he both suffered and did not suffer,[133] for through the eternal tranquillity of his divine impassibility he took upon himself our passibility and redeemed it. In the nature of the case this is not something about which a logical account can be given, for logically impassibility and passibility exclude one another.[134] Rather is it to be understood dynamically and soteriologically on the ground of what has actually taken place in the vicarious life and passion of God's incarnate Son. Nor can God be thought of as 'impassible' in the Greek or Stoic sense, but on the contrary as God who in his measureless love and compassion has stooped to take upon himself our passion, our hurt and suffering, and to

---

[130]Isaiah 63.9.

[131]Athanasius, *Con. Ar.*, 3.31ff, 41ff, 55ff; cf. 1.60; *Ad Adel.*, 4ff; *Ad Epict.*, 5ff; *Con. Apol.*, 1.10f; 2.1f; 10f. Refer to G. D. Dragas, *op. cit.*, pp. 242–280.

[132]Gregory Naz., *Or.*, 30.5f; 45.22 & 28. See the sensitive account of this by D. B. Harned, *Creed and Personal Identity. The Meaning of the Apostles' Creed*, 1981, p. 67f.

[133]Athanasius, *Con. Apol.*, 1.11; cf. *Con. Apol.*, 2.2f, 11f; *Ad Epict.*, 6.

[134]Cf. the logical arguments advanced in Theodoret's third Dialogue which inevitably imply a dualist interpretation of the incarnation – *MPG*, 83.220–317. Contrast Athanasius, *Ad Epict.*, 7.

exhaust it in his divine impassibility (τὸ παθητὸν ἐν ἀπαθείᾳ)[135] in such a way that he masters and transmutes it within the embrace of his own immutable peace and serenity. It is an essential aspect of the atoning exchange in Jesus Christ that through his sharing in our passion (πάθος) he makes us share in his own imperturbability (ἀπάθεια). As Didymus expressed it, he 'translates us into his own imperturbable tranquility'.[136]

It is basically the same argument that is to be applied to the atoning exchange between ignorance and wisdom in Christ – a problem that was much discussed in the fourth century, for the Arians had appealed to passages in the Gospels such as those in which it was said of Jesus that he increased in wisdom and even was lacking in knowledge.[137] Athanasius handled this question in entire consistency with his arguments about what the Son of God had done in making himself one of us and one with us in what we actually are in order to save us. That is to say, while the Son or Word of God who is of one and the same being as the Father enjoys a relation of mutual knowing between himself and the Father, nevertheless in his self-abasement in the form of a servant he had condescended, for our sakes, really to make our ignorance along with other human limitations his own, precisely in order to save us from them.[138] 'He incorporated the ignorance of men in himself, that he might redeem their humanity from all its imperfections and cleanse and offer it perfect and holy to the Father.'[139] The fact that Christ was both God and man, and thus acted as God and as man, led some theologians in the fourth century to make ambiguous statements about the 'economic ignorance' of Christ,[140] and sometimes even to speak of it as unreal.[141] Gregory Nazianzen,[142] and Gregory Nyssen,[143] both insisted on the

[135]Athanasius, *Con. Apol.*, 2.11.

[136]Thus Didymus, *De Trin.*, 3.12; εἰς ἀπάθειαν μετέστησεν. Cf. also 1.26 and *De Sp. St.*, 1.11 for this interpretation of the divine ἀπάθεια.

[137]Luke 2.52; Mark 13.32.

[138]Athanasius, *Con. Ar.*, 3.42–53.

[139]Athanasius, *Ad Ser.*, 2.9.

[140]Hilary, *De Trin.*, 9.58–75; Evagrius/Basil, *Ep.*, 8.6–7; Basil, *Ep.*, 236.2.

[141]Cf. Didymus, *De Trin.*, 3.22.

[142]Gregory Naz., *Or.*, 30.15.

[143]Gregory Nyss., *Adv. Apol.*, 24, Jaeger, 3.1, p. 167f.

reality of our Lord's ignorance as essential to his humanity; but it was Cyril of Alexandria who developed the soteriological approach of Athanasius most fully. For him the ignorance of Christ was just as essential to his amazing self-abasement or κένωσις as his physical imperfections and limitations, all of which are to be predicated of his one incarnate reality (μία φύσις σεσαρκωμένη). It was an economic and vicarious ignorance on our Lord's part by way of a deliberate restraint on his divine knowledge throughout a life of continuous *kenosis* in which he refused to transgress the limits of the creaturely and earthly conditions of human nature.[144]

As the Word or Mind of God become flesh Jesus Christ was the incarnate wisdom of God, but incarnate in such a way as really to share with us our human ignorance, so that we might share in his divine wisdom. That was not just an appearance of ignorance on his part, any more than his incarnating of the Word or Mind of God was only in appearance. Had either been in appearance only, it would have emptied the economic condescension of the Son to save and redeem of any reality. Unless the Son of God had assumed the whole nature of man, including his ignorance, man could not have been saved. The wonderful exchange that lies at the heart of the interaction of incarnation and atonement operates right here, as at every other point in the relation between God and sinful human being, for the human mind is an absolutely essential element in creaturely being. Hence God in Christ Jesus took it up into himself along with the whole man, in order to penetrate into it and deal with the sin, alienation, misunderstanding, and darkness that had become entrenched within it. Jesus Christ came among us sharing to the full the poverty of our ignorance, without ceasing to embody in himself all the riches of the wisdom of God, in order that we might be redeemed from our ignorance through sharing in his wisdom. Redemption was not accomplished just by a downright *fiat* of God, nor by a mere divine 'nod',[145] but

---

[144]Cyril of Alex., *Quod unus sit Christus*, MPG, 75.1332; *Con. Theod.*, MPG, 76.416; *Adv. Nest.*, MPG, 76.155; *Adv. anthr.*, MPG, 76.100–104; *De rect. fid.*, MPG, 76.1353; *Thes.*, MPG, 75.368–380; 421–429, etc. For a fuller discussion consult *Theol. in Reconcil.*, pp. 163–7.

[145]Athanasius, *De inc.*, 44.

by an intimate, personal movement of the Son of God himself into the heart of our creaturely being and into the inner recesses of the human mind, in order to save us from within and from below, and to restore us to undamaged relations of being and mind with himself. Thus throughout his earthly life Christ laid hold of our alienated and darkened human mind in order to heal and enlighten it in himself. In and through him our ignorant minds are brought into such a relation to God that they may be filled with divine light and truth. The redemption of man's ignorance has an essential place in the atoning exchange, for everything that we actually are in our lost and benighted condition has been taken up by Christ into himself in order that he might bring it under the saving, renewing, sanctifying, and enlightening power of his own reality as the incarnate wisdom and light of God.

(c) The third form of the atoning exchange to which some consideration must now be given is that which is conveyed in the concept of *theopoiesis* (θεοποίησις) and which is perhaps its most comprehensive expression. 'He was made man that we might be made divine.'[146] It is important to note that the interchange spoken of here is essentially of a soteriological nature, and must be understood from that perspective. This was made very clear by Athanasius. 'The Word was made flesh in order to offer up this body for all, so that we, partaking of his Spirit, can be made divine, a gift which we could not otherwise have gained had he not clothed himself in our created body; it was thus that we began to be called 'men of God' and 'men in Christ'. But as we, in receiving the Spirit do not lose our own proper being, so the Lord when he was made man for us, and bearing a body, was no less God. He was not diminished by the envelopment of the body, but on the contrary he deified it and rendered it immortal.'[147] There are but two aspects of this *theopoiesis* which call for consideration here.

In the first place, there is no suggestion that this interaction between Christ's deity and our humanity, results in any change

[146] Athanasius, *De inc.*, 54.

[147] Athanasius, *De decr.*, 14. See further *De syn.*, 51; *Con. Ar.*, 1.9, 37–43, 46–50; 2.47, 53, 59, 63–70, 74, 76–78; 3.17, 19–25, 34, 39f, 53; 4.33; *Ad Adel.*, 4; *Ad Epict.*, 5ff; *Ad Ser.*, 1.24.

in divine or human being (οὐσία), for as he is not less divine in becoming man, so we are not less human in being brought under the immediate presence and power of his divine being. What makes us 'divine' is the fact that the Word of God has come to us and acts directly upon us,[148] or more concretely the fact that in Jesus Christ the Son of God has become man and thus brought us into kinship with himself.[149] In other words, our 'deification' in Christ is the obverse of his 'inhomination'. This is a deification, however, which more than recreates our lost humanity, for it lifts us up in Christ to enjoy a new fullness of human life in a blessed communion with divine life.

In the second place, the concept of *theopoiesis* is closely related to the reception of the Holy Spirit, for to have the Spirit dwelling in us is to be made partakers of God beyond ourselves. This is made possible through the atoning exchange that took place in the incarnation. In the words of Irenaeus, 'The Lord has redeemed us through his own blood, giving his soul for our souls, and his flesh for our flesh, and has poured out the Spirit of the Father for the union and communion of God and man, imparting indeed God to men by means of the Spirit, and on the other hand attaching man to God by his own incarnation, and bestowing upon us at his coming immortality durably and truly through communion with God.'[150] It was because of the incarnation that the Holy Spirit descended upon man in Christ and became accustomed to dwell in humanity, and thus on the other hand that man was accustomed to receive God and have him dwelling in him.[151] That is certainly how Athanasius understood the way in which the Holy Spirit is mediated to us by and through the humanity of Christ who sanctified himself in the Spirit that we might be santified in him. We recall that in explaining what Christ meant by his self-sanctification for our sakes, Athanasius put the following words in his mouth: 'As the Father's Word, I give to myself, when becoming man, the Spirit; and I sanctify myself, become man, in him, that henceforth in me, who am the truth, all may be sanctified.'

[148] Athanasius, *Con. Ar.*, 1.38; 3.38; *Ad Afr.*, 7; *De syn.*, 51.
[149] Athanasius, *Con. Ar.*, 1.38–39.
[150] Irenaeus, *Adv. haer.*, 5.1.1., vol. 2, p. 315.
[151] Irenaeus, *Adv. haer.*, 3.18.1, vol. 2, p. 92; 3.21.2, p. 107.

Then he added, 'If then for our sakes he sanctifies himself, and does this when he is become man, it is very plain that the Spirit's descent on him in Jordan was a descent upon us because of his bearing our body. This did not take place for the promotion of the Word himself, but for our sanctification, that we might share in his anointing, and of us it might be said, 'Do you not know that you are God's Temple, and the Spirit of God dwells in you?' For when the Lord, as man, was washed in Jordan, it was we who were washed in him and by him. And when he received the Spirit, it was we who by him were made recipients of him.'[152] This twofold movement of the giving and receiving of the Spirit áctualised within the life of the incarnate Son of God *for our sakes* is atonement operating within the ontological depths of human being. It constitutes the 'deifying' content of the atoning exchange in which through the pouring out of the same Spirit upon us we are given to participate. The indwelling of the Spirit mediated to us through Christ is the effective counterpart in us of his self-offering to the Father through the eternal Spirit.[153] In other words, Pentecost must be regarded, not as something added on to atonement, but as the actualisation within the life of the Church of the atoning life, death and resurrection of the Saviour.

---

[152]Athanasius, *Con. Ar.*, 1.46f – the biblical reference is to 1 Cor.3.16 – this is an Athanasian passage which we shall consider later; cf. *Con. Ar.*, 3.24–5.
[153]Hebrews 9.14.

6

The Eternal Spirit

'And in the Holy Spirit, the Lord, the Giver of Life, who proceeds from the Father, who with the Father and the Son together is worshipped and glorified; who spoke by the prophets.'

At the Council of Nicaea in 325 A.D. the Fathers spoke of the Holy Spirit only in the last single sentence: 'We believe in the Holy Spirit'. Brief as this was, it brought into sharp focus the universal emphasis in the New Testament upon the personal and divine nature of the Holy Spirit who, with the Father and the Son, is both the subject and object of faith, he through whom and in whom we believe in Jesus Christ and are saved. In him God himself is immediately present in our midst, miraculously and savingly at work, and through him God reveals himself as *Lord*, for God himself is the content of what he does for us and communicates to us. The Spirit is not just something divine or something akin to God emanating from him, not some sort of action at a distance or some kind of gift detachable from himself, for in the Holy Spirit God acts directly upon us himself, and in giving us his Holy Spirit God gives us nothing less than himself. Since God is Spirit, the Giver of the Spirit and the Gift of the Spirit are identical.[1] Thus in the Nicene Creed belief in the Holy Spirit is bracketed together with belief in the Father and in the Son, as belief in one God and Lord.[2]

[1] Athanasius, *Ad Ser.*, 1.30; Epiphanius, *Haer.*, 74.7.
[2] See Epiphanius' emphasis upon a three-fold πιστεύομεν in this respect, *Haer.*, 73.25; 74.14; and Basil, *Ep.*, 236.6.

The personal divine nature of the Spirit as himself the Lord was made clear in the apostolic witness from the very beginning through the designation 'holy' (ἅγιος) rendering the Hebrew *qadosh* (קָדוֹשׁ). *Qadosh* (קָדוֹשׁ) had been used in the Old Testament Scriptures to speak of the utterly transcendent, unfathomable nature, and the unapproachable glory and majesty of God. 'Holy, holy, holy is the Lord of hosts, the whole earth is full of his glory.'[3] Thus in the Isaianic tradition *qadosh* was used to refer to the Lord as 'the Holy One of Israel', not least in connection with the redeeming activity of God in the life and history of his people,[4] and sometimes to name his Spirit as 'Holy Spirit'.[5] It was doubtless because of his wholly other and incomparable nature that the Greek Old Testament and the New Testament alike passed over the more commonly used Greek word ἱερός in preference for the relatively rare word ἅγιος with which to express the holiness and otherness of the Deity. The name 'Holy Spirit' thus gave expression to the recognition that the immanence of the Spirit was the immanence of the Spirit in his irreducible transcendence.

Moreover, the Hebrew word for 'spirit', *ruach* (רוּחַ), unlike the word for 'spirit' (πνεῦμα) in classical Greek thought and literature,[6] carried an active and concrete sense, so that in linking 'holy' (קָדוֹשׁ) and 'spirit' (רוּחַ) together, the Old Testament clearly intended the mighty living God, the presence of whose Spirit is to be understood as at once intensely personal reality and dynamic event. The Spirit of God is not the emission of some divine force detachable from God but the confrontation of human beings and their affairs with his own Self in which he brings the impact of his divine power and holiness to bear directly and personally upon their lives in judgment and

---

[3]Is., 6.3; see also Lev., 11.45f; 19.2; 20.7, etc.

[4]Cf. Is., 1.4; 5.19, 24; 10.17, 20; 12.6; 7.7; 29.19, 23; 30.11f; 31.1; 37.23; 40.25; 41.14, 16, 20; 43.3, 14f; 45.11; 47.4; 48.17; 49.7; 54.5; 60.9, 15; cf. Mk. 1.24; Lk. 4.34; Jn 6.69; Acts 3.14; 1 Jn 2.20.

[5]Is. 63.10f; Ps. 51.11.

[6]Of course, πνεῦμα like רוּחַ literally meant 'wind' or 'breath', but whereas in classical Greek that original nuance was thinned out, it was largely retained in Hebrew and thus in the biblical use of πνεῦμα, as in John 3.8, or Acts 2.1f. For a carry over of the original nuance of πνεῦμα, see Gregory Nyss., *Or. cat.*, 2.

salvation alike. That conception of God's Spirit was greatly accentuated through the intimate association of the Word (דָּבָר) and the Spirit (רוּחַ) of God in his revealing and saving activity and its promised fulfilment in the Messiah as the Bearer of the Spirit and Word of God.[7] It was this decidedly Hebraic approach that characterised the New Testament teaching about the Holy Spirit as the sanctifying, life-giving and redeeming outreach of God through his Word toward mankind, drawing them into communion face to face with himself.[8] Just as the God of the old and new covenants and the Lord Jesus Christ were worshipped as sublimely and incomparably *holy*, so the Spirit of God in virtue of his intrinsically holy nature drew to himself the same awe and adoration, for in the Spirit it was none other than the Lord God, almighty and all-holy, who was personally and objectively present meeting and speaking with his people.

I

It was squarely in line with these biblical convictions about the Holy Spirit that the Nicene fathers confessed, 'We believe in one God ... and in one Lord Jesus Christ ... and in the Holy Spirit'. They thereby acknowledged that faith in the Holy Spirit is to be held in a *trinitarian* frame in accordance with the ordinance of holy baptism into the *one name* of Father, Son and Holy Spirit, and with the rule of faith handed down to them from the apostles. As Basil expressed it, 'We are bound to be baptised in the terms we have received and to profess belief in the terms in which we have been baptised.'[9] Thus explicit assertion of the clause on the Spirit filled out the Church's understanding of the Godhead, and gave centrality to the doctrine of the divine Τριάς or *Trinity*. It reinforced the

---

[7] See Is. 11.1ff; 42.1ff; 44.3; 48.16; 59.21; 61ff; 63.7ff, etc.
[8] Cf. K. L. Schmidt, 'Das Pneuma Hagion als Person und als Charisma', *Eranos Jahrbuch*, 1945 (XIII), pp. 190ff; and A. I. C. Heron, *The Holy Spirit*, 1983, pp. 1–60.
[9] Basil, *Ep.*, 125.3.

teaching of the New Testament that God *is* Spirit and is truly known and worshipped as such, for *Spirit* is the specific nature of God's eternal being (οὐσία), whether as Father, Son or Holy Spirit, and therefore that Father, Son and Holy Spirit in themselves and their interrelations are to be understood and expressed only in an essentially *spiritual* way.

The effect of the doctrine of the Spirit on the doctrine of the Father and the Son may be discerned in the statement of Athanasius that while Christ is the only Εἶδος or 'Form' or 'Image' of Godhead, the Spirit is the Εἶδος or 'Image' of the Son.[10] The idea that the Spirit is the 'Image' of the Son may be rather puzzling until it is realised that the Spirit himself is *imageless*. This implies that, since the Father and the Son and the Holy Spirit are of one and the same nature,[11] it must be in an *ineffable*, *imageless* and wholly *spiritual* way that we are to think of them and of their relations with one another in the Holy Trinity.[12] In order to perceive him, Epiphanius once said, we must use our ears rather than our eyes, for we know him only through his Word and see him only with the mind,[13] for 'God is Spirit', who may be known only through Christ the living Word and the one Form or Image of the invisible God.[14]

In the second chapter it was pointed out that when divine revelation employs the terms 'Father' and 'Son' of God, we have to think of them as referring *imagelessly* to the Father and the Son, without the intrusion of creaturely images or material forms of thought.[15] It is by linking together in our minds the

[10]See *Con. Ar.*, 3.6, 10; *Ad Ser.*, 1.19f; cf. Didymus, *De Trin.*, 2.5, 11, and John of Damascus, *De fide*, 1.13.

[11]Cf. Cyril of Jer., *Cat.*, 16.3: 'The one Father, the one Son, and the one Spirit belong essentially and inseparably together.'

[12]Cf. Eusebius, *De eccl. theol.*, 1.12; Gregory Naz., *Or.*, 24.4; 28.12; 29.2, 8; 30.17; 31.7, 33; Basil, *Hom.*, 111; Cyril of Jer., *Cat.*, 11.11, 19; Epiphanius, *Haer.*, 70.5.

[13]Epiphanius, *Haer.*, 70.4–8.

[14]Cf. Ps. Athanasius, *Con. Sabellianos*, 5ff (*MPG*, 28.105f) which is evidently a variation on Basil's *Homily* 111.

[15]See Athanasius, *Con. Ar.*, 1.15, 21; *De decr.*, 24; *De syn.*, 42 & 51. See Basil, *Con. Eun.*, 2.16; *De Sp. St.*, 15, 84; Gregory Nyss., *Con. Eun.*, II.6, 4; Didymus, *De Sp. St.*, 57. In fact imagelessness is implied by the concept of God as 'Light' as well as 'Spirit' – cf. Athanasius, *Ad Ser.*, 1.19, 30; Basil, *De Sp. St.*, 47. 64; Epiphanius, *Haer.*, 70.5, etc.

imaging of the Father by the Son and the imaging of the Son by the Spirit, that we are enabled to refer images taken from our human relationships to the Godhead in a spiritual and not in a material or creaturely way.[16] The Son is of the being of God in the same sense as the Spirit, and the Spirit is of the being of God in the same sense as the Son. Thus the doctrine of the *homoousion* of the Spirit, with its unequivocal assertion of the Deity of the Holy Spirit, that emerged in this period between Nicaea and Constantinople,[17] helped the Church to grasp more appropriately and more spiritually, and therefore more adequately, the *homoousion* of the Son to the Father and indeed the ultimate relations of being within the Holy Trinity. It was as such that the doctrine of the Holy Spirit was brought to full dogmatic expression within the trinitarian faith of the Church, with as firm a place in the mind of the Church as the doctrine of the Son.[18]

This was a basic point that Athanasius pressed home in his synodal letter of 369 (to which we have already referred), in view of the semi-Arian denial of the Deity of the Spirit. 'For this synod of Nicaea is in truth a proscription of every heresy. It also upsets those who blaspheme the Holy Spirit, and call him a creature. For the fathers, after speaking of the faith in the Son, immediately added: "And we believe in the Holy Spirit", in order that by confessing perfectly and fully the faith in the Holy Trinity they might make known the exact form of the faith of Christ, and the teaching of the Catholic Church. For it is clear both among you and among all, and no Christian can have a doubtful mind on this point, that our faith is not in a creature, but in one God, Father Almighty, Maker of all things visible and invisible: and in one Lord Jesus Christ his only begotten Son, and in one Holy Spirit: one God, known in the holy and perfect Trinity, baptised into whom, and in him united to the Deity, we believe that we have inherited the kingdom of the heavens, in Christ Jesus our Lord, through whom to the Father

---

[16]This would also prevent any 'silly' transference of male or female gender into Deity – Gregory Naz., *Or.*, 31.7.

[17]Cf. Epiphanius, *Anc.*, 7, 46, 69f; *Haer.*, 69.17f, 32f; 74.6, etc.

[18]See Didymus, *De Trin.*, 2.6ff; Epiphanius, *Haer.*, 73.15ff, 24f, 34f, and especially the long refutation of the 'Pneumatomachians', 74.1–14.

be the glory and the power for ever and ever.'[19]

At the Council of Nicaea itself, as Basil and Epiphanius pointed out,[20] there had been no controversy with regard to the Holy Spirit, for in the context of the ongoing evangelical and doxological life and faith of the Church, the Holy Spirit was inseparably associated with the Father and the Son in praise and worship as the divine Source of salvation and renewal.[21] When controversy did break out after 350, however, the assertion that the Holy Spirit is really a creature was denounced by Athanasius as a subversion of the foundations of the faith, for it divided the Holy Trinity and undermined holy baptism, and he appealed, not only to the tradition of the Catholic Church, but to the biblical and apostolic message that lay behind it which he set himself to clarify.[22] It was only after clear knowledge of the Father and of the Son had been given, as Gregory Nazianzen was later to say, that in the economy of God's self-revelation the Deity of Holy Spirit indwelling the Church was becoming clearly known, and worship of God the Father, God the Son, and God the Holy Spirit, was clarified as that of three Persons, one Godhead.[23]

Of primary importance in the tradition of the Church was the record in the Gospel according to St Matthew of the command given by the risen Christ to the whole Church to baptise in the name of the Father, Son and Holy Spirit, which looks back to the actual baptism of Jesus himself in the river Jordan, when he was acknowledged by the Father as his beloved Son, with the descent of the Holy Spirit upon him anointing him as the Christ. Within the New Testament, however, there were triadic formulae which entered into the central stream of the apostolic faith and message, worship and tradition, and which were spelled out in the theology of the early Church. Of special theological significance were three explicit formulae:

[19]Athanasius, *Ad Afr.*, 11; see *Ad Ant.*, 3; and Epiphanius, *Haer.*, 73.34.
[20]Basil, *Ep.*, 125, 159.2, 226.3; *Ep. ad Epiph.*, 258.2; Epiphanius, *Haer.*, 74.14.
[21]Hence the stress upon μία δοξολογία, as with Epiphanius, *Anc.*, 24; *Haer.*, 62.3, 8; 69.29, 33, 56, 75; 74.14; 76. *Ref. Aet.*, 10, 21, 30; *Exp. fidei*, 17, etc.
[22]Athanasius, *Ad Ser.*, 1.1–33; cf. Epiphanius, *Anc.*, 65ff & *Haer.*, 74.2ff.
[23]Gregory Naz., *Or.*, 34.26–28.

(1) The baptismal formula, Matthew 28.19: 'In the name of the Father, and of the Son and of the Holy Spirit'.

(2) The familiar benediction from 2 Cor. 13.14: 'The grace of the Lord Jesus Christ, and the love of God and the communion of the Holy Spirit, be with you all.'

(3) Then the passage from 1 Cor. 12.4–6, much discussed in the early Church: 'There are diversities of gifts, but the same Spirit; and there are diversities of administrations, but the same Lord; and there are diversities of operations, but it is the same God who works all in all.'

Karl Ludwig Schmidt in our day, like Gregory Nazianzen and Didymus in the fourth century, has called attention to the fact that in these three formulae there is a variation in the order in which 'Father', 'Son' and 'Holy Spirit' appear.[24] The fact that 'Father', 'Son', and 'Holy Spirit' are each mentioned first seems to indicate that the order used does not detract from full equality between the three divine Persons. While in the regular liturgy of the Church, the Father comes first, as in the rite of holy baptism, in the benediction as in the evangelical message of the Church, widely reflected in the post-apostolic period, as Oscar Cullmann has pointed out,[25] it is the Son who is mentioned first, for faith in God the Father and in God the Holy Spirit was regarded as a function of, and included within, faith in Jesus Christ as Saviour and Lord. In the spiritual life and service of members of the Church, however, the immediate focus is upon the gifts and operations of the Spirit. While this variation was recognised by Athanasius, and was certainly in accord with his understanding of Christian faith and life, he nevertheless warned, in the face of Sabellian heresy, against changing the order in which the Persons of the Trinity are mentioned in holy baptism.[26]

There are, however, other triadic formulations in the New Testament which had their measure of impact in pre-Nicene

[24]K. L. Schmidt, *op. cit.*, pp. 215f. See Gregory Naz., *Or.*, 36.15; and Didymus, *De Trin.*, 1.18, who puts this down to the indivisible nature of the divine Persons and the indifference of their order.

[25]O. Cullmann, *Early Christian Confessions.*

[26]Athanasius, *Ad Ser.*, 4.5. Also Basil, *Ep.*, 125.3.

and post-Nicene theological development of the apostolic message and tradition.[27] Notably the following:

> (1) Acts 2.32f: 'This Jesus God raised up, and of that we are all witnesses. Being therefore exalted at the right hand of God, and having received from the Father the promise of the Holy Spirit, he has poured out this which you see and hear.'
>
> (2) 1 Peter 1.2: 'Chosen and destined by God the Father and sanctified by the Spirit for obedience to Jesus Christ and for sprinkling with his blood: May grace and peace be multiplied to you.'
>
> (3) 2 Thess. 2.13f: 'But we are bound to give thanks to God always for you, brethren beloved by the Lord, because God chose you from the beginning to be saved, through sanctification by the Spirit and belief in the truth. To this he called you through our gospel, so that you may obtain the glory of our Lord Jesus Christ.'
>
> (4) Ephesians 2.18: 'For through him (Christ Jesus) we both have access in one Spirit to the Father.'
>
> (5) Ephesians 4.4–6: 'There is one body and one Spirit, just as you were called in one hope that belongs to your call, one Lord, one faith, one baptism, one God and Father of us all, who is above all and through all and in all. But grace was given to each of us according to the measure of Christ's gift.'

That is to say, the message of the Gospel as handed on by the apostolic tradition, is one in which the Father, the Son and the Holy Spirit together belong to the essential faith and experience of the Church as it is rooted and grounded in Christ. Witness is borne to this trinitarian belief in the earliest surviving hymns after apostolic times, such as the morning hymn Δόξα ἐν ὑψίστοις Θεῷ found in the *Codex Alexandrinus* appended to the Psalter,[28] and the evening hymn Φῶς ἱλαρὸν ἁγίας δόξης

---

[27] See K. L. Schmidt, *op. cit.*, pp. 209f, 216ff.

[28] Also *Apost. Const.*, 7.47: 'Glory to God in the highest ... God Father Almighty, Lord only begotten Son, Jesus Christ, and Holy Spirit, Lord and God.' Refer to Epiphanius, *Haer.*, 74.10.

mentioned by Basil.[29] The universality of this trinitarian outlook is evident also from other early writings as well.[30] The Nicene theologians found that this biblical witness to Father, Son and Holy Spirit already embodies triadic or trinitarian understanding of the one being of God and in fact cannot be properly grasped without or apart from a doctrine of the Trinity. Indeed a definite doctrine of the Trinity was found to arise out of faithful exegetical interpretation of the New Testament and out of the evangelical experience and liturgical life of the Church from the very beginning. It made explicit what was already implicit in the fundamental deposit of faith.[31] It was with the formulation of the *homoousion* clarifying and expressing the essential connection of the Son to the Father upon which the very Gospel rested, and with the application of the *homoousion* to the Holy Spirit to express his oneness in being with the Godhead of the Father, that the theological structure of the trinitarian understanding of the Godhead unfolded and established itself firmly within the mind of the Church. The concept of consubstantiality carried within it also the concept of the coinherence of the three divine Persons in the one identical being of God.[32] That is to say, through the *homoousion* the incarnational and saving self-revelation of God as Father, Son and Holy Spirit was traced back to what God is enhypostatically and coinherently in himself, in his own eternal being as Father, Son and Holy Spirit.[33]

[29]Basil, *De Sp. St.*, 73: 'We hymn Father and Son and Holy Spirit Divine'.

[30]See *Didache*, 7.1; Ignatius, *Magn.*, 13.1; *Polc. martyr.*, 14.3; Justin Martyr, *Apol.*, 1.6, 13, 61, 65; Athenagoras, *Leg.*, 6, 10, 12, 24; Irenaeus, *Adv. haer.*, 1.2ff, vol. 1, p. 90ff; 3.1f, 4, vol. 2, pp. 22ff; 4.1f, pp. 146ff; 4.53.1, p. 261f; 5.20.1f, pp. 377f; *Dem.*, 5f; Hippolytus, *Apost. Trad.*, 3, 8, 21; Novatian, *De Trin.*, 7, 16, 29f; Tertullian, *Adv. Prax.*, 2–5, 8f, 11ff, 25, 30, etc.; Origen, *De prin.*, 1.3.5, 7f; 4.2f; 6.2; 2.2.2; 3.5.8; 4.3.14f; 4.1, 3; *In Jn.*, 2.6; 6.17, etc.

[31]This was evidently the intention behind the gloss found in some Vulgate MSS upon 1 John 5.6f which was made to read: 'There are three that bear witness in heaven, the Father, the Word and the Spirit, and these three are one; there are three that bear witness on earth, the Spirit, the water and the blood, and these three agree in one.'

[32]See Athanasius, *Ad Ser.*, 1.27; 2.3, 5; 3.1; Epiphanius, *Haer.*, 63.6; 65.1ff; 74.12; 76.2; 76.35; *Exp. fidei*, 14.

[33]Athanasius, *Con. Ar.*, 3.1ff; Epiphanius, *Anc.*, 2–7, 10, 67, 72, 81; *Haer.*, 62.1ff; 64.9; 72.11; 73.20; 74.9, 11ff; 76.30; 77.22; Gregory Naz., *Or.*, 29.16, 20;

Following upon the Council of Nicaea, in the process of the continuing struggle against Arianism, which remained rampant largely due to the political theologians of those days, it became evident that denial of Deity to the Son entailed denial of Deity to the Spirit. The Spirit and the Son were so deeply intertwined in the message of the Gospel that acceptance of the full Deity of the Son carried with it acceptance of the full Deity of the Spirit, so that the traditional recognition of the Holy Spirit as Lord had to be given theological formulation parallel to that of the Son. This explains in part why formally the doctrine of the Spirit developed from the doctrine of the Son.[34] In this context, however, what was primary was once again the evangelical faith and the doxological approach of the Church in the response of worship and prayer to the holy and saving presence of God through Christ and in the Spirit – access to the Father through Christ and in one Spirit. This is the aspect of post-Nicene doctrine that we have most clearly set forth in the *De Spiritu Sancto* of Basil of Caesarea.[35] The theologians then proceeded to give credal expression to agreed convictions about the Holy Spirit which paralleled those which Nicaea had formulated about the Son in his relation to God the Father, for it became clear that the truth and effectiveness of the Gospel rest not only on the oneness in being and agency between the incarnate Son and God the Father but on the oneness in being and agency between the Spirit and both the Son and the Father. Thus Cyril of Jerusalem taught his catechumens: 'Believe also in the Holy Spirit, and hold concerning him the same opinion which has been delivered to you concerning the Father and the Son ... with the Father and the Son he is exalted with the glory of the Godhead.'[36]

31.10; *Schol.*, *MPG*, 36.911; cf. Gregory's defence of Basil against the charge of 'economising the truth' regarding the Deity of the Spirit, *Ep.*, 58; *Or.*, 43.68.

[34]Athanasius, *Ad Ser.*, 3.1ff.

[35]Basil appealed for support in his views to Irenaeus, Clement, Origen and Dionysius of Alexandria – *De Sp. St.*, 72.

[36]Cyril of Jer., *Cat.*, 4.16. Thus also Amphilochius, *Ep. syn.*, 2. Cf. the Byzantine Liturgy (F. E. Brightman, *Eastern Liturgies*, p. 382): 'Let us love one another that we may confess with one mind, the Father, the Son and Holy Spirit, Trinity consubstantial and undivided.' And the Roman adaptation of

It was with Athanasius, Basil, Gregory Nazianzen, and Epiphanius, particularly, that a more rigorous theological formulation of faith in the Holy Spirit took place.[37] Athanasius' approach to the doctrine of the Spirit was entirely consistent with his approach to the doctrine of the Son or Logos of God. In accordance with the teaching of the New Testament, he turned sharply away from any conception of the Logos as a cosmological principle (or of λόγοι σπερματικοί, 'seminal reasons', immanent in the universe) occupying an intermediate status between God and creation. Likewise Athanasius would have nothing to do with any attempt to reach an understanding of the Spirit beginning from manifestations or operations of the Spirit in creaturely existence, in man or in the world. Instead, as we shall see, he took his controlling point of reference from what he called 'the propriety' of the Spirit to God on the divine side of the line dividing between the Creator and the creature, and therefore from the inner relation of the Son to the one being of the Godhead. The Holy Spirit no less than the Son is the *self-giving* of God: in him the Gift and the Giver are identical.[38] Precisely because the Holy Spirit *is* the Spirit of the Father and of the Son, Athanasius developed the doctrine of the Spirit from his essential relation to the one God and his undivided co-activity with the Father and the Son, and specifically from his inherence in the being of the eternal Son. The Spirit is not outside the being of the Word or Son but inherent in him as he is inherent in God the Father, and as the Father is in him, and so through the Son the Spirit is inherent in the Father. 'The Holy and Blessed Trinity is indivisible and one in himself. When mention is made of the Father, there is included also his Word

---

the *Gloria* (C. E. Hammond, *Liturgies Eastern and Western*, p. 296): 'Lord God, Lamb of God, Son of the Father ... you alone are holy, you alone are Lord, you alone, O Christ, with the Holy Spirit, are most high in the glory of the Father.'

[37] Refer to Athanasius, *Ad Ser.*; Basil, *De Sp. St.*, & *Con. Eun.*, 3; Gregory Naz., *Or.*, 31, 37, 41; Gregory Nys., *De Sp. St.*, *De Trin.*, *Con. Eun.*, 1; and Epiphanius, *Anc.*, 65ff, *Haer.*, 74. See *Theol. in Reconstr.*, pp. 209–258; *Theol. in Reconcil.*, pp. 231–9; and also T. C. Campbell, 'The Doctrine of the Holy Spirit in the Theology of Athanasius', *SJT*, vol. 27, 1974. pp. 408–440.

[38] Athanasius, *Ad Ser.*, 1.30; 3.1, 16; cf. Cyril of Jer., *Cat.*, 16.24.

and the Spirit who is in the Son. If the Son is named, the Father is in the Son, and the Spirit is not outside the Word. For there is from the Father one grace which is fulfilled through the Son in the Holy Spirit; and there is one divine nature and one God "who is over all and through all and in all" '.[39] 'The Father does all things through the Word and in the Holy Spirit. Thus the unity of the Holy Trinity is preserved.'[40] Since the activity of the Trinity is one, the operations of the Spirit are not to be regarded in any way as on a lower level than that of the Father or of the Son, for they are all operations in the one God and from the one God.[41] Thus it is understandable that in the order of Athanasius' development of formulated doctrine, controlled knowledge of the Spirit is taken from controlled knowledge of the Son and of the Father through the Son.[42]

The doctrine of the Holy Spirit is derived, therefore, not merely from biblical statements, nor from doxological formulae alone, but from the supreme truth that God reveals himself through himself, and therefore that *God himself* is the content of his revelation through the Son and in the Spirit.[43] That is to say, far from being an extraneous intrusion, the doctrine of the Spirit was developed naturally and properly out of the inner structure of knowledge of the one God grounded in his *self*-revelation and *self*-communication as Father, Son and Holy Spirit. That is the structure that was brought into light at the Council of Nicaea through the formulation of the *homoousion* of the Son. All that remained to be done after Nicaea was to show that this approach applied equally to the doctrine of the Holy Spirit sent from the Father through the Son, and so Athanasius had little hesitation in applying the term ὁμοούσιος to the Spirit as well as to the Son.[44] And here he was followed by other post-Nicene theologians, particularly by Didymus,[45]

---

[39] Athanasius, *Ad Ser.*, 1.14 & Ephesians 4.6; see also *Ad Ser.*, 1.20f; 3.5
[40] Athanasius, *Ad Ser.*, 1.28.
[41] Athanasius, *Ad Ser.*, 1.31.
[42] Athanasius, *Ad Ser.*, 1.2, 20; 3.1–5; 4.4, 17, etc.
[43] Athanasius, *Ad Ser.*, 1.31–33.
[44] Athanasius, *Ad Ser.*, 1.2, 27; 3.1; cf. *Ad Jov.*, 1, 4.
[45] Didymus, *De Trin.*, 1.19; 1.33f; 1.36; 2.4; 2.6.6; 2.6.15; 2.6.22; 2.13; 2.25f; 3.1.2; 3.2.35, 46; 3.12.25f; 3.18; *De Sp. St.*, 17.

Evagrius,[46] Gregory Nazianzen,[47] and Epiphanius.[48] Moreover, since the Father, Son and Holy Spirit are one perfect, indivisible Godhead,[49] it was natural that the term ὁμοούσιος should come to be applied to the Trinity as a whole.[50]

It was clear to these theologians, however, that it is only in and through the Son, the one and only Son, that the εἶδος of Godhead is made known, for it is specifically in Jesus Christ, the incarnate Son, that God has communicated himself to us creaturely human beings within the conditions and structures of our earthly existence and knowledge. Thus it is only in him who is both ὁμοούσιος with the Father and ὁμοούσιος with us, that we may really know God as he is in himself and in accordance with his nature. But it is on that ground, the same ground where we know the Father through the Son, that we may also know the Spirit, for it is in the Spirit sent to us by the Father through the Son that knowledge of God is mediated and actualised within us.[51] Thus knowledge of the Spirit as well as of the Father is taken from and is controlled by knowledge of the Son.[52] The Holy Spirit does not bring to us any independent knowledge of God, or add any new content to God's self-revelation.[53] He comes to us as the Spirit of the Father and of the Son, revealing the Father in the Son and the Son in the Father, and thus as himself God through whom God reveals himself. 'The holy and blessed Trinity is indivisible and one in himself. When mention is made of the Father, there is included also his Word, and the Spirit who is in the Son. If the Son is named, the Father is in the Son, and the Spirit is not outside the Word.'[54]

[46]Evagrius/Basil, *Ep.*, 8.10f.

[47]Gregory Naz., *Or.*, 31.10.

[48]Epiphanius, *Anc.*, 6, 74, 120; *Haer.*, 73.34f; 74.12; 76.11, 16.

[49]Athanasius, *Ad Ser.*, 1.33.

[50]Thus Didymus, *De Trin.*, 1.17f; 1.34; 1.36; 2.1; 2.4; 2.6.9; 2.14; 2.18; *De Sp. St.*, 7; Basil, *De fide*, 4; Amphilochius, *Fragm.*, 13, *MPG*, 39.111; Epiphanius, *Anc.*, 2, 5–7, 74; *Haer.*, 57.4; 72.1; 74.14; 86.16; *Exp. fidei*, 14; Theodoret, *Hist. eccl.*, 5.9.11; Cyril of Jer., *Ep. ad Const.*, 8; Ps. Macarius, *Hom.*, 17.15.

[51]Epiphanius, *Haer.*, 73.15f; 74.4ff, 10, 13f; 76. *Ref. Aet.*, 7, 29; 86.32; *Anc.*, 19. 67ff, 72f.

[52]See *Theol. in Reconstr.*, p. 213f; *God and Rationality*, pp. 165ff.

[53]Athanasius, *Ad Ser.*, 3.1ff.

[54]Athanasius, *Ad Ser.*, 1.14.

Knowledge of the Father, knowledge of the Son, and knowledge of the Holy Spirit cannot be separated from one another, for God is known only through the one movement of self-revelation from the Father, through the Son and in the Holy Spirit. It was with this understanding of the oneness of God's triadic revelation of himself through himself that Athanasius found it intrinsically and conceptually necessary to apply the Nicene *homoousion* to the relation of the Spirit to God the Son and of the Spirit to God the Father.

The Nicene doctrine of the Spirit was given further emphasis or content in two different directions or respects in the period between the Councils of Nicaea and Constantinople. First, in relation to the holy sacraments or mysteries. This is the aspect of the doctrine of the Spirit that had been developed by Cyril of Jerusalem in his famous *Catecheses*, especially 4, 16, & 17. And secondly, in relation to ascetical theology and the doxological tradition of the Church. This is the teaching presented by Basil of Caesarea, in his *De Spiritu Sancto*, in which he sought to show that the oneness of the doxology ascribed by the Church to the Father, Son and Holy Spirit points to a transcendent oneness of nature and being in the communion of the Godhead. The Holy Spirit was thus to be regarded by the Church as 'completing the blessed and adorable Trinity'.[55] With this understanding shared by the Cappadocian and Alexandrian theologians the decisive affirmations about the Holy Spirit were evidently made by Epiphanius of Constantia (or Salamis, as it was known in the New Testament) in the *Anchoratus* of 374 A.D., in which the various clauses of the Nicene-Constantinopolitan Creed were clearly anticipated.[56] It was this Athanasian doctrine and tradition mediated mainly through Epiphanius (not forgetting

[55]Basil, *De Sp. St.*, 45; cf. *Hex.*, 2.6, and *Ep.*, 243, where Basil refers to the Holy Spirit as συμπληρωτικὸν τῆς Ἁγίας Τριάδος and κοινωνὸν τῆς θείας καὶ μακαρίας φύσεως; and to Athanasius, *Ad Ser.*, 1.25.

[56]Epiphanius, *Anc.*, 119–120; cf. also *Anc.*, 2–11, 67; *Exp. fidei*, 14ff. Compared with these formulations, the credal statements of Cyril of Jerusalem, to which some scholars trace the Creed of Constantinople, are relatively slight. But refer to the long discussion by J. N. D. Kelly, *Early Christian Creeds*, 1950, pp. 297ff, 338ff.

Didymus, Gregory Nazianzen and Basil) that evidently influenced the formulations of Constantinople in 381 A.D.[57]

II

We must now probe into the main features of this Nicene-Constantinopolitan doctrine of the Spirit and offer an interpretative account of them.

(1) God is Spirit and the Holy Spirit is God

The inclusion in the Creed of the clauses on the Holy Spirit tells us two main things at once: that the very nature of God as God is *Spirit*, and that *the* Spirit with the Father and the Son belongs to the eternal being and inner life of the Godhead.[58]

In the Holy Scriptures and in the writings of the Church fathers, the word 'spirit' was often used in an absolute sense of God, in respect of his infinite, transcendent, invisible, immaterial, immutable nature, in sharp contrast to the contingent, transient and limited nature of creaturely beings.[59] Spirit characterises what God is in himself, in the boundless perfection of his holy being, but it also characterises what God is in his limitless freedom toward every thing that is not God, in bringing it into being out of nothing, in sustaining it in creaturely relation to himself, and in sovereign interaction with it.[60] 'God is Spirit'.[61] In this absolute sense, 'Spirit' simply refers to Deity, without distinction of Persons, and is equally

[57]Compare the Athanasian *Tomus ad Antiochenos*, 3.5, 11, emanating from the Council of Alexandria in 362, and the synodal Letter from the Council of Constantinople in 382, *ap.* Theodoret, *Hist. eccl.*, 5.9; and see H. B. Swete, *The Holy Spirit in the Ancient Church*, pp. 210–229.

[58]Athanasius, *Con. Ar.*, 3.15, 24; *Ad Ser.*, 1.11–14, 17, 22, 24–28; 3.1–5; 4.3, 6f; *Ad Jov.*, 1.4; *Ad Afr.*, 11.

[59]E.g., Isaiah 31.3; 51.11.

[60]E.g., Psalm 104.29–30.

[61]John 4.24.

applicable to the Father, the Son and the Holy Spirit.[62] 'God is Spirit, Spirit beyond all spirit and Light beyond all light.'[63] Hence when Christ as the Son or Word of God was sometimes spoken of as 'Spirit', it was meant, not to equate him with the Holy Spirit, but to designate his divine nature.[64] It was thus that Gregory Nazianzen could speak of the anointing of the incarnate Son with the Spirit, as his being anointed 'with his own Deity'.[65]

This application of the word 'Spirit' in an absolute sense to Father, Son and Holy Spirit, must not be understood to rule out distinction between the Persons (ὑποστάσεις) of the Father, Son and Holy Spirit, for it was meant to designate the nature of the one being (οὐσία) of the Godhead which they have in common.[66] As Athanasius pointed out to Serapion, when reference is made in the Scriptures to the Holy Spirit, distinguishing him from the Father and the Son, the word 'Spirit' is always qualified with some particularising expression such as 'of God', 'of the Father', 'of the Son', or as 'the Spirit' or 'Holy Spirit',[67] yet in such a way that the Persons of the Father, Son and Holy Spirit are never separated in being or activity, for the Holy and blessed Trinity is intrinsically one and indivisible.[68] However, the definite place given in the Church's confession of faith to the Holy Spirit as inhering and coinhering with the Father and the Son in one indivisible Godhead,[69] emphasises the conviction that in his eternal nature *God is*

---

[62]See Origen, *De prin.*, I.1–4; Eusebius, *De eccl. theol.*, 3.5; Gregory Nyss., *Ant. con. Eun.*, 2.14, Jaeger, vol. 2, p. 389; Cyril of Jer., *Cat.*, 11.5ff; 17.34; Epiphanius, *Haer.*, 73.16–18; 74.7; *Anc.*, 70; Didymus, *De Trin.*, 2.5.

[63]Epiphanius, *Haer.*, 70.5.

[64]See Athenagoras, *Leg.*, 10; Theophilus, *Ad Aut.*, 2.10; Tertullian, *Adv. Prax.*, 26f; *Apol.*, 23; Adamantius, *Dial.*, 5.11; Hilary, *De Trin.*, 2.24, 26; 8.23f; 9.3, 14; Gregory Naz., *Or.*, 38.13; Ep. 101; Amphilochius, *ap.* Theodoret, *Dial.*, 1, *MPG*, 83.99, etc.

[65]Gregory Naz., *Or.*, 10.4; 30.21; see also Athanasius, *Con. Ar.*, 1.46; 4.36; *Con. Apol.*, 2.3.

[66]Epiphanius, *Anc.*, 73; *Haer.*, 62.1ff; 69.53; 74.10.

[67]Athanasius, *Ad Ser.*, 1.4–7; see Cyril of Jer., *Cat.*, 16.3; 17.4.

[68]Athanasius, *Ad Ser.*, 1.14, 20, 27f; 30f; 3.5f; 4.7; *Con. Ar.*, 3.15, etc. Cf. Basil, *Hom.*, 111.4–6.

[69]For this concept of coinherence see Hilary, *De Trin.*, 3.1–4.

Spirit,[70] and therefore that he is to be known and thought of by us in a reverent and spiritual way without the crude use of creaturely or material images.[71]

In utter differentiation from all created nature, the nature of God is so incomparable with anything we know, that it is not fitting for us to ask human questions about the Godhead – God may be known, not from without, but only from what he is within himself.[72] The doctrine of the Spirit thus raised again an epistemological issue that had come to the fore earlier in the century when Arians operated with the principle that what they could not humanly conceive could not be.[73] That is to say, they equated the limits of their understanding with the limits of reality, and thereby laid down conditions for their understanding of God and their interpretation of divine revelation.[74] It became increasingly evident to the Nicene theologians, however, that all such ways of thought shattered themselves upon the transcendent Lordship of the Holy Spirit which means that God can be known only through and out of himself.[75] Thus the questions we ask of God are turned back upon ourselves, for the Holy Spirit stands for 'the unconditionality and irreversibility of the Lordship of God in his revelation'.[76]

It is clear that without the Spirit the doctrine of God would not stand as a coherent whole in our faith.[77] On the other hand,

[70]Eusebius, *Hist. eccl.*, 3.5; Athanasius, *Con. Ar.*, 2.33, 41; 3.1–6; *De decr.*, 26; *Ad Ser.*, 1.26; Cyril of Jerusalem, *Cat.*, 17.34; Basil, *De Sp. St.*, 9.22, 25, 53; Gregory Nyss., *Con. Eun.*, 2.14; cf. Origen, *In Jn.*, 13.21f; Novatian, *De Trin.*, 5ff; Tertullian, *Adv. Prax.*, 26; Hilary, *De Trin.*, 2.26; 3.4; 4.6.

[71]Athanasius, *Ad Ser.*, 1.17–25.

[72]Athanasius, *Ad Ser.*, 1.15, 18; 4.2–5; *Con. Ar.*, 1.15, 20ff, 57; 2.36; Gregory Naz. *Or.*, 30.20; 31.7; Hilary, *De Trin.*, 2.29ff; 4.1; 5.20f.

[73]Basil had to deal with the same kind of questioning on the part of Eunomius, in which he presupposed that what he could not measure by human comprehension or understand by reasoning is wholly non-existent – *Con. Eun.*, 2.24.

[74]Hilary, *De Trin.*, 1.13, 15, 3.1, 20, etc.

[75]See Hilary, *De Trin.*, 12.55f.

[76]Thus Karl Barth in his account of the Nicene doctrine of the Spirit – *C.D.*, 1.1, pp. 468f.

[77]Hilary, *De Trin.*, 2.29: 'The Spirit is joined with the Father and the Son in our confession of faith and cannot be excluded from a true confession of the

the inclusion of the doctrine of the Holy Spirit in the doctrine of the triune God means that the Spirit is to be understood not from some external relation but from his unique *internal* relation to the Father.[78] It will be remembered that for Athanasius the devout and accurate way to know God is not from his works of creation which are external to him, but from his eternal Son for that is to know him as he really is in himself in accordance with his divine nature as Father.[79] Likewise the devout and accurate way to know the Holy Spirit is not by beginning with manifestations or operations of the Spirit in creaturely existence which is external to God but from the propriety of the Spirit to the eternal being of God, as the Spirit of the Father and the Son, and thus from his *internal* relations within the Godhead.[80]

This is an approach that was carried further by Epiphanius. Just as we know the Father and the Son only from within their mutual relation of knowing and being, and as through the Spirit that knowledge of God by himself is revealed to us, so we may know the Spirit of the Father and the Son only as he dwells in us and brings us into the communion of the Holy Trinity. That is to say, our approach to the doctrine of the Holy Spirit must be from his inner '*enhypostatic*' relation to the triune being of God.[81] The emphasis here was undoubtedly upon the objectivity of the Spirit, for even while we partake of the Spirit of God through his dwelling in us, that is an objective inwardness grounded in the mutual indwelling of the Father, Son and Spirit in the Godhead. As Athanasius expressed it: 'Our being in the Father is not ours, but is the Spirit's who is in us and dwells in us . . . It is the Spirit who is in God, and not we viewed in our own selves.'[82] For us to be in the Spirit or to have the Spirit dwelling in us means that we are made partakers of God beyond ourselves, and even share in the inwardness of God

---

Father and the Son – take away a part and the whole faith is marred.' Cf. H. B. Swete with reference to Athanasius, *op. cit.*, p. 220.

[78] Athanasius, *Con. Ar.*, 3.3–6, 24f; *Ad Ser.*, 1.14, 25; 3.5f; 4.3f.

[79] Athanasius, *De decr.*, 30f; *Con. Ar.*, 1.33f.

[80] Athanasius, *Con. Ar.*, 3.15, 24f; *Ad Ser.*, 1.25; 3.5.

[81] Epiphanius, *Haer.*, 57.4f; 62.1f, 6; 74.9ff; 72.22; *Anc.*, 5, 10f, 67f, 72, 81; cf. Didymus, *De Trin.*, 3.37–38; Cyril of Jer., *Cat.*, 6.6; 7.11; 16.1ff; 17.1ff.

[82] Athanasius, *Con. Ar.*, 3.24–25.

himself – a concept which we shall discuss below.[83] The Nicene theologians could not forget that the Spirit dwells in us only as he who utterly transcends all creaturely existence, so that they could only think of the Holy Spirit dwelling in them by thinking of themselves as dwelling in God, for, as Athanasius argued, 'the Holy Spirit is partaken but does not partake'.[84]

Regarded in this way, from his internal relation to the Godhead, the Holy Spirit is to be understood as the presence to us of the Lord God in the full reality of his divine life and being – the presence to us of the Holy Spirit is the immediate presence of God Almighty and All-Holy, in his ultimate majesty, glory and power, in his sheer Deity, in his utter Godness and Holiness. The Holy Spirit, then, is none other than the living dynamic reality of God Almighty, the transcendent Lord of all being, from whom we derive our own being and existence, to whom we are altogether indebted, and before whom we can only prostrate ourselves in sheer wonder, adoration and worship. The godliness (εὐσέβεια) and reverence (εὐλάβεια) inspired in us and called forth from us by the Holy Spirit are reflected above all in the *Ad Serapionem* of Athanasius, who was clearly overcome with awe and astonishment at the fact that in sending to us his Spirit God has given us, not just something of himself, but his very Self. In the Lord the Giver of Life, God himself is the content of his giving. 'When the Holy Spirit is given to us ("Receive the Holy Spirit",[85] said the Saviour) *God is in us*; for so John wrote, "If we love one another, *God* dwells in us; hereby we know that we dwell in him and he in us, because he has given us of his Spirit."[86] But when *God* is in us, the Son also is in us. For the Son himself said, "The Father and I will come and make our dwelling with him."[87] Furthermore, as the Son is life – for he says "I am the life"[88] – we are said to be quickened by the Spirit.'[89] It is not merely his divine power or operation, but

[83]See *Theol. in Reconcil.*, pp. 231–239.
[84]Athanasius, *Ad Ser.*, 1.27 – see the whole argument from 1.23; and Gregory Naz., *Or.*, 41.9.
[85]John 20.22.
[86]1 John, 4.12f.
[87]John, 14.6.
[88]John 14.6.
[89]Athanasius, *Ad Ser.*, 1.19; cf. 1.20.

God himself, the almighty Creator, who is present to us in the sheer reality of his own transcendent being. Hence Didymus was clearly critical of a distinction between the energies or operations of God and the immediate activity of his being, such as was put forward by Basil,[90] for it would damage a proper understanding of the real presence of God to us in his Spirit.[91]

The Nicene theologians could not forget the word of the Lord Jesus which resounded throughout the early Church that, while evil-speaking against himself may be forgiven, blasphemy against the Holy Spirit will never be forgiven.[92] This had the effect of reinforcing in the Church veneration, adoration, and worship of the Spirit as very God, God in his unlimited Godness and majesty, God in his utter holiness, sublimity and lordship. Of one and the same being with the Father and the Son, the Holy Spirit is to be worshipped and glorified together with the Father and the Son, and to be confessed as God.[93] Hence the place of the *Trisagion* in the Christian liturgy directed to the Father, Son and Holy Spirit, echoing within the praises of the Church on earth the ceaseless hymn of angels and seraphim around the throne above.[94]

[90]Basil, *Ep.*, 234.1; cf. 235.2; 236.1ff; *Con. Eun.*, 2.32.

[91]Thus Didymus, *De Sp. St.*, 23ff, 60f; *De Trin.*, 2.6.7, could speak of the indwelling presence of the Holy Spirit as the presence of God *secundum substantiam*, and not merely *secundum operationem*. Contrast Basil, *Ep.*, 234.1–3; 235.2f; *Con. Eun.*, 1.14, 23; 2.32; *De obs. se*, 7, Athens ed., 54, p. 36; cf. Gregory Naz., *Or.*, 38.7. Athanasius, *De decr.*, 11, cannot be understood in this way. See further *Theol. in Reconst.*, pp. 210, 213f; *Theol. in Reconcil.*, pp. 235f; and E. L. Mascall, *Existence and Analogy*, 1949, pp. 148ff.

[92]Matt. 12.31f; Mark 3.28f; Luke 12.10 – see Athanasius, *Con. Ar.*, 1.50; *Ad Jov.*, 1; *Ad Afr.*, 11; *Ad Ser.*, 1.1f; 3.7; 3.8ff, 16ff, Athens ed., 33, p. 139f, 143ff; Basil, *De Sp. St.*, 46, 70, 75; *Hom.*, 111.5ff; *Con. Eun.*, 2.33; *Or.*, 35; *Ep.*, 152.3; 188.1; 251.4; Gregory Nyss., *De Sp. St.*, Jaeger, 3.1, p. 106f; Gregory Naz., *Or.*, 31.30; Didymus, *De Trin.*, 2.26; 3.2.54; 3.40; *De Sp. St.*, 1, 63; *Con. Eun.*, Athens ed., 44, p. 259; Amphilochius, *Con. haer.*, 17; *Ep. syn.*, 4; Epiphanius, *Anc.*, 69, 116; *Haer.*, 54.2; 74.6, 14; Cyril of Jer., *Cat.*, 4.16; 5.5; 16.1, 6, etc.

[93]Athanasius, *Ad Jov.*, 4; *Ad Ser.*, 1.31; Basil, *De Sp. St.*, 3, 26, 64, 73; *Ep.*, 90.2; 159.2; 258.2; Gregory Naz., *Or.*, 31.12, 28; Gregory Nyss., *De Sp. St.*, Jaeger, 3.1., pp. 92ff, 108ff; *Ep.*, 24; Amphilochius, *MPG*, 39.97B; Didymus, *De Trin.*, 2.21f; *Con. Eun.*, Athens ed., 44, pp. 245, 247; Epiphanius, *Anc.*, 70, 117, 119; *Haer.*, 70.6f; Cyril of Jer., *Cat.*, 4.16; 16.1ff.

[94]*Apost. Const.*, 8.12; Serapion, *Euch.*, 13, Athens ed., 43, p. 76; Basil, *Lit.*, Athens ed., 56, p. 28f (cf. Brightman, *op. cit.*, p. 402); *De Sp. St.*, 38; Gregory

Two distinctive implications of this approach to the doctrine of the Holy Spirit call for particular consideration.

On the one hand, the Holy Spirit guards the ultimate mystery and ineffability of God in virtue of the fact that while it is in the Spirit that we are confronted with the ultimate being and presence of God, he is not approachable in thought or knowable in himself.[95] The Holy Spirit is *Spirit,* not only in his being or οὐσία, which he has in common with the Father and the Son, but in his distinctive ὑπόστασις or personal mode of being as *the Spirit,* for in being named 'Holy Spirit' he is distinguished from the personal modes of being of the Father and the Son while perfectly ὁμοούσιος with them.[96] He is 'Spirit of Spirit, for God is Spirit (Πνεῦμα ἐκ Πνεύματος, Πνεῦμα γὰρ ὁ Θεός)'.[97] While the Father and the Son, whose being is Spirit, are revealed to us in their distinctive ὑποστάσεις as through the Spirit we are given to share in the knowing of the Son by the Father and of the Father by the Son, the Holy Spirit is not directly known in his own *hypostasis* for he remains veiled by the very revelation of the Father and the Son which he brings.[98] He is the invisible Spirit of truth sent from the Father in the name of the Son, not in his own personal name as the Holy Spirit, and thus does not speak of himself but speaks of the Father and of the Son what he receives from them.[99] He does not show us himself, and so the

Nyss., *Con. Eun.,* 1.23; Athanasius, *In ill. om.,* 6; Epiphanius, *Haer.,* 76. *Ref. Aet.,* 10; *Anc.,* 9, 26, 69; Didymus, *De Trin.,* 2.7, 19; Cyril of Jer., *Cat.,* 23.6; Gregory Naz., *Or.,* 34.13; 38.8; & 45.4: 'This then is the Holy of Holies, completely veiled by the seraphim, and glorified with a thrice-repeated 'holy' joined together in one ascription of Lordship and Deity.' Cited by John of Damascus, *De fide,* 3.10. Cf. also the discussion of Isaiah's vision, 6.1ff, in Ps. Athanasius, *De Trin. et Sp. St.,* 16 and *De Inc. et con. Ar.,* 10.

[95]Basil, *De Sp. St.,* 44, 53. Cf. 22: 'His proper and peculiar title is "Holy Spirit", which is a name specially appropriate to everything that is incorporeal, purely immaterial and indivisible.'

[96]Epiphanius, *Haer.,* 73.16, 25; 74.10ff; *Anc.,* 8, 72ff.

[97]Epiphanius, *Haer.,* 73.17; 74.7 – the corresponding passage in *Anc.,* 70, however, reads, Πνεῦμα ἐκ Πατρός, etc.

[98]See Didymus, *De Trin.,* 3.36ff; Epiphanius, *Anc.,* 6f, 10f, 67f, 73; Cyril of Jer., *Cat.,* 16.3, 5, 13, 24.

[99]John 14.16f, 25f; 15.26f; 16.13f. See Athanasius, *Ad Ser.,* 1.20; 3.1; *Con. Ar.,* 1.15; 3.44; Hilary, *De Trin.,* 7.20; 8.20; Didymus, *De Sp. St.,* 30–38; Cyril

world cannot receive him or know him.[100] He shows us the face of the Father in the Son, and shows us the face of the Son in the Father. Thus it could be said of the Holy Spirit that he is the Face of the Father, in that he makes the Face of the Father to be seen in the Son.[101] 'While there are three Persons really subsisting in God, there is but one εἶδος deriving from the Father, shining in the Son and becoming manifest through the Spirit.'[102] By his very mode of being as Spirit of Spirit he hides himself from us behind the Father in the Son and behind the Son in the Father, so that we do not know him face to face in his own ὑπόστασις.[103] Through him the Word of God became flesh and dwelt among us, but he was not himself that Word. Through him the Son of God became incarnate, but he did not incarnate himself among us. He is the one Spirit in whom the Father communicates himself to us through his Son, and in whom we have access through the Son to the Father. He is the invisible light in whose shining we see the uncreated light of God manifest in Jesus Christ, and is known himself only in that he lights up the face of God in the face of Jesus Christ.[104] The Holy Spirit is indeed personally present among us, but in his *transparent and translucent mode of being*,[105] who as ὁμοούσιος with the Father and the Son throws his eternal light upon the Father in the Son and upon the Son in the Father. 'Our mind, enlightened by the Spirit, looks toward the Son, and in him as in an image, sees the Father.'[106] In

---

of Jer., *Cat.*, 16.14; Epiphanius, *Haer.*, 48.12; 62.4, 7; 69.18, 34; 74.1, 4, 6, 9ff; 76.4, 7; *Anc.*, 6ff, 11, 73, 120; Gregory Nyss., *De Sp. St.*, Jaeger, 3.1, p. 108, etc.

[100]John 14.17. Cf. A. I. C. Heron, *op. cit.*, p. 56: 'The Spirit mirrors Christ himself, but to the "world" the mirror conveys no image.'

[101]Thus Cyril of Alex., *Thes.*, 34.

[102]Ps. Athanasius/Basil, *Con. Sab.*, 12. Cf. Gregory Nyss., *De Trin.*, Jaeger, 3.1, p. 13.

[103]See Gregory/Basil, *Ep.*, 38.4.

[104]Basil, *De Sp. St.*, 47: ' "No one knows the Father but the Son" (Matt. 11.27). And "no man can say that Jesus is Lord but in the Holy Spirit" (1 Cor. 12.3). For it is not said through the Spirit but in the Spirit, and "God is Spirit, and they who worship him must worship him in Spirit and in truth" (John 4.24), as it is written "in thy light we shall see light" (Ps. 36.9), namely by the illumination of the Spirit, "the true light that enlightens every man that comes into the world" (John 1.9).'

[105]Cf. Basil, *De Sp. St.*, 22f; 46f.

[106]Basil, *Ep.*, 236. Also *De Sp. St.*, 64: 'It is impossible to see the image of the

this way God the Father, the Son and the Holy Spirit in their indivisible Triunity shine through him to us in their three-fold light. 'When the Spirit is in us, the Word also who gives the Spirit, is in us, and in the Word is the Father. So it is as it is said: "We will come, I and the Father, and make our abode with him." For where the light is, there is also the radiance; and where the radiance is, there also is its activity and luminous grace.'[107] Thus also Gregory Nazianzen: 'No sooner do I conceive of the one than I am enlightened by the radiance of the three; no sooner do I distinguish them than I am carried back to the one. When I think of any one of the three I think of him as the whole, and my vision is filled, and the greater part of what I conceive escapes me. I cannot grasp the greatness of that one so as to attribute a greater greatness to the others. When I contemplate the three together, I see but one luminary, and cannot divide or measure out the undivided light.'[108] The three Persons of the Holy Trinity are thus to be heard and known, worshipped and glorified by us 'as one Person (πρόσωπον)'.[109]

Through the ineffability of his own personal mode of being, then, the Holy Spirit confronts us with the sheer ineffability of God, for in him we are in immediate touch with the ultimate being and acts of the All-Holy and Almighty before whom all our forms of thought and speech break off in wonder and adoration. To cite once more Athanasius' observation to Serapion: 'Thus far human knowledge goes. Here the cherubim spread the covering of their wings.'[110]

---

invisible God, except in the illumination of the Spirit. And in directing our gaze upon the image, we cannot sever the light from the image, for that which causes our seeing is necessarily seen with what is seen. Thus rightly and appropriately it is through the shining of the Spirit that we see the brightness of God's glory, and through the express Image are led up to him of whom he is the express Image and exact Seal.'

[107]Athanasius, *Ad Ser.*, 1.30 & 1.19.

[108]Gregory Naz., *Or.*, 40.1 See also *Or.*, 39.11; Ps. Gregory Naz., *Ep.*, 243; Gregory Nyss., *De Sp. St.*, Jaeger, 3.1, p. 108f; Epiphanius, *Haer.*, 69.33; 70.5; 74.7f, 10; *Anc.*, 61; Didymus, *Con. Eun.*, Athens ed., 44, p. 255f.

[109]Didymus, *De Trin.*, 2.36; and Cyril of Alex., *In Jn.*, 15.1.

[110]Athanasius, *Ad Ser.*, 1.17. Hence the inherent difficulty we have in formulating a doctrine of the Spirit, for the Holy Spirit is God of God present to us in his mode of being as Spirit and thus precisely as the unknowable. See

On the other hand, the Holy Spirit is the pledge that while the eternal being of God infinitely transcends our comprehension he is not ·closed to us, for the Holy Spirit is the outgoing movement of his being whereby he makes himself open to our knowing. That God is ineffable does not mean that he is unintelligible,[111] for he is intrinsically intelligible and knowable, and as such is the active· ground and source of our knowing of him through Jesus Christ the Word made flesh and in the Holy Spirit whom he mediates to us. Basil could thus speak of the Spirit as 'the Spirit of knowledge' (τὸ τῆς γνώσεως Πνεῦμα), for it is '*in himself* that he shows the glory of the only Begotten and *in himself* that he bestows the knowledge of God upon true worshippers. Thus the way of the knowledge of God lies from one Spirit through the one Son to the one Father.'[112] The fact that the Holy Spirit in his personal mode of being and activity is ὁμοούσιος with the Father and the Son assures us that the presence of the Spirit mediates to us the truth of God's self-revelation, so that far from being empty of content it is replete with the Word of God. The Word and the Spirit of God coinhere inseparably in one another.[113] 'What is spoken from God is said through Christ and in the Spirit.'[114] Thus since there is only one activity of God, and only one movement of divine self-revelation, from the Father, through the Son and in the Spirit,[115] the ineffability of God is not a negative but a positive ineffability, for it is in making himself actually known to us through the Son and in the Spirit that God reveals himself as infinitely greater than we can conceive. Only the Spirit of God who knows what is in God can reveal him to us, for he searches

---

'The Epistemological Relevance of the Spirit', *God and Rationality*, pp. 165–192.

[111]Basil, *Ep.*, 235.2: 'We confess that we know what is knowable of God, and yet that what we know reaches beyond our comprehension.'

[112]Basil, *De Sp. St.*, 47.

[113]Athanasius, *Ad Ser.*, 1.14, 19, 21, 30f; 4.4.

[114]Athanasius, *Ad Ser.*, 1.14.

[115]Athanasius, *Ad Ser.*, 1.19ff, 27f, 30f; 3.5; Didymus, *De Sp. St.*, 34–39; *De Trin.*, 2.1; Basil, *Con. Eun.*, 3.4; Gregory/Basil, *Ep.*, 189.6f; Gregory Nys., *non tres dei*, Jaeger, vol. 3.1, pp. 47f, 55f; cf. *Ex comm. not.*, Jaeger, 3.1, pp. 3f; *De Sp. St.*, Jaeger, 3.1, pp. 97–100, 105ff, 109; Gregory Naz., *Or.*, 31.6, 16.

the very depths of God.[116] Since he is sent to us from the Father in the name of Christ, in order to bear witness to him, and as the Spirit of truth to lead us into all truth, the Holy Spirit marvellously gives us access to the intrinsic intelligibility of God, while nevertheless preserving inviolate the ultimate mystery and ineffability of his divine being. 'Coming from the Father and the Son he alone is the Guide to the truth ... the Teacher of the apostles, the luminous Source of evangelical dogmas, the Composer of holy things, the true Light from true Light.'[117] It is through communion with him, who is in Christ and is himself God of God, that we are lifted up to have knowledge of God as he is in himself, and at the same time are restrained by the sheer holiness and majesty of God's being as unapproachable light from transgressing the bounds of reverent and lawful inquiry.

(2) The Holy Spirit is distinctively personal reality along with and inseparable from the Father and the Son

The Nicene pronouncement that the incarnate Son is ὁμοούσιος τῷ Πατρί had the effect not only of giving definite assertion to the Deity of Christ but of greatly reinforcing the biblical conception of the personal nature and activity of God the Father Almighty. As we have seen in our discussion of the *homoousion*, it made clear that what God the Father is toward us in Jesus Christ he is inherently and eternally in himself. He himself is the living content of his Word and Grace in the Person Jesus Christ: the Revealer and what he reveals, the Giver and what he gives, are identical. The 'I am' of God and the 'I am' of the Son are inseparably one, for the Father is in the Son and the Son is in the

[116] I Cor. 2.10f. This passage had a powerful influence on Nicene theology – see Athanasius, *In ill. om.*, 1; *Exp. fidei*, 2; *Ad Ser.*, 1.6, 15, 22, 26; 3.1; 4.1; Basil, *De Sp. St.*, 10, 38, 40, 50; *Con. Eun.*, 1.14; Gregory Nyss., *Con. Eun.*, 2, Jaeger, I, pp. 289, 340; 3, 1, II, p. 160; Gregory Naz., *Or.*, 28.6; 30.15; 40.9; 43.65; Amphilochius, *Fr.*, 5; Cyril of Jer., *Cat.*, 4.16; 6.6; 11.13; 16.23; Didymus, *Con. Man.*, 40; *De Trin.*, 1.9, 15; 2.2f, 5, 6.14f, 7.8; 3.37; *De Sp. St.*, 15, 31, 40, 54f; *Con. Eun.*, Athens ed., pp. 232, 251f, 255, 260; Epiphanius, *Anc.*, 7, 12, 15f, 68, 117; *Haer.*, 74.1, 5, 11, 13; 76.29.

[117] Epiphanius, *Anc.*, 73; cf. 15f; *Haer.*, 74.10; 76. *Ref. Aet.*, 29.

Father. While they are personally other as Father and as Son, they are indivisibly one in their divine being. Thus in the mind of the Nicene Church the incarnation stood for the acute personalisation of the nature and activity of God.[118] The application of the *homoousion* by Athanasius to the relation of the Holy Spirit to Christ and through him to the Father had the same effect in reinforcing the biblical conception of the personal nature and activity of the Spirit and intensifying it in the faith of the Church.[119] It was thus that the *homoousion* applied to the Spirit as well as the Son became what Epiphanius called 'the bond of faith' (σύνδεσμος τῆς πίστεως).[120]

What prompted this definite and explicit emphasis upon the oneness in being, nature and activity of the Spirit with the Son and the Father, was the idea put forward by semi-Arians, '*Tropici*' and others, that the Holy Spirit was not God of God but an impersonal creaturely force emanating from God and detachable from him.[121] As Athanasius pointed out in his *Letters to Serapion on the Holy Spirit*, such a conception of the Spirit was a serious violation of the oneness of the Church's faith in the oneness of the Holy Trinity in whose name baptism was dispensed. 'The Trinity is not only in name and form of speech but in truth and actual existence. For as the Father is he who is, so also is his Word one who is, and God over all. Nor is the Holy Spirit without actual existence, but exists and has true being.'[122] 'As baptism, which is given in Father, Son and Holy Spirit, is one; and as there is one faith in the Trinity (as the apostle said), so the Holy Trinity, being identical with himself and united within himself, has in him nothing which belongs to created things. This is the indivisible oneness of the Trinity; and faith in him is one.'[123]

When the attack upon the Deity of the Holy Spirit was

---

[118]See again Athanasius, *Con. Ar.*, 1.9, 46; 3.1–6; *De syn.*, 41–53; *Ad Ser.*, 1.27; 2.2, 5.

[119]Athanasius, *Ad Ser.*, 1.25–33; 3.1.

[120]Epiphanius, *Anc.*, 6.

[121]Athanasius, *Ad Ser.*, 1.2, 9–10.

[122]Athanasius, *Ad Ser.*, 1.28.

[123]Athanasius, *Ad Ser.*, 1.30.

renewed by Eunomius and other Anomoean churchmen,[124] their teaching was formally condemned by a Council presided over by Athanasius at Alexandria in 362. They accepted belief 'in a Holy Trinity, not a Trinity in name only, but one really existing and subsisting: a Father really existing and subsisting, and a Son really and substantially existing and subsisting, and a Holy Spirit really existing and subsisting himself ... They acknowledged a Holy Trinity but one Godhead and one Principle, and that the Son is consubstantial with the Father, as the fathers declared; while the Holy Spirit is not a creature, nor external but proper to and inseparable from the being of the Father and the Son.' In rejecting the idea that the Son was non-substantial and that the Spirit was impersonal, they went on to assert: 'we believe that there is one Godhead and that he has one nature, and not that there is one nature of the Father, from which that of the Son and the Holy Spirit are different.' It was then accepted that 'three Persons' (τρεῖς ὑποστάσεις) and 'one Being' (μία οὐσία) could be held together in an orthodox and proper understanding of the Holy Trinity, which would avoid unipersonal notions of God on the one hand and divisive or tritheistic notions of God on the other hand.[125]

It soon became clear, however, that, due to the subtle philosophical and logical arguments put forward by Eunomius and his followers, effective refutation called for further qualification in the use of theological terms. Athanasius was accustomed to use theological terms in an open flexible way that allowed the objective realities they intend to govern their use and meaning, and so he avoided formal definitions and logico-analytical distinctions that had little or no basis in fact.[126] He could thus find genuine agreement with people across merely terminological difference. However, when differences of this

---

[124]See especially Eunomius, *Apologia 1* of 360, *MPG*, 30.835ff, and *Apologia 2* of 378, preserved in the *Con. Eun.* of Gregory Nyss., Jaeger, 1 & 2.

[125]Athanasius, *Ad Ant.*, 5–6.

[126]See *Theol. in Reconcil.*, pp. 242f. Thus also Gregory Naz., *Or.*, 31.11: 'God is three "Properties", "Hypostases" or "Persons" – call them what you will, we will not quarrel over names as long as they intend the same thing – but one in being – that is the Godhead.' And 43.68: 'Salvation lies not in terms but in the reality they express.'

kind were deployed as cover for heresy, the need for greater precision and agreement in the use of theological terms became urgent. At this juncture the Cappadocian theologians, standing on the shoulders of Athanasius, made an impressive contribution in refuting Eunomius and helping to regularise the use of apposite theological terms in the doctrine of the Trinity.[127]

It was thus that Basil came to write his great work *On the Holy Spirit* at the request of Amphilochius.[128] While he was strangely hesitant in applying the term ὁμοούσιος directly to the Holy Spirit, he insisted on the divine personal nature of the Spirit. This was everywhere evident in the Church's worship in which the Holy Spirit was glorified and adored equally with the Father and the Son and in the indivisible oneness of the Holy Trinity, as also in the traditional understanding and experience of the Holy Spirit as sharing completely in the indivisible activity of the Holy Trinity, not least through his creative and sanctifying operations. Moreover, Basil showed, the Spirit has the same relation to the Son as the Son has to the Father, so that one Form of Godhead is beheld in the Father, Son and Holy Spirit. Thus while they are personally distinct they are inseparably united in the 'I am' of God, in the uncompounded nature and communion of the Godhead, and in his one activity toward the world.[129] Far from having a created nature or being an impersonal force, 'the Spirit is living being (οὐσία ζῶσα), Lord of sanctification, from which his kinship with God becomes disclosed, while his ineffable mode of existence (τρόπου ὑπάρξεως) is preserved.'[130]

Like Athanasius, then, Basil held that the Holy Spirit has real personal objective subsistence in God in identity of being with the undivided Trinity, and that he exercises divine functions in his own Person.[131] In the interest of more effective expression,

[127]Basil, *Con. Eun.*, 1–3, Athens ed., 52, pp. 157–227; *Antir.*, pp. 143–156; Gregory Nyss., *Con. Eun.*, Jaeger, 1 & 2. See also Didymus, *Con. Eun.* (Ps. Basil, *Con. Eun.*, 4–5), Athens ed., 44, pp. 223–261.

[128]Basil, *Ep.*, 231.

[129]Basil, *De Sp. St.*, 16f, 37, 41–47; *Ep.*, 159; 189.5–8.

[130]Basil, *De Sp. St.*, 46; *Con. Sab.*, 6. Cf. Gregory Nyss., *Con. Eun.*, 1, Jaeger, 1, p. 89; *non tres dei*, 3.1, p. 56.

[131]E.g., Basil, *Hex.*, 2.6.

however, he drew a significant distinction between οὐσία as referring to the one being of God, and ὑποστάσεις as referring to the Persons of the Trinity, which helped to regularise the formulation μία οὐσία, τρεῖς ὑποστάσεις, 'One Being, three Persons'.[132] While οὐσία was used to refer to the one being of the Godhead common to the three divine Persons, ὑπόστασις was used to refer to them in their differences from one another and in their relations with one another in accordance with their particular modes of subsistence in God as Father, Son and Holy Spirit.[133] For this purpose Basil drew into the reference of ὑπόστασις the terms πρόσωπον or 'face' and ὄνομα or 'name',[134] in order to give a more adequate expression to the peculiar mode of personal subsistence (τρόπος ὑπάρξεως) of Father, Son and Spirit in the one being of the Godhead.[135] The concept of τρόπος ὑπάρξεως may have been meant to take over Athanasius' notion of τρόπος Θεότητος or a 'mode of deity substantially and truly subsisting in the Godhead', and apply it to the personal distinctions within God without introducing any idea of division in the oneness of his being.[136]

This interpretative development by Basil of Nicene and Athanasian trinitarian teaching[137] was supported and extended by his fellow Cappadocians, the two Gregories and Amphilochius.[138] The effect of this on the doctrine of the Holy Spirit was to deepen and intensify understanding of the

---

[132]Basil, *De Sp. St.*, 7; *Ep.*, 52, 69, 125, 210, 214, 236, 258; *Hom.*, 111; cf. Athanasius, *Ad Ant.*, 5–6, 11; *In ill. om.*, 6; Epiphanius, *Haer.*, 73.16; Gregory Naz., *Or.*, 21.35; 31.7–16; 43.30; Gregory/Basil, *Ep.*, 38; *Ex comm. not.*, Jaeger, 3.1, pp. 21–33.

[133]Basil, *Ep.*, 214.4; 236.6. See also Gregory Naz., *Or.*, 25.16, 26.19, 29.2; 31.29; 32.21; Gregory Nyss., *Or. cat.*, 1f. Consult again the clarification offered by G. L. Prestige, *God in Patristic Thought*, pp. 168f, 188ff, 244ff.

[134]See also Gregory Naz., *Or.*, 20, *MPG*, 35, 1072; 39.11; 42.16, etc., but he differed from Basil in not using the expression τρόπος ὑπάρξεως.

[135]Basil, *De Sp. St.*, 46; *Ep.*, 38.1–4; 9.2; 125.1; 236.6; cf. *Con. Eun.*, 1.19; 2.29; Gregory Nyss., *Con. Eun.*, 1, Jaeger, 1, p. 89; and cf. his careful analysis in *Ex com. not.*, 3.1, pp. 19–33.

[136]See Athanasius, *Exp. fidei*, 2; *Con. Ar.*, 3.15; 4.2; *De syn.*, 52; and cf. his use of ὕπαρξις and ὑπάρχειν, *Ad Ser.*, 1.28, which may well have influenced Basil.

[137]Compare Basil, *Ep.*, 52, with Athanasius, *De syn.*, 45–51.

[138]Cf. the statement attributed to Amphilochius (*Fragment* 15, *MPG*,

intrinsically divine and personal nature of the Holy Spirit. We may let Gregory Nyssen speak for this. 'We regard God's Spirit as accompanying the Word and manifesting his energy, and not as a mere influence or breath ... but as a power having real existence in his own right and in his own distinctive ὑπόστασις who cannot be separated from God in whom he is or from the Word whom he accompanies. Far from being contingent, he exists hypostatically with his own freedom to choose, move and act as he wills, and with the power to carry out every purpose.'[139] As Gregory understood it, it is because the Holy Spirit comes to us and acts upon us from the inner communion of Father and Son in the one Godhead of the Holy Trinity that we have such sublime and exalted conceptions of him as he is in his own Person and in his life-giving power.[140]

Much the same conception of the fully personal nature and activity of the Holy Spirit – but with a distinctly Hebraic slant in the way he related the 'I am' of the one God to his *ousia* and thought into each other the notions of face, name and ὑπόστασις[141] – had been offered by Epiphanius in his *Anchoratus* before the publication of Basil's *De Spiritu Sancto*, and in his *Panarium haeresium* four years later. This was a direct development of Athanasian teaching in the light of the *Tomus ad Antiochenos*, but it is clear that he and Basil were familiar with each other's views.[142] He also held that the Nicene ὁμοούσιος implied a distinction of Persons in God, for one Person cannot

39.112): 'When I speak of one God, I am not denying the ὑποστάσεις, but by the word "God" I am signifying his community of being (τὸ κοινὸν τῆς οὐσίας). Whenever I speak of ὁμοούσιον I do not refer to one Person but to the consubstantiality of three, Father, Son and Holy Spirit, for one Person is not said to be consubstantial with himself. The difference applies to Persons, not to the being, for Father, Son and Holy Spirit are names of a mode of subsistence or relation, but not of being as such (τρόπου ὑπάρξεως ἤγουν σχέσεως ὀνόματα, ἀλλ' οὐκ οὐσίας ἁπλῶς).' This passage, however, does not appear in the critical edition of Amphilochius' works by C. Datema, *Cor. Chr.*, *Ser. Gr.*, vol. 3.

[139]Gregory Nyss., *Or. cat.*, 2.

[140]Gregory Nyss., *De Trin.*, Jaeger, 3.1, pp. 6–15; *non tres dei*, pp. 47–57; *De Sp. St.*, pp. 99f, 105ff. Refer to D. B. Harned, *op. cit.*, p. 87f.

[141]Cf. Epiphanius, *Anc.*, 6, 8; *Haer.*, 57.10; 62.7f; 63.7; 69.36, 67, 72; 73.16; etc.

[142]Basil, *Ep.*, 258.

be consubstantial with himself, and insisted that each of the three Persons has real, substantial, true and perfect subsistence in the one being of God, and indeed that the whole being of the Spirit is the same as the whole being of the Son and the whole being of the Father. Each is whole and perfect God.[143] Accordingly, the Holy Spirit is honoured adored, glorified and worshipped by the Church along with God the Father and God the Son. Understood in this light the formulation 'one Being, three Persons' was quite acceptable to Epiphanius, although he understood οὐσία in the earlier Nicene way as expressing being in its internal relations and as having a personal slant.[144] Thus like Athanasius he could handle the terms οὐσία and ὑπόστασις more flexibly in the light of what was being intended at the time.[145] Epiphanius certainly brought the development of the Nicene belief in the Holy Spirit to its conclusion in a full and unambiguous assertion of the Deity of the Holy Spirit. 'We call the Father God, the Son God, and the Holy Spirit God ... When you pronounce the *homoousion*, you declare that the Son is God of God and the Holy Spirit is God of the same Godhead.'[146] In his own distinctive Person the Holy Spirit is whole God, God of God, of one and the same being with the Father and the Son, and in his own peculiar activity as the Holy Spirit, the one indivisible Trinity is fully and unreservedly participant.

The teaching of Epiphanius, however, was not without its own characteristic nuances. (1) Unlike the Cappadocians, he did not speak of the different Persons of Father, Son and Holy Spirit as 'modes of existence' in the one being of God, but preferred to speak of them as 'enhypostatic' (ἐνυπόστατος) in God, that is, as having real, objective personal being in God and as coinhering hypostatically in him. This was a more concrete and less abstract way of speaking of the living individuality and reality of the divine Persons in the one being of God, which led up to the teaching of Cyril of Alexandria.[147] (2) His understanding of the

---

[143]Epiphanius, *Haer.*, 62.3ff; 65.1–8.
[144]Epiphanius, *Anc.*, 81; *Haer.*, 73.34.
[145]E.g. Epiphanius, *Haer.*, 69.72.
[146]Epiphanius, *Anc.*, 2.
[147]Epiphanius, *Anc.*, 5–10, 67, 72, 74, 81; *Haer.*, 57.4f; 62.1ff, 6; 65.1ff;

homoousion as applying not only to each Person but to the inner relations of the Trinity as a whole, deepened his notion of the coinherence of Father, Son and Holy Spirit in their enhypostatic relations, in respect of which he could speak of the Holy Spirit as 'in the midst (ἐν μέσῳ) of the Father and the Son', or as 'the bond of the Trinity (σύνδεσμος τῆς Τριάδος)'.[148] There is no suggestion of any subordinationism in God, for whatever the Father is, this the Son is and this the Spirit is in the Godhead. Their being of the Father and with the Father is beyond beginning and beyond time (ἀνάρχως καὶ ἀχρόνως) – there is no 'before' or 'after' in God.[149] 'There never was when the Spirit was not' (οὐδὲ ἦν ποτὲ ὅτε οὐκ ἦν Πνεῦμα).[150] (3) The Holy Spirit dwells in and flows from the inner being and life and light of the Holy Trinity, where he shares fully in the reciprocal knowing and communing of the Father and the Son. It is as such that he comes into the midst (ἐν μέσῳ) of us, proceeding from the Father, receiving from the Son, revealing God to us and making us partake in him of God's knowing of himself.[151] (4) Like Athanasius, Epiphanius abhorred any partitive thinking of God either as he is in himself or as he is toward us. Thus he regarded God's self-giving to us in the Holy Spirit in an essentially unitary way. The Gift and the Giver are one. There are diverse operations of the Spirit, but they are intensely personal, for the triune God is directly and creatively at work in them all. There is only one grace (ἓν χάρισμα) and one Spirit (ἓν Πνεῦμα), for God himself in the fullness of his triune being is

---

69.21, 40; 70.6; 72.5, 11; 74.9; 76. *Ref. Aet.*, 2f, 12, 18; 77.32; 77.22; cf. Athanasius, *De syn.*, 42; *Con. Ar.*, 4.2; *Con. Apol.*, 1, 20.

[148]Epiphanius, *Anc.*, 4, 7f, 10; *Haer.*, 62.4; 74.11; cf. Gregory Naz., *Or.*, 31.8f; Basil, *De Sp. St.*, 38, 43, 45f.

[149]Epiphanius, *Anc.*, 46; *Haer.*, 57.4; 62.3; 69.36; 70.8; 73.36; 74.1; 76.6, 21. Cf. his reference to the Son and the Spirit as the one ultimate Source, πηγὴ ἐκ πηγῆς, with the Father, *Haer.*, 69.54.

[150]Epiphanius, *Anc.*, 74, 120; *Haer.*, 74.10. Cf. Gregory Naz., *Or.*, 29.3; 31.4.

[151]Epiphanius, *Anc.*, 6ff, 11, 15, 67, 70f, 115; *Haer.*, 57.9; 62.4; 64.9; 69.18, 43; 74.4, 10; 76. *Ref. Aet.*, 7, 21, 29, 32. Cf. Athanasius, *Con. Ar.*, 1.20, 33, and Hilary, *De Trin.*, 2.3; and Basil, *Hom.*, 111.7: 'The Son includes the Spirit in his and the Father's Communion.'

present in all his acts of creating, revealing, healing, enlightening and sanctifying.[152]

Epiphanius presented his doctrine of the Spirit, then, in an understanding of the whole undivided Trinity, and not just of the Father, as the Μοναρχία. He laid the strongest emphasis upon the perfect Triunity of God, with no suggestion that in him there is any detraction from the reality, wholeness or perfection of the enhypostatic nature and distinctiveness of any one of the divine Persons in relation to another, and thus not of the Son nor of the Spirit in relation to the Father. 'In proclaiming the Μοναρχία we do not err, but confess the Trinity, Unity in Trinity and Trinity in Unity, one Godhead of the Father, Son and Holy Spirit'.[153] 'There is one true God, Trinity in Unity; one God, Father, Son and Holy Spirit.'[154] Epiphanius' formulation of belief in the Holy Spirit along these lines led directly up to the Council of Constantinople in 381. 'We believe in one Holy Spirit, the Lord and Giver of Life, who proceeds from the Father and with the Father and the Son is worshipped together and glorified, who spoke through the prophets.'[155]

Like Epiphanius Didymus of Alexandria applied the Nicene *homoousion* to the whole Trinity,[156] and adopted the principle: one οὐσία, three ὑποστάσεις.[157] And like Epiphanius he made frequent use of the concept of ἐνυπόστατος[158] but unlike Epiphanius and like the Cappadocians he could use the expression τρόπος ὑπάρξεως in characterising the peculiar

---

[152]Epiphanius, *Anc.*, 7f, 67f, 70f, 119f; *Haer.*, 69.17, 52; 70.5; 72.4f; 73.16, 18; 74.5, 7, 11f; *De fide*, 14.

[153]Epiphanius, *Haer.*, 62.3.

[154]Epiphanius, *Anc.*, 2. See also 6, 10, 24, 26, 28, 67, 73f, 81, 117f; *Haer.*, 57.4, 8; 62.3, 8; 69.33, 44, 54, 56, 62, 68, 74ff; 72.1; 73.16, 34; 74.11; 76.6; *De fide*, 14.

[155]Epiphanius, *Anc.*, 119; cf. 120; *Haer.*, 66.70ff, 84; 67.3; 74.10; 76. *Ref. Aet.*, 36, etc.

[156]Didymus, *De Trin.*, 1.16ff, 20, 24f, 27, 34; 2.1, 4ff, 6f, 13f, 18, 27; 3.7, 15; *Con. Eun.*, Athens ed., 44, p. 238.

[157]Didymus, *De Trin.*, 1.16 – but he preferred to speak of 'one Godhead (μία Θεότης) and three Persons', e.g., *De Trin.*, 2.27.

[158]Didymus, *De Trin.*, 1.16, 26; 2, 1ff, 8, 10; 3.19, 37; *Con. Eun.*, Athens ed., 44, pp. 239, 253.

modes of existence of the divine Persons in God.[159] He insisted
with Athanasian and Epiphanian energy upon the oneness and
identity in being and lordship of the Father, Son and Holy
Spirit, for each Person is wholly and perfectly God, and thus
upon the indivisible nature of God's being.[160] The Father is in
himself the whole divine nature, but this is true also of the Son
and of the Spirit. The Father is not Father apart from the Son,
and the Son is not Son apart from the Father, nor are they what
they are as Father and Son apart from the Spirit, while the Holy
Spirit is not what he is as Holy Spirit apart from the Father and
the Son, for they all coinhere consubstantially and inseparably in
the one being of God. The Godhead is intrinsically trinitarian,
and the Trinity is essentially one, a Unity in Trinity and a
Trinity in Unity.[161]

At the same time, Didymus was deeply concerned to rebut a
Sabellian unipersonalism and, like the Cappadocians, to keep
constantly in view the reality and objective existence, the
peculiar nature and specific properties, of the three Persons or
ὑποστάσεις and their inter-personal relations (σχέσεις) in the
one being of God.[162] He took the concept of the *homoousion* so
seriously that he maintained that the different ὑποστάσεις are
wholly alike and perfectly equal in power and honour, so that
the Father is not greater than the Son, and that as in the holy
Scriptures each of the divine Persons may be mentioned first.[163]

---

[159]Didymus, *Con. Eun.*, Athens ed., 44, p. 226f; for cognate expressions see
De Trin., 1.9; 2.1, 12.

[160]See the recurring emphasis on *una substantia* in Didymus *De Spiritu
Sancto*, extant only in Jerome's Latin translation, 16–19, 21f, 24f, 32, 36f, 40,
53, 58.

[161]Didymus, *De Trin.*, 1.9f, 11, 15f, 18f, 25, 27; 2.1, 3f, 5ff, 15, 18, 26f; 3.2,
15f, 24, 47, 55; *De Sp. St.*, 30–39; *Con. Eun.*, Athens ed., 44, pp. 246f, 255ff.

[162]*De Trin.*, 1.9, 11f, 15f, 18f, 21, 26f, 30, 34f; 2.1ff, 5ff, 8, 12, 19, 27; 3.1f, 18,
23f, 38, 40f, 45; *De Sp. St.*, 27, 30. See Gregory Naz., *Or.*, 29.16; 31, 8–20.

[163]Didymus, *De Trin.*, 1.16, 18, 26f; cf. 3.1f, 13, 18; *De Sp. St.*, 36. John
14.28, 'the Father is greater than I', is explained in terms of the incarnational
condescension of the Son 'for our sakes'. Thus also Hilary, *De Trin.*, 9.51, 54f;
cf. 3.65; *De syn.*, 64; and Amphilochius, *ap.* Theodoret, *Dial.*, 1, *MPG* 83.99.
According to Athanasius 'greater than I' refers to the filial relation of the Son
to the Father, not to any inequality in divine nature – *Con. Ar.*, 1.58; cf.
Epiphanius, *Haer.*, 69.43, 53. Basil and others explained that the Father is
'greater' in that he is the 'Source' (πηγή) and 'Cause' (αἰτία) of the Son – *Con.*

In all his extant writings Didymus kept the focus of his attention mainly on the Holy Spirit. This was consistent with his evangelical piety and with a spiritual inwardness which was nourished through the 'mystical tradition' of the inspired Scriptures of the Old and New Testaments, in which the Holy Spirit continues to speak personally (ἐκ προσώπου) to the Church.[164] He thought of the Holy Spirit predominantly as the intrinsically Holy One, the ultimate Source of all Holiness. It is as such that he comes to dwell in us, while dwelling in God, and is present in all divine acts of creation, revelation, redemption, justification, and sanctification, not in part but in the wholeness of his Deity. Hence Didymus regarded the Holy Spirit as personally subsisting in all God's gifts, and as directly present in his own being, in such a way that in him the divine Giver and the Gift are one.[165] This intensely personalised conception of the Holy Spirit was clearly related to his doctrine of the Spirit as deriving consubstantially, though timelessly and without beginning, from the Person (ἐκ τῆς ὑποστάσεως) of the Father, and even from the Person (ἐκ τῆς ὑποστάσεως) of the Son.[166] What this means for the doctrine of the procession of the Spirit we shall have to consider later, but for Didymus himself it meant that the experience of the Holy Spirit and filial relation to the Father through the Son were inseparably associated.[167]

It was in continuation of this Nicene tradition and with a Hebraic and Biblical frame of mind that Cyril of Jerusalem sought to present to his catechumens the Christian doctrine of the Holy Spirit. He held that, since the Holy Scriptures of both Testaments are inspired by the Spirit, it is by adhering to what they say of the Spirit that we may speak rightly and worthily of him.[168] Indeed it is only through the living Spirit himself that we may discourse wisely about him. Hence Cyril refused to say

Eun., 1.25; Evagrius/Basil, *Ep.*, 8.5f; Gregory Nyss., *Ex comm.*, Jaeger ed., 3.1, p. 24f; cf. Gregory Naz., *Or.*, 29.15; 30.7; and John of Damascus, *De fide*, 1.8.

[164]See for example Didymus, *De Trin.*, 1.36.

[165]Didymus, *De Trin.*, 2.1–3; *De Sp. St.*, 3ff; 16–25; 32–40; 57–61.

[166]Didymus, *De Trin.*, 1.15, 18, 26, 36; 2.1ff, 5; 3.3, 5, 38; *De Sp. St.*, 26, 37; cf. *Con. Eun.*, Athens ed., 44, p. 251.

[167]Didymus, *De Sp. St.*, 34–37.

[168]Cyril of Jer., *Cat.*, 4.16, 33; 11.12; 16.1–4, 16ff, 24.

anything about the Holy Spirit except what had been revealed. 'The Holy Spirit himself spoke the Scriptures; he also spoke about himself as much as he pleased, or as much as we could receive. Let only those things be spoken therefore which he himself has said, for whatever he has not said, we dare not say.'[169] We are told by the Lord Jesus himself that there is one God, the Father, the Son and the Holy Spirit. 'It is sufficient for us to know this. Do not inquire speculatively into his nature or ὑπόστασις, for if it had been written, we would speak about it; let us not *dare* to go beyond what has been written. It is sufficient for our salvation to know that there is Father, Son and Holy Spirit.'[170] This perhaps explains why Cyril, unlike other contemporary theologians, did not speak of the Spirit, or of the Son, expressly as ὁμοούσιος,[171] although he clearly held that both the Spirit and the Son are inseparably one in being and agency with the Father, with emphatic rejection of both tritheist and Sabellian heresies which separated or confused the three Persons of the Godhead.[172]

Within these constraints, however, Cyril felt that he had to be very definite and emphatic about the fact that the Holy Spirit, far from being an impersonal cosmological force like the Stoic πνεῦμα, is living, acting, rational, speaking, personal or *enhypostatic* reality, subsisting objectively in the one indivisible Godhead of the Trinity.[173] He strung together phrase after phrase in his determination to press home the truth that, supremely great and unsearchable power of God though he is, the Holy Spirit is intrinsically and fully personal in his divine mode of being.[174] 'With the Father and the Son he is exalted with the glory of the Godhead ... For there is one God, the Father of Christ; and one Lord Jesus Christ, of the only God the only begotten Son; and one Holy Spirit, who sanctifies and deifies all.'[175] 'The Father through the Son bestows all things;

[169]Cyril of Jer., *Cat.*, 16.2 and 13.
[170]Cyril of Jer., *Cat.*, 16.24.
[171]But cf. Sozomen, *Hist. eccl.*, 7.7, for a reported change in Cyril's views.
[172]Cyril of Jer., *Cat.*, 16.3–4; 17.34; cf. 17.4f, 34.
[173]Cyril of Jer., *Cat.*, 16.3f, 12, 24; 17.2, 5.
[174]Cyril of Jer., *Cat.*, 16.3, 13; 17.2, 5, 28, 33f.
[175]Cyril of Jer., *Cat.*, 4.16; cf. 6.1, 6f; 16.3.

the gifts of the Father are none other than those of the Son, and those of the Holy Spirit; for there is one salvation, one power, one faith; one God the Father, one Lord, his only begotten Son, one Holy Spirit, the Paraclete.'[176] He is living, subsisting, active Spirit, intrinsically personal, equal in honour with the Father and the Son, and always present together with them. As such he is not only living and rational being himself, but the creative and sanctifying Source of all things made by God through Christ. That is to say, Cyril thought of the Holy Spirit as spiritualising, enlightening and rationalising, and thus the one personalising being, to whom all other spiritual and rational natures are indebted.[177]

Here as everywhere in the fourth century the teaching of the Greek fathers implied that the immediate presence of God, far from overwhelming creaturely being, actually sustains it. That holds good, as Basil and Didymus pointed out, even with regard to the guilty who fall under the judgment of God.[178] The teaching of Cyril of Jerusalem was strikingly clear about the Holy Spirit in this respect. He spoke of the life-giving presence of God in the world as *the grace of the Holy Spirit* which like rain does not change when it comes down but adapts itself to the nature of each thing that receives it. While one in his own nature, and undivided in himself, the Holy Spirit divides to each one his grace, and at the will of God and in the name of Christ works many excellencies.[179]

We must think of the Holy Spirit, then, as the creative, energising, enlightening presence of God who freely interacts with his human creatures in such a way as to sustain their relation to himself as the source of their spiritual, personal and rational life. According to Cyril it is distinctive of the presence and operation of the Holy Spirit that while he comes to us and acts upon us in the sheer unlimited power of God, he does not

[176]Cyril of Jer., *Cat.*, 16.24.

[177]Cyril of Jer., *Cat.*, 4.16; 16.3; 17.2, 5, 28, 33f.

[178]Basil, *De Sp. St.*, 38–40; Didymus, *De Trin.*, 2.6. Contrast the claim of A. Grillmeier, with reference to the teaching of Athanasius, that 'the bright Light of the Logos swallows up all created light' – *Christ in Christian Tradition*, 1965, p. 215.

[179]Cyril of Jer., *Cat.*, 16.11–13, with reference to 1 Cor. 12.1–11.

overwhelm us with might and violence, for his coming is altogether of a different kind. As Cyril characteristically expressed it: 'His coming is gentle. Our perception of him is fragrant; his burden is very easy to bear; beams of light shine out with his coming. He comes with the compassion of a true Guardian, for he comes to save and to heal, to teach, to admonish, to strengthen, to exhort, to enlighten the mind.'[180] This linking of the Holy Spirit to light was fairly common among the fourth century fathers, who often pointed to the behaviour of created light as a way to help people grasp something of the silent, impalpable way in which God operates throughout his creation.[181] Thus the Holy Spirit as well as the Word made flesh could be described as 'life–giving light'.[182] As Jesus embodied in himself the life that is the light of men, so the Holy Spirit was regarded as functioning with that kind of quiet but utterly supreme power. If it is only the almighty who can be infinitely gentle, the Holy Spirit may well be characterised as the gentleness of God the Father Almighty.

We may associate this Cyrilian understanding of the distinctive properties of the Holy Spirit with that of Basil about the way in which 'the Holy Spirit perfects rational beings, completing their excellences'.[183] Since the Holy Spirit cannot be separated in being or agency from the Father and the Son, he is united with them in being the source (πηγή) and cause (αἰτία) of all things, as in their original creation. However, Basil drew a distinction between the work of the Father as 'the original cause' (τὴν προκαταρκτικὴν αἰτίαν) of all created things, and the work of the Son as 'the operative cause' (τὴν δημιουργικὴν αἰτίαν), and the work of the Holy Spirit as 'the perfecting cause' (τὴν τελειωτικὴν αἰτίαν).[184] 'The first principle of existing things is one, creating through the Son and perfecting through the Spirit.'[185] Basil thought of the specific work of the Holy Spirit

---

[180]Cyril of Jer., *Cat.*, 16.16.
[181]See, for example, Basil, *Hex.*, 2.3–8; *De Sp. St.*, 22f.
[182]Gregory Naz., *Or.*, 31.3, 29; 41.9, 14.
[183]Basil, *De Sp. St.*, 61.
[184]Basil, *De Sp. St.*, 38; see also 48–56.
[185]Basil, *ibid.*, 38. Cf. Gregory Nyss., *non tres dei*, Jaeger, 3.1, p. 47ff; and

as the sovereign freedom of God to be present to his creatures in
the world in order to realise and bring to completion the
creative purpose of God in which creatures are established in
enduring relations with the holiness and Lordship of God.[186]
The words he chose to use here, τελειοῦν, τελειωτικός, carry the
double significance of completing (or perfecting) and
sanctifying.[187] They were particularly relevant in respect of the
will of God to be present to his rational or human creatures in
order to bring to fruition his holy purpose in their relations with
himself. Through the indescribable mode of his presence in the
Holy Spirit God unceasingly supports his creatures in their
existence, and in virtue of his presence within them realises their
relation to himself and so becomes the very principle of their
life, and the source of their enlightenment. Moreover by his
presence the Holy Spirit is the 'place' (τόπος) where men may
meet with God and are enabled to have communion with him,
receive his revelation and worship him.[188] Basil's friend,
Gregory Nazianzen, could even speak of the relation which
God establishes with us in this way through his Spirit as a
relation of himself to himself.[189] Thus in upholding living,
rational creatures from below and within them and in bringing
them to their true end or τέλος in God the Holy Spirit makes
them participate in the very life and holiness of God himself.
Their 'perfection' (τελείωσις) is their 'sanctification'
(τελείωσις).[190]

If we are to follow this development in the doctrine of the
Holy Spirit in the teaching of people like Basil and Cyril of
Jerusalem, we must not lose sight of the profound
Christological perspective in which it took its rise with
Athanasius. That is to say, it is only in the light of the coinherent

Gregory Nazianzen's distinction between αἴτιος, δημιουργός, and
τελειοποιός, *Or.*, 34.8.

[186]Basil, *De Sp. St.*, 49, 51f, 55ff, 61f.

[187]Basil, *ibid.*, 38–40.

[188]Basil, *ibid.*, 46–49, 55, 61–64.

[189]Gregory Naz., *Or.*, 31.12. This Cappadocian teaching clearly underlies
Karl Barth's doctrine of the Spirit, *CD*, I.1, pp. 450ff, 471f.

[190]Basil, *Con. Eun.*, 3.5; *In Ps.*, 48.1f; also Athanasius, *Con. Ar.*, 2.41f, 46;
3.22; *Ad Ser.*, 1.6, 9, 22f, 29; 2.7; 4.7, etc.

relation of the Holy Spirit with the incarnate Son that we may adequately appreciate his rationalising and personalising presence in human beings as he brings them into sanctifying fellowship with God. The 'perfecting cause' is to be understood in conjunction with the incarnation of God's 'operative cause' in Jesus Christ. Through him the eternal Son became man without overriding or diminishing the reality of the human person or ὑπόστασις, but on the contrary gave it real subsistence *in* himself. That is to say, in Epiphanian and Cyrillian language, the human nature of Jesus was personalised or given enhypostatic (ἐνυπόστατος) reality in the Person of the Son of God become man. That took place in Jesus in an utterly unique way. Yet we are all persons in our creaturely beings, for through the personalising activity of the Word and Spirit of God we have authentic personal existence in relation to God and in relation to one another. We are persons, however, not in an independent, but in a dependent or contingent way, as *personalised persons*. Each human being is a *persona personata*, to use the Latin; but God alone is properly and intrinsically Person. As the fullness of personal being he is the creative Source (πηγή) and Author (αἴτιος) of all other personal reality. He alone is personalising Person, *persona personans*. It was precisely in terms of that personalising activity that the Son of God 'came down from heaven, and was made flesh by the Holy Spirit and of the Virgin Mary, and was made man'. Far from the presence of the Deity of the Son overwhelming or displacing the rational human person in Jesus, his human mind and human soul, the exact opposite took place. And so it must be said that no human being has such a full and rich personal human nature as Jesus. It is surely in that light that we must think of the saving and renewing activity of God through Jesus and in his Spirit proclaimed to us in the Gospel. Far from crushing our creaturely nature or damaging our personal existence, the indwelling presence of God through Jesus Christ and in the Holy Spirit has the effect of healing and restoring and deepening human personal being.[191] This personalising activity of the Spirit is to be understood in connection with his *naming* activity

[191]Cf. Epiphanius on this, *Anc.*, 68; *Haer.*, 74.4.

in baptism. Just as the Spirit of God is *named* 'Holy Spirit' in disclosure of his distinct personal identity, so in holy baptism the Spirit seals us with the name of God in adopting us as sons of God, and through his mysterious presence within us as the Spirit of the Son and of the Father enables us to cry 'Abba, Father'.[192] That is what it means to be at once 'in Christ' and 'in the Spirit', for it is through Christ and in the Spirit that we are granted personalising communion with the ever-living God in the perfection of his triune personal being.[193]

(3) The Procession of the Holy Spirit

It was Athanasius, as we have seen, who laid down a firm foundation for the doctrine of the Holy Spirit in showing that our knowledge of the Spirit, in his relation to God and in his own divine nature as Spirit in God, must be taken from our knowledge of the Son, and in applying to the Holy Spirit the ὁμοούσιος as it had been applied to the Son.[194] 'The Holy Spirit proceeds from the Father (παρὰ τοῦ Πατρὸς ἐκπορεύεται), and belonging to the Son (καὶ τοῦ Υἱοῦ ἴδιον ὄν) is from him given (παρ' αὐτοῦ δίδοται) to the disciples and all who believe on him.'[195] 'The Spirit proceeds from the Father and receives from him (καὶ ἐκ τοῦ αὐτοῦ λαμβάνει) and gives.'[196] 'The Spirit receives from the Son (ἐκ τοῦ Υἱοῦ λαμβάνει).'[197] 'If the Son is of (ἐκ) the Father and is proper to his being (ἴδιος τῆς οὐσίας αὐτοῦ), the Spirit who is said to be of (ἐκ) God must also be proper to the Son in respect of his being (ἴδιον εἶναι κατ' οὐσίαν τοῦ Υἱοῦ).'[198] 'Because the Spirit is one and, what is more, is proper to the Word who is one, he is proper to God who is one

---

[192]Rom. 8.15; Gal. 4.6; Cyril of Jer., *Procat.*, 1ff; *Cat.*, 1.1ff; 3.1ff; 7.14; 17.4, 6; 21.1ff; 23.5.

[193]This is surely part of the meaning of θεοποίησις in Greek patristic theology – Athanasius, *De decr.*, 14, 31; *Con. Ar.*, 1.9, 39, 78; 2.59, 70; 3.19, 33, 53; 4.21f; *Ad Ser.*, 1.23ff; *De syn.*, 51; *Ad Adel.*, 4; *Ad Max.*, 2, etc.

[194]Athanasius, *Ad Ser.*, 1.27; 3.1.

[195]Athanasius, *Ad Ser.*, 1.2; cf. 3.1; 4.3.

[196]Athanasius, *Ad Ser.*, 1.11.

[197]Athanasius, *Ad Ser.*, 1.20; 3.1; 4.1f.

[198]Athanasius, *Ad Ser.*, 1.25; 3.1; 4.3f.

and ὁμοούσιον with him . . . In nature and being he is proper to and not foreign to the Godhead and being of the Son and is thus of the Holy Trinity.'[199]

The ground for this doctrine of the Holy Spirit in his ontological relation to the Father and the Son had already been prepared by Athanasius in his encounters with the Arians.[200] The Son is not different in being (ἑτερούσιος) from God or foreign (ἀλλότριος) to his nature, but is of one being (ὁμοούσιος) and of one nature (ὁμοφυής) with him. Likewise we must think of the Holy Spirit as ὁμοούσιος with God, for he cannot be divided from the Son, since the Holy Trinity is indivisible and of one nature (ὁμοφυής).[201] While Basil of Caesarea and Cyril of Jerusalem were strangely hesitant about affirming the consubstantiality of the Holy Spirit, Gregory Nazianzen had no hesitation in following Athanasius. 'Is the Spirit God? Most certainly. Is he ὁμοούσιος, then? Yes, if he is God'.[202] However, when the concepts of ὁμοούσιος and of ἐνυπόστατος were brought together to speak of the oneness of being and inner hypostatic reality of the three divine Persons in God, as they were with great power by Epiphanius, then the way was open for a deeper understanding of the Triunity of God and for a doctrine of the procession of the Spirit from the being of the Father parallel to that of the Son affirmed at the Council of Nicaea.

In applying the ὁμοούσιος to the relation of the incarnate Son to God the Father, the Nicene theologians gave precise expression to their conviction that what God is toward us in his revealing and saving work in Jesus Christ he is inherently in his own eternal being as God. Thus they affirmed at the same time that he was 'from the being of the Father (ἐκ τῆς οὐσίας τοῦ Πατρός), God of God, Light of Light, true God of true God'. A two-way movement of thought was involved there: what God is toward us, he is in himself, and what he is in himself he is

---

[199]Athanasius, *Ad Ser.*, 1.27; 3.1; 4.3.

[200]Athanasius, *Con. Ar.*, 1.15, 47f; 1.50, 56; 2.18; 3.15, 24, 25, 44; cf. also the addendum to the *Ad Ser.*, 4.8–23, Athens ed., 33, pp. 133–149; and *Con. Apol.*, 1.9.

[201]Athanasius, *Con. Ar.*, 1.58; *Ad Ser.*, 1.17, 28; 3.1.

[202]Gregory Naz., *Or.*, 31.10.

toward us. The Father and the Son coinhere in one another in the one being of God, but, as Epiphanius and Didymus would have it, coinhere 'enhypostatically', that is in respect of their distinct personal or hypostatic realities each of which is 'whole God' (ὅλος θεός). It became clear, as we have seen, that the Nicene belief in the Holy Spirit, parallel to belief in the Father and the Son, involved the same double movement of thought, for there is a coinherent relation between the Holy Spirit and God the Son, just as there is a coinherent relation between the Son and the Father. The overwhelming conviction about the Holy Spirit in the evangelical experience and doxological understanding of the Church, was that all his distinctive operations, in speaking, saving, enlightening, sanctifying and liberating us, are *divine acts*: *in the Spirit* our creaturely beings come under the immediate impact of the holy being of God, the almighty Creator and Source of all being. Hence the Holy Spirit is acknowledged to be in his own nature and being what he is toward us in all his divine acts of blessing and grace, for along with the Son he belongs to and flows from the inner being and nature of the Godhead. 'When you pronounce the ὁμοούσιον, you assert that the Son is God of God, and that the Holy Spirit is God of the same Godhead.'[203]

Here too a double movement of thought is involved: what the Holy Spirit is toward us, he is in himself, and what he is in himself he is toward us. The Holy Spirit is ever with the Father and the Son, coinhering with them in the one being of God, but coinhering 'enhypostatically' with them in such a way that in the one being of God, the Holy Spirit is always Holy Spirit, as the Father is always Father and the Son is always Son, each being 'true and perfect God', as Epiphanius loved to express it.[204] That is to say, the Holy Spirit belongs to the inner being of the one God, and to the constitutive internal relations of the Godhead as Father, Son and Holy Spirit. He is central to the Triunity of God, for God the Father is not the Father nor God the Son the Son, without God the Holy Spirit. There is, then, only one divine activity, that of God the Father through the Son

[203]Epiphanius, *Anc.*, 6.
[204]Epiphanius, *Anc.*, 10, 81; *Haer.*, 69.44, 56; 72.1; 76.21; *Exp. fidei*, 18.

and in the Spirit, for whatever the Father and the Son are, the Holy Spirit is, except 'Father' and 'Son'.[205]

That is why, as we have seen, Gregory Nazianzen could speak of the Holy Spirit as intermediate between the Father and the Son,[206] and why Basil could speak of the κοινωνία of the Spirit with the Father and the Son, and find in that κοινωνία the very unity of the Godhead.[207] Similarly Epiphanius, as we have seen, spoke of the Holy Spirit as 'in the middle of the Father and the Son', and even as 'the bond of the Trinity'.[208] This is the conception of the Spirit which was later taken up by Augustine in his doctrine of the Holy Spirit as 'the consubstantial communion of the Father and the Son', and as 'the mutual love wherewith the Father and the Son reciprocally love one another'.[209] It was along this line that the developing Nicene theology came to recognise that the coinherent relations of the Father, Son and Holy Spirit, revealed in the saving acts of God through Christ and in the Spirit, are not temporary manifestions of his nature, but are eternally grounded in the intrinsic and wholly reciprocal relations of the consubstantial Trinity.[210] 'God is one, the Father in the Son, the Son in the Father with the Holy Spirit ... true enhypostatic Father, and true enhypostatic Son, and true enhypostatic Holy Spirit, three Persons, one Godhead, one being, one glory, one God. In thinking of God you conceive of the Trinity, but without confusing in your mind the Father, the Son and the Holy Spirit.

---

[205]Gregory Naz., *Or.*, 41.9: 'All that the Father has the Son has also, except being the unbegotten; and all that the Son has the Spirit has also, except being begotten.' See also 31.9.

[206]Gregory Naz., *Or.*, 31.8.

[207]Basil, *De Sp. St.*, 30, 38, 45ff, 68; cf. Athanasius, *Ad Ser.*, 1.20; 3.1; Gregory Nyss., *Con. Eun.*, Jaeger, 2, p. 328; Hilary, *De Trin.*, 2.33.

[208]Epiphanius, *Anc.*, 4, 7f; *Haer.*, 62.4; 74.11.

[209]Augustine, *De Trin.*, 6.7; 15.27, 50.

[210]Evidently the term περιχώρησις came into theological use through Gregory Nazianzen, *Or.*, 18.42; 22.4; *Ep.*, 101.6. See the comments of G. S. Kirk and J. E. Raven (*The Presocratic Philosophers*, 1957, pp. 373, 380), with reference to the *Scholia* on Gregory's *Orationes*, *MPG*, 36.991. For earlier thought in this direction see Athenagoras, *Suppl.*, 10; Irenaeus, *Adv. haer.*, 3.6.2, vol. 2, p. 22f; Dionysius of Alex., *ap.* Athanasius, *De decr.*, 26; Hilary, *De Trin.*, 3.4; 4.10.

The Father is the Father, the Son is the Son, the Holy Spirit is the Holy Spirit, but there is no deviation in the Trinity from oneness and identity.'[211]

It is in the light of this developed doctrine of the Triunity of God, which holds together the conceptions of the identity of the divine being and the intrinsic unity of the three divine Persons, that we may best consider the issue of the procession of the Holy Spirit.

We learn from Athanasius that it was within such a context of the divine Trinity and Unity that the question of the procession of the Holy Spirit had been raised by Dionysius of Alexandria well before the Council of Nicaea. In a defence of the Μοναρχία against both tritheism and unipersonalism, he insisted on taking into account the Holy Spirit, including 'both whence and through whom he proceeded', and so pointed to the κοινωνία of the Father and the Son 'in whose hands is the Spirit, who cannot be parted either from him who sends or from him who conveys him'.[212] This was the position adopted by Athanasius himself,[213] but it was greatly strengthened by his doctrine of the coinherence of the divine Persons. 'The Spirit is not outside the Word but being *in* the Word he is *in* God through him'.[214] Moreover, since he felt that knowledge of the Spirit is properly taken from knowledge of the Son on the ground of this inherence of the Spirit in the Son and in God, he could not but understand the gift of the Spirit as coming to us 'through and from' Christ as well as 'from the Father', for like the Son the Spirit is 'in God' and 'of God'.[215] Thus for Athanasius the procession of the Spirit from the Father is inextricably bound up with 'the generation of the Son from the Father which exceeds and transcends the thoughts of men'.[216] Since it would not be reverent, therefore, to ask how the Spirit proceeds from God, Athanasius did not and would not entertain the question. Thus

---

[211]Epiphanius, *Anc.*, 10.

[212]Athanasius, *De sent. Dion.*, 17; cf. also *De syn.*, 26.

[213]Athanasius, *Exp. fidei*, 4.

[214]Athanasius, *Ad Ser.*, 3.5; οὐ γὰρ ἐκτός ἐστι τοῦ Λόγου τὸ Πνεῦμα, ἀλλά, ἐν τῷ Λόγῳ ὄν, ἐν τῷ Θεῷ δι' αὐτοῦ ἐστιν.

[215]Athanasius, *Con. Ar.*, 1.47f, 50; 2.18; 3.3ff, 15, 25; *Ad Ser.*, 1.2, 15, 20; 4.3.

[216]Athanasius, *De decr.*, 12.

the problem of a so-called 'double procession' of the Spirit just did not arise for him.[217] However, he was bound to understand the Spirit's being 'of God' and 'from God', and even 'from and through' the Son, in the light of the Nicene ὁμοούσιον and the explanation that 'from the Father' meant 'from the *being* of the Father' (ἐκ τῆς οὐσίας τοῦ Πατρός). Hence Athanasius' application of ὁμοούσιος to the Holy Spirit had the effect, not only of asserting that the Spirit is also of one being with the Father, but of implying that the procession of the Spirit is from the *being* of the Father (ἐκ τῆς οὐσίας τοῦ Πατρός), and not from what came to be spoken of as the ὑπόστασις *of the Father in distinction from, though inseparable from, his* οὐσία *as God*.[218] For Athanasius the fact that the Son and Spirit are both *of the being* of God the Father meant that there is one activity of God which is manifested in the distinctive operations of the three divine Persons and always takes the form of a unitary movement 'from the Father, through the Son and in the Spirit'.[219]

That trinitarian pattern was taken over from Athanasius by the Cappadocian theologians, but, as we have seen, they called for a clear distinction between οὐσία and ὑπόστασις in order to bring more sharply into focus the Persons of the Father, the Son and the Holy Spirit in their different modes of existence and identifying particularities. Thus the specific relation of the Son to the Father from whom he is begotten precisely as *Son*, is quite different from the relation of the Spirit to the Father from whom he proceeds precisely as *Spirit* like breath from his mouth.[220] This clear distinction between 'Paternity', 'Filiation' and 'Spiration' had the effect of shifting the main weight of emphasis (at least in the order of knowing) onto the three ὑποστάσεις who, nevertheless, in virtue of their common divine

[217]Athanasius, *Con. Ar.*, 1.17f; 4.5; *Ad Ser.*, 1.15ff, etc. Cf. Cyril of Jerusalem, *Cat.*, 11.9.

[218]Athanasius, *Ad Ser.*, 1.0, 22, 25, 27; 2.5; 3.1. His thought was quite clear on this matter, although, as in the Nicene anathemas, he could use οὐσία and ὑπόστασις as more or less equivalent, *De decr.*, 20; *De syn.*, 41; *Ad Ser.*, 2.5.

[219]Athanasius, *Ad Ser.*, 1.9, 12, 14, 20, 24, 28, 30; 3.5; 4.6.

[220]Basil, *De Sp. St.*, 46; *Con. Eun.*, 2.28; *Ep.*, 214.4; 236.6; Gregory Nyss., *Or. cat.*, 2; Gregory Naz., *Or.*, 41.9, 14.

nature possess one identical divine being (μία οὐσία).[221] The community of nature is not disrupted by the distinction of the Persons, nor are the particularising notes of the Persons confounded in the community of their being.[222] The Son derives from the Father in a way appropriate to the Son as Son, by generation, and the Spirit derives from him in a way appropriate to the Spirit as Spirit, by procession, the Son unoriginally begotten and the Spirit unbegottenly proceeding, both quite ineffably.[223]

However, when the Cappadocians argued for this doctrine of 'one Being, three Persons' (μία οὐσία, τρεῖς ὑποστάσεις) on the principle that the οὐσία has the same relation to the ὑπόστασις as the common to the particular, they were tempted to account for the oneness and threeness of God through recourse to the dangerous analogy of three different people having a common nature. Understandably this laid them rather open to the suspicion of advocating some form of tritheism – three gods with a common nature – which they strongly rejected, as we can see in Gregory Nyssen's book, *That there are not three Gods*.[224] They sought to preserve the oneness of God by insistng that God the Father, who is himself without generation or origination, is the one Principle or Origin (ἀρχή) and Cause (αἰτία) of the Son and the Spirit, although in such a way that there is no interval of existence, time or space between them and no 'before' or 'after' in the order of their being. This involved a unique notion of cause, as comprising and continuous with its effects.[225] This way of regarding the Father as the unifying

---

[221]See especially Basil's *Epistles* 125, 214, 236, and Gregory/Basil, *Ep.*, 38.

[222]See Gregory/Basil, *Ep.*, 38.4, where mention is made of 'a conjoined separation and a separated conjunction' in God. Similarly Gregory Naz. referred to the three ὑποστάσεις as 'divided without division, and united in division', *Or.*, 39.11; also *Or.*, 31.14; *Or.*, 41.9.

[223]See Gregory Naz., *Or.*, 29.8f; 30.19; 31.8f; 39.12.

[224]See Basil, *Hom. con. syc.*, Athens ed., 54, pp. 234–237; *Ep.*, 8, 31, 189, etc.

[225]Basil, *Con Eun.*, 1.19, 25; Gregory Nyss., *Con. Eun.*, 1.36, 39, 42; Gregory/Basil, *Ep.*, 38.4, 7. However, so far as the external relations of God are concerned, the Son and the Spirit are inseparably conjoined with the Father in constituting one ἀρχή and αἰτία – Basil, *De Sp. St.*, 37; Gregory Nyss., *Con. Eun.*, 1.36; 3.64; *De Sp. St.*, Jaeger, 3.1, pp. 97ff, 105ff; *non tres dei*, Jaeger, 3.1, pp. 47ff; Gregory/Basil, *Ep.*, 38.4, etc.

Principle in the Godhead was strongly put forward by Gregory Nyssen, who could speak of the Son and the Spirit as 'caused' (αἰτιατοί) by the Father, not in respect of their nature but in respect of their mode of existence. And yet at the same time he thought of the being of the Holy Spirit as grounded through the being of Son in the being of the Father.[226]

A double problem arises here which is very evident in Gregory Nyssen's account of the procession of the Spirit. 'The Holy Spirit, from whom the supply of all good things in the creation has its source, is attached to the Son with whom he is inseparably apprehended. He depends for his being on the Father as Cause, from whom he also proceeds. It is the identifying mark of his hypostatic nature that he is known after and with the Son, and that he derives his subsistence from the Father.'[227] Thus the Cappadocian rebuttal of the charge that their differentiation between three ὑποστάσεις, with their distinct modes of existence, implied three ultimate divine Principles (ἀρχαί), and their attempt to secure the oneness (ἕνωσις) of the Godhead by referring the three Persons to a single Principle (ἀρχή) or Cause (αἰτία) in the Father, were made at the expense of a damaging distinction between the Deity of the Father as wholly underived or 'uncaused', and the Deity of the Son and of the Spirit as eternally derived or 'caused'.[228] Moreover, in differentiatng the Persons of the Holy Trinity they cast the internal relations between the Father, the Son and the Holy Spirit into the consecutive structure of a causal series or a 'chain' of dependence 'through the Son',[229] instead of conceiving of them more, like Athanasius, in terms of their coinherent and undivided wholeness, in which each Person is 'whole of the whole'.[230] It would have been better if the

---

[226]Gregory Nyss, *non tres dei*, Jaeger, 3.1, p. 56f; see also *Con. Eun.*, 1.25, 33ff, 42; *Con. Eun.*, 2, Jaeger, 1, pp. 264ff; *Con. Eun.*, 3.5, 4; *Or. cat.*, 1ff.

[227]Gregory/Basil, *Ep.*, 38.4.

[228]Gregory Naz., *Or.*, 29.3; 31.13f. At the same time Gregory can refer to the Godhead as the Μοναρχία *Or.*, 2.38; 31.14; 39.12; 41.9.

[229]Gregory/Basil, *Ep.*, 38.4; Basil, *De Sp. St.*, 13, 45f, 58f; *Con. Sab.*, 4; Gregory Nyss., *Con. Eun.*, 1, 36; *Adv. Maced.*, 13; and *non tres dei*, Jaeger, 3.1, p. 56, where, however, Gregory suggests that the notion of 'cause' may ultimately be dispensable.

[230]Athanasius, *Con. Ar.*, 1.16; 3.1ff; 4.1ff; *Ad Ser.*, 1.16, 29, etc. While

Cappadocians had paid less attention to the concept of causality in God, and given more attention to what Athanasius called 'the living will of God'.[231] Once again it was Gregory Nazianzen who was closest to him in this respect, in affirming the identity of being, movement and will in God.[232]

While Gregory Nazianzen offered much the same teaching as his fellow Cappadocians, he exercised more flexibility in the use of theological terms, and had a more Athanasian conception of the unity of God and of the Godhead as complete not primarily in the Father but in each Person as well as in all of them.[233] He could also employ causal language in referring the Deity of the Son and of the Holy Spirit to one Principle or ἀρχή in the Godhead,[234] but he was more aware of the difficulties involved. 'I would like to call the Father greater', he wrote, 'in that both the equality and the being of the equal ones are from him. But I am alarmed at the word "principle" (τὴν ἀρχὴν), lest I make him the Principle of inferiors, and insult him through the idea of precedence in honour . . . For there is no greater or less in respect of the being of consubstantial Persons.'[235] 'We do not honour the Father, by dishonouring his Offspring with unequal degrees of Deity . . . To subordinate any of the three is to overthrow the Trinity.'[236] While Gregory nevertheless spoke of the Father as the ἀρχή and the αἰτία in order to secure the unity of the Godhead, actually he *thought* of them as referring to *relations* or σχέσεις subsisting in God which are beyond all time (ἀχρόνως), beyond all origin (ἀνάρχως), and beyond all cause (ἀναιτίως).[237] This conception of divine relations was later

Athanasius did on occasion use αἴτιος of the Father, it was without any notion of causal structure or subordination in the Trinity – *De syn.*, 46f. In *Con. Ar.*, 2.54, αἰτία means 'reason' rather than 'cause'.

[231] Athanasius, *Con. Ar.*, 2.2, 31; *De syn.*, 23; cf. *Con. Ar.*, 3.58ff. Here he was followed by Cyril of Alexandria, *Thes.*, *MPG* 75.97A, 105C, 249A.

[232] Gregory Naz., *Or.*, 20.7; cf. 29.6; and Basil, *De Sp. St.*, 21.

[233] Gregory Naz., *Or.*, 30.20; 37.33ff; 38.8; 39.10f; 40.41ff; 42.16; 45.4.

[234] Gregory Naz., *Or.*, 1.38; 2.38; 20.7; 29.3, 15, 19; 30.19f; 31.8–14; 32.30, 33; 34.8, 10; 39.12; 40.41ff; 41.9; 42.15ff.

[235] Gregory Naz., *Or.*, 40.43; and see 29.15.

[236] Gregory Naz., *Or.*, 43.30.

[237] Gregory Naz., *Or.*, 29.2ff, 16; 30.11, 19f; 31.9, 14, 16. Cf. also Gregory Nyss., *Con. Eun.*, 1.22; *De fide*, Jaeger, 3.1, p. 65; and Basil, *De Sp. St.*, 14f;

taken up by Cyril of Alexandria, but reinforced by his rejection of any notion of causality within the Holy Trinity.[238]

There is the further problem, however, as to whether the being or existence of the Son and the Spirit is to be traced back to the *Person* or ὑπόστασις of the Father.[239] Gregory Nyssen sought to clear up this point, although he was not always consistent. Thus in his little work on 'Common Notions' he pointed out that the word 'God' (Θεός) signifies being (οὐσία) and does not refer to Person (πρόσωπον), which implies that the Father is not God in virtue of his Fatherhood but in virtue of his being; otherwise neither the Son nor the Holy Spirit would be God. And yet, on the other hand, he could say at the same time that in the Holy Trinity everything proceeds from the Father as the centre of unity, who is properly called 'God' for it is in his ὑπόστασις that the ἀρχή of Deity is lodged.[240] The upshot of this train of reasoning would appear to be that the Son and the Spirit are held to derive, not their Deity from the Father, but only their Persons (ὑποστάσεις) or their distinctive modes of existence (τρόποι ὑπάρξεως), for the οὐσία of Deity is one and the same in all. It is properly in that respect that they may be regarded as derived from and as causally dependent on the ὑπόστασις or πρόσωπον of the Father.[241]

In their attempt to give the doctrine of the Trinity more precise definition in the terms used, which would bring out the distinctive individualities and objectivities of the three divine Persons, the Cappadocian theologians left the Church with a twofold problem, as to the significance of the Fatherhood of

Con. Eun., 1, Athens ed., 52, p. 164.

[238]Cyril Alex., *Thes.*, *MPG*, 75, 10.125f, 128f; 32.553; cf. *Dial. de Trin.*, *MPG*, 75, 2.721, 744f, 769.

[239]See Gregory Naz., *Or.*, 31.14.

[240]Gregory Nyss., *Ex com. not.*, Jaeger, 3.1, pp. 19–25; cf. *De Sp. St.*, Jaeger, 3.1, pp. 13ff; and *Ex com. not.*, Jaeger, 3.1, p. 25, where he speaks of the Son as generated and Spirit as proceeding from the Person (πρόσωπον) of the Father.

[241]Gregory Nyss., *non tres dei*, Jaeger, 3.1, pp. 55ff. The same ideas are found in several fragments once attributed to Amphilochius, e.g.: 'The difference is in the Persons, not in their being (οὐσία), for 'Father', 'Son' and 'Holy Spirit' are names of a mode of existence or relation, but not at all of being (οὐσίας).' *MPG*, 39, 112.

God, and as to the oneness of the Trinity. As we have already noted, 'Father' was constantly used in the early Church in two ways, with reference to the Godhead and to the Person of the Father. They were never separated from one another, but with the Cappadocian theologians these two senses of Paternity were completely conflated. As the same time, their way of distinguishing between the οὐσία as a generic concept and ὑπόστασις as a particular concept, imported a shift in approach: from emphasis upon the ὁμοούσιος as the key to the identity, intrinsic oneness, and internal relations of the Holy Trinity, to emphasis upon the three diverse ὑποστάσεις as united through the Μοναρχία of the Father and through having one being in common.[242] Thus the main thrust of the Cappadocian teaching, even with reservations and qualifications, was to make the first Person of the Trinity or the ὑπόστασις of the Father the sole Principle or Cause or Source of Deity (ἀρχή, αἰτία, πηγή Θεότητος). Although it could be claimed that everything of the Father belongs to the Son and everything of the Son belongs to the Father,[243] the general trend was to weaken the Athanasian axiom that whatever we say of the Father we say of the Son and the Spirit except 'Father'.[244] For Athanasius, as for Alexander, the idea that the Father alone is ἀρχή in this sense was an Arian concept.[245] He, on his part, held that since the whole Godhead is in the Son and in the Spirit, they must be included with the Father in the one originless ἀρχή of the Holy Trinity.[246] Admittedly, the Cappadocian way of expounding the doctrine

[242]But see Basil, *Con. Eun.*, 1.23, where he appeared to modify the notion of generic unity toward one of identity (ταὐτότης).

[243]Gregory/Basil, *Ep.*, 38.8.

[244]Thus also Epiphanius, *Haer.*, 70.8. Cf. Ps. Athanasius, *Quaest. al.*, 5, *MPG*, 28.784. It was Gregory Nazianzen who stood closest to Athanasius in this as in other respects – see again, *Or.*, 21.13, 34; 31.9, 14; 34.8ff; 40.41; 41.9; 42.15ff, etc.

[245]See the Letter of Arius to Eusebius, *ap.* Theodoret, *Hist. eccl.*, 1.4; Athanasius, *De syn.*, 16. Thus also Hilary, *De Trin.*, 4.13; and Epiphanius, *Haer.*, 69.8, 78; cf. also 73.16 & 21.

[246]Athanasius, *Ad Ant.*, 5; *Con. Ar.*, 4.1–4. Thus also Epiphanius, *Haer.*, 69.29; 73.16; *Exp. fidei*, 14. He laid considerable emphasis on one ultimate lordship and sovereignty of the undivided Trinity – see *Haer.*, 57.4; 62, 2f; 63.8; 69.33, 44, 73, 75; 73.15f; 74.14.

of the μία οὐσία, τρεῖς ὑποστάσεις helped the Church to have a richer and fuller understanding of the three Persons of the Holy Trinity in their distinctive modes of existence. However this was done at the cost of cutting out the real meaning of οὐσία as *being in its internal relations*, and of robbing οὐσία of its profound personal sense which was so prominent at Nicaea. Moreover, the Cappadocian interpretation concealed a serious ambiguity. From one point of view the so-called 'Cappadocian settlement' meant the rejection of subordinationism, but from another it implied a hierarchical structure within the Godhead – an ambiguity that kept disconcerting thought within the Church and opening the way for division.

Meantime the effect of the neo-Nicene discussions on the conception of the procession of the Spirit became apparent in the thought of Didymus the Blind. As we have seen, he wisely tied the doctrine of *one Being, three Persons* into the doctrine of the consubstantiality of the Trinity as a whole. While the Father, Son and Holy Spirit are quite distinct, each is nevertheless God of God in the fullest and most perfect sense, indivisibly coinhering in the others within the oneness and identity of their divine nature and being. He was closest to Gregory Nazianzen in the way he thought of the Son and the Spirit as deriving hypostatically, by way of generation and procession beyond all time and beyond all beginning, from the Father. 'We confess that the Holy Spirit is God, consubstantial with the Father and the Son and with them without any beginning (συνανάρχως), who proceeds from God the Father consubstantially.'[247] However, he often stressed that this meant procession from the ὑπόστασις of the Father.[248] As the Son derives from the Father through generation in a way appropriate to him as Son (υἱϊκῶς), so the Spirit derives from the Father through procession in a way appropriate to him as Spirit (πνευματικῶς), but neither in an operative nor in a creative way (δημιουργικῶς).[249] On a rare occasion Didymus could speak of

[247]Didymus, *De Trin.*, 2.26.

[248]Didymus, *De Trin.*, 1.10, 15, 32, 34f; 2.1f, 4f; 2.6, 22; 2.7, 12; 3.2f, 5, 38; *De Sp. St.*, 26; 34f; *Con. Eun.*, Athens ed., 44, pp. 225f.

[249]Didymus, *De Trin.*, 2.1f, 5; 2.6.8, 22, etc.

these trinitarian relations in causal terms, but that way of thinking did not have the importance for him that it had for the Cappadocians.[250]

The significance of Didymus lies in the fact that, basically Athanasian though he was, he tended to replace the Nicene formula 'from the being of the Father' (ἐκ τῆς οὐσίας τοῦ Πατρός) with 'from the Person of the Father' (ἐκ τῆς ὑποστάσεως τοῦ Πατρός).[251] Nevertheless he upheld the truth that in his being the Holy Spirit is of one being with God and is God of God, and must be thought of, therefore, as present to us in his actual being and not just through his operations, for *God himself* is the content of his self-giving to us in the Spirit. Hence he identified the procession of the Spirit from the Person of the Father as an eternal procession 'from God', for the Spirit and the Son coexist consubstantially and naturally, and proceed simultaneously and continuously from the Father within the unity of the Holy Trinity.[252]

There is little hint here of the idea, later associated with the Cappadocians, that the procession of the Holy Spirit from the Father implied procession from the Father *only*. Didymus' position was not altogether clear, but he evidently wanted to avoid any conception of the oneness of the Godhead which defined it in terms of the derivation of the Son and the Spirit from the *Person* of the Father as the one Source or ἀρχή of *Deity*, and thus to avoid any subordinationist distinction between the underived Deity of the Father and the derived Deity of the Son and of the Holy Spirit. The Son and the Spirit do derive their distinctive modes of existence and their distinctive properties through their generation and procession from the Person of the Father, but that is not to be equated with the *causation of their being*. Thus Didymus could even speak of the procession of the Spirit from the Person of the Son as well as from the Person of

---

[250]Didymus, *Con. Eun.*, Athens ed., 44, p. 251 – this is the work in which the influence of Basil on him is most evident.

[251]However, see Didymus, *De Trin.*, 2.5, where he combined ἐκ τῆς ὑποστάσεως τοῦ Πατρός and ἐκ τῆς οὐσίας τοῦ Πατρός in the source of the Spirit's procession. Cf. *Epistola Eusebii*, *ap.* Theodoret, *Hist. eccl.*, 1.11.

[252]Didymus, *De Trin.*, 2.2, 15.

the Father within the indivisible consubstantiality of the Holy Trinity, without any suggestion that the Spirit came into being through the Son or that there are two ultimate divine Principles, for procession from and through the Son relates to the inherence of the Spirit in the Son and to their community of nature with the Father.[253]

This problematic situation over the procession of the Holy Spirit was considerably clarified through Epiphanius by returning to the basic position laid down by Athanasius, and building upon it. Athanasius had taught that the Spirit is ever in the hands of the Father who sends and of the Son who gives him as his very own, and from whom the Spirit on his part receives. Since the Spirit like the Son is of the being of God, and belongs to the Son, he could not but proceed from or out of the being of God inseparably from and through the Son. In the nature of the case, the idea that the Spirit derives his *being* from the Person of the Son just does not and could not arise for Athanasius.[254] That also holds true for Epiphanius. Thus in the *Anchoratus* we read that 'The Holy Spirit is ever with the Father and the Son, proceeding from the Father and receiving from the Son.'[255] He thought of procession, whether of the Son or the Spirit, as taking place enhypostatically in God beyond all beginning and all time (ἀνάρχως καὶ ἀχρόνως).[256] That has to be understood, as we have seen, within the context of Epiphanius' doctrine of the Triunity of three coequal and coeternal enhypostatic Persons in the Godhead, in whose midst the Holy Spirit is 'the bond of the Trinity'. In that light Epiphanius thought of the Holy Spirit, not only as having his personal subsistence 'out of the Father through the Son' (ἐκ Πατρὸς δι᾽ Υἱοῦ), but as 'out of the being' (ἐκ τῆς οὐσίας) or 'out of the same being' (ἐκ τῆς

[253]Didymus, *De Trin.*, 2.1; 2.2, 5; 2.26f; *De Sp. St.*, 26. Heron rightly points out that Didymus rejected any kind of subordinationism in the Trinity – *Ekkl. Pharos*, 1971, p. 16; *Kerygma und Logos*, edit. by A. H. Ritter, 1979, p. 308.

[254]Athanasius, *De sent. Dion.*, 1.17; *Exp. fidei*, 4; *Con. Ar.*, 1.16, 20, 46ff, 50; 2.18, 28; 3.1ff, 15, 24ff, 44ff; *Ad Ser.*, 1.2, 15f, 20ff; 3.2ff; 4.3f.

[255]Epiphanius, *Anc.*, 6; cf. 9 & 11; and *Haer.*, 76. *Ref. Aet.*, 15, 22, 28, 31, 35; thus also Gregory Nyss., *Adv. Maced.*, 10.

[256]Epiphanius, *Haer.*, 62.3; 63.7; 69.18, 36; 73.11, 26; 76.6; 76. *Ref. Aet.*, 5, 21, 28; 78.3.

αὐτῆς οὐσίας) of the Father and the Son, for the Holy Spirit *is* God. Thus it may be said that the Holy Spirit proceeds as Light and Truth 'from both' the Father and the Son.[257] It was, then, in these terms that Epiphanius interpreted and filled out the succinct Athanasian statement that 'the Holy Spirit proceeds from the Father and receives from the Son', but in such a way that the enhypostatic realities and distinctive properties of the Father, the Son and the Holy Spirit always remain the same in the equality and consubstantiality of the Holy Trinity.[258] And it was in these terms that he put forward the credal statement about the Holy Spirit which was taken over by the Council of Constantinople in 381. 'We believe in one Holy Spirit, the Lord and Giver of life, who proceeds from the Father, who with Father and the Son together is worshipped and glorified, who spoke through the prophets.'[259]

In their doctrine of the Holy Spirit the fathers of Constantinople were undoubtedly indebted to the Cappadocian theologians, particularly to Gregory Nazianzen who presided over their early sessions.[260] It is significant, however, that it was the line of development from Athanasius through Epiphanius that was finally decisive for them, not least in their statement of the procession the Spirit 'from the Father'. This was intended to be parallel to the Nicene statement about the generation of the Son 'from the Father', without the addition of any qualification along Cappadocian lines, although of course the doctrine of 'one Being, three Persons' was given conciliar authority.[261]

---

[257]Epiphanius, *Haer.*, 62.4; 69, 54, 56, 63; 73.12, 16; 74.7f; 74.14; 76.11; *Anc.*, 71f.

[258]Epiphanius, *Anc.*, 72ff; *Haer.*, 74.9ff, 12.

[259]Epiphanius, *Anc.*, 119. In the following chapter a fuller statement is found which was designed for instruction.

[260]See Gregory Naz., *Or.*, 42.15ff, in which he obviously had some misgivings about what was being put forward at the Council.

[261]See the synodical Letter from the Council of Constantinople, *ap.* Theodoret, *Hist. eccl.*, 5.9: 'There is one Godhead, power and being of the Father, the Son and the Holy Spirit, equal in honour, dignity and sovereignty in three perfect ὑποστάσεις and three perfect πρόσωπα.' And see also the rider to the Council found in the correspondence of Damasus of Rome anathematising those who do not confess that the Holy Spirit is of one and the

This determination to keep close to the basic position adopted at Nicaea was surely providential. The Cappadocian attempt to redefine οὐσία as a generic concept, with the loss of its concrete sense as being with internal relations, meant that it would be difficult if not impossible for theology to move from the self-revelation of God in his evangelical acts to what he is inherently in himself. If God's Word and act are not inherent (ἐνούσιοι) in his being or οὐσία, as Athanasius insisted, then we cannot relate what God is toward us in his saving revelation and activity to what he is in himself, or vice versa.[262] The Cappadocian way of taking a middle path between unipersonalism and tritheism (through grounding the unity of the Godhead in the Father as the unique and exclusive Principle of the Godhead and thus as the one Cause of the being and existence of the Son and the Spirit) gave rise to a serious impasse. In view of the suggestion that the Spirit proceeds from the Father only, Western Churchmen felt obliged to hold that the Spirit proceeds from the Son as well as from the Father, otherwise the Son would not be regarded as really God of God, God in the same sense as the Father. But in view of this reaction, Eastern Churchmen felt they had to reject any idea of a procession of the Spirit from the Son as well as the Father, for that appeared to assume two ultimate divine Principles in God – hence they opted for a doctrine of the procession of the Spirit *from the Father only*. That was a dilemma that would not have arisen had the Church in East and West kept closer to the Athanasian doctrine of the Holy Spirit in this line of development through Epiphanius and the Council of Constantinople to the teaching of Cyril of Alexandria.

It may be worth referring at this point to Cyril of Jerusalem who held a doctrine of the procession of the Spirit that was untroubled by the problem we have been discussing. 'The Holy

---

same being and power as the Father and the Son, the consubstantial Trinity to be worshipped in three perfect Persons – Theodoret, *ibid.*, 5.11.

[262]This became very clear in the claim of pseudo-Dionysius that mystical theology must reach beyond the notion of *Fatherhood* in its thought of God as a superessential undifferentiated *ousia* not nameable or knowable in its internal relations – *De div. nom.*, 1.5ff; 2.1ff; *Theol. myst.*, 1f.

Spirit is ever one and the same, living and personally subsisting and always present together with the Father and the Son – not as if uttered like breath from the mouth and lips of the Father and the Son, only to be dispersed into the air – but as enhypostatic being, speaking and operating, dispensing and fulfilling the saving economy which comes to us from the Father, the Son and the Holy Spirit, and is indivisible, harmonious and one.'[263]

III

Before we conclude this account of Pneumatology in fourth century Greek patristic thought, we ought to draw attention, if only briefly, to several aspects of the Holy Spirit's activity within the life of the Church which are of importance for what we shall consider in the next chapter.

The first aspect can be indicated by bringing together the statements in the Nicene-Constantinopolitan Creed about the Holy Spirit as 'the Lord' and as he 'who spoke by the prophets'.[264] That is to say, the Holy Spirit meets us as coming from the 'I am' of the Lord God Almighty.[265] He is 'the Lord the Spirit',[266] the sovereign divine Subject (Κύριος) who speaks to us in Person and establishes fellowship with us. He is 'speaking Spirit', the very Spirit who spoke to the people of God through the prophets in the Old Covenant, and who now speaks to us through Christ in the New Covenant.[267] We have already had occasion to consider the essential unity of the Spirit and the Word of God, who inhere in one another in God, but the issue that concerns us now is the bearing of that upon reverence for the Holy Scriptures of the Old and New Testaments. The Nicene confession of belief in the Holy Spirit who spoke through the prophets has to do with the unity of

[263]Cyril of Jersualem, *Cat.*, 17.5.

[264]See Epiphanius, *Haer.*, 66.72f, 84; 74.7; *Anc.*, 119f.

[265]See Didymus, *Con. Eun.*, Athens ed., 44, pp. 253, 255, 277; cf. Athanasius, *De decr.*, 22; *De syn.*, 35; *Con. Ar.*, 1.46; 3.6f; *Ad Afr.*, 4; Epiphanius, *Anc.*, 70; *Haer.*, 58.10; 62.4; 63.7; 74.7; 76. *Ref. Aet.*, 29. etc.

[266]2 Cor. 3.17. Cf. Athanasius, *Ad Ser.*, 1.4ff; *Con. Ar.*, 1.11; *Ep.*, 1.8f; Basil, *De Sp. St.*, 52f.

[267]E.g., Cyril of Jer., *Cat.*, 4.16, 33; 11.12; 16.1ff, 16f, 24, 26ff; 17.5.

God's self-revelation through Israel and the incarnation, and thus with the divine inspiration of all the Holy Scriptures. The fathers were not very interested in the mechanics of inspiration or with its supernatural features, but they were deeply moved by the fact that in and through these Scriptures it is none other than God himself who continues to speak in the Spirit as the Lord, with the unrestricted majesty and holiness of his being. If we turn here for guidance to Didymus as one steeped in the Holy Scriptures, we find him piling up different expressions to convey the conviction that it is none other than the direct Word of God that we hear in the Bible.[268] Thus he could speak of the Word of God in the inspired Scriptures as the θεολογία of the Spirit,[269] for in them there speaks the living Spirit who searches the deep things of God and reveals them to us.[270] That is to say, the Word of God which we hear in the Scriptures is not some static Word, but Word brought to us from the mouth of the living God by his life-giving Breath or Spirit – θεόπνευστος Word.[271]

Of primary importance in all discussions about the Holy Spirit were the Johannine passages about the mission of the Spirit from the Son as well as the Father, in which the Spirit is said to speak not of himself but of what he has received from the Son. This indissoluble relation between the Word and the Spirit figured very prominently in Athanasius' letters to his friend Serapion.[272] Thus it was quite fitting that a close association of this kind between the Spirit and the Word of Christ should be reflected in the *Euchologion of Serapion* in which we have the earliest form of the Epiclesis. In it prayer is offered for the gift of the Spirit that the Lord Jesus and the Holy Spirit may speak in those who worship, enabling them to declare the holy mysteries and join in the Trisagion; but in the Epiclesis itself it is the Word,

---

[268]Didymus, *De Trin.*, 1.15–18, 25f; 2.2, 6, 21f; *Con. Eun.*, Athens ed., p. 242, etc.

[269]Didymus, *De Trin.*, 1.18, 26, 35.

[270]Didymus, *De Trin.*, 1.18; 2.3, 5, 16; 3.37; *De Sp. St.*, 15, 32, 55, etc.

[271]Didymus, *De Trin.*, 1.18; 2.11; *Con. Eun.*, Athens ed., 44, p. 242; *In Ps.*, 17.16; 39.8; 41.2; 64.10; 92.1, etc.; see also Epiphanius, *Anc.*, 72, 75; *Haer.*, 74.9.

[272]Athanasius, *Ad Ser.*, 1.2f, 6, 11, 33; 3.2; 4.3f.

without mention of the Spirit, that was invoked.[273] It was otherwise with the Epiclesis in the Jerusalem rite, where it is the Holy Spirit who is invoked, but where, as we have seen, the Holy Spirit was thought of by Cyril as 'speaking Spirit' who mediates Christ and his Word to the faithful.[274] It is because the Word and the Spirit mutually inhere in one another that the Holy Spirit is not dumb but eloquent of Christ the incarnate Word. He is the one Spirit of God who was present and active in the Church of the Old Testament and in the New Testament Church alike – 'who spoke by the prophets'.

If we consider the statements that the Holy Spirit is the Lord, the Giver of life, and who proceeds from the Father, in the light of the Athanasian and Epiphanian addition that 'he receives from the Son', we come close to our Lord's designation of the Holy Spirit as the *Paraclete* whom he sends to act in his place. The Spirit is so closely related to the being and activity of the incarnate Son from whom he is sent to us by the Father and from whom he receives, that in a real sense he is Christ's *Alter Ego* or *Alter Advocatus*, glorifying Christ and acting in his place.[275] The Paraclete is the living and life-giving Spirit of God who mediates to us the life of God, glorifies Christ as the Son of the Father, by throwing his radiance upon him, who thus actualises among us the self-giving of God to us in his Son, and resonates and makes fruitful within us the intervening, atoning and intercessory activity of Christ on our behalf. It was quite in line with this biblical teaching that Hippolytus had called him 'the high-priestly Spirit'.[276] The vicarious advocacy of the Paraclete was a favourite theme with the Nicene and post-Nicene fathers.[277] Here we have in Greek patristic theology a

---

[273]Serapion, *Euch.*, 13, Athens ed., 43, p. 76f.

[274]Cyril of Jer., *Cat.*, 23.7. Cf. also *Apost. Const.*, 8.12; *The Liturgy of St Mark*, xvii, Brightman, *op. cit.*, p. 134.

[275]Gregory Naz., *Or.*, 30.14; 31.3, 30; 34.13; 41.12.

[276]Hippolytus, *Apost. Trad.*, 3.5. Cf. Hilary, *De Trin.*, 8.19; 12.55; *De syn.*, 11, 29, 54f; Cyril of Jer., *Cat.*, 16.20; 17.4, 9; and Tertullian, *De praescr. haer.*, 13.

[277]Thus Basil, *De Sp. St.*, 23, 44, 46; *Con. Eun.*, 2.32f; 3.1ff; Gregory Nyss., *Ref. Eun.*, Jaeger, 2, pp. 389ff; Gregory Naz., *Or.*, 30.14; 31.3, 12, 26ff; Epiphanius, *Haer.*, 66.19; 73.15, 25; 74.12f; *Anc.*, 8, 67; Didymus, *De Trin.*, 2.2, 6, 16, 19; 3.38; *De Sp. St.*, 25–37, etc.

clear development of the teaching of St Paul in Romans 8, where he speaks of the Holy Spirit as interceding for us, and where, interestingly, St Paul used an even stronger word, ὑπερεντυγχάνειν, of the Spirit than he used of Christ, in order to reinforce what he says of the vicarious activity of the Spirit. That is what happens, St Paul claimed, when we pray, for as we engage in prayer, the prayers of the whole creation are penetrated by the intercessory, intervening activity of the Spirit.[278] Hence with Gregory Nazianzen the office of the Paraclete was linked especially to prayer and worship, for through the Spirit the heavenly advocacy and intercession of Christ our great high Priest are made to echo inaudibly within us, so that our praying and worship in the Spirit are upheld and made effective by him through a relation of God to himself.[279] And with Epiphanius the conjunction of the vicarious activity of Christ and of the indwelling Spirit was held to apply specifically to the Epiclesis as well as generally to the sanctifying and upholding of the life of the faithful in Christ.[280]

In all his activity the Holy Spirit comes to us from the inner communion of the Father, Son and Holy Spirit. He is the bond (σύνδεσμος) of the Holy Trinity dwelling in the midst of the Father and the Son, but also the bond (σύνδεσμος) of truth and faith who creates unity among us and brings us into communion with the Father, Son and Holy Spirit, into whose one name we are baptised. He is the very life of God himself, and is thus the living content of the whole self-giving of God to us through the Son and in one Spirit.[281] It is then in the Holy Spirit that we have communion or κοινωνία in the mystery of Christ, and are made members of his Body. The personalising incorporating activity of the Spirit creates, not only reciprocity between Christ and ourselves, but a community of reciprocity among ourselves, which through the Spirit is rooted in and reflects the trinitarian relations in God himself. It is thus that the Church comes into being and is constantly maintained in its

---

[278]Romans 8.14–26. See Origen, *De Or.*, 2.14.
[279]Gregory Naz., *Or.*, 30.14; 31.12; Basil, *De Sp. St.*, 50.
[280]Epiphanius, *Anc.*, 68.72; cf. *Haer.*, 55.5; and Basil, *De Sp. St.*, 66f.
[281]Epiphanius, *Anc.*, 5–8; *Haer.*, 62.4; 73.36; 74.11; cf. 70.1.

union with Christ as his Body. This is the Church of the triune God, embodying under the power of the Spirit, the Lord and Giver of life, the divine *koinonia* within the conditions of human and temporal existence. For the Church to be *in the Spirit* in an objective and ontological sense, is to be *in God*. It belongs to the nature and life of the Church in space and time to partake of the very life and light and love which God is. It is thus an imperative inherent in the being of the Church ever to keep the unity of the Spirit in the bond of peace, and thereby to mirror in itself the oneness of the Holy and Blessed Trinity.

It is on this trinitarian ground that we shall go on to consider the Nicene doctrine of the One Church in the following chapter.

7

The One Church

'And in one holy catholic and apostolic Church. We confess one baptism for the remission of sins; we look for the resurrection of the dead and the life of the world to come.'

The Nicene-Constantinopolitan Creed did not repeat the expression 'we believe' (πιστεύομεν) before the article on the Church, but it was nevertheless implied, as it had been in the Creed of Nicaea.[1] The significance of this would appear to be two-fold. In the first place, the clauses on the Church do not constitute an independent set of beliefs, but follow from belief in the Holy Spirit, for *holy* Church is the fruit of the *Holy* Spirit, the result of his sanctifying activity in mankind, and as such is, as it were, the empirical correlate of the *parousia* of the Spirit in our midst. If we believe in the Holy Spirit, we also believe in the existence of one Church in the one Spirit. Belief in 'one, holy, catholic and apostolic Church' is thus regarded in the Creed as a function of belief in the Spirit or rather of belief in the Father, Son and Holy Spirit. In the second place, the clauses on the Church are to be reckoned as belonging to the articles of saving faith, for they have to do with the Gospel. Just as there is 'one Lord', 'one baptism' and 'one faith', so there is 'one body'.[2] They are central to the Church's confession of faith in the Holy Trinity and cannot be treated as affirmations having significance in themselves apart from their integration with the substance of the evangelical and apostolic *kerygma*. This relation of the

[1] Thus Epiphanius, *Haer.*, 73.25; 74.13; cf. also 72.1f; and Basil, *Ep.*, 236.6.
[2] Eph. 4.5; see Epiphanius, *Anc.*, 7, 118; *Haer.*, 74.11.

clauses on the Church to the main content of belief confessed in the Creed sets the context and tone of what must be said about the Church and the way in which it is to be understood. The Church has imprinted upon it through holy baptism the seal and character of the Holy Trinity, and as such it is to be honoured and revered.[3]

It was undoubtedly St Paul's teaching about the *Church as the Body of Christ* together with *baptism in the name of the Father, the Son and the Holy Spirit*, that provided the basic convictions on which the early patristic doctrine of the Church, and of its unity and universality, took shape. It was the empirical community of men, women and children called into being through the proclamation of the Gospel, indwelt by the Holy Spirit in whom it is united to Christ and through him joined to God. Far from being a human institution it was founded by the Lord himself and rooted in the Holy Trinity. As Ignatius of Antioch taught, the members of the Church are united with Jesus Christ just as he is united with the Father. Hence whatever the Church does from beginning to end is done 'in the Son and the Father and the Spirit'.[4] The Church is what it everywhere is in the world as a manifestation of the saving union with God incarnate in Jesus Christ. Although for the purpose of preserving the empirical oneness of the Church in face of heretical dissension he kept pointing to the bishop as the focal point of unity,[5] Ignatius clearly thought of the Church's relation to Christ as overarching everything else: 'Wherever Jesus Christ is, there is the universal Church (ἡ καθολικὴ ἐκκλησία)'.[6]

Basically the same teaching about the Church is found in other texts deriving from the early centuries.[7] While they do

[3]Epiphanius, *Anc.*, 7f; *Exp. fidei*, 18, 25; cf. also, *MPG*, 42.876f.

[4]Ignatius, *Eph.*, 5.1; *Magn.*, 13.1; *Trall.*, 11.2; *Smyrn.*, 12.2.

[5]Ignatius, *Eph.*, 5.6; *Smyrn.*, 8.2; *Trall.*, 2.3; *Magn.*, 3.6; Philad., 7.

[6]Ignatius, *Smyrn.*, 8.2. See Irenaeus, *Adv. haer.*, 3.15.2, vol. 2, p. 79f, where we learn that 'catholics' was a nickname given by Valentinian Gnostics to members of the Church evidently because, unlike themselves, they believed in the universal range of redemption.

[7]Consult Clement, *Ep. 1*, 46.5–7; *Ep. 2*, 14.1–4; Hermas, *Shepherd, Vis.*, 1.1; 2.4; 3.3; *Sim.*, 9.17f; *Didache*, 9f; Justin, *Dial.*, 42, 63; Hippolytus, *In Dan.*, 1.9.8; 1.17.8ff; 4.37.2; Tertullian, *De bap.*, 6; Clement of Alex., *Paed.*, 1.6; *Strom.*, 7.5, 14, 17, 26; Origen, *Con. Cel.*, 6.48, 79 – but Origen fostered the

not contain any explicit ecclesiology, scattered throughout them we find similar conceptions of the Church as the living Body of Christ into which believers are incorporated through his life-giving Spirit, and are thus regarded as constituting a dynamic, spiritual magnitude, enshrining an altogether new, indeed divine, dimension in the world.[8] That is what was meant by 'holy Church' as the direct fruit of God's Holy Spirit. All members of the Church are united to Christ and organically cohere with and in him as one Body in one Spirit. It was thus, for example, that Irenaeus, as we shall see, used to speak of a oneness and communion with Christ in the most realist sense, for there takes place in him a soteriological and ontological unification of people in whose midst God himself dwells through the presence of his Spirit. This Body is what it is through the incarnation of the Son of God in Christ who has gathered up and reformed the human race in himself, and through the astonishing event at Pentecost when God poured out his own Spirit upon the apostles and disciples of the Lord Jesus thereby giving birth or rather rebirth to the Church and making it participate in his own divine life and love.[9] All this was, of course, in line with Pauline and Johannine teaching in the New Testament, in which Christological and Pneumatological conceptions of the Church were blended together.

At this stage in the early centuries, due in part at least to its conflict with Gnosticism, the Church began to be more conscious of itself and its evangelical mission as one holy catholic and apostolic. The main focus in its own self-understanding as a believing and worshipping community

---

idea that the Church as the Body of Christ is animated by his soul, which was to have a disastrous effect in Western conceptions of the Church.

[8]In his Montanist period Tertullian went so far as to say that 'properly and principally the Church is the Spirit himself in whom is the Trinity of the one God – Father, Son and Holy Spirit'. *De pud.*, 21; cf. *De or.*, 2.

[9]For Irenaeus the Church was the gathering together of two covenants and two peoples into one under the Word of God, the Lord Jesus Christ, as its one Householder, *Adv. haer.*, 4.18.1, vol. 2, p. 169; 4.39.1, p. 235; 4.49.1, p. 372; 5.17.4, p. 372. The old and new covenants are 'of one and the same substance (*unius et eisudem substantiae*)', *Adv. haer.*, 4.18.1, vol. 2, p. 168.

centred upon the apostolic κηρύγματα (in Irenaeus' sense),[10] that is, upon 'the word and truth of the Gospel' handed down from the apostles, rather than upon a definite ecclesiology. What might be said of the Church itself, for example in connection with its developing institutions, was felt to be entirely subordinate to the living Word and Truth of the Lord Jesus Christ who with his Spirit dwells in the Church thereby making it a servant of his mission and kingdom. Otherwise the Church would not be what it is as the Body of Christ in the world.

It is noteworthy that there were no writings specifically devoted to the nature and function of the Church in the early centuries, apart from the brief tractate of Cyprian *On the Unity of the Church*. References to the Church, of course, were made in connection with baptism and the eucharist, and the traditional ordinances of divine worship, in which the oneness of the apostolic and catholic Church was everywhere taken for granted. The fact that there were no monographs on the doctrine of the Church as such, therefore, was not without significance, for it reflected a situation in which the Lord Jesus Christ and the Holy Spirit occupied the unqualified centre of Christian faith and life empirically as well as spiritually.

As the understanding of the Church was developed in that Christocentric way and with general acknowledgement of the Pauline doctrine of the Church as the Body of Christ, it was baptism in the one name of the Father, Son and Holy Spirit by which people were admitted into the Church that provided it with its trinitarian structure. It was at baptism, of course, that catechetical instruction in the Gospel was regularly given to neophytes under the guidance of 'the rule of faith', so that it was naturally in connection with baptism that the early formulations of the Church's beliefs arose. It was in that distinctively trinitarian context that place was given to the *Church* itself in the basic articles of belief. This is what we find, for example, in the *Epistola Apostolorum* with its statement of belief in 'the Father, the Pantocrator, and in Jesus Christ our Saviour, in the Holy Spirit the Paraclete, in the holy Church and

[10]As in Irenaeus' Ἀπόδειξις τῶν κηρυγμάτων, cited as *Demonstratio*.

in the remission of sins.'[11] A similar correlation of belief is found in *The Apostolic Tradition* of Hippolytus, where one of the questions put to the catechumen in the rite of baptism was: 'Do you believe in the Holy Spirit and in the holy Church, and in the resurrection of the flesh?'[12]

In the *Demonstration of Apostolic Preaching* by Irenaeus, on the other hand, in which 'the rule of order and faith' follows the trinitarian form, Father, Son and Holy Spirit, mention is made of a 'community of union between God and man', but *not* of the 'Church'.[13] Evidently, the Church did not need to be mentioned, for it was taken for granted as the corporate manifestation in space and time of the divine covenant of redemption fulfilled in the incarnation and of the oneness of the communion of the faithful in God the Father, the Son and the Holy Spirit.[14] Through baptism the Church does not exist in its own name but in the supreme name of the Father, Son and Holy Spirit, by which it has been sealed, and thus precisely as the Church looks beyond itself to its transcendent Source and Ground in the Holy Trinity.[15] Hence from beginning to end Irenaeus was concerned in this work with the truth of the Gospel proclaimed by the apostles, that access to the Father is mediated through the Son and in the Holy Spirit, and that a community of union is thus activated between God and man.

If there was no explicit mention of the Church in that context, it was surely because Irenaeus' sights were set on the one and only God, the Father, Son and Holy Spirit, infinitely exalted above and beyond the Church, but in whom the Church dwells through its worship, and from whom it lives. Thus the Church may be described as the place in space and time where knowledge of the Father, the Son and the Holy Spirit becomes grounded in humanity, and union and communion with the Holy Trinity becomes embodied within the human

---

[11]See M. R. James, *The Apocryphal New Testament*, pp. 485ff.

[12]Hippolytus, *Apost. Trad.*, 21; Cyprian, *Ep.*, 70.1; 72.26; 74.4.7, 11; 76.1, 8. See also the brief confession of faith in the Der Balyzeh papyrus, cited by J. N. D. Kelly, *Early Christian Creeds*, 1949, p. 89.

[13]Irenaeus, *Dem.*, 6; cf. also 31, 94 & 98.

[14]Irenaeus, *Dem.*, 6ff, 31, 37f, 47ff, 98ff.

[15]Cf. Tertullian, *De bap.*, 6.

race. Expressed the other way round, the Church is constituted by the Holy Spirit as the empirical counterpart of his sanctifying presence and activity in our midst, for in the Spirit we are made members of Christ the incarnate Son and through him have access to the Father. The 'one holy Church' is thus, as it were, the complement of the 'one Holy Spirit'. As Irenaeus in his major work expressed it: 'This Gift of God has been entrusted to the Church, as breath was to the first created man, that all members receiving it may be vivified, and the communication of Christ has been distributed within it, that is, the Holy Spirit, the earnest of incorruption and the confirmation of our faith, and the ladder of ascent to God ... For where the Church is, there is the Spirit of God; and where the Spirit of God is, there is the Church, and every kind of grace; but the Spirit is truth.' As such the Church is constituted by Christ to be the receptacle of the Gospel proclaimed and handed on by the apostles, which Irenaeus described as a continuously 'rejuvenating deposit' (*depositum juvenescens et juvenescere faciens*).[16] It is significant, as we have already noted, that while Irenaeus regarded the Church thus entrusted with the Gospel as the empirical *vis-à-vis* of the Holy Spirit, he nevertheless thought of it as oriented so completely beyond itself that he spoke of the *Gospel* as 'the pillar and ground of the Church (στύλος καὶ στήριγμα ἐκκλησίας)'[16] rather than like St Paul of the *Church* as 'the pillar and bulwark of the truth (στύλος καὶ ἑδραίωμα τῆς ἀληθείας)'.[17] It was ultimately in the Gospels themselves that Irenaeus located the vivifying deposit committed to the Church, and handed on by the apostles.[18]

In this conception of the Church Irenaeus was clearly drawing out the implications of the New Testament injunction about 'the faith once for all delivered to the saints', to which we have already given attention at several points.[19] His prime concern was for the original *datum* of divine revelation in Jesus Christ and his Gospel upon which the very existence and

---

[16]Irenaeus, *Adv. haer.*, 3.28.1, vol. 2, p. 132f.

[17]1 Tim. 3.15.

[18]Irenaeus, *Adv. haer.*, 3.11.11, vol. 2, p. 47; cf. 5.1, *praef.*, pp 313f; 5.20.1f, pp. 377f.

[19]Jude 3.

continuity of the Church as the Body of Christ in the world depended, and which exercised the regulative force of a 'canon of truth' in all its witness, preaching and teaching.[20] According to the teaching of St Paul, not least in the Pastoral Epistles, the Church had been entrusted with a sacred deposit (παραθήκη) enshrined in the apostolic foundation of the Church laid by Christ himself and empowered through his indwelling Spirit of truth, which the Church was bound to guard inviolate, and for which it had to render an account before God.[21] In the last analysis 'the deposit of faith', as it came to be called, was equated with the whole living fact of Christ and his saving acts, in the indivisible unity of his Person, Word and Life, as through the resurrection and the sending of his Spirit he fulfilled and unfolded the content of his self-revelation as Saviour and Lord within the apostolic nucleus of the Church. He allowed it to take authoritative shape in the apostolic mind and embody itself in the apostolic mission, in such a constitutive way that the identity and continuity of the Church and its teaching in history became inseparably bound up with it. Thus in the inspired witness, teaching and preaching of the apostles we do not have to do with Christ apart from his Word or with the Word apart from Christ, nor with Christ apart from his Truth or with the Truth apart from Christ. He is the incarnate embodiment of the Word and Truth of God in his own personal being, who continues in the power of his resurrection to make his mighty acts of redemption effective in the life and faith of all who are baptised into him and who draw near to the Father through his atoning sacrifice.

When, with the pouring out of the Holy Spirit upon the Church, Christ thus clothed with his Gospel indwelt the Church and united it to himself as his Body, the Word and Truth of the Gospel embodied uniquely in Christ also became embodied in a subsidiary way in the apostolic foundation of the Church. This does not mean that the self-revelation of Christ entrusted to the

[20]Consult here again my essay, 'The Deposit of Faith', *SJT*, 36, 1983, pp. 1–28.

[21]1 Tim. 6.20; 2 Tim. 1.12ff; 2.2, 4; 4.3; Titus 1.9, 13; cf. 2 Thess. 2.15; 3.6; Gal. 1.9; 2.2, 9; 1 Cor. 11.23; 15.3; 2 Cor. 11.3f; Rom. 6.7; 1 Tim. 4.6; and Hebrews 3.1; 4.14; 10.23.

apostles was resolved, as it were without remainder, into their witness to Christ, nor therefore that the deposit of faith may be identified as such with the teaching and preaching of the apostles, for it continues to remain identical with the incarnate self-communication of God in Jesus Christ mediated after the resurrection and ascension through the apostles. It does mean, however, that from that time onward people may have access to the deposit of faith only in the form which, under the creative and renewing impact of the risen Lord and his Spirit, it has assumed once and for all in the apostolic foundation and tradition, i.e. through the apostolic interpretation of the Gospel mediated to us in the Scriptures of the New Testament and through baptismal incorporation into Christ in the midst of his Church where he continues to make himself known from faith to faith and to be savingly at work in the power of his indwelling Spirit.

This means that the deposit of faith is to be understood as spanning two levels. On its primary level it is identical with the whole saving economy of the incarnate, crucified and risen Son of God. On its secondary level it is identical with the faithful reception and interpretation of the Gospel as under the inspiration of the Holy Spirit it took definitive form in the apostolic nucleus established by Christ for this very purpose, that is, in the apostolic foundation of the Church and thus in the New Testament Scriptures. From the beginning these two levels were inseparably coordinated in the deposit of faith, the second being governed and structured through the revelatory impact of the first upon it, so that it pointed away from itself to Christ. Thus the New Testament *kerygma* referred not merely to the proclamation about Christ but to the *reality* proclaimed, Jesus Christ who continues to be present and savingly at work through the *kerygma*. That is surely how the original Christians regarded the deposit of faith, as finally inseparable from the very living substance of the Gospel and the saving event of Christ crucified, risen and glorified, but as once and for all entrusted to the Church through its apostolic foundation in Christ, informing, structuring and quickening its life and faith and mission as the Body of Christ in the world. This was a sacred gift that the Church had to treasure above all else, guarding it intact against all misunderstanding and serving its faithful transmission to future generations through divinely appointed ordinances binding the Church in every age to its apostolic foundation in Christ as the ground of its continuity and renewal in history. While the deposit of faith was replete with the truth as it is in Jesus, embodying kerygmatic, didactic and theological content, by its very nature it could not be resolved into a system of truths or a set of normative doctrines and formulated beliefs, for the truths and doctrines and beliefs entailed could not be abstracted from the embodied form which they were given in Christ and the apostolic foundation of the Church without loss of their real substance. Nevertheless in this embodied form 'the faith once for all delivered to the saints' constituted the regulative basis for all explicit formulation of Christian truth, doctrine and belief in the deepening understanding of the Church and its regular instruction of catechumens and the faithful.

It was just such an understanding of the deposit of faith embodied in the apostolic foundation of the Church in Christ that held a central place in Irenaeus' conception of the Gospel and the mission of the Church. For him the incarnation of the Lord and the message of salvation, fact and meaning, the Word and the word, the Truth and truths, were all intrinsically integrated and might not be torn apart without serious distortion of the faith. What Christ has done for us in his saving work he has embodied in his own Person as Saviour and continues to be as saving act of God on our behalf and as Word of salvation to us. As the Word of God, by whom all things visible and invisible were created, himself become flesh for our sake, Christ is also the Word who in being proclaimed to us remains the mighty saving act of God.[22] Thus the message of Christ must be regarded as more than a message of who he was and what he has done for us, for it is so integrated with him that it is itself the saving Word and power of God constantly at work among his people precisely as Word, and effectively operative in the faith of the Church, anchoring it and giving it substance in the Person of Christ as Saviour and Lord.

[22]Irenaeus, *Adv. haer.*, 3.9–11, vol. 2, pp. 30–36.

It was in accordance with that embodied nature of the Word and truth of the Gospel that Irenaeus thought of the Church. As the Body of Christ the Church embodies 'the union and communion between God and man' brought about through the incarnation of the Lord and the atoning redemption he effected for all mankind.[23] And as such it continues to embody the deposit of faith or the saving truth of the Gospel as the God-given source of its renewal and the inner secret of its identity and continuity in space and time.[24] Hence when the Gospel of the incarnation came under attack from the dualist speculations of the Gnostics, which threatened to tear apart Jesus from Christ[25] and thus dismember the embodiment of the truth in Christ and in the Church as his Body, he set about defending the integration of the Gospel with Christ and the continuity of the Church with its apostolic foundation in Christ, for the very substance of the Gospel and the identity of the Church as the one depository of apostolic truth were at stake.

We are not concerned here with the arguments which Irenaeus developed in his defence of the integrity of the Church and the unvarying nature of its faith and teaching,[26] or with his view of Church order, tradition and succession upon which he laid such weight in dissociating the authentic apostolic deposit of faith from heretical deviation. Our interest lies rather in his doctrine of the Church as the community called to believe in Jesus Christ as Lord and Saviour, and brought into union and communion with God the Father through baptism and the regenerating gift of the Holy Spirit. By its very nature, therefore, the Church is tied up with the tradition of the apostolic Message or Gospel which is handed on from generation to generation with baptism: instruction in the faith which was once for all delivered to the saints and baptism in the name of the Father, Son and Holy Spirit are thus inseparable. Through baptism established in faith and through faith

---

[23]Irenaeus, *Adv. haer.*, 5.1.1ff, vol. 2, pp. 314ff.

[24]Irenaeus, *Adv. haer.*, 3. *praef.* & 3, vol. 2, pp. 1 & 12; 3.38.1, 2, pp. 131f.

[25]Irenaeus, *Adv. haer.*, 3.11.10, vol. 2, pp. 45f; 3.17.8, p. 89; cf. 4.3.2, pp. 148f.

[26]Irenaeus, *Adv. haer.*, 1.3f, vol. 1, pp. 92–97; 3.12.9f, vol. 2, p. 62; 4.53.1f, pp. 261f; 57.1ff, pp. 273ff; 5.19.1f, pp. 377ff.

perfected in baptism the Church continues everywhere and always to be informed and moulded by the truth of God's self-revelation through Christ and in the Spirit, and is committed to the preservation of its unity and identity by constant reference to 'the kerygma of the truth' or 'the canon of the truth' embedded in its apostolic foundation, and handed on through baptism.[27]

Irenaeus' theological interpretation of the truth of the Gospel and his elucidation of the conceptual content of the deposit of faith, had the effect of bringing to light in incipient credal form the trinitarian pattern of belief which was eventually to come to explicit expression in the Nicene Creed.[28] Hence in so far as the Church continued through baptism and faith to be 'one and the same' with its apostolic foundation in Christ Jesus,[29] and thus continued as the 'union and communion between God and man'[30] to embody the truth of the Gospel in its empirical existence, it was bound to understand itself more and more as founded and rooted in the Holy Trinity. It belongs to the very nature of the Church, therefore, constantly to confess belief in the Father, the Son and the Holy Spirit, for it *is* the Church of the Triune God. In the words of St Paul: 'There is one body and one Spirit, just as you were called to one hope that belongs to your call, one Lord, one faith, one baptism, one God and Father of all, who is above all and through all and in all.'[31]

The primary constitutive facts, then, are the one faith and one

[27]Irenaeus, *Adv. haer.*, 1.1.20, vol. 1, pp. 87f; 1.15, p. 188; 2.8.1, p. 272; 2.40.1–41.3, pp. 347–52; 3.1–5, vol. 2, pp. 2–20; 3.11.7, p. 41; 3.12.6f, pp. 58f; 3.15.1, p. 79; 3.38.1f, pp. 131f; 4.57.2, 4, pp. 274ff; 5. *praef.*, pp. 313f; 5.20.1f, pp. 377ff; and *Dem.*, 1–7, 100.

[28]For early formulations of trinitarian belief, see Irenaeus, *Adv. haer.*, 1.2, vol. 1, pp. 90f; 3.1f.4, vol. 2, pp. 2ff, 25f; 4.1f, pp. 146ff; 4.53.1, pp. 261f; 5.20.1f, pp. 377f; *Dem.*, 6; cf. also *Adv. haer.*, 2.41.1, vol. 1, p. 349; 3.1.2, vol. 2, p. 6; 3.4.1, pp. 15f; 3.17.6, pp. 87f; 3.19.3, p. 97; 4.11.5, pp. 161f; 4.34.1ff, pp. 213–218; 4.53.1f, pp. 261f; 4.63.2, p. 296; 5.1ff, pp. 314ff; 5.6.1, p. 333; 5.18.1f, p. 374; 5.36.1, p. 429.

[29]Irenaeus, *Adv. haer.*, 1.3.3, vol. 1, p. 94; 1.10.3, p. 97; 3. *praef.*, 2, vol. 2, p. 1; 3.12.9, p. 62; 3.28.1, p. 131; 5.20.1f, p. 378; cf. Hegesippus, *ap.* Eusebius, *Hist. eccl.*, 4.22.

[30]Irenaeus, *Adv. haer.*, 5.1.2, vol. 2, p. 315; *Dem.*, 6, 31.

[31]Ephesians, 4.4–6; cf. Irenaeus, *Haer.*, 2.2.5, vol. 1, pp. 256f; 4.34.2, vol. 2, p. 214; 4.49.2, p. 255; 5.18.1, p. 374; *Dem.*, 5.

baptism, coordinated to the activity of the one Spirit, the one Lord and the one Father. The true Church is marked by its unity and holiness, and by its fidelity to the Holy Trinity. One Church is to be understood strictly in that context of belief in the Holy Trinity. Thus with reference to the biblical injunction that three witnesses are required to attest the truth of some matter,[32] Tertullian explained that at baptism, 'after the attestation of belief and the promise of salvation have been pledged under the sanction of three witnesses, mention must also be made of the Church, for wherever there are the three, the Father, the Son and the Holy Spirit, there is the Church which is a body constituted by three.'[33] Since God the Father has communicated himself to us through the saving economy of his Son, the Word made flesh in Jesus Christ, it is the incarnate Son who naturally constitutes the real focus for the doctrine of the Trinity, and the regulative centre with reference to which all the worship, faith and mission of the Church take their shape: from the Father, through the Son and in the Spirit, and to the Father, through the Son and in the Spirit. It is correspondingly the New Testament teaching about the Church as the Body of Christ incarnate, crucified and risen, that provides the immediate focus and controlling centre of reference for a doctrine of the Church founded and rooted in the self-communication of the Holy Trinity. It was a Christocentric doctrine of the Church along these lines, reached under the constraint of God's revealed nature as the consubstantial communion of Father, Son and Holy Spirit in one indivisible Trinity, that was brought to fruition in the mind of the Church through the work of the great Greek theologians of the fourth century, but as a by-product of their determination to preserve the evangelical substance of the faith.

At the Council of Nicaea the Church was not actually given a place in the Creed itself among the articles of saving faith, but mention was made of 'the holy catholic and apostolic Church' in the anathematisation of heresies appended to the Creed. When it became clear that the trinitarian faith of the catholic

[32]Deut. 19.15; Matt. 17.16; 2 Cor. 13.1.

[33]Tertullian, *De bap.*, 6; cf. *De or.*, 2. Nevertheless Tertullian did not think of the Church as included within the *regula fidei*.

and apostolic Church was at stake over the issue of the Deity of the Holy Spirit, as we saw in the last chapter, the Council added clauses confessing belief in the Holy Spirit equally with the Father and the Son. The time was then ripe for appropriate statements to be made about the Church which the Council of Constantinople set out in clear strong terms, 'And in one holy catholic and apostolic Church'. Theological expression was thus given to the Church among the articles of saving faith, in the light of the rule of truth handed down from the apostles in connection with baptism in the name of the Father, Son and Holy Spirit, but now also in the light of the Church's matured convictions about the Holy Spirit and the Holy Trinity. As Epiphanius made very clear shortly before the meeting of the Council, one Church, one baptism, and one faith are bound up with belief in one Father, one Son, one Holy Spirit, a Trinity in Unity.[34]

In order to understand this development we must refer once again to the key-concept used in the resolution of the doctrine of Christ, the *internal relation of the Son to the Father*, for that must also govern the doctrine of the Church as the Body of Christ the incarnate Son. Since the Sonship of Christ falls *within* and not outside the Godhead, everything we say of the Church must be consistent with the consubstantial oneness between the Son and the Father and be an expression of the union and communion between God and man effected in the incarnate life and reconciling work of the Mediator. That is to say, the doctrine of the Church must be expounded in terms of its *internal relation*, and not some external relation, to Jesus Christ, for it is in Christ and his inherent relation to the Father and the Holy Spirit that the essential nature of the Church is to be found.

Athanasius pointed to the very heart of the matter in the incarnation of the Son of God, which by its very nature involved the union of God and man in Christ, and at the same time our 'deification' or adoption as sons of God in Christ.[35]

---

[34]Epiphanius, *Anc.*, 118.

[35]Athanasius, *De decr.*, 14, 31; *Con. Ar.*, 1.9, 37ff, 42f, 46ff; 2.47, 53, 59, 63ff, 69f, 74, 76ff; 3.17, 19–25, 32f, 39f; 4.29, 33–36; *De syn.*, 51; *Ad Adel.*, 4; *Ad Ser.*, 1.24.

That was the inner force of Athanasius' doctrine of the Church as the Body of Christ. 'Because of our relation to his body, we have become God's Temple, and in consequence are made God's sons, so that even in us the Lord is now worshipped.'[36] It is not due to some external relation in moral resemblance to Christ that the Church is his Body, but due to a real participation in him who is consubstantial with God the Father.[37] Thus in an explanatory paraphrase of our Lord's high-priestly prayer for oneness between believers and himself parallel to that between him and the Father,[38] Athanasius wrote: 'You, Father, are in me, for I am your Word, and since you are in me and I am in them because of the body, and since through you the salvation of mankind has been perfected in me, I ask that they also may become one according to the body that is in me and according to its perfection, in order that they too may be made perfect and through unity with it may be made one and the same thing; and that through being upheld by me they may all be one body and one spirit and may reach the status of a perfect man. For through partaking of the same body they become one body, having the one Lord in ourselves.'[39] This does not mean, Athanasius added, that the relation between us and Christ is precisely the same as that between the Son and the Father, although it is grounded upon it, for there is no identity in nature or equality between us and Christ as there is between him and the Father. The union between us and Christ is not one of nature but one of adoption and grace effected through the gift of the Spirit who comes to dwell in us as he dwells in God. 'Apart from the Spirit we are strange and distant from God, but in partaking of the Spirit we are united to the Godhead.'[40] Since this takes place in Christ, the incarnate Son, however, it involves a somatic and not just a spiritual union in and with him.[41] Thus

[36]Athanasius, *Con. Or.*, 1.43; cf. 47, and *In Ps.*, 67.30.

[37]See Athanasius, *In Ps.*, 21.22.

[38]John 17, 21–23.

[39]Athanasius, *Con. Ar.*, 3.22. Note that the words rendered 'perfect' (τέλειος), 'make perfect' (τελειοῦν) and 'perfection' (τελείωσις) in this passage carry the meaning of perfection, or completion, *and* consecration.

[40]Athanasius, *Con. Ar.*, 3.24.

[41]Athanasius, *Con. Ar.*, 3.22f. See Athanasius' discussion of the analogical

with reference to our Lord's teaching about himself as the true Vine, Athanasius wrote: 'As the branches are of one substance (ὁμοούσια) with the vine, and are of the vine, so we also having bodies that are connate (ὁμογενῆ) with the Lord's body, receive out of his fullness and have that body as the root of our resurrection and salvation.'[42] Thus the body of Christ which he took from us is the first fruit of the Church for it has already been raised up with him and made to sit with him in heavenly places.[43]

It was characteristic of Athanasius that he conceived of the union between Christ and the members of his Body as established by incarnation and atonement, since, as we have already seen, for Athanasius atonement had to be understood as having taken place *within* the incarnate Person of Christ as the one Mediator between God and man. What the Son of God became in his incarnation and what he has done for us in his redeeming activity are essentially one – that is why, Athanasius pointed out, the apostle spoke of the incarnation (ἐνανθρώπησις) of Christ and his high-priesthood (ἀρχιερωσύνη) as having functioned together.[44] That is to say, 'Christ in us' and 'Christ for us' are completely interlocked in the oneness (ἕνωσις) that lies at the core of the Church as the Body of Christ. This was made very clear by Athanasius in his long exegetical arguments with the Arians over biblical passages that spoke of the humiliation of Christ and his human life in the form of a servant, which instead of disparaging his nature as the Son of God, as Athanasius showed, referred to his merciful condescension in self-abasement and to his deliberate identification with us in our flesh of sin, in order to make our misery, death and judgment his own, and thus through atoning

---

nature of this relation involving unlikeness as well as likeness, *Con. Ar.*, 3.17–22, and Arian reduction of it to mere similarity, *Con. Ar.*, 3.1ff.

[42] Athanasius, *De sent. Dion.*, 10; also *ap.* Theodoret, *Dial.* 1, *MPG*, 83.89–92. The word 'root' (ῥίζα) here is the same as *arche* (ἀρχή) elsewhere, as in *Con. Ar.*, 1.48.

[43] Eph. 2.6; cf. *De inc. et con. Ar.*, 12, attributed to Athanasius.

[44] Athanasius, *Con. Ar.*, 2.10; cf. 4.6.

reconciliation to heal, renew and sanctify us and restore us to union with God.[45]

Of particular importance for his doctrine of the Church was the incarnational and soteriological interpretation which Athanasius gave to the favourite text of the Arians: 'The Lord created me a beginning (ἀρχήν) of his ways, for his works.'[46] For Athanasius this had to do with the humanity of Jesus Christ which was specifically brought into being by God *for our sakes* to be the one Principle or Head of the whole economy of incarnation, redemption, regeneration and sanctification. He was made the ἀρχή of the new humanity. As the incarnate Son of God he became one body with us in order to gather up our corrupt humanity into bodily existence in himself, healing and renewing it within himself through the perfection and holiness of his own human nature and life. Moreover, he makes our humanity in him partake of the Holy Spirit with which he has been anointed and sanctified *as man* for our sakes, and thereby unites it through himself with the Godhead.[47] It is that perfected or consecrated humanity in Jesus Christ which constitutes the life-giving substance of the Church and the perpetual source of its renewal. The Church is thus to be regarded as constituting all who are reconciled to God in one body through the Cross and are made one in Christ, united with his humanity in such a way that he now comprises both in himself, their humanity and his own, as 'one new man', for he is in them as they are in him.[48]

Actually the various references which Athanasius made to the Church throughout his writings were only of an incidental nature. That was not without significance, however, for his thought was always centred on Christ the Lord of the Church, and on the self-offering and self-consecration which he made for our sakes within the humanity which he took from us. We are so deeply rooted in Christ and united together with him

---

[45]For example, Phil. 2.9f, *Con. Ar.*, 1.37–45; or Heb. 1.4, *Con. Ar.*, 1.53–64; Heb. 3.2, *Con. Ar.*, 2.1–11.

[46]Prov. 8.22; Κύριος ἐκτισέν με ἀρχὴν ὁδῶν αὐτοῦ εἰς ἔργα αὐτοῦ; *Con. Ar.*, 2.18–82.

[47]See especially Athanasius, *Con. Ar.*, 1.46–50.

[48]Eph. 2.14f; Athanasius, *Con. Ar.*, 2.55; cf. also 1.50; 2.45; 4.36.

through incarnation and atonement and are so joined to God through the presence of his Holy Spirit imparted to us by Christ, that we are made to dwell in God. However, as Athanasius reminds us, 'our being in the Father is not ours but is the Spirit's who is in us and abides in us . . . It is the Spirit, then, who is in God, and not we viewed in ourselves.'[49] That is clearly how Athanasius looked upon the Church, not as viewed in itself, but as hid with Christ through his Spirit in God the Father. Thus the Church does not live in its own name but in the name of the Father, the Son and the Holy Spirit sealed upon it in holy baptism. In other words, the Church really is the one Church of Christ when it looks away from itself to its objective source and ground in the Godhead, and dwells in the Holy Trinity, for it is in the Father, Son and Holy Spirit that the Church and its faith are rooted and founded.[50] Athanasius certainly mentioned 'the Catholic Church' a great many times, but almost invariably in order to refer to the universal faith of the Church or the one unvarying truth of the Gospel with which the Church is entrusted. It was always the objective reality of the self-revealing and self-giving of the Father through the Son and in the Holy Spirit that occupied the centre of his vision. The Church is truly Church in so far as it dwells in the Holy Trinity and embodies the truth of the Gospel in its empirical life and worship.

It was much the same teaching about the Church that was offered by the Cappadocians, but again only incidentally. Thus Gregory Nazianzen could speak of the Church as 'the great Body of Christ',[51] or of the members of Christ, like the members of our body, as 'combined, joined and bound together by the harmony of the Spirit so as to be constituted one perfect Body really worthy of Christ himself, our Head.'[52] And Gregory Nyssen wrote: 'There is no other way to have God than to be united to him. And no one may be united to him otherwise than by being concorporate with him (σύσσωμος τῷ αὐτῷ), as Paul expressed it, for in being conjoined to the one

[49]Athanasius, *Con. Ar.*, 3.24f.

[50]Athanasius, *Con. Ar.*, 1.34; 4.21; *Ad Ser.*, 1.28; 3.6; 4.7.

[51]Gregory Naz., *Or.*, 21.7.

[52]Gregory Naz., *Or.*, 2.3; cf. 32.10.

Body of Christ by way of participation (διὰ τῆς μετουσίας), we all become his one Body ... He is the Head, therefore, from whom the whole body is continuously built up, for he takes up into himself all who become united to him through communion with his Body (διὰ τῆς κοινωνίας τοῦ σώματος) and makes them members of his own Body, so that while there are many members there is but one Body.'[53]

Little more was added to this doctrine of the Church by Basil, although he obviously took for granted that the Church is the Body of Christ in which individual believers are knit into unity with one another in Christ.[54] A rich account of this conception of the Church was nevertheless offered by him in the *De Spiritu Sancto* where it was presented from the perspective of the indwelling of the Holy Spirit in each member and in the Church as a whole. 'All members together complete the Body of Christ in the unity of the Spirit ... And as parts in the whole so are we individually in the Spirit, for we were all baptised in one Body into one Spirit.'[55] It was distinctive of Basil that he spoke of the Holy Spirit as 'the space (χώρα) where people are sanctified', and as 'the proper place (ὁ τόπος ἴδιος) where there is true worship', i.e., the worship of the Father and the Son in and with the Holy Spirit. 'The Spirit is indeed the place of the saints, and the saint is the place proper to the Spirit, as he devotes himself to the indwelling of God, and is called his Temple.'[56] That is to say, for Basil, the Church exists and is defined in its worship of the Father, Son and Holy Spirit, and as in the Spirit it participates in the κοινωνία which the three Persons of the Holy Trinity have with one another.[57] Through the indwelling Spirit, who himself completes the adorable and blessed Trinity, the worshipping Church is, so to speak, the doxological correlate of the Triunity of God.[58]

If we look to the West during this period, the best indication

[53]Gregory Nyss., *In illud, Tunc ipse*, *MPG*, 44.1317, with reference to Col. 1.24; 1 Cor. 12.27; Eph. 2.20 & 4.15f.
[54]Basil, *Ep.*, 113; 146.1; 203.3; 243.1; 266.1.
[55]Basil, *De Sp. St.*, 61; and 1 Cor. 12.25; cf. 28.
[56]Basil, *De Sp. St.*, 62–64; cf. 3, 13, 16, 22, 45ff, 58, 67f.
[57]Basil, *De Sp. St.*, 37f, 43, 45f, 48, 59f, 62f, 68.
[58]Cf. Basil, *Hex.*, 6; *De Sp. St.*, 45; cf. *Ep.*, 233.4.

of how the doctrine of the Church was developing is found in the thought of Hilary, which was clearly influenced on the one hand by Irenaeus and on the other hand by Athanasius and the Cappadocians. With them he had a strong sense of the oneness of the Church in Christ who took all humanity into himself.[59] And like Athanasius Hilary thought of Christ as constituting the Church in himself. 'He is himself the Church, embracing it all in himself through the mystery of his Body.'[60] The members of the Church ordained by the Lord and established by the apostles are not a collection of congregations but have a natural unity for they form one body through one faith and one baptism and through eucharistic communion with Christ, and thus exhibit a profound unity that arises ultimately from the Holy Trinity.[61] It should be noted, however, that in Hilary's ecclesiology we evidently see the beginning of a distinction between the Church as an external fellowship of believers, and the Church as a mystical body, which appears to reveal the influence of Origen, but which was to become characteristic of the Roman doctrine of the Church.[62]

Before we go further it must be pointed out that in this conception of the Church embedded in Nicene theology nothing was affirmed about the structure or organisation of the Church as having to do with the essential content of saving faith. The nearest approach to that at an earlier point was found in North Africa in connection with a growing legalist conception of the Church in the face of laxity and schism. In his pre-Montanist Catholic period Tertullian used to insist that the Church was a body bound together not only by piety but by 'unity of discipline',[63] which was consistent with his conception of the deposit of faith, in rather sharp contrast to that of Irenaeus, as a fixed set of formal propositions constituting the

[59]Hilary, *In Ps.*, 51.16; *De Trin.*, 11.16; cf. 2.24.

[60]Hilary, *In Ps.*, 125.6. This concept was taken up and developed by Augustine, *De Trin.*, 4.8, 12; 4.9.12; *In Jn. ev.*, 21.8; 8.1; *In Ps.*, 26.2; 29.2; 30.2; 54.3; 56.1; 60.1; 90.2; 143.1, etc.

[61]Hilary, *De Trin.*, 6.9f; 7.4; 8.7–19, 32ff; 11.1; *In Ps.*, 91.9; 121.5.

[62]Hilary, *In Ps.*, 127.8; 128.9; 131.23; 132.6; 138.29.

[63]Tertullian, *Apol.*, 39.1.

regula fidei.[64] It was much in the same vein that Cyprian published his important tract *On the Unity of the Church*, which he wrote in order to meet the threat of schism, but even in it Cyprian was concerned, not so much with ecclesial structure as with the necessity of preserving the unity of the Church which he likened to the 'seamless robe of Christ'. He held that the inherent oneness of the Church operates within it as a 'sacrament', and appealed in support to the teaching of St Paul that 'there is one body and one Spirit, one hope of your calling, one Lord, one faith, one baptism, one God.'[65] Cyprian venerated the unity of the Church as an intrinsic principle handed down by the Lord through the apostles, and identified it in practice with the episcopate functioning within the continuing life and mission of the Church as a 'sacrament of unity'. He traced this unifying character of the episcopate back to a single source in the principate of Peter, and described it in corporate terms as held *in solidum* by all bishops both individually and conjointly.[66]

There was no suggestion in Cyprian's account of the leadership given to Peter at the outset of the Church's mission of any primacy in authority or of any succession in office, but he was clearly influenced by Roman conceptions of society and law in the way he thought of membership within the Church as constituting a closed community under the authority of the bishop.[67] The social and juridical issues latent in this conception of the Church, not least with regard to questions of validity and authority, were thrown increasingly into prominence through controversy in Rome and North Africa and came to exercise a determining role in the formation of the Latin doctrine of the Church, as a divinely instituted society in the world under the universal headship of the bishop of Rome, and with canonically defined structures of unity, continuity and authority.

Ecclesiological developments in the East took a rather

[64]Tertullian, *De pr. haer.*, 13f; *Adv. Prax.*, 2; *De virg. vel.*, 1; *De an.*, 2; *De spec.*, 4, etc. See my essay 'The Deposit of Faith', *op. cit.*, pp. 15f.

[65]Eph. 4.4; Cyprian, *De un. eccl.*, 4; cf. also 23.

[66]Cyprian, *De un. eccl.*, 5: *Episcopatus unus est, cuius a singulis in solidum pars tenetur*; cf. also *Ep.*, 33.1; 55.24; 66.8.

[67]Cyprian, *De. un. eccl.*, 17; *Ep.*, 49.2; 66.1.

different line from those which we have just been considering in the West. As we have already found in the writings of the Greek fathers, primacy was given to *the truth of the Gospel* to which all organisational and juridical questions were entirely subordinate. It was of course this emphasis upon 'the faith of the Catholic Church' that was to give the Orthodox Church its distinctive character. Nevertheless, while it was unthinkable that the organisation of the Church could have a place among the articles of saving faith, those articles were regarded as having important implications for the ordering of the life and mission of the Church, which were expressed in the form of canons appended to conciliar decisions on doctrine. Thus they were given a *quasi de fide* status, but within an essentially trinitarian understanding of the Church in which Church authority and government were construed in terms of κοινωνία rather than in terms of hierarchical structure.[68]

Here too, of course, the episcopate was everywhere acknowledged to have had a central role in the life and mission of the Catholic Church from apostolic times. As such, however, it was held to be subordinate to the apostolic foundation of the Church, as well as to the Lord Jesus Christ the one Head of the Church. Quite typical for the whole Church in the East was the exhortation of Ignatius of Antioch at the end of the first century. 'See that you all follow the bishop, as Jesus follows the Father, and the presbytery as if it were the apostles. And reverence the deacons as the command of God. Let no one do any of the things pertaining to the Church without the bishop, or by one whom he appoints. Wherever the bishop appears let the congregation be present, just as wherever Jesus Christ is, there is the Catholic Church. It is not lawful to baptise or hold an *agape* without the bishop; but whatever he approves, this is also pleasing to God, that everything which you do may be secured and established.'[69] However, this conception of the bishop did not carry with it the idea that the Church over which he presided

---

[68]See my contribution, 'The Trinitarian Foundation and Character of Faith and Authority in the Church', to *Theological Dialogue between Orthodox and Reformed Churches*, ed. by T. F. Torrance, Edinburgh, 1985, pp. 79–120.

[69]Ignatius, *Ad Smyrn.*, 8.1–2.

was endowed with the grace of the Holy Spirit as a possession to be dispensed under his authority, far less the idea that the bishop himself constituted the link between Christ and the faithful. Rather was the Church regarded as wholly subject to the sovereignty of the Spirit, while its bishops were but servants (δοῦλοι) of Christ called to act like deacons ministering to others as good stewards of the manifold grace of God.[70]

The Church in the East as well as in the West had clearly to wrestle with the interrelation between doctrine and structure, or faith and order, as it faced up to the problem that arose out of its expansion throughout the Mediterranean world. How was it to take root and develop within nations and societies which had already been shaped by patterns of culture and codes of law? That is basically the same question which we have already had to consider in connection with how the *Gospel* was to take root and be brought to faithful expression within the framework of Graeco-Roman culture and thought, when the answer had to be given: only by transforming the foundations upon which pre-Christian culture and thought rested. And that meant that theology had to penetrate into and overcome the epistemological, anthropological and cosmological dualisms which permeated the Graeco-Roman world, and which in their clash with Christianity gave rise to Gnosticism outside the Church and Arian and other heresies within the Church, threatening its foundations in the Gospel. That is certainly what was at stake in the Council of Nicaea, when it was precisely in overcoming dualist patterns of thought that the classical theology of the Church came to its clear and structured articulation.

Throughout the fourth century after the Nicene Council it was made abundantly clear that in accordance with its apostolic and catholic faith the Church regarded itself as wholly centred in the Lordship of Christ, and his reign as the enthroned and exalted Κύριος Χριστός who was and is and ever will be coequal and coeternal with the Father and the Holy Spirit in the supreme sovereignty and power of the Holy Trinity. In the life and

---

[70] I Peter 4:10: διακονοῦντες ὡς καλοὶ οἰκονόμοι ποικίλης χάριτος Θεοῦ. Cf. *Royal Priesthood, SJT Occasional Papers*, 3, 1955.

mission of the empirical Church on earth it was the kingdom of Christ that was predominant, for all power in heaven and earth had been given to him, and things visible and invisible, earthly and heavenly, were subject to him. They had in any case been created by him as the Word of God. What gave concrete shape and structure to the faith of the Catholic Church was the incarnation, the economic condescension of God in Jesus Christ to be one with us in the concrete realities of our human and social life, and his saving activity within the structures of our creaturely existence in space and time.

However, the question had to be asked: Was the incarnation merely a temporary episode in the economic purpose of God, or was it permanent? That was the issue at stake in the idea evidently put forward by Marcellus of Ancyra, to which reference has several times been made in earlier chapters. Although he supported the Nicene *homoousion*,[71] Marcellus held that the kingdom of Christ would eventually be handed over to the Father, who would then be 'all in all', which implied that the whole incarnational economy would come to an end.[72] Such an idea, it was felt, would call in question the coeternity and coequality of the three divine Persons, but would also strike at the very root of belief in the Church as the Body of Christ, the incarnate, crucified and risen Son of God who will come again to make all things new. Hence it was decidedly rejected at the Council of Constantinople, along with Arian, Sabellian, Apollinarian and Macedonian heresies, in the affirmation 'whose kingdom shall have no end (οὗ τῆς βασιλείας οὐκ ἔσται τέλος)', for as there is one Godhead, so there is one power, sovereignty and glory, one lordship and one kingdom.[73] It was thus that the recognition of the finality and everlasting nature of the saving economy embodied in the Lord Jesus Christ profoundly affected the Church's understanding of itself as the one people God incorporated into Christ as his Body, and as the

[71]Thus Athanasius, *Ap. con. Ar.*, 23, 32, 45, 47; but cf. Basil, *Ep.*, 69, 125.1, 263.5, 265.3.

[72]Theodoret, *Hist. eccl.*, 2.6; Socrates, *Hist. eccl.*, 2.19; Epiphanius, *Haer.*, 72.1–12; Cyril of Jer., *Cat.*, 15.27. For earlier hints of this notion see Novatian, *De Trin.*, 31; and Tertullian, *Adv. Prax.*, 4.

[73]Theodoret, *Hist. eccl.*, 5.9–11.

dwelling-place of the Spirit of the Father and the Son, the 'place' (χώρα and τόπος) where the one God, Trinity in Unity and Unity in Trinity, brings us into union with himself in such a way that we may partake of the eternal communion of Father, Son and Holy Spirit in the Godhead. As united to Christ in his incarnate reality the Church constitutes the sanctified community within which we may draw near to the Father through the Son and in the Spirit and share in the eternal life, light and love of God himself. That was surely the primary truth embedded in the mind and worship of the Catholic Church in the fourth century, and was rightly given precedence over all questions of external form, organisation and structure. If it was, as they believed, the empirical Church that had been incorporated into Christ as his Body, then the real structure of the Church was lodged in Christ himself, and had to be lived out in space and time through union and communion with the risen, exalted and advent Lord whose kingdom will have no end.

How far did the Catholic Church manage to translate its theological victories over the dualist patterns of thought in the culture of that ancient world into its own empirical life and order? Was it able to transform society, and resist the inroad of dualist paradigms into its ecclesial structures? Certainly in the period preceding and following the Councils of Nicaea and Constantinople the answer must be largely in the affirmative. However, radically dualist modes of thought taken over from Hellenism in the second and third centuries, not least by Alexandrians, laid the basis for serious problems. Thus both Clement and Origen operated with a radical Platonic disjunction between a sensible world (κόσμος αἰσθητός) and an intelligible world (κόσμος νοητός),[74] which led them to draw a damaging distinction between a physical or sensible Gospel (σωματικόν, αἰσθητὸν εὐαγγέλιον) and a spiritual or eternal Gospel (πνευματικόν, αἰώνιον εὐαγγέλιον), and to claim that the former will pass away, for it is only a shadowy representation of the latter. It was thus inevitable that a corresponding distinction

---

[74]E.g. Clement, *Strom.*, 5.6–14; Origen, *In Jn.*, 1.7–9, 24; 6.5; *De prin.*, 4.3.13.

would be drawn between a visible earthly Church regarded as a passing similitude of the real thing, and the invisible Church of enduring spiritual reality, which Origen spoke of as the mystical 'bride of Christ'.[75]

It was when this dualist way of thinking was found to affect the very core of Christian belief in the incarnation, by driving a sharp line of demarcation between the Son and God the Father, that the Nicene Fathers inserted the *homoousion* into the midst of the Creed, which not only secured the supreme truth of the Deity of Christ but had the effect of undermining dualist concepts and establishing a realist and unitary basis for the interpretation and proclamation of the gospel of the incarnation of the Son and Word of God in Jesus Christ. Hence for Nicene ecclesiology the focus of attention was on the incorporation of believers into the Body of Christ on the ground of the reconciliation with God which he had accomplished in and through his bodily death and resurrection. That is to say, it was precisely the visible, empirical Church in space and time that was held to be the Body of Christ. It should now be clear, on the other hand, that any failure to grasp the implications of this Nicene theology for a realist and unitary doctrine of the Church, opened the door for the identification of the real Church with a spiritualised timeless and spaceless magnitude, and for the on-going life and mission of the empirical Church to be regarded as subject to the laws that control human society in this world. In other words, it would result in a state of affairs in which the dualist sub-structure prevailing in Graeco-Roman institutions of society and law would inevitably entangle the Church in a distinction between a juridical Society on the one hand, and a mystical body on the other hand, but that would involve the rejection of the doctrine that through the sanctifying and renewing presence of the Holy Spirit, *the empirical Church is the Body of Christ*. Thus Nicene theology became strengthened in its belief that 'the reality of the Church is the earthly-historical form of the existence of Jesus Christ, the one holy catholic and apostolic Church.'[76]

---

[75]Origen, especially, *In Cant.*, 2–3.
[76]I have borrowed this form of words from Karl Barth, for it gives accurate

In order to clarify our understanding of the Nicene-Constantinopolitan doctrine of the Church we must probe again into the crucial issues that were brought to light during and following the Council of Nicaea in the drawn-out debates between Nicene theologians and Arian or semi-Arian churchmen. It became more and more evident to the catholic fathers that there was a profound interconnection between ecclesiology and Christology as well as pneumatology, the key to which, as in the doctrine of the Holy Trinity, was the Nicene *homoousion*. In its own way and on its own creaturely level the doctrine of the Church, like the doctrines of Christ and the Spirit, had to do with the evangelical substance of the faith. The cardinal point upon which everything hinged was the internal relation of Christ to the being of the Father and thus the internal relation of the atonement to the incarnate Person of Christ, the one Mediator between God and man. Likewise, the basic principle in the doctrine of the Church upon which it depended was its internal relation to Jesus Christ, for it is in him that the very being of the Church is rooted. Thus through the communion of the Holy Spirit imparted to it by Christ, the Church is united to Christ as his body, but in such an interior ontological and soteriological way that Christ himself is both the Head and the Body in one.

The crucial problem in the doctrine of the Church that confronted the Nicene theologians in the fourth century may be set out in the following way. **Arianism** held that the relation between the Son and the Father was merely of an external or moral kind contingent upon the divine will, and not internal to the one being of the Godhead. Correspondingly, it operated with an external relation between the saving work and the Person of Christ, and thus also with an external or moral relation between the Church and Christ. Hence the Church was regarded, not as the Body of Christ, but as a community formed through the voluntary association of like-minded people. **Nicene Theology**, on the other hand, held that the relation

---

expression to the Greek patristic concept of the empirical nature of the Church which Jesus Christ has formed and continually renews as his Body. See Barth, *CD.*, 4.1, p. 643.

between the incarnate Son and the Father was internal to the one eternal being of God, and was not an external creaturely or moral relation but one intrinsic to the essential nature of God. Correspondingly, it operated with an internal ontological relation between the Person and work of Christ, and thus with an internal relation between the Church and Christ of a dynamic and ontological kind established through the reconciling and incorporating activity of the incarnate Son and the communion of the Holy Spirit.

It was early Christian understanding of the incarnation and atonement in their mutual involution in the one Mediator between God and man, the man Christ Jesus, that gave rise to the classical doctrine of the Church. Through the pouring out of the Holy Spirit upon it, the Church was constituted the unique 'place' where access to the Father through the Son was grounded in space and time among the nations of mankind. In one Spirit the reconciling exchange between Christ and sinful men and women was actualised in their existence individually and conjointly, and thus the Church was called out from the midst of mankind into being as the Body of Christ in the world, united to him and unified in him. The central point upon which the doctrine of the Church as the Body of Christ hinged was located in the mystery of union and communion with Jesus Christ the incarnate Son of God who was himself of one being (ὁμοούσιος) with God the Father.

The continuing actualisation of the Church takes place through holy baptism, when by the power of the Spirit people are initiated into union with Christ, sealed in the name of the Father, the Son and the Holy Spirit, and are given to share in the communion of the Holy Trinity. We shall consider the significance of the credal statement 'one baptism for the remission of sins' later, but at this juncture it may be noted that the union in which the Church is implicated is characterised by ontological depth reaching back into God himself. Through the communion of the Holy Spirit the Church is united to Christ and grounded in the hypostatic union of God and man embodied in him, and through Christ and in the Spirit it is anchored in the consubstantial union and communion of the Father, Son and Holy Spirit in the Holy Trinity.[77]

We are now in a better position to consider the formal confession of belief '**in one holy, catholic and apostolic Church**', with a view to throwing some of the ideas that have come before us into sharper relief.

(1) The Oneness of the Church

The Creed is here speaking of the visible or empirical Church, which has come down in history from the apostles, and places it within the frame of its belief in 'the Holy Spirit, the Lord and Giver of Life, who proceeds from the Father, who with the Father and the Son together is worshipped and glorified, who spoke by the prophets'. That is to say, the existence of the Church is not the product of human activity, but is to be traced back to the Lord himself, in the sovereign self-giving of God in his Spirit, who through his Word calls the Church into being and by his own breath makes it alive with the very life of God. In biblical language, the actual Church to which we belong has not been made by human hands but derives from God himself, for it is the work of his Holy Spirit.[78] This divine origin, or supernatural formation of the Church, was thrust into the centre of Nicene thought with considerable force in the face of heretical claims that the Holy Spirit was a creature, for that had the effect of rejecting the union of the Church with God.[79]

It follows from this that the Church throughout all its manifestations in space and time is intrinsically and essentially *one*, for it is constituted as Church through the presence of the one Lord and his one Spirit – that was the point of the insistence by Ignatius and Irenaeus that wherever Christ is, and wherever his Spirit is, there only is the Church. We shall return to the oneness of the Church when we come to consider the 'one baptism for the remisison of sins.' The early Church was deeply

[77]Cf. 'The Mystery of the Kingdom', *Conflict and Agreement in the Church*, vol. 2, 1960, pp. 82–92.

[78]Acts. 4.10f; 7.48; 17.24; cf. Matt. 12.42f; Mk. 15.58; Lk. 20.17f; 2 Cor. 5.1; 2 Pet. 2.4ff; Heb. 9.11, 24.

[79]See, for example, Athanasius, *Con. Ar.*, 1.34; 2.69; *De syn.*, 36; *Ad Ser.*, 1.2–11, 20–25, 29f.

aware of another aspect of the Church in its embrace of the people of God under the old covenant as well as the new. The very term ἐκκλησία used of the Church had already carried that notion of oneness within it from apostolic times, but it was reinforced by the fathers of Constantinople in their belief that it was one and the same Holy Spirit who spoke in the prophets and in the apostles. Cyril of Jerusalem who was present at the Council used to speak of the ἐκκλησία in ancient times as 'the first Church', and of the ἐκκλησία in Christian times as the 'second holy Church' called 'the Catholic Church' which owed its increase throughout the world to the fact that the one Church in Judaea had been cast off.[80] Irenaeus, who had the strongest sense of the oneness of the Church spanning the Old Testament and the New Testament, cited an earlier source to the effect that through one Head in their midst the two peoples scattered to the ends of the earth are assembled into one God.[81] For Irenaeus there was only one Church stretching from Adam to Christ, but gathered up in him as its Head. In the run-up to the Council of Constantinople it was especially Epiphanius who gave expression to this all-embracing unity, when he connected the Church in its different forms under the old and new covenants with the one self-revelation of the Holy Trinity, and described it as the Mother of the faithful, but without playing down the unique character of the holy Catholic Church due to the incarnation.[82] The Council of Constantinople itself spoke of the Church at Jerusalem as 'the Mother of all the Churches'.[83]

(2) The Holiness of the Church

As the one people of God the Church is called out of the world and separated from secular society for fellowship with God. Its holiness does not derive from any moral goodness or purity of its members, but from the holiness of God the Father, the Son

[80]Cyril of Jer., *Cat.*, 17.24f.

[81]Irenaeus, *Adv. haer.*, 5.18.1, vol. 2, p. 372; see also 4.8.1, p. 169; 4.18.1, p. 168; 4.39.1, p. 233; 4.49.1, p. 255; cf. Clement Alex., *Strom.*, 7.17, etc.

[82]Epiphanius, *Exp. fidei*, 1f, 6, 14, 18f, 25; *Anc.*, 118f.

[83]Theodoret, *Hist. eccl.*, 5.9; cf. Cyril of Jer., *Cat.*, 18.26.

and the Holy Spirit. The holiness of the Church is thus objectively grounded in the utterly transcendent holiness, glory and purity of God's being. It is precisely as the Holy One who dwells in unapproachable light that God seeks and establishes fellowship with his human creatures, coming into their midst always as the Lord whose awful presence among them opposes and judges their impurity and sin, yet in such a way that he does not annihilate them but gathers them to himself within the embrace of his covenant mercies and grace. Thus in the language of the Old Testament revelation, God sanctifies himself in the midst of his people, implicating them in his own divine holiness and constituting them on earth as the living sanctuary where he has put his name and which he has bound to himself through his steadfast love, and within which he is unceasingly worshipped and glorified: 'Holy, Holy, Holy is the Lord God Almighty, the whole earth is full of his glory.'[84] The counterpart to that after the incarnation of the Holy One, as Didymus pointed out, is the self-sanctification of Christ on behalf of his Church in whose midst he is worshipped and glorified as the Holy Lord.[85]

It will be convenient to recall again the way in which Athanasius expressed this truth through a paraphrase of our Lord's words, 'For their sakes I sanctify myself, that they may be sanctified in the truth'.[86] 'I, being the Father's Word, give to myself become man, the Spirit, and myself, become man, do I sanctify in him, that henceforth in me, who am the truth (for "thy Word is truth") all may be sanctified. If, then, for our sakes he sanctified himself, and does this when he is become man, it is very clear that the coming of the Spirit upon him was a coming upon us because of his bearing our body. It did not take place for the sake of the Word but for our sanctification, that we might share in his anointing.'[87] Since the Church was brought into being through his assumption of our fallen and enslaved humanity into himself, the self-sanctification of Christ as the

[84]Is. 6.3.

[85]Didymus, *De Trin.*, 2.6.6–7, with reference to Rev. 4.8: 'Holy, Holy, Holy, is the Lord God Almighty, who was and is and is to come.'

[86]John 17.19.

[87]Athanasius, *Con. Ar.*, 1.46f.

Holy One in its midst brings the holiness of the Holy Spirit to bear upon it in conviction and judgment of its unrighteousness, but nevertheless in such a way that the Church is justified in Christ and made holy with his holiness.[88] As Origen once expressed it, all our righteousness (and sanctification) derives from Christ himself who *is* Righteousness in his own being (τὸ γὰρ αὐτοδικαιοσύνη ἡ οὐσιώδης Χριστός ἐστιν).[89]

The holiness of the Church, then, is not its own but derives from God himself through the grace of the Lord Jesus Christ and the communion of the Holy Spirit. Through the self-sanctification of Christ in its midst and the pouring out of the Holy Spirit upon it, the Church has been chosen by God and set apart as a spiritual house and a royal priesthood to offer spiritual sacrifices acceptable to God through Jesus Christ. Since it is thus implicated in the awesome holiness of God, the Father, the Son and the Holy Spirit, the Church of Christ inevitably attracts awe and veneration to itself, not for its own sake, but as the community in which God has put his name, as the Body with which Christ identifies himself in the world, and as the unique place where God is immediately present to us through the Holy Spirit in his very own being as God. In its derivation from the holiness of the Triune God, the holiness of the Church was held to be divine in its essential character, so that to speak evil of the Church was regarded as tantamount to speaking evil of Christ himself, and close to blasphemy against his Holy Spirit. Hence for the Church to usurp the place of Christ in any way or to arrogate to itself the holiness and authority that belong to him alone, would be nothing less than an affront upon the holiness and majesty of God himself.

(3) The Catholicity of the Church

In its original use 'catholic' meant 'universal', and as such could be applied to the all-inclusive range of redemption or resurrection[90] or divine providence,[91] and was applied even to

[88]Didymus, *De Trin.*, 2.6.6–7; 2.7.4; *De Sp. St.*, 53f, etc.

[89]Origen, *In Jn.*, 6.6, with reference to 1 Cor. 1.30.

[90]E.g., Irenaeus, *Adv. haer.*, 3.15.2, vol. 2, p. 79f; Theophilus, *Ad Aut.*, 1.23; Justin, *Dial.*, 81.

[91]Clement Alex., *Strom.*, 6.16; Origen, *In. Jer.*, 3.1.

God by Didymus.[92] It was very naturally, and most generally, applied to the Church.[93] In its association with the epithets 'one' and 'holy', however, 'catholic' became intensified in its meaning. To be catholic the Church must be one and holy, for unity and holiness interpenetrate each other in the essential nature of the Church as the Body of which Christ is the organising Head, and which through the indwelling of the Holy Spirit is united to the one and only God, the Holy Trinity. In this context, then, the Catholic Church is to be understood as embracing all dimensions of the people of God and their existence throughout space and time, for by the very nature of its unique foundation by Christ upon his apostles, and in virtue of the faith once and for all delivered to it by the apostles, the Church must ever be one and the same in all ages and places.[94] Certainly the main stress in the notion of the Catholic Church found in the great Nicene fathers, as we have noted in the case of Athanasius,[95] was the close correlation between the catholicity of the Church and the identity of the apostolic faith which, owing to its objective ground in God's one self-revelation through the Son and in the Spirit, can never alter its nature. That was what the Nicene-Constantinopolitan Creed was about, the restoring of the Church to its ancient health and true godliness.[96]

Cyril of Jerusalem defined the catholicity of the Church for his catechumens in a rather wider way. 'Now the Church is called Catholic because it is spread throughout the world, from one end of the earth to the other; and because it teaches universally and completely one and all the doctrines which people ought to know about things visible and invisible, heavenly and earthly; and because it subjects to godliness every class of men, governors and governed, learned and unlearned

[92]Didymus, *De Trin.*, 2.4.

[93]Ignatius, *Smyrn.*, 8.2; Polycarp, *apud* Eusebius, *Eccl. hist.*, 4.15.1; *Der Balyzeh Papyrus*, Denz-Schoen., *Enc.*, 2, p. 18, etc.

[94]Cf. for example, Epiphanius, *Anc.*, 82; 118ff; *Haer.*, 31; 34.21; 61.2; *Exp. fidei*, 18, 22ff. This was the aspect of catholicity later made prominent by Vincent of Lerins, *quod semper, quod ubique, et quod ab omnibus creditum est* – *Comm.*, 2.

[95]E.g., Athanasius, *Con. Ar.*, 1.14.

[96]Theodoret, *Hist. eccl.*, 5.9.

alike; and because it universally treats and heals all sorts of sins committed by soul or body, and possesses in itself every kind of virtue that is named, both in deeds and words, and in all kinds of spiritual gifts. And it is rightly called Church (ἐκκλησία), *because it calls forth and assembles together all men.*'[97]

While the Church fathers and theologians of the Nicene-Constantinopolitan period thought of catholicity mainly in terms of the oneness and identity of the Church's faith throughout the world (οἰκουμένη), we must not lose sight of the profound bearing of catholicity upon the rejection of all dualist patterns of thought that kept on giving rise to schismatic movements within and outside the borders of the Church. At its deepest level the catholicity of the Church has to do with its commitment to the universal range of the incarnation and the atonement, for he who became flesh in Jesus Christ was identical with the very Word of God by whom all things visible and invisible were created and in whom they continue to consist. That implied that the Gospel of redemption through the life, death, and resurrection of Christ proclaimed by the Church had a completely universal range. As the fathers of the second century saw so clearly, to separate redemption from creation was to limit the saving range of the incarnation and atonement and thereby to destroy the essential message of the Gospel. At that level, then, 'catholic' describes those people who remained faithful to the apostolic tradition in believing that Jesus Christ the incarnate Son of God died and rose again for all people irrespective of who they are. Catholicity of that kind, of course, was far removed from the kind of universalism advocated by Origen in his concept of the final restitution (ἀποκατάστασις) of all things in God.[98] The rejection of cosmological and epistemological dualism cut away the ground from beneath conceptions of a twofold Gospel and a twofold Church, and it became increasingly clear that the oneness of the Church arises out of the interlocking of the incarnation and the atonement or

[97]Cyril of Jer., *Cat.*, 18.23.

[98]Origen, *De prin.*, 3.5.1–8; 3.6.1–9; cf. 2.3.5; *In Jn., 1.16;* cf. Epiphanius, *Haer.*, 64.31f. See also Gregory Nyss., *Or. cat.*, 26; *Con. Eun.*, 3.1, Jaeger, 2, p. 21; *De Op.*, 17.2; *De an. et res.*, *MPG*, 46.129–160; Didymus, *In Ac.*, 3.21, Athens ed., 49, p. 28, etc.

the indivisibility of the Person and work of Christ as the one Mediator between God and man. This one Church is intrinsically catholic because it is the one Body of Christ in whom the fullness of the Godhead dwells bodily, in whom all things visible and invisible are gathered up and reconciled to God, and because as the Body of such a Christ the Church is itself the fullness of him who fills all things.[99]

The catholicity of the Church, then, refers to the intensive wholeness and fullness of the Church in Christ, to the coordination of the Church, everywhere, in every place, and throughout all space and time, with the wholeness and fullness of Christ himself. The catholic Church does not live out of itself but out of Christ; nor does it derive inspiration from its own spirit but only from the one Spirit of the living God. It does not act in its own name and authority but only in the name and authority of the Father, Son and Holy Spirit. But throughout all its life the intensive oneness or wholeness of the Church in Christ unfolds as under the imperative of the Holy Spirit it seeks to be obedient to its commission to proclaim the Gospel to all mankind. 'The Church is firmly established; it is "founded on the rock", and the gates of hell shall not prevail against it.'[100]

(4) The Apostolicity of the Church

In its simplest sense the apostolicity of the Church refers back to the original foundation of the Church once for all laid by Christ upon the apostles,[101] but it also refers to the interpenetration of the existence and mission of the Church in its unswerving fidelity to that apostolic foundation. As the incarnate Son of the Father Jesus regarded himself as having been anointed by the Spirit and clothed with his power for the fulfilment of his unique evangelical mission.[102] With its completion in the cross and resurrection, he commissioned his disciples as apostles to act

[99]See Col. 1.19; 2.9; Eph. 1.23.

[100]Athanasius, *Con. Ar.*, 4.34; cf. Hilary, *De Trin.*, 6.37; both with reference to Matt. 16.18.

[101]Matt. 7.5; 1 Cor. 3.10f; Eph. 2.20f; cf. Matt. 16.13–23; 1 Pet. 2.4–9.

[102]Lk. 4.18f.

in his name, thereby linking their subordinate mission with his own supreme mission: 'As the Father has sent me, so I send you'. At the same time he breathed his Spirit upon them, thereby constituting their sending by him as the empirical counterpart to the sending of the Holy Spirit by the Father in the name of the Son, which took place as Jesus had promised on the day of Pentecost.[103] Jesus was the Apostle in the absolute sense.[104] The apostles, however, were sent out by him as his chosen witnesses whose word he promised to empower as his own, and thus to unfold in them his own self-revelation. That was the peculiar function of the apostles, to be the link between Christ and the Church, the hinge on which the incarnational revelation objectively given in Christ was grounded and realised within the continuing membership of the Church. The apostolate was designed and formed by Christ to be the nucleus of the Church concorporate with himself within which his own self-witness was integrated with inspired witness to him and translated into the appropriate form (i.e. the New Testament Scriptures) for its communication in history. As such the apostolate in its embodiment of the truth of the Gospel or the deposit of faith constituted the unrepeatable foundation on which the Church was built, and to which the Church was committed ever afterwards to refer as its authoritative norm for the understanding and interpretation of the Gospel. That was the apostolic Church which Christ sent out into the world with the command to teach all nations, baptising them in the name of the Father, Son and Holy Spirit, and with the promise that he himself, to whom all power in heaven and earth had been given, would always be with it right to the end of time.

Let us recall again at this point the way in which Irenaeus thought of the deposit of faith embodied in the apostolic foundation of the Church as having a continuously rejuvenating force (*depositum juvenescens et juvenescere faciens*).[105] But let us also recall his determination to make clear that it was not the Church itself that is the pillar and ground of the truth but 'the

---

[103]John 17.18; 20.21; cf. 14.25f; 16.12; Lk. 24.49; Acts 1.2–8.
[104]Heb. 3.1.
[105]Irenaeus, *Adv. haer.*, 3.28.1, vol. 2, p. 131.

Gospel and the Spirit of life'.[106] He realised that the apostolic deposit of faith must be understood as spanning two levels, the authoritative reception and interpretation of it embodied in the apostolic foundation of the Church, and the objective and life-giving reality on which it rested, the whole saving fact of Christ himself. The former is entirely subordinate to the latter, for it is only in Christ and not out of itself, and only through union and communion with Christ in its faith and mission and not through its own piety, that the Church is continuously sustained.

In that light the apostolicity of the Church will be seen to refer to its grounding and rooting in Christ through the foundation he laid for it in his apostles, to whom he gave magisterial authority over the Church,[107] and through whom the Word and truth of the Gospel were to be transmitted.[108] But the apostolicity of the Church will also be seen to refer to the character and imprint of its distinctive apostolic origin, and to the nature of the Church as continuously embodying the apostolic witness and testimony in its life and mission, for it is through faithful transmission of the preaching and teaching of the apostles that the Church is itself constantly renewed and reconstituted as Christ's Church. That the Church is *apostolic* as well as one, holy and catholic, signifies, therefore, that it is ever one and the same with the Church once for all founded by Christ in the apostolate. Just as the Holy Trinity is ever identical with himself, as Jesus Christ is the same yesterday, today and for ever, and as there is only one and the same Spirit of God in the Church of Old Testament and of the New Testament, so the Church of Christ is one and the same today with what it was in its apostolic foundation. That is to say, apostolicity has to do with the continuing *identity* of the Church as the authentic Body of Christ in space and time.

The apostolicity of the Church, thus understood, clearly has a significant bearing on how we are to understand the oneness, holiness, and catholicity of the Church, all of which have to be gaged with reference to the normative authority of the apostles,

---

[106]Irenaeus, *Adv. haer.*, 3.11.11, vol. 2, p. 47, with reference to 1 Tim. 3.15.
[107]Matt. 17.18; Luke 22.29f; John 17.18, 20.21ff.
[108]Acts 1.8; Matt. 28.19f; Mark 16.15f, etc.

that is, with reference to the apostolic Scriptures and their witness to Christ. The one, holy, catholic and *apostolic* Church is the Church continuously occupied with the interpretation, exposition and application of Holy Scripture, for it is in that way that the Church opens its mind and life to the direction and correction of the Word of God. And that was precisely what the Church was doing, not least in the theologically turbulent years between the Nicene and the Constantinopolitan Councils. I refer to the constant exegetical activity undertaken by the Church fathers in their attempt to bring to consistent expression the internal connections of the Gospel and thus, not only to clarify and defend the apostolic and catholic faith in the face of heretical disruption, but to provide the Church with a structural framework within which its members could mediate upon the Holy Scriptures, worship the Holy Trinity, proclaim the Gospel of forgiveness, reconciliation and sanctification, and so fulfil its mission in obedience to the command of Christ. That was not by any means a formal hermeneutical operation, for the Holy Scriptures were revered and interpreted within the living witness of the worshipping people of God, and with prayer for guidance by the Spirit of truth.

Accordingly, as the bishops and theologians assembled in Council they sought to yield themselves to the control of the apostolic tradition in order to keep in tune at every debatable point with the witness and testimony of the apostles. Hence on every crucial issue Nicene theology and the Nicene formulations of the deposit of the faith were checked and established strictly in accordance with the teaching of the Holy Scriptures, even though basic points of connection had sometimes to be expressed through the coining of new terms in order to clarify and preserve genuine faithfulness within the worship and mind of the Church to the proclamation and teaching of the Gospel embodied in the New Testament. That does not mean that the Nicene and Constantinopolitan fathers were engaged in any kind of 'biblicist' formalisation of the Gospel. They were concerned in wrestling with the Holy Scriptures to express what they were *compelled* to think and hold within the context of the apostolic tradition under the impact of

God's self-revelation through the Word and Spirit of Christ, and on that basis alone, to confess their faith in the Father, the Son and the Holy Spirit. And thereby they sought to provide continuing generations of people in the Church with an evangelical and apostolic framework within which continuing interpretation of Holy Scripture, proclamation of the truth of the Gospel, and instruction in the faith could be carried out.

This brings us to the concluding statement of the Nicene-Constantinopolitan Creed in which the whole declaration of belief is directed to its actual evangelical import in the daily life of the people of God.

'We confess one baptism for the remission of sins; we look for the resurrection of the dead and the life of the world to come.'

It was through baptism, to cite Irenaeus to this effect once again, that 'the rule of truth' (κανὼν τῆς ἀληθείας) was received by the Church to be retained unchanged. This was a doctrinal instrument inherited from the foundation of the Church which enabled it to interpret the Holy Scriptures in accordance with their objective intention in God's self-revelation and thereby to discern how each expression of the Gospel taken from the Scriptures fits into the coherent pattern of its essential message. It is thus through baptismal discipling of that kind, in accordance with the command of the risen Lord,[109] that the faith of the Church is transmitted in such a way as ever to be one and the same (*una et eadem fides*).[110] It is not surprising that Origen could speak of the rule of truth as 'the supreme summary of the faith (μέγιστον τῆς πίστεως κεφάλαιον)', for it contains all that we need to believe in order to be saved.[111] It was undoubtedly the inner connection between baptism and the

[109]Matt. 28.19f.

[110]Irenaeus, *Adv. haer.*, 1.1.14, vol. 1, p. 67; 1.1.20, pp. 87ff; 1.3, pp. 93f; cf. Tertullian, *De virg. vel.*, 1.

[111]Origen, *In Jn.*, 32.16; cf. 6.6; 13.16; *De prin.*, 1.1. Cf. the second creed of Sirmium: τὸ δὲ κεφάλαιον πάσης τῆς πίστεως καὶ ἡ βεβαιότης ἐστὶν ἵνα Τριὰς ἀεὶ φυλάττηται, καθὼς ἀνέγνωμεν ἐν τῷ εὐαγγελίῳ, with reference to Matt. 29.19 – Socrates, *Hist. eccl.*, 2.30.

wholeness of the apostolic and catholic faith, not least in respect of belief in the Holy Trinity included in baptism, that lay behind the confession or acknowledgement of 'one baptism' in the Creed. The expression was taken from the Pauline passage regularly cited in this connection: 'There is one body, and one Spirit, as you are called in one hope of your calling; one Lord, one faith, one baptism, one God and Father of all, who is above all and through all and in you all.'[112] Thus the whole substance of the Gospel of grace could be regarded as concentrated in 'one baptism for the remission of sins'.[113]

Athanasius claimed that it is in baptism that 'the fullness of the mystery (τὸ πλήρωμα τοῦ μυστηρίου) is lodged, for it is given in the name of the Father, Son and Holy Spirit.[114] That helps to explain why the Creed spoke only of 'one baptism', and not also of 'one eucharist', as might have been expected. In its correlation with the Holy Trinity baptism was regarded as the great seal, or the all-embracing sacrament bound up with one Body, one Spirit, one Lord, one faith, and one God and Father, while the eucharist was regarded as celebrated only within the Church's participation in the great mystery of baptism and as properly included within it. Certainly many of the early Church accounts of the eucharist such as we have from Justin Martyr, Hippolytus or Cyril of Jerusalem are what might be called 'baptismal eucharists'. Another factor helping to explain the fact that the Creed did not explicitly refer to 'one eucharist' is simply because the eucharist did not figure *expressis verbis* in the paradigmatic text cited from St Paul.[115]

One baptism, understood through this Pauline passage, pointed in the first place directly to Jesus Christ as the one Lord of the Church, for it was through his vicarious activity in life, death and resurrection that the Church came into being. Christ himself was both the ontological ground and the unifying core of the Church which he appropriated to himself as his own

---

[112]St Paul, Eph. 4.4–6.

[113]Athanasius, *Con. Ar.*, 2.41–42; cf. *Ad Ser.*, 1.6, 29f; 3.6. See also Tertullian, *De bap.*, 6.12, 15; *De virg. vel.*, 2; Hilary, *De Trin.*, 8.7; 11.1; Epiphanius, *Anc.*, 118; *Haer.*, 62.4.

[114]Athanasius, *Con. Ar.*, 2.42.

[115]Ephesians 4.4–6.

peculiar possession (ἰδιοποίησις), and identified with himself as his own Body.[116] Hence baptism in his name signified incorporation of the baptised into Christ as members of his Body. To speak of the Church in this way is certainly to make use of figurative or analogical language, but there is rather more to it than that, for a relation in *being* between Christ and his Church is clearly entertained. That was understood by the early Church very realistically as a *somatic* and not just a *pneumatic* reality, for the Church is not the Body of the Spirit but the Body of Jesus Christ, the Word made flesh. The mystery of the Church has to do with its profound ontological relation to Christ 'in whom the fullness of the Godhead dwells bodily (σωματικῶς)'.[117]

On the other hand, one baptism pointed to one Spirit, for it is in one Spirit as well as through Christ that the Church has access to the Father. It is through the κοινωνία of the Holy Spirit that the Church shares in the incarnate mystery of Christ, and through his power and operation within it that the unity of the Church as the Body of Christ is progressively actualised among the people of God. The Church was thus respected as the Temple of God in which he dwells through his Spirit. And as Jesus promised his disciples, with the coming and presence of the Paraclete to act in his name, he himself would return as the risen and ascended Lord to dwell in the Church, along with God the Father.[118] It is through the Spirit sent by the Father in the name of the Son and who himself receives from the Son, that Christ continues to be mediated to his Church. It was understandable, therefore, that theologians like Epiphanius should think of the Holy Spirit, not only as 'the bond of the Holy Trinity', but as 'the bond of unity', 'the bond of truth' and 'the bond of faith' within the Church, for it is in and through him that the reciprocity between God and man established in Christ is progressively deepened and realised within the membership of the Church in its worship of the Holy Trinity.[119] That is to say,

[116]Cf. the risen Lord's word to Saul, 'Why do you persecute me?' Acts 9.4.
[117]Col. 2.9.
[118]John 14.16ff; 16.7f; 17.21f.
[119]Epiphanius, *Anc.*, 5–10; *Haer.*, 62.4; 73.36; 74.11; cf. 70.1.

the Holy Spirit is not only the bond of unity between the three divine Persons in the one being of God, but the bond of unity between God and human beings as they are baptised into the one Lord and are united with him and one another in one faith. Since it is none other than the one Spirit of the Holy Trinity who has been sent to dwell within the Church and lead it into all truth, the Church is made more and more open to the one God and Father of all, who is above all, and through all and in all, and is thus more and more universalised or 'catholicised' as the one Body of him whose fullness fills all in all.[120]

What then are we to understand by 'one baptism for the remission of sins' (ἓν βάπτισμα εἰς ἄφεσιν ἁμαρτιῶν)? Baptism in the name of the Father, Son and Holy Spirit initiates people into the sphere in which all the divine blessings of forgiveness of sins, resurrection and eternal life are bestowed and become effective, but does the emphasis fall on baptism as an objective event in Christ or as a subjective event in our experience of Christ through the Spirit? No doubt baptism properly understood involves both, but a noticeable difference in emphasis already arose in the early Church, for example in the teaching of Cyril of Jerusalem compared to that of Athanasius. With Cyril there was clearly a greater stress upon baptism as a mystical replica of what took place in Christ, an interiorisation in the soul of the spiritual reality signified by baptism.[121] With Athanasius, however, there was a considerable stress on the fact that even when we consider our adoption in Christ to be sons of God as taking place in the Spirit, we must think of that not as viewed in ourselves, but as viewed in the Spirit who is in God.[122] For Athanasius the decisive point, to which we have referred already, was that in his baptism in the Jordan the incarnate Son of God received the Spirit upon the humanity he had taken from us, not for his own sake, but for our sake. That is to say, it was our humanity that was baptised, anointed, sanctified and sealed in him. Thus when he was baptised for us we were

[120]Eph. 1.22f & 4.6.

[121]Cyril of Jer., *Cat.*, 1, 3, 17.14f, 18, 19 & 20. Cyril's credal phrase, καὶ εἰς ἓν βάπτισμα μετανοίας, *Cat.*, 19.9, is more subjective than that of Constantinople.

[122]Athanasius, *Con. Ar.*, 3.24–25.

baptised in him.[123] Our baptism in the name of the Holy Trinity, therefore, is to be understood as a partaking through the Spirit in the one unrepeatable baptism of Christ which he underwent, not just in the Jordan river, but throughout his life and in his death resurrection, on our behalf.[124] That vicarious baptism was the objective truth behind the ἓν βάπτισμα of the Creed in which its depth of meaning was grounded.

It is often overlooked that in speaking of Christian baptism the New Testament Scriptures used the unusual word βάπτισμα and never the common word βαπτισμός. That is highly significant, for while βαπτισμός referred to a repeatable *rite* of ablution or ceremonial cleansing,[125] βάπτισμα regularly referred not to the rite itself but to the reality signified in baptism, that is, the unique saving event in Christ on which the rite rested. In this respect βάπτισμα was precisely like κήρυγμα which did not refer to proclamation as such but to the reality proclaimed, for it was not proclamation that was the saving event but Jesus Christ himself, a point with which, as we saw earlier, Irenaeus was very familiar in his concept of 'the κήρυγμα of truth'. In preaching it was the objective reality of Christ acting on our behalf and proclaiming himself, Christ clothed with his own truth, that was signified by κήρυγμα. It was not otherwise with βάπτισμα in which we are directed through the rite of baptism to its objective ground and reality, Christ clothed with the saving truth of his vicarious life, death and resurrection.

It is interesting to note that while Josephus could speak of John's baptism as βαπτισμός,[126] the New Testament never did, but right from the start spoke of it as βάπτισμα. That is to say, even John's baptism was not presented as a mere rite, but as a rite transformed and fulfilled in Christ, when he submitted to be baptised at the hands of John to fulfil all righteousness and to be consecrated by the Spirit as the Lamb of God come to bear away the sins of the world through the atoning sacrifice he was to

[123]Athanasius, *Con. Ar.*, 1.46–47; cf. also 1.12, 15f, 43, 48ff, 60; 2.14, 18, 59, 61; 3.16, 19, 24f, 33; *Ad Ser.*, 1.29ff.
[124]Mk. 10.38f; Lk. 12.50.
[125]Mk. 7.4 or Heb. 6.2.
[126]Josephus, *Antiquities of the Jews*, 18.5.2.

offer on the Cross. Hence as in the evangelical account of John the Baptist preaching (κηρύσσειν) and baptising (βαπτίζειν) were correlated with each other, so in the writings of the New Testament κήρυγμα and βάπτισμα were linked intimately together, for they shared the same semantic reference to the saving reality of Christ and his Gospel. It is in that way that St Paul's teaching about baptism, in the sixth chapter of his Epistle to the Romans, for example, is surely to be understood, in which the implied rite was, so to speak, stereoscopically related to the reality discerned through it. It was not the rite of baptism which he had primarily in mind but what had once and for all taken place in the Lord Jesus Christ on our behalf, and in which he had already implicated us; for as at the Jordan it was our humanity which was baptised in him, so it was our humanity that was crucified and resurrected in him. When he died for us and was buried, we died and were buried with him, and when he rose again from the grave, we were raised up with him – that is the truth sealed upon us in 'one baptism'. Jesus Christ underwent that one baptism vicariously as Redeemer, but by uniting us to himself through his Spirit he makes us participate in it receptively as those whom he has redeemed. The central truth of baptism, therefore, is lodged in Jesus Christ himself and all that he has done for us within the humanity he took from us and made his own, sharing to the full what we are that we may share to the full what he is. *Baptism is the sacrament of that reconciling and atoning exchange in the incarnate Saviour*. When we understand baptism in that objective depth, we are directed away from ourselves to what took place in Christ in God. Hence St Paul was accustomed to speak of our dying and rising in Christ in the aorist tense.[127] However, if we think of baptism not objectively as βάπτισμα but subjectively as βαπτισμός, then the only meaning we can give to it will be in terms of what we do or experience, or in terms of the efficacy of its valid performance as a rite.

If Athanasius and Epiphanius are true guides here, it is basically in that biblical, objective sense of βάπτισμα that we must understand the Nicene-Constantinopolitan doctrine of

[127]E.g. Eph. 2.1–6.

one baptism for the remission of sins. It was not the baptismal
rite itself (βαπτισμός) that they had primarily in mind, but the
one baptism correlated to one Body, one Spirit, one Lord, one
faith and given in the one name of the Holy Trinity.[128] This
objective reference of one baptism in Christ carried with it the
inference already drawn in the New Testament that baptism is
necessarily once for all and cannot be repeated. Repetition
would be tantamount to crucifying the Son of God afresh.[129]
When ideas of rebaptism or second baptism were thrown up in
connection with schismatic movements they were firmly
rejected by the Church.[130] Thus a very strong injunction to
maintain the traditional practice of 'one baptism' is to be found
in the *Apostolic Constitutions*, with the terse pronouncement that
'those who attempt to baptise people already initiated crucify
the Lord afresh, slay him a second time, dishonour the Spirit,
and affront the sacred blood of Christ'.[131] That is a clear
indication of the seriousness with which the biblical and catholic
doctrine of ἓν βάπτισμα promulgated at Constantinople was
taken.

The doctrine of 'one baptism' must also be understood in its
inherent relation to 'one faith'. Basil once wrote to a friend that,
'we are bound to be baptised in the terms we have received and
to profess belief in the terms in which we are baptised, and as we
have professed belief in him, so to give glory to Father, Son and
Holy Spirit.'[132] It was on the ground of that intrinsic
connection between one baptism and one faith, that the Nicene
theologians refused to accept Arian 'baptism' as Christian, for it
was not baptism in the name of the Triune God, but in the name
of the Father and two creatures, or in the semi–Arian case, in the
name of the Father and the Son and a creaturely Spirit. Hence
repentant heretics were required to receive Christian baptism,

---

[128]Thus Cyril of Jer., *Cat.*, 16.4: 'We preach one God, by one Son, with the
Holy Spirit. The faith is indivisible, the worship of God is not divided.'
[129]Hebrews 6.4–6.
[130]See the stress on one unrepeatable baptism in the anonymous *De
rebaptismate* of the third century, and my discussion of it, *Theol. in Reconcil.*,
pp. 90ff.
[131]*Apost. Const.*, 6.15.
[132]Basil, *Ep.*, 125.3.

for that was the one and only true baptism, and their baptism in
the one name of the Holy Trinity could in no sense be regarded
as a second baptism.[133] This was fully supported by Athanasius.
'As baptism, which is given in the Father, Son and Holy Spirit is
one, and there is one faith in the Trinity (as the apostle said), so
the Holy Trinity, being identical with himself, and united
within himself, has in him nothing in common with creaturely
realities. This is the indivisible oneness of the Trinity, and faith
in him is one.'[134] It was also recognised, of course, that to
invoke the name of the Holy Trinity in an attempted second
baptism was to call in question its invocation in the first instance,
and thus consequently in any repetition as well. The 'seal' or
'character' of the Holy Trinity conferred in baptism upon the
baptised is by its very nature unrepeatable and indelible.[135]

In concluding this chapter we must now give some
consideration to the *evangelical content* of one baptism, namely,
the remission of sins, the resurrection of the dead and the life of
the world to come. The forgiveness of sins was associated with
baptism from the very beginning,[136] and, as we learn from
Irenaeus, was soon given a place in the rule of truth. 'We must
hold the rule of truth without deviation . . . First of all it bids us
bear in mind that we have received baptism for the remission of
sins, in the name of the Father, and in the name of the Son of
God, who was incarnate and died and rose again, and in the
Holy Spirit of God. And that this baptism is the seal of eternal
life, and is the new birth unto God, that we should no longer be
the sons of mortal men, but of the eternal and perpetual
God.'[137] The clauses in the Creed of Constantinople were
clearly put forward as a concentrated form of that part of the

[133]No distinction was drawn in the East, as it was in the West, between the
efficacy and the validity of baptism, for such a dualist conception of baptism
imported a detachment of the one baptism from its objective ground and truth
in Christ.

[134]Athanasius, *Ad Ser.*, 1.30; *Con. Ar.*, 2.42; 4.25; *De syn.*, 36; see also Cyril
of Jer., *Cat.*, 1.7; 4.37; 16.3f; 17.36; Epiphanius, *Exp. fidei*, 13; and *MPG.* 42,
876.

[135]See Epiphanius, *Exp. fidei*, 14, 25; *Anc.*, 7f, 25; Cyril of Jer., *Cat.*, 1.2f, 17;
3.3f, 12; 4.16f; 5.6; 16. 24; 17.35f; 22.7.

[136]Acts. 2.38.

[137]Irenaeus, *Dem.*, 3; cf. *Haer.*, 1.1.20, vol. 1, p. 87f.

received rule without deviation from its essential content. In baptism we are united to Christ through the Holy Spirit in such a way that we partake of the whole substance of the Gospel, for all grace and truth are embodied in him. We may recall the point made by Irenaeus in this connection, when he claimed that the incarnate Son is called and actually is '*Salvation, Saviour* and *Saving Activity*' and that thus he is 'salvation made flesh'.[138] In other words, saving grace is not something detached from Christ which can be dispensed at will, but is identical with Christ in the unity of his Person, Word and Act.[139] It is through the *one baptism* which we have in common with Christ, or rather which he has in common with us, that we share in all that God has in store for us. Because baptism is one (the baptism with which Christ was baptised for our sakes, and the baptism in which we are given to share in all he was, is and will be) to be baptised is much more than to be initiated into the sphere where forgiveness is proclaimed and dispensed in the Church. It is to be 'delivered out of the power of darkness and translated into the kingdom of God's dear Son in whom we have redemption through his blood, even the forgiveness of sins'.[140] It is to have our frail transient existence taken up into Christ himself in such a way that, without any loss to our creaturely reality but rather with its perfecting through his Spirit, it is united to God and established in union with his eternal reality.[141]

It is understandable, then, that in passages to which reference has already been made Athanasius should have said about baptism in the name of the Holy Trinity, that it is 'the fullness of the mystery', and that 'the components of the whole of our faith are anchored in it'.[142] The remission of sins, the resurrection of the dead, and the life of the world to come, belong together to the very core of that mystery, for they are the saving benefits that flow from union with Christ through one baptism and one Spirit, and are enjoyed in one Body. They are not benefits that we may have outside of Christ but only in Christ, and so they

---

[138]Irenaeus, *Adv. haer.*, 3.11.2, vol. 2, pp. 35f.
[139]Cf. Athanasius, *Con. Ar.*, 1.47ff; 2.41ff.
[140]Col. 1.13f.
[141]Athanasius, *De decr.*, 14; *Con. Ar.*, 3.33.
[142]Athanasius, *Con. Ar.*, 2.42; 4.21.

may not be experienced in separation from one another for they cohere indivisibly in him. Nor may they be enjoyed in the experience of separated individuals, but only as individuals share together in the one baptism of Christ and his Spirit. People are certainly baptised one by one, yet only in such a way that they are made members of the one Body of Christ, share in his benefits as a whole, and share in them together with all other members of Christ's Body. Hence it was surely not without intention that acknowledgement of one baptism for the remission of sins, the resurrection of the dead and the life of the world to come, were inserted into the Creed at this point in association with belief in one Church.

The linking together of forgiveness of sins with the resurrection was particularly important, for it meant that forgiveness was not in word only but enacted in the concrete reality of human physical existence. Behind that, of course, lay the great emphasis on the early Church, not least in its opposition to the docetic and dualist ideas put forward by Gnostic thinkers, upon the fact that in Jesus Christ the Word had become *flesh*, and that he rose again in *flesh* or in *body* from the dead.[143] In his incarnate life, death and resurrection the Son of God established a binding relation between his divine reality and mankind; he not only bridged the gap between the creature and the Creator but triumphed completely over the separation between man and God due to human sin and alienation. The resurrection of Christ demonstrated the fact that all division between man and God has now been removed in atoning reconciliation through the blood of Christ. Moreover, the resurrection of Christ in *body* demonstrated that the saving work of Christ on our behalf was fulfilled within the concrete reality of our actual human existence, and in such a way as to set it upon an entirely new basis in the regeneration or renewal of human being in the risen Lord. That was the great message of forgiveness proclaimed at once by the apostles on the day of Pentecost and sealed by the gift of the Holy Spirit in baptism.

[143]See Ignatius, *Smyrn.*, 3.1ff, 7.1, 12.2; Hermas, *Sim.*, 5.6.7; Clement, *Ep. 2.*, 6.6, 9.1–5; Justin, *De res.*, 8–10; Irenaeus, *Adv. haer.*, 2.44.1, vol. 1, p. 360; 4.31.3, vol. 2, p. 204; 5.2.1, p. 318; 5.15.1, p. 364; 5.31.1f, pp. 411f. Cf. also Tertullian, *De carn. Chr.*, and *De res. carn.*, *passim*.

To be united to the crucified and risen Christ through the baptism of his Spirit, necessarily carries with it sharing with him in the resurrection of the dead and the life of the world to come. 'Our resurrection is stored up in the Cross', as Athanasius once expressed it.[144] Through his incarnation the Son of God took up into himself our physical existence enslaved to sin, thereby making our corruption, death and judgment his own and offering himself as a substitute for us, so that through the atoning sacrifice of his own life, he might destroy the power that corruption and death have over us. Through the resurrection of our physical human nature in himself Christ has set us upon an altogether different basis in relation to God in which there is no longer any place for corruption and death.[145] 'Now that the Saviour is risen in his body, death is no longer terrible; for all who believe in Christ trample over it as if it were nothing, and choose rather to die than deny their faith in Christ. They know that when they die, they are not lost, but live and become incorruptible through the resurrection.'[146] Thus the central focus of Christian belief is upon the incarnate, crucified and risen Saviour, for he has burst the bands of death and brought life and immortality to light – that is the forgiveness of sins and resurrection of the dead into which we are once for all baptised by the Holy Spirit. Far from being just a promise for the future, it is an evangelical declaration of what had already taken place in Christ, and in him continues as a permanent triumphant reality throughout the whole course of time to its consummation, when Christ will return with glory to judge the quick and the dead, and unveil the great regeneration (παλιγγενεσία) which he has accomplished for the whole creation of visible and invisible realities alike.

It is important to recall that the apostolic witness to Christ did not speak of his advent (παρουσία), any more than of his kingdom (βασιλεία), in the plural, for strictly speaking there is only one saving παρουσία of the incarnate Son which reaches from his coming in great humility to his coming again with

[144]Athanasius, *Con. Ar.*, 1.43.
[145]Athanasius, *De inc.*, 9.
[146]Athanasius, *De inc.*, 27.

great glory – 'whose kingdom shall have no end.'[147] The term παρουσία was used in the New Testament to speak of all three: the coming, arrival, and presence of Christ; and thus not only of the presence of one who has come but of the presence of one who is to come again. His presence is an advent and his advent is a presence. 'The hour comes and now is', as Jesus once said.[148] It is instructive to find that the plural word, 'advents' or παρουσίαι, was not found in Christian literature for more than a century after the ascension of Christ, when it was used to distinguish between his first coming and his second coming.[149] In one revealing statement, however, Justin Martyr spoke of what takes place *in the midst of Christ's parousia* (ἐν τῷ μεταξὺ τῆς παρουσίας αὐτοῦ).[150] In other words, here and now in the on-going life of the Church we live in the midst of the advent-presence of Christ, already partake of the great regeneration (παλιγγενεσία) of the future, and share in its blessings with one another. Because the Church is the Body of the risen and ascended Christ who will come again, all that is said about one baptism for the remission of sins is proleptically conditioned by the future. Hence due to its union with Christ through one baptism and one Spirit the Church cannot but look through its participation in the saving death of Christ to its participation in his resurrection from the dead, and thus look forward in expectation to the general resurrection[151] at the return of its risen Lord and Saviour when its whole existence will be transformed and it will enjoy to the full the sanctity and eternal life of God himself. As St Paul wrote to the Ephesians: 'Christ loved the Church, and gave himself for it; that he might sanctify

---

[147]See Epiphanius, *Anc.*, 119f; *Exp. fidei*, 17; and *MPG*, 42.885.

[148]John 4.23.

[149]For example, Justin Martyr, *Apol.*, 1.52; *Dial.*, 14, 32, 40, 49, etc.; Hippolytus, *De Chr. et ant.*, 44; *In Dan.*, 4.18, 23, 39, etc.

[150]Justin, *Dial.*, 51.

[151]Cf. Epiphanius, *Anc.*, 119; ὁμολογοῦμεν ἓν βάπτισμα εἰς ἄφεσιν ἁμαρτιῶν, προσδοκῶμεν ἀνάστασιν νεκρῶν καὶ ζωὴν τοῦ μέλλοντος αἰῶνος. This was paraphrased in 120 as: καὶ εἰς ἓν βάπτισμα μετανοίας, καὶ εἰς ἀνάστασιν νεκρῶν, καὶ κρίσιν δικαίαν ψυχῶν καὶ σωμάτων, καὶ εἰς βασιλείαν οὐρανῶν καὶ εἰς ζωὴν αἰώνιον.

and cleanse it with the washing of water by the Word, that he might present it to himself as a glorious Church.'[152]

'No Christian can have a doubtful mind on this point, that our faith is not in a creature, but in one God, Father Almighty, Maker of all things visible and invisible, and in one Lord Jesus Christ his only begotten Son, and in one Holy Spirit: one God known in the holy and perfect Trinity, baptised into whom, and in him united to the Godhead, we believe that we also have inherited the kingdom of the heavens, in Christ Jesus our Lord, through whom to the Father be the glory and the power for ever and ever. Amen.'[153]

[152]Eph. 5.25ff.
[153]Athanasius, *Ad Afr.*, 11.

8

The Triunity of God

'We believe in one God the Father Almighty . . . and in one Lord Jesus Christ, the only begotten Son of God . . . And in the Holy Spirit, the Lord and Giver of life.'

(1) Athanasius

'There is one eternal Godhead in Trinity, and there is one Glory of the Holy Trinity (ἀΐδιος καὶ μία Θεότης ἐστὶν ἐν Τριάδι, καὶ μία δόξα τῆς ἁγίας Τριάδος) . . . If theological truth is now perfect in Trinity, this is the true and only divine worship, and this is its beauty and truth, it must have been always so (Εἰ γὰρ νῦν ἐν Τριάδι ἡ θεολογία τελεία ἐστί, καὶ αὕτη ἡ ἀληθὴς καὶ μόνη θεοσέβειά ἐστι, καὶ τοῦτό ἐστι τὸ καλὸν καὶ ἡ ἀλήθεια: ἔδει τοῦτο οὕτως ἀεὶ εἶναι).'[1] 'There is one Form of Godhead (ἓν εἶδος Θεότητος), which is also in the Word; and one God the Father, existing in himself as he transcends all things, and manifest in the Son as he pervades all things, and in the Spirit as in him he acts in all things through the Word. Thus we confess God to be one through the Trinity (Οὕτω γὰρ καὶ ἕνα διὰ τῆς Τριάδος ὁμολογοῦμεν εἶναι τὸν Θεὸν), and claim that our understanding of the one Godhead in Trinity (τὴν μίαν ἐν Τριάδι Θεότητα) is much more godly than the heretics' conception of Godhead with its many forms and its many

---

[1] Athanasius, *Con. Ar.*, 1.18. Note that Τριάς and Μονάς in Greek are more concrete expressions than *Trinitas* and *Unitas* in Latin.

parts.'[2] These sentences of Athanasius take us into the very heart
of Christian belief in God and worship of him as triune. Since
there is only one Form of Godhead in the indivisible unity of his
self-revelation as Father, Son and Holy Spirit, we believe that he
is *eternally triune in himself*. It is indeed *through the Trinity* that we
believe in the *Unity* of God, but it is also through
acknowledgement of the oneness and identity of being in the
Son and the Spirit with the Father, that faith in the Holy Trinity
takes its perfect and full form.[3] This is the doctrine of God as
Trinity in Unity and Unity in Trinity. It was characteristic of
Athanasius, therefore, that he should have equated θεολογία, in
its deepest sense as the knowledge and worship of God as he is
known through Jesus Christ and in the Holy Spirit and as he is
eternally in himself, specifically with the doctrine of the Holy
Trinity.[4]

Athanasius' approach to the knowledge of God was strictly
through the Son, and not otherwise. 'In beholding the Son, we
see the Father, for our conception and understanding of the Son
are knowledge of the Father, because he is the proper Offspring
from his being.'[5] That is why Athanasius insisted that 'it is more
godly and accurate to signify God from the Son and call him
Father, than to name him from his works and call him
Unoriginate.'[6] The Son is certainly different (ἕτερος) from the
Father, but as the Offspring of the Father's being and ὁμοούσιος
with him, the Deity of the Son and the Deity of the Father are
one and the same.[7] That is to say, for us to know the Son is to
know the Father in accordance with what he is in his own
essential nature, in the indivisibility of the Father from the Son
and of the Son from the Father, and thus to know God in the
internal relations of his eternal being.[8]

That true knowledge of God is knowledge of him as he is

[2] Athanasius, *Con. Ar.*, 3.15.
[3] Athanasius, *Ad Afr.*, 11.
[4] Likewise, Gregory Naz., *Or.*, 31.3 – see also *Or.*, 6.22, Athens ed. 59,
pp. 22f; and 25.17, p. 199.
[5] Athanasius, *Con. Ar.*, 1.16; cf. *De syn.*, 48.
[6] Athanasius, *Con. Ar.*, 1.34; and *De decr.*, 31.
[7] Athanasius, *Con. Ar.*, 1.9, 39, 58, 61; 3.4, 6.
[8] Athanasius, *Con. Ar.*, 1.14–19, 25–34; 2.57f; 3.1–6; 4.1–10; *De syn.*, 41–54.

intrinsically Father and Son *in his own being* was powerfully developed by Athanasius in the third book of his *Contra Arianos*. 'We are allowed to know the Son in the Father, because the whole being of the Son (σύμπαν τὸ εἶναι) is proper to the Father's being (οὐσία) ... For whereas the Form of the Godhead of the Father is the being (τὸ εἶναι) of the Son, it follows that the Son is in the Father and the Father is in the Son.' Then with reference to the words of the Lord 'I and the Father are one', and 'I am in the Father and the Father in me', Athanasius pointed out that 'they show the identity of the Godhead and the oneness of the being (τὴν ταυτότητα τῆς Θεότητος τὴν δὲ ἑνότητα τῆς οὐσίας δείξῃ)'.[9] 'They are two, for the Father is Father and is not also Son, and the Son is Son and is not also Father; but the nature is one and all that is the Father's is the Son's ... The Son and the Father are one in propriety and peculiarity of nature and in the identity of the one Godhead (ἕν εἰσιν αὐτὸς καὶ ὁ Πατὴρ τῇ ἰδιότητι καὶ οἰκειότητι τῆς φύσεως, καὶ τῇ ταυτότητι τῆς μιᾶς Θεότητος). The Godhead of the Son's is the Father's; whence also it is indivisible; and thus there is one God and none other but he. And so since they are one, and the Godhead himself is one, the same things are said of the Son as are said of the Father, except his being said to be "Father"'.[10] 'Since the Son is the Father's Image, it must necessarily be understood that the Godhead and propriety of the Father is the being of the Son (ἡ Θεότης καὶ ἡ ἰδιότης τοῦ Πατρὸς τὸ εἶναι τοῦ Υἱοῦ ἐστι). And this is the meaning of "who being in the form of God" and "the Father in me". Nor is this Form of God merely partial, but the fullness of the Father's Godhead is the being of the Son, and the Son is whole God (τὸ πλήρωμα τῆς τοῦ Πατρὸς Θεότητός ἐστι τὸ εἶναι τοῦ Υἱοῦ, καὶ ὅλος Θεός ἐστιν ὁ Υἱός) ... For the propriety of the Father's being is the Son ... the Form of the Father's Godhead is the Son (τὸ γὰρ ἴδιον τῆς τοῦ Πατρὸς οὐσίας ἐστὶν ὁ Υἱός ... τὸ γὰρ εἶδος τῆς τοῦ Πατρὸς Θεότητός ἐστιν ὁ Υἱός).'[11]

Quite clearly, Athanasius' approach to the doctrine of the Holy Trinity took its start and controlling norm from the

[9] Athanasius, *Con. Ar.*, 3.3.
[10] Athanasius, *Con. Ar.*, 3.4–5.
[11] Athanasius, *Con. Ar.*, 3.5f.

revealing and saving acts of God in the 'incarnate παρουσία' of his only begotten Son in Jesus Christ, and moved through the ὁμοούσιος τῷ Πατρί to its ultimate ground in the eternal relations and distinctions within the one οὐσία of the Godhead. The Nicene formulation of the ὁμοούσιον gave exact expression to the supreme truth of the Gospel that God himself is the content of his revelation and that the Gift which God bestows upon us in his Grace is identical with himself the Giver of the Gift – the point to which Athanasius gave such attention in his doctrine of θεοποίησις. The ὁμοούσιον undoubtedly provided the controlling centre of his thought, for it gave clear and decisive account of the underlying oneness in being and activity between the incarnate Son and God the Father upon which everything in the Gospel depended. At the same time, however, it carried within it the conception of coinherent relations within the one being of God to which the distinctions in the self-revelation of God in the 'saving economy' as Father, Son and Holy Spirit pointed, and upon which they were grounded. For Athananius this coinherence was not merely a linking or intercommunication of the distinctive properties of the three divine Persons but a completely mutual indwelling in which each Person, while remaining what he is by himself as Father, Son, or Holy Spirit, is wholly in the others as the others are wholly in him.[12] Thus within his supreme incarnational perspective, soteriological and ontological factors were always combined in his development of the Nicene doctrine of God.

This Christological approach to the understanding of the Holy Trinity was very evident in Athanasius' *Letters on the Holy Spirit* written between 356 and 361 at the request of his friend Serapion, Bishop of Thmuis, in order to deal with an outbreak of semi-Arian rejection of the Deity of the Holy Spirit on the ground that he was of a *different being (*ἑτερούσιος*)* from the

---

[12]While the actual term 'coinherence' was not used by Athanasius, it was certainly he who developed the conception of coinhering relations in God. Cf. Hilary *De Trin.*, 3.1 for a succinct statement of the idea that the three divine Persons who, while retaining their distinct existence and condition, 'reciprocally contain one another, so that one permanently envelops, and is also permanently enveloped by, the other, whom yet he envelops.' See further 3.2–4 & 9.69.

Father and the Son. Since this clearly threatened the doctrine of the Holy Trinity, and of course the integrity of holy baptism, by tearing the Unity of God asunder, Athanasius combatted it with basically the same Christological, soteriological and ontological arguments that he had deployed in his long debates with the Arians.[13] He maintained against the semi-Arians that it is precisely with the doctrine of the consubstantiality and Deity of the Holy Spirit that the proper understanding of the Holy Trinity is brought to its completion in the theology and worship of the Church. Hence Athanasius could say in his Encyclical Letter to the Bishops of Africa in 369, that the Nicene doctrine of 'the one God known in the Holy and Perfect Trinity' (instead of detracting from the evangelical content of the apostolic κήρυγμα of Christ as Lord and Saviour) has the effect, as the fathers of Nicaea had already perceived, of making known 'the exact form (χαρακτῆρα) of the faith of Christ and the teaching of the Catholic Church.'[14]

Just as we take our knowledge of the Father from our knowledge of the Son, so we must take our knowledge of the Spirit from our knowledge of the Son, and in him from our knowledge of the Father: that is, from the inner relations which the Father, Son and Holy Spirit have with one another in the one indivisible being of the Holy Trinity.[15] Prompting Athanasius' argumentation was the soteriological insight that, unless in the Holy Spirit we have a divine and not a creaturely relation to God, the substance drops out of the Gospel, just as it would if the Son were not of one being and agency with God the Father. Everything hinges, then, upon the truth that the Holy Spirit has the same oneness in being with the Son as the Son has with the Father. Since the Son is of the being (ἐκ τῆς οὐσίας) of the Father and belongs to his being, so the Spirit of God who is one with the being of the Son must be, with him, of the being and one with the being of Father.[16] 'Since the Spirit is one, and, what is more, since he is proper to the Word who is one, he is proper to God who is one, and one in being

[13] Athanasius, *Ad Ser.*, 1.2ff.
[14] Athanasius, *Ad Afr.*, 11.
[15] Athanasius, *Ad Ser.*, 2.3–4; 3.1, 3.
[16] Athanasius, *Ad Ser.*, 1.4–14, 23ff, 27.

(ὁμοούσιος) with him.'[17] 'For the Holy and Blessed Trinity is indivisible and one in himself. When the Father is spoken of, there is included his Word as well, and the Spirit who is in the Son. If the Son is named, the Father is in the Son, and the Spirit is not outside the Word. For there is from the Father one grace which is fulfilled through the Son and in the Holy Spirit; and there is one divine nature and one God "who is over all and through all and in all"'.[18] Thus Athanasius expounded his doctrine of the coinherent relations of the Spirit with the Father and the Son,[19] along the same lines in which he had earlier worked out the mutually interpenetrating and indwelling relations between the Son and the Father.[20] The Holy Trinity is thus homogeneous and unitary, not only in the oneness of his activity (μία ἐνέργεια) toward us, but in the indivisibility of his own eternal being.[21] This was the teaching, Athanasius claimed, which in accordance with the apostolic faith had been delivered by tradition from the fathers. Far from being an extraneous invention, it derived from the Lord Jesus Christ who in his own Person taught the woman of Samaria and us through her, 'the perfection of the Holy Trinity, as being an indivisible and single Godhead (τὴν τῆς Ἁγίας Τριάδος τελειότητα, ἀδιαίρετον ὑπάρχουσαν καὶ μίαν Θεότητα)'.[22]

It is important to note that at this juncture in the argument of the *Ad Serapionem*, Athanasius returned to the point he had made in the first letter about the way Arians had misunderstood 'the incarnate presence of the Word (τὴν ἔνσαρκον παρουσίαν τοῦ Λόγου)',[23] in order to reestablish the incarnational and soteriological basis of the Gospel in the inseparable relation between the Son and the Father, for it is on the same ground that we are to interpret the mission of the Spirit in proceeding from the Father and receiving from the Son.[24] Thus in his second

[17]Athanasius, *Ad Ser.*, 1.27; 3.1.
[18]Athanasius, *Ad Ser.*, 1.14; & 16–17, 21, 29.
[19]Athanasius, *Ad Ser.*, 1.19–21; 3.3ff.
[20]Athanasius, *Con. Ar.*, 3.1–6.
[21]Athanasius, *Ad Ser.*, 1.2, 9, 14, 16f, 20, 28–33; 3.6.
[22]Athanasius, *Ad Ser.*, 1.33.
[23]Athanasius, *Ad Ser.*, 1.3 & 9.
[24]Athanasius, *Ad Ser.*, 1.33 & 3.1.

letter Athanasius was concerned to show not only that the same things are said of the Son as are said of the Father, but that the Father and the Son inhere in one another, for the Son is 'from the being of the Father (ἐκ τῆς οὐσίας τοῦ Πατρός)', and 'of one being with the Father (ὁμοούσιος τῷ Πατρί)'.[25] It is on that inner divine basis, and not on any creaturely basis outside of God, that the life and work of Christ the incarnate Son of God are to be understood as that of the one Mediator between God and men, who is himself God and man. The truth of the Gospel depends on the integrity of that consubstantial relation between Christ and God. And so Athanasius went on to point out that after having fulfilled his human economy, the incarnate Son now sits at the right hand of the Father, 'being in the Father and the Father in him, as always was and is for ever.'[26] That is to say, Athanasius insisted that the union between the incarnate Son and the Father, far from being merely a transient episode in time, is ontologically and eternally real in the Godhead. For Athanasius, then, the ὁμοούσιον provided the all-important point of reference for his understanding of God's self-revelation, from the Father, through the Son and in the Spirit, and of the eternal oneness of God in the Holy Trinity. It is on that ground and in that light that we are to understand the mission of the Holy Spirit from the Father and the gift of the Holy Spirit by the Son.

In his third and fourth letters, then, Athanasius was concerned to offer an account of the doctrine of the Spirit based on the teaching of Jesus himself, in St John's Gospel, 15.26 and 16.13–15, but interpreted in accordance with the principle that 'from our knowledge of the Son, we will be able to have true knowledge of the Spirit, for the Spirit has to the Son the same proper relation as we have learned that the Son has to the Father.'[27] Since he referred to what he had already written, it will be convenient for us at this point to recall what he said. 'The Holy Spirit proceeds from the Father (παρὰ τοῦ Πατρὸς ἐκπορεύεται), and belonging to the Son (τοῦ Υἱοῦ ἴδιον ὄν) is

[25] Athanasius, *Ad Ser.*, 2.2–5.
[26] Athanasius, *Ad Ser.*, 2.7.
[27] Athanasius, *Ad Ser.*, 3.1.

given from him (παρ' αὐτοῦ δίδοται) to the disciples and all who believe on him.'[28] 'The Spirit proceeds from the Father and receives from him (ἐκ τοῦ αὐτοῦ λαμβάνει) and gives.'[29] 'The Spirit receives from the Son (ἐκ τοῦ Υἱοῦ λαμβάνει).'[30] 'If the Son is of (ἐκ) the Father and is proper to his being (ἴδιος τῆς οὐσίας αὐτοῦ), the Spirit who is said to be of (ἐκ) God must be proper to the Son in respect of his being (ἴδιον εἶναι κατ' οὐσίαν τοῦ Υἱοῦ).'[31] 'Because the Spirit is one and, what is more, is proper to the Word who is one, he is proper to God who is one and ὁμοούσιον with him . . . in nature and being he is proper to and not foreign to the Godhead and being of the Son and thereby also of the Holy Trinity.'[32]

These ideas were then taken up again by Athanasius, with renewed insistence upon the Deity of the Holy Spirit and his absolute distinction from all creaturely beings. On the one hand, he emphasised that there is an inseparable ontological relation between the Spirit and the Son, in virtue of which the Son imparts the Spirit out of himself, while the Spirit at the same time receives from the Son. On the other hand, he emphasised that since everything that is the Son's belongs to the Father, the Holy Spirit who is the Spirit of the Son belongs to the Father and is of one being with him. Thus while it is ultimately from the Father that the Holy Spirit proceeds, 'because of his proper relation to the Son he is given *from* him to all (διὰ τὴν πρὸς τὸν Υἱὸν ἰδιότητα αὐτοῦ, καὶ ὅτι ἐξ αὐτοῦ δίδοται πᾶσι).'[33] This teaching was further reinforced by showing that the Son and the Spirit, while distinct from one another, inhere in one another in God, so that there is only one divine activity. This is true of the act of creation: 'The Father creates all things through the Word in the Spirit'; but it is also true of all spiritual gifts which are given in the Trinity: 'For the Father himself through the Word in the Spirit works and gives

---

[28]Athanasius, *Ad Ser.*, 1.2; cf. 3.1; 4.3.
[29]Athanasius, *Ad Ser.*, 1.11.
[30]Athanasius, *Ad Ser.*, 1.20; cf. 3.1; 4.1f.
[31]Athanasius, *Ad Ser.*, 1.25; 3.1; 4.3f.
[32]Athanasius, *Ad Ser.*, 1.27; 3.1; 4.3.
[33]Athanasius, *Ad Ser.*, 3.1.

all things.'[34] This activity, however, is the activity of an eternal unchanging Trinity in whom the Spirit coexists eternally with the Word and is in him. 'As it always was, so it now is; as it now is, so it always was, that is the Trinity, and in it the Father, Son and Holy Spirit.'[35] 'In the Godhead alone the Father is properly Father, and since he is the only Father, he is and was and always will be. The Son is properly Son, and the only Son. And in them it holds good that the Father is always Father, and the Son is always Son, and the Holy Spirit is always Holy Spirit. We believe him to be God, and to be given from the Father through the Son. Thus the Holy Trinity remains invariable, known in one Godhead.'[36]

This trinitarian theology of Athanasius carried with it a profound revision in the meaning of οὐσία and ὑπόστασις as used in Christian theology, which was signalled by an agreement on the formula 'one οὐσία, three ὑποστάσεις' reached at the Council called by Athanasius in 362, and which he explained in the *Tomus ad Antiochenos*. As G. L. Prestige expressed it: 'While hypostasis lays stress on concrete independence, ousia lays it on intrinsic constitution. Hypostasis means "a reality *ad alios*", ousia "a reality *in se*"; the one word denotes God as manifest, the other connotes God as being. Athanasius taught that in God one and the same identical "substance" or object, without any division, substitution, or differentiation of content, is permanently presented in three distinct objective forms.'[37] In some contexts, when speaking of the being of God, Athanasius used the term οὐσία in its simplest sense as that which is and subsists by itself, and as more or less equivalent to ὑπόστασις in its simplest sense.[38] That had to be changed and deepened, however, in the light of God's self-revelation as the Creator who is beyond all created being or οὐσία, and who alone is οὐσία in the strict sense, for he is the

---

[34] Athanasius, *Ad Ser.*, 3.5; cf. 4.3–5.

[35] Athanasius, *Ad Ser.*, 3.7.

[36] Athanasius, *Ad Ser.*, 4.6.

[37] G. L. Prestige, *God in Patristic Thought*, ed. 1950, p. xxix; see also pp. 168ff, 188; and my *Theology in Reconciliation*, 1975, pp. 218ff, 226ff, 231ff, 234ff.

[38] Athanasius, *Con. Ar.*, 1.11; 2.10; 3.63; *De decr.*, 22, 27; *De syn.*, 35, 41; *Ad Afr.*, 4, 8; *Ad Ser.*, 2.5.

only one who really and truly *is*.[39] This change was especially
necessary in view of the fact that God reveals himself to us
through the Son and the Spirit who inhere in his own eternal
being. He thus gives us such access to himself through Christ
Jesus and in one Spirit, that we may know God, in some
measure, as he really is in himself, in the inner relations of his
own triune being.[40] Thus when associated with God's self-
revelation in three distinct objective ὑποστάσεις as Father, Son
and Holy Spirit, οὐσία signifies the one eternal being of God in
the indivisible reality and fullness of his intrinsic personal
relations as the Holy Trinity. Far from being an abstract or
general notion, therefore, οὐσία as applied to God had an
intensely personal and concrete meaning. It will be recalled that
this was very evident in his distinctive conception of the
ἐνούσιος λόγος and ἐνούσιος ἐνέργεια of God,[41] for God's
activity in *self*-revelation and *self*-giving through the Son and in
the Holy Spirit, is as indivisibly one toward us as is the one οὐσία
of the Godhead from which it issues and to which it directs us,
while that one οὐσία is disclosed to be as intensely personal in
itself as it is in its manifestation to us in the coinherent relations
of the three divine Persons.[42]

This revised understanding of οὐσία was retained by
Athanasius in his conception of the *one being* of God, even when
he agreed to the formula μία οὐσία, τρεῖς ὑποστάσεις. It is surely
in that light that his teaching about the Unity and Trinity of
God, particularly as filled out and reinforced by his doctrine of
the Holy Spirit, is properly to be appreciated. For Athanasius,
however, the concept of Triunity was already embedded in his
understanding of the ὁμοούσιον which, with its rejection of any
notion either of undifferentiated or of partitive relations
between the three divine ὑποστάσεις, carried with it the
conception of eternal distinctions and internal relations in the
Godhead as wholly and mutually interpenetrating one another

[39] Athanasius, *Con. gent.*, 2, 35, 40; *De inc.*, 17; *Con. Ar.*, 1.20; 3.22; *De decr.*,
11; *In ill. om.*, 1.
[40] Athanasius, *Con. Ar.*, 1.9ff, 14ff, 24f; 2.1f, 22, 31ff; 3.1ff, 15ff, 24f; 4.1, 5, 9;
Ad Ser., 1.14, 19ff, 25; 3.5f.
[41] See Athanasius, *De syn.*, 34, 41; *Con. Ar.*, 2.2; 4.1; *Ad Ant.*, 5.
[42] Athanasius, *Exp. fidei*, 1–4; *In ill. om.*, 1–6; *Con. Ar.*, 3.1ff.

in the one identical perfect being of the Father, Son and Holy
Spirit. It was thus through the Trinity, Athanasius held, that we
believe in the Unity of God, and yet it is only in recognition of
the indivisible oneness and identity of being in the Son and the
Spirit with the Father that we rightly apprehend the Holy
Trinity.[43]

It is also in this light that we are to understand how
Athanasius regarded the divine Μοναρχία. He certainly
thought of the Father as the ἀρχή of the Son in that he eternally
begot the Son. He thus declared 'we know only one ἀρχή', but
he immediately associated the Son with that ἀρχή, for 'we
profess to have no other form of Godhead (τρόπον Θεότητος)
than that of the only God'.[44] While the Son is associated with
the ἀρχή of the Father in this way, he cannot be thought of as an
ἀρχή subsisting in himself, for by his very nature he is
inseparable from the Father of whom he is the Son. By the same
token, however, the Father cannot be thought of as ἀρχή apart
from the Son, for precisely as Father he is Father of the Son. 'The
Father and the Son are two, yet the Monad of Godhead is one
and indivisible. And thus we preserve the one ἀρχή of the
Godhead, and not two ἀρχαί, so that there is strictly a
Μοναρχία.'[45] It is surely in this light also that we are to
understand the *Tomus ad Antiochenos* in which Athanasius joined
with others in acknowledging 'a Holy Trinity, but one
Godhead, and one ἀρχή, and that the Son is of one being with
the Father, while the Holy Spirit is proper to and inseparable
from the being of the Father and the Son.'[46] While accepting
the formulation of μία οὐσία, τρεῖς ὑποστάσεις he had such a
strong view of the complete identity, equality and unity of the
three Persons within the Godhead, that he declined to advance a
view of the Monarchy in which the oneness of God was defined
by reference to the **Person** of the Father. While the Father was
on occasion denoted as the αἴτιος and the ἀρχή of the Son that

[43] Athanasius, *Con. Ar.*, 3.1ff; 4.1ff; *Ad Ser.*, 1.16, 20, 28; 3.1, 6; cf. *De inc. et
con. Ar.*, 10: Μία γὰρ ἡ Θεότης καὶ εἷς Θεὸς ἐν τρισὶν ὑποστάσεσι, which is
certainly Athanasian if not directly from the Patriarch's pen.

[44] Athanasius, *Con. Ar.*, 1.14; 3.15.

[45] Athanasius, *Con. Ar.*, 4.1; cf. 2–3.

[46] Athanasius, *Ad Ant.*, 5.

was meant to express the truth that the Father is *Father* of the Son and that the Son is *Son* of the Father, but not to withdraw anything from the complete equality of the Son with the Father, for the Sonship of the Son is as ultimate as the Fatherhood of the Father. 'The same things are said of the Son as are said of the Father, except his being said to be "Father" '.[47] The Μία 'Αρχή or Μοναρχία is identical with the Trinity, the Μονάς with the Τριάς, and it is precisely in the Τριάς that we know him to be Μονάς. Athanasius actually preferred to speak of God as Μονάς rather than as 'Αρχή, since his understanding of the Μονάς was essentially as the Τριάς: God is eternally and unchangeably Father, Son and Holy Spirit, three divine Persons who, while always Father, Son and Holy Spirit, in their co-indwelling and interpenetrating relations *are the Triune God.* The Μοναρχία or the Μονάς is essentially and intrinsically trinitarian in the inner relations of his eternal οὐσία.[48] An early statement attributed to him appears to represent his concept of the Triunity of God rather faithfully. 'The Trinity praised, worshipped and adored, is one and indivisible and without degrees (ἀσχημάτιστος). He is united without confusion, just as the Monad is distinguished in thought without division. For the threefold doxology "Holy, Holy, Holy is the Lord" offered by those venerable living beings, denotes the three perfect Persons (τρεῖς ὑποστάσεις τελείας), just as in the word "Lord" they indicate his One Being (μίαν οὐσίαν).'[49]

(2) Basil, the Gregories and Didymus

When we turn from Athanasius to Basil of Caesarea we find a rather different approach in which theological motivation came not so much from soteriological and ontological convictions as from spiritual and moral conceptions of an Origenistic kind about the Christian way of life under the transforming power of the divine energies and the sanctifying and deifying activity of

[47] Athanasius, *Con. Ar.*, 3.3f; *De syn.*, 49; cf. *Con. Ar.*, 2.54; 3.1; 4.3; *De decr.*, 16; *De syn.*, 46; *Ad Ant.*, 5.
[48] Athanasius, *Con. Ar.*, 4.1, 3; *De decr.*, 26; *In sent. Dion.*, 17, etc.
[49] Athanasius, *In ill. om.*, 6.

the Holy Spirit. When the basic assumptions of this approach came under threat from Eunomians and Sabellians alike, he turned for help to the *De synodis* of Athanasius[50] in a reappropriation of the Nicene doctrine of the ὁμοούσιον to combat the impious idea that the Son was brought into being out of nothing, 'to remove the idea of the identity of hypostasis (τὴν ταὐτότητα τῆς ὑποστάσεως), and bring to perfection the conception of the Persons (τελείαν τῶν προσώπων τὴν ἔννοιαν)'. 'The same thing is not ὁμοούσιον with itself, but only one thing with another. The word has therefore an excellent and devout use, defining both the proper character of the hypostases and setting forth the invariance of their nature (τῶν τε ὑποστάσεων τὴν ἰδιότητα διορίζουσα καὶ τῆς φύσεως τὸ ἀπαράλλακτον παριστῶσα).'[51] Basil's thought did not move at the same deep soteriological and ontological level as that of Athanasius, but with the help of primary Nicene convictions he gave his own distinctive devotional approach a strong trinitarian underpinning resting on our Lord's institution of baptism in the one name of the Father, Son and Holy Spirit, that was nevertheless impressive.[52] This was particularly evident in his doxological and liturgical arguments for the 'godly co-numbering' of the Holy Spirit *with* the Father and the Son in conjoint worship, adoration and invocation of the Holy Trinity, which he elaborated in the *De Spiritu Sancto*.[53] He held that, far from being alien to the divine nature, the Holy Spirit has an ineffable mode of existence (τρόπος ὑπάρξεως) as ὑπόστασις in the indivisible κοινωνία of divine nature with the Father and the Son.[54] On the other hand, however, Basil strangely avoided any overt assertion that the Holy Spirit is *God*,[55] and hesitated to speak of him as ὁμοούσιος, preferring instead terms like ὁμότιμος, ὁμόδοξος, ὁμόθρονος, although he

[50]See especially Athanasius, *De syn.*, 45–51.

[51]Basil, *Ep.*, 52.3.

[52]Basil, *De Sp. St.*, 24–36, 66ff; cf. *De fide*, 4.

[53]Basil, *De Sp. St.*, 3, 13ff, 28, 35–38, 43–49, 62f, 64, 68.

[54]Basil, *De Sp. St.*, 7, 13f, 30, 37f, 42, 45, 48, 60, 63, 68.

[55]But cf. his citation from Origen about 'the Godhead of the Holy Spirit', *De Sp. St.*, 73. *Epistle* 8, which does speak quite unequivocally of the Holy Spirit as consubstantial with God and as God, was not by Basil but by Evagrius Ponticus.

did once refer to the Holy Trinity as ὁμοούσιος in connection with baptism.[56]

There can be no question, of course, about Basil's belief in the Deity of the Holy Spirit, not only because as Ἅγιον Πνεῦμα he is of the same transcendent spiritual nature as the Father and the Son,[57] but because the Holy Spirit is inseparably and equally, though distinctively, Creator with the Father and the Son in being the one Cause (αἰτία) of all that is.[58] Here he deployed one of the main arguments of Athanasius, in insisting that 'the relation of the Spirit to the Son is the same as that of the Son to the Father. And if the Spirit is coordinate with the Son, and the Son with the Father, it is clear that the Spirit is also coordinate with the Father'.[59] Hence while the three Persons are to be distinguished from one another, they belong inseparably together. 'In the divine and uncompounded nature the oneness consists in the communion of the Godhead (ἐν τῇ κοινωνίᾳ τῆς Θεότητός ἐστιν ἡ ἕνωσις). One is the Holy Spirit, and while we speak of him singly he is conjoined to the one Father through the one Son, and through himself completes the adorable and blessed Trinity ... As there is one Father, one Son, so there is one Holy Spirit.'[60] In Basil's thought the Holy Spirit is indivisibly linked to and comes from the κοινωνία of the Father and the Son, and is as such the immediate Source of our communion with the Holy Trinity.[61]

It was in his Epistles, however, that Basil offered more precise accounts of how he thought of the Holy Trinity as *three Persons and one Being*.[62] While he was clearly anxious to keep in full accord with the teaching of the Nicene Council,[63] he felt that the defence of Nicene theology required a clear distinction to be made between the terms οὐσία and ὑπόστασις, for their identity could be used, though diversely, by Sabellians and Eunomians

---

[56]Basil, *De fide*, 4; cf. the interpolation Τριὰς ὁμοούσιος in Hippolytus, *Apost. Trad.*, 21. Refer again to Gregory Naz., *Ep.*, 58 and *Or.*, 43.68.

[57]Basil, *De Sp. St.*, 22 & 45f.

[58]Basil, *De Sp. St.*, 19ff, 37ff.

[59]Basil, *De Sp. St.*, 43; cf. Athanasius, *Ad Ser.*, 1.21f, 25f, 31f, etc.

[60]Basil, *De Sp. St.*, 45.

[61]Basil, *De Sp. St.*, 30, 38, 45, 48, 63f, 68.

[62]Basil, *Epistles* 52, 69, 125, 210, 214, 236; and Gregory/Basil, *Ep.*, 38.

[63]Basil, *Ep.*, 52, 92, 125, 128, 140, 159, 204; Gregory/Basil, *Ep.*, 38.

in support of their heretical ideas.[64] In any case, a suggestion along those lines had evidently been put forward at the Council of Alexandria in 362 with regard to the formula 'one Being, three Persons'.[65] Controversy, especially with Eunomius, convinced Basil that μία οὐσία and τρεῖς ὑποστάσεις considered on one and the same level involved a logical absurdity, but that it was another matter when they were considered on different levels. Hence he distinguished οὐσία from ὑπόστασις by relating them to one another as the general (τὸ κοινόν) to the particular (τὸ ἴδιον) on two different levels, and differentiated the three ὑποστάσεις from one another on one and the same level in accordance with their peculiar modes of existence (τρόποι ὑπάρξεως) and particular characteristics (ἰδιώματα, ἰδιότητα, γνωρίσματα, χαρακτηριστικά), in terms of 'Paternity', 'Sonship' and 'Sanctity' (πατρότης, υἱότης, ἁγιασμός or ἁγιωσύνη).[66] In so doing, however, Basil sometimes tended to define the different ὑποστάσεις in terms of their ἰδιώματα or ἰδιότητα with little significant reference to their inherence in one οὐσία, although he could also claim that each πρόσωπον has a natural existence in a real ὑπόστασις.[67] To undergird this way of thinking his brother Gregory resorted to Athanasian language in showing how the three divine Persons are inwardly and inseparably interrelated. 'All that is seen in the Father is seen in the Son, and all that is the Son's is the Father's, since the whole Son dwells in the Father and on his part has the whole Father in himself. Wherefore the Person (ὑπόστασις) of the Son is, as it were, Form and Face (μορφὴ καὶ πρόσωπον) of the knowledge of the Father; and the Person (ὑπόστασις) of the Father is known in the Form (μορφή) of the Son, while the particularities (ἰδιότητα) contemplated in them are due to the clear distinction of their Persons (ὑποστάσεις).'[68]

However, in spite of this approach to the Athanasian doctrine of coincidence which Basil evidently shared, his proposal that

[64]Basil, *Ep.*, 52.2f; 124.3; 210.3–5; 265.2; *Hom.*, 111.

[65]Athanasius, *Ad Ant.*, 6, 11.

[66]Gregory/Basil, *Ep.*, 38.1ff; Basil, *Ep.*, 125.1f; 214.3f; 236.6; *De Sp. St.*, 7; *Con. Eun.*, 2.28. Consult Methodios Fouyas, *op. cit.*, pp. 53ff.

[67]Basil, *Ep.*, 210.5.

[68]Gregory/Basil, *Ep.*, 38.8.

οὐσία should be treated as an abstract generic term modified the
earlier notion of God's οὐσία by equating it with the notion of
φύσις or nature common to the three divine Persons.[69] That
change was made at the expense of the more personal concrete
understanding of οὐσία as characterised by intrinsic relations,
which could not but affect their doctrine of God. Together with
Basil's rather sharp distinction between the transcendent being
of God which is quite unknowable and the divine energies
whereby God reveals himself to us,[70] this interpretation of μία
οὐσία and τρεῖς ὑποστάσεις had the effect both of shifting the
weight of emphasis from identity of being to equality between
the Persons, and of transferring the element of concreteness in
the doctrine of God almost entirely on to the differentiating
particularities of Father, Son and Holy Spirit.[71]

It will help to refer back at this juncture to the account we had
to offer of the Cappadocian doctrine of the Spirit in the sixth
chapter,[72] in order to appreciate the distinctive slant that their
teaching gave to the doctrine of the Trinity. In face of the charge
of tritheism which their shift in emphasis prompted,[73] the
Cappadocians sought to establish a doctrine of the unity of God
by anchoring it in the *Father* as the one Principle or Origin
(ἀρχή) and Cause (αἰτία) of the Son and the Spirit.[74] Although
they held that the Son and the Spirit are eternally caused by the
Father in such a way that there is no separation between cause
and effect and that thus their derivation from the Father is
without beginning (ἀνάρχως), they nevertheless thought of the
internal relations between the three Persons of the Trinity as
constituting the consecutive structure of a causal series or, as it

[69]Basil, *Con. Eun.*, 2.28; *Ep.*, 236.6; cf. Gregory/Basil, *Ep.*, 38.3f: (κοινὴ
φύσις, κοινότης τῆς φύσεως); and also Evagrius/Basil, *Ep.*, 8.2.

[70]Basil, *Con. Eun.*, 1.12, 14f; 2.32; *Ep.*, 234.1; 235.2f.

[71]But cf. Basil's *Homily*, 23.4, where he was forced to make some appeal to
ταὐτότης; more characteristic was his argument with Eunomius, *Con. Eun.*,
2.28.

[72]See above p. 236–242.

[73]Evagrius, *Ep.*, 8.2; Basil, *Ep.*, 131.2; 189.2f; *Hom. con. syc.*, 1ff, Athens ed.,
54, pp. 234ff.

[74]Gregory/Basil, *Ep.*, 38.4, 7; Basil, *Con. Eun.*, 1.25; 2.12; 3.1; *Hom.*, 24.4. A
similar idea had already been put forward by Dionysius of Alexandria, *apud*
Athanasius, *De sent. Dion.*, 17.

were, a 'chain' of dependence (ὥσπερ ἐξ ἀλύσεως).[75] This idea was given some prominence in the teaching of Gregory Nyssen who argued that the being of the Spirit was caused by and grounded in the existence of the Son whose being in turn was caused by and grounded in the Father.[76] The point that Basil and his brother clearly wished to express was that the distinctive mode of existence of the Son derives from the Father, for he is Son of the Father, and the distinctive mode of the Holy Spirit in his indivisible union with the Son is also derived from the Father. However, with their generic conception of the οὐσία of God, they were led to say that the Son and the Spirit owe their being (τὸ εἶναι) to the *Person* (ὑπόστασις) or (πρόσωπον) of the Father.[77] This clearly affected the very root of the doctrine of the procession of the Spirit. 'The Holy Spirit is attached to the Son with whom he is inseparably apprehended, and has his being in dependence upon the Father as Cause. He also proceeds from him with the identifying mark of his hypostatic nature that he is known after and with the Son, and that he derives his subsistence from the Father.'[78]

Both the Gregories seem to have had second thoughts about this account of trinitarian relations between the three Persons which traced, not just the mode of existence, but the existence itself or the very being of the Son and of the Spirit to the ὑπόστασις rather than the οὐσία of the Father. Gregory Nyssen drew a distinction between existence and the manner of existence,[79] and pointed out that 'God' (Θεός) signifies being and does not refer to Person (πρόσωπον), which implies that the Father is not God in virtue of his Fatherhood but in virtue of his

---

[75]Gregory/Basil, *Ep.*, 38.4; Basil, *De Sp. St.*, 13, 45f, 58f; *Con. Eun.*, 3.1; *Con. Sab.*, 4.

[76]Gregory Nyss., *Con. Eun.*, 1.36, 42; *Adv. Maced.*, 12f; *non tres dei*, Jaeger, 3.1, p. 56; see again Gregory/Basil, *Ep.*, 38.4. In Gregory Nazianzen's thought this conception of consecutive causes within the Trinity was modified by his doctrine of continuous subsistent relations, e.g., *Or.*, 31.9, 14, 33.

[77]Gregory/Basil, *Ep.*, 38.4ff; Gregory Nyss., *Ex com. not.*, Jaeger, 3.1, p. 25; cf. Gregory Naz., *Or.*, 31.14.

[78]Gregory/Basil, *Ep.*, 38.4.

[79]Gregory Nyssen, *non tres dei*, Jaeger, 3.1, p. 56: ἄλλος οὖν ὁ τοῦ τί ἐστι καὶ ἄλλος ὁ τοῦ πῶς ἐστι λόγος.

being.[80] And Gregory Nazianzen pointed out that 'Father' is not a name for being (οὐσία) but for the relation (σχέσις) that the Father bears to the Son, or the Son has with the Father.[81] This strange lapse from the Nicene doctrine that the Son proceeds from the *being* of the Father (ἐκ τῆς οὐσίας τοῦ Πατρός), together with the introduction of causality into the conception of inter-hypostatic relations in the Holy Trinity, replacing the Athanasian understanding of the one being (οὐσία) of God as having intrinsic constitutive relations, created a problematic state of affairs. It put forward a somewhat divergent notion of the Unity and Triunity of God, and opened up the way for serious misunderstanding and division over the doctrine of the procession of the Holy Spirit.

Generally speaking Gregory Nazianzen fell in with the line of thought put forward by Basil and his brother about the Holy Trinity, for he was anxious lest he should think of the Father so much in terms of οὐσία as not to think of the others in terms of ὑπόστασις, but make them 'powers of God existing but not subsisting in him' (δυνάμεις Θεοῦ ἐνυπαρχούσας, οὐχ ὑφεστώσας).[82] 'The three (Persons)', he wrote, 'have one nature, namely, God, but the ground of their unity is the Father, out of whom and towards whom the subsequent Persons are reckoned.'[83] He also employed the language of causality in referring the Son and the Spirit to one Principle or ἀρχή in the Father,[84] but with a more Athanasian conception of the oneness of God and of the Godhead as complete not primarily in the Father but in each Person as well as in all of them.[85] The Trinity is adored in the Unity just as the Unity is adored in the Trinity.[86] The Μονάς and the Τριάς are identical, for while the

[80]Gregory Nyss., *Ex comm. not.*, Jaeger, 3.1, pp. 19–25; *De Sp. St.*, 3.1, pp. 13ff.

[81]Gregory Naz., *Or.*, 29.16; 31.14, 16.

[82]Gregory Naz., *Or.*, 31.32.

[83]Gregory Naz., *Or.*, 42.15.

[84]Gregory Naz., *Or.*, 1.38; 2.38; 20.7; 29.3, 15, 19; 30.19f; 31.8–14; 32.30, 33; 34.8, 10;40.41ff; 42.15ff.

[85]Gregory Naz., *Or.*, 30.20; 31.9f, 14, 16; 37.33ff; 38.8; 39.10f; 40.41ff; 42.16; 45.4.

[86]Gregory Naz., *Or.*, 6.22; 25.17; 29.2f; 34.8f; 39.10; 40.41; 42.16.

one God is three, the three are one. 'The Godhead is one in three, and the three are one, in whom the Godhead is, or to be more precise, *who are the Godhead*.'[87] 'When you read "I and the Father are one", keep before your eyes the oneness of being (οὐσία); but when you see "We will come to him and dwell with him", remember the distinction of πρόσωπα; and when you see the names, Father, Son, and Holy Spirit, think of the three ὑποστάσεις.'[88] As for Athanasius, so for Gregory Nazianzen, it was the ὁμοούσιον that provided the key to the divine Triunity.[89] Thus he was rather nearer to Athanasius than his fellow Cappadocians in adopting a soteriological and ontological approach governed by the evangelical significance of the ὁμοούσιον which he had no hesitation in applying to the Holy Spirit as well as to the Son. 'The three are one in Godhead, and the one three in properties. Thus neither is the oneness of a Sabellian sort nor are the three subject to an evil (Eunomian) division, What then? Is the Spirit God? To be sure! Is he then ὁμοούσιον? Yes if he is God.'[90]

Gregory Nazianzen was clearly rather worried about the element of Origenist subordinationism that had cropped up in the Cappadocian doctrine of the Holy Trinity in which he shared with the others in speaking of the Father as 'greater' than the Son and the Spirit, while nevertheless trying to do justice to the unity and equality of the three divine Persons. What alarmed him was the application of the concept of 'principle' or ἀρχή to the Father in distinguishing him from the Son and the Spirit, for that appeared to imply the impossible idea of precedence in honour and even unequal degrees of Deity within the Holy Trinity. Hence Gregory insisted that to subordinate any of the three divine Persons to another was to overthrow the doctrine of the Trinity.[91] His answer to the difficulties that had cropped up in the context of contemporary debates was that Father, Son and Holy Spirit must be thought of as **relations** or

[87]Gregory Naz., *Or.*, 39.11.

[88]Gregory Naz., *Or.*, 34.13.

[89]Gregory Naz., *Or.*, 31.17ff; 34.13; 39.11; 40.41, 45; 42.16.

[90]Gregory Naz., *Or.*, 31.9f. See *Ep.* 58 in which Gregory showed that he wanted a profounder doctrine of the Spirit than that put forward by Basil.

[91]Gregory Naz., *Or.*, 40.43; 43.30; cf. 29.15.

σχέσεις eternally and substantially subsisting in God which are strictly beyond all time (ἀχρόνως), beyond all origin (ἀνάρχως) and beyond all cause (ἀναιτίως).[92] It is significant that Gregory avoided the Basilian notion of τρόπος ὑπάρξεως altogether, for as he understood them the relations between the divine Persons are not just modes of existence but substantial relations which belong intrinsically to what Father, Son and Holy Spirit are in themselves as distinctive hypostatic realities as well as in their objective reciprocal relations with one another. The relations between them are just as substantial as what they unchangeably are in themselves and by themselves. Thus the Father *is* Father precisely in his indivisible ontic relation to the Son and the Spirit, and the Son and the Spirit *are* what they are as Son and Spirit precisely in their indivisible ontic relations to the Father and to one another.

It may well be claimed that Gregory's understanding of the Holy Trinity registered a significant deepening of the Athanasian conception of the divine οὐσία as being considered in its internal relations, for it was cast in a more dynamic form. In the Godhead all subsistent relations are dynamic, mutually interpenetrating, unitary and without opposition in their reference to one another.[93] Here we have presented a rather more satisfactory view of the Triunity of God than that of the other Cappadocians, for the Μοναρχία is not limited to one Person: it is a Unity constituted in and by the Trinity.[94] 'To us', Gregory declared, 'there is one God, and one Godhead, and all that issues from him is referred back to him so as to be one with him, although we believe that there are three. And one is not more and another less God, nor is one before and another after. They are neither divided in will nor separated in power; nor are any of the distinguishing marks of separated individualities to be

[92]Gregory Naz., *Or.*, 23.8, 11; 29.2ff, 16; 30.11, 19f; 31.9, 14, 16; 42.15ff. Cf. Athanasius, *De syn.*, 16.

[93]Gregory Naz., *Or.*, 20.7–11; 23.8; 31.6–9; 35.1–4; 41.9; 42.15.

[94]Gregory Naz., *Or.*, 29.2; 31.14; 40.41; 42.15–16. This means that the Trinity as a whole must be thought of as the one divine Principle or ἀρχή – cf. the remarkable statement in one of Gregory's songs: ῎Αναρχον, Ἀρχή, Πνεῦμα, Τριὰς τιμία,// ἀναίτιον, γεννητόν, ἐκπορεύσιμον · // Πατὴρ τὸ μέν · τὸ δ᾽ Υἱός, αὐτὸς καὶ Λόγος · τὸ δ᾽ οὐ μὲν Υἱός, Πνεῦμα, δ᾽ οὐσίας μιᾶς.' Athens ed. 61, p. 146.

found there, but divided as the Persons are, the entire and undivided Godhead is one in each person.'⁹⁵ 'But each of these Persons is entirely one with those with whom he is conjoined, as he is with himself, because of the identity of being and power that is between them (ἀλλὰ τὸ ἓν ἕκαστον αὐτῶν ἔχει πρὸς τὸ συγκείμενον οὐχ ἧττον ἢ πρὸς ἑαυτό, τῷ ταὐτῷ τῆς οὐσίας καὶ τῆς δυνάμεως). This is the account of the oneness (ὁ τῆς ἑνώσεως λόγος) so far as we have apprehended it. If this account has force, thanks be to God for the insight; if it does not, let us seek for a stronger one.'⁹⁶ It may be noted that Gregory Nazianzen's concept of subsistent relations in the Trinity (with his hint of an analogical openness of the human person to 'that Mind, Word and Spirit, who is one kindred Deity'?)⁹⁷ was later taken up and developed by Augustine and given an important place in western trinitarian theology.⁹⁸

This understanding of the coinherence of subsistent trinitarian relations in God clearly set the doctrine of the procession of the Holy Spirit on a rather different basis, that of a Μοναρχία which is not limited to one Person and in which there is no partition of οὐσία.⁹⁹ The Holy Spirit certainly proceeds from the Father, but because of the Unity of the Godhead in which each Person is perfectly and wholly God, he issues from out of the midst of the relation between the Father and the Son as he who is of the Father and of the Son. On this basis it is not easy to see why the problem of the *filioque* arose! All we can say about the Spirit, Gregory claimed, is that while the Son is the 'Begotten', the Holy Spirit is the 'Emission' (ἔκπεμψις) or the

⁹⁵Gregory Naz., *Or.*, 31.14; cf. also 25.16; 26.19. In *Or.*, 36.15, he drew attention to the significant fact that the New Testament itself varied the order in which Father, Son and Holy Spirit were mentioned.

⁹⁶Gregory Naz., *Or.*, 31.16; cf. 42. 15ff.

⁹⁷Gregory Naz., *Or.*, 12.1; *Car.*, 38, *MPG* 37.1325–6.

⁹⁸Augustine, *De Trin.*, 5–7; *De civ. Dei*, 10; *In Jn.*, tr. 39; *In Ps.*, 68.1, 5; *Ep.*, 170, 238–241; cf. Thomas Aquinas, *S. Theol.*, Ia. *xxvi–xxx*; *De pot.*, 1–2. See also J. N. D. Kelly, *Early Christian Doctrines*, 1958, pp. 271ff; E. L. Mascall, *The Triune God, An Ecumenical Study*, 1986, pp. 11–22; and T. F. Torrance, 'Toward an Ecumenical Consensus on the Trinity', *Theol. Zeitschr.*, vol. 31, 1975, pp. 337–350; *Reality and Scientific Theology*, 1985, 'The Trinitarian Structure of Theology', pp. 160–206.

⁹⁹Gregory Naz., *Or.*, 29.2; 40.41; cf. 2.36 where he referred to the blessed Trinity as ἀρχή.

'Proceeding' (ἐκπόρευσις). He issues from the Father not as a son (υἱϊκῶς), nor as an offspring (γεννητῶς), but by way of procession (ἐκπορευτῶς), that is, in an altogether unique and ineffable way in accordance with his distinctive nature (ἰδιότης) or Person (ὑπόστασις) as he who is intrinsically *Holy* and indeed 'Holiness himself' (αὐτοαγιότης).[100]

The problematic situation that resulted from this neo-Nicene discussion of the Holy Trinity was very evident in the teaching of Didymus of Alexandria. In accordance with the Athanasian tradition he made the ὁμοούσιον central to all his thought, insisting on the oneness, identity and indivisibility of the being and lordship of the Godhead.[101] He may well have been the first theologian to have used the formula, μία οὐσία, τρεῖς ὑποστάσεις, although he preferred to speak of μία Θεότης rather than μία οὐσία.[102] He applied the ὁμοούσιον to the Trinity as a whole,[103] and held that the three ὑποστάσεις are wholly alike and perfectly equal in power and honour, for the Father is not greater than the Son, so that as in the Holy Scriptures each of the divine Persons may be mentioned first.[104] The Father is in himself the whole divine nature, but this is true also of the Son and the Holy Spirit. The Father is not Father apart from the Son, and the Son is not Son apart from the Father, nor are they what they are as Father and Son apart from the Holy Spirit, while the Spirit is not what he is as Holy Spirit apart from the Father and the Son, for they all coinhere consubstantially and inseparably in the one being of God. The Godhead is intrinsically a Trinity, and the Trinity is essentially one, a Unity in Trinity and a Trinity in Unity.[105]

At the same time Didymus was deeply concerned to rebut a Sabellian unipersonalism, and like the Cappadocians, to keep constantly in view the distinctive and objective existence, the

[100]Gregory Naz., *Or.*, 25.16; 29.2ff; 31.8f; 39.12.

[101]See the recurring emphasis on *una substantia* in the *De Sp. St.* of Didymus, extant only in Latin, 16–19, 21f, 24f, 32, 36f, 40, 53, 58.

[102]Didymus, *De Trin.*, 1.16, 18f, 36; 2.6.7, 16ff, 14 *fin*, 15; 2.27, etc.

[103]Didymus, *De Trin.*, 1.16ff, 20, 24f, 27, 34; 2.1.4ff, 13f, 18, 27; 3.7, 15; *Con. Eun.*, Athens ed., 44, p. 238.

[104]Didymus, *De Trin.*, 1.16, 18, 26f; cf. 3.1f, 13, 18; *De Sp. St.*, 36.

[105]Didymus, *De Trin.*, 1.9f, 11, 15f, 18f, 25, 27; 2.1, 3f, 6.7ff, 15f, 18; 26f; 3.2, 15f, 24, 55; *De Sp. St.*, 30–39; *Con. Eun.*, Athens ed., 44, pp. 246f, 255ff.

peculiar nature and characteristics, of the three Persons or ὑποστάσεις and their inter-personal relations (σχέσεις) in the one being of God.[106] He made some use of the Basilian expression τρόπος ὑπάρξεως, but strengthened it and cognate expressions with the term ἐνυπόστατος to make sure that these distinctive modes of existence were not just identifying characteristics but objective personal realities in God.[107] Here his views were clearly close to those of Gregory Nazianzen, in his thought of the Son and the Spirit as deriving hypostatically by way of generation and procession beyond all time (ἀχρόνως) and beyond all beginning (ἀνάρχως) from the Father. 'We confess that the Holy Spirit is God, consubstantial with the Father and the Son and with them without beginning (συνανάρχως), who proceeds from the Father consubstantially.'[108] As the Son derives from the Father through generation in a way appropriate to the Son (υἱϊκῶς), so the Spirit derives from the Father in a way appropriate to the Spirit (πνευματικῶς), but neither in an operative or creative way (δημιουργικῶς).[109] Thus he thought of the Holy Spirit, along with the Son, as enhypostatic reality who, while dwelling eternally in God, is directly present among us in his own being, and personally subsists in all God's self-giving to us in such a way that in him the Gift and the Giver are identical.[110]

It was in this intensely personalised form that Didymus held that the Holy Spirit derives consubstantially and eternally from the Person (ἐκ τῆς ὑποστάσεως) of the Father and even from the Person (ἐκ τῆς ὑποστάσεως) of the Son.[111] By this Didymus evidently meant to say that our experience of the Holy Spirit

[106]Didymus, *De Trin.*, 1.9, 11f, 15f, 18f, 21, 26f, 30, 34f; 2.1ff, 5ff, 8, 12, 19, 27; 3.1f, 18, 23f, 38, 40f, 45; *De Sp. St.*, 27, 30.

[107]Didymus, *Con. Eun.*, Athens ed., 44, pp. 226f; for cognate terms see *De Trin.*, 1.9; 2.1, 12, and for ἐνυπόστατος, see *De Trin.*, 1.16, 26; 2.1ff, 8, 10; 3.19, 37; *Con. Eun.*, 44, pp. 239, 253.

[108]Didymus, *De Trin.*, 2.26; cf. 1.15; 3.2, 8.

[109]Didymus, *De Trin.*, 2.1f, 5; 2.6, 8, 22, etc. In the *Con. Eun.*, the work in which the influence of Basil is most apparent, he spoke of the inner trinitarian relations in causal terms – Athens ed., 44, p. 251.

[110]Didymus, *De Trin.*, 2.1–3; *De Sp. St.*, 3ff, 16–25; 32–40, 57–61.

[111]Didymus, *De Trin.*, 1.15, 18, 26, 36; 2.1ff, 5; 3.3, 5, 38; *De Sp. St.*, 26, 37; cf. *Con. Eun.*, Athens ed. 44, p. 251.

and our filial relation to the Father through the Son are inseparably associated.[112] However, at this juncture Didymus clearly diverged from the Athanasian tradition in replacing the Nicene formula 'from the *being* of the Father (ἐκ τῆς οὐσίας τοῦ Πατρός)' with 'from the *Person* of the Father (ἐκ τῆς ὑποστάσεως τοῦ Πατρός)'. Sometimes, however, Didymus could qualify this in such a way as to show that procession from the Father must be understood to take place in accordance with the oneness of his Godhead.[113] And at one point he combined the two formulae,[114] but this was rather an exception to his main thrust. He certainly believed that the Holy Spirit together with the Son is of one being with God and is God of God, and that the procession of the Spirit from the Person of the Father is a continuous relation within the Unity of the Holy Trinity.[115] His position was far from being clear, but it would appear that he wanted to avoid any subordinationist distinction between the underived Deity of the Father and the derived Deity of the Son or of the Holy Spirit, on the one hand; and yet to say, on the other hand, that the Son and the Spirit derive their particular modes of existence and their distinctive properties through their generation and procession from the *Person* of the Father. In other words, the generation of the Son and the procession of the Spirit from the ὑπόστασις of the Father are not to be equated with the *causation of their being*, but only with the *mode* of their hypostatic differentiation within the one being of the Godhead. Thus Didymus could speak of the procession of the Spirit from the Person of the Son as well as from the Person of the Father within the indivisible consubstantiality of the Holy Trinity, without any suggestion that the Spirit came into *being* through the Son or that there are two ultimate divine Principles (ἀρχαί), for procession from and through the Son relates to the inherence of the Spirit in the Son and to their community of being and nature with the Father.[116] This means that the statements by

[112]Didymus, *De Sp. St.*, 34–37.

[113]Didymus, *De Trin.*, 2.2: ἐκπόρευσις . . . ἀπὸ τοῦ ἑνὸς Πατρὸς καθ᾿ ἕνωσιν τῆς ἑαυτοῦ Θεότητος cf. 2.39; 3.38.

[114]Didymus, *De Trin.*, 2.5; cf. *Ep. Euseb.*, Theodoret, *Hist. eccl.*, 1.11.

[115]Didymus, *De Trin.*, 2.2, 15.

[116]Didymus, *De Trin.*, 2.1; 2.2, 5; 2.26f; *De Sp. St.*, 26.

Didymus about the procession of the Spirit from the Father and the Son should not be understood to lend any support for later arguments for or against the *filioque*.

(3) Epiphanius and the Council of Constantinople

It was Epiphanius the Bishop of Salamis who did more than any other to clarify the problematic trends that had become apparent in doctrines of the Spirit and the Holy Trinity. As a Jewish-Christian theologian he brought to theology a strong Hebraic slant in which he related the 'I am' of the one being of God to what the Holy Scriptures proclaim of him as Father, Son and Holy Spirit, and thought into each other more fully the notions of πρόσωπον, ὄνομα, and ὑπόστασις.[117] God was thus believed to be hypostatically and always in himself the Trinity of divine Persons indwelling one another in full accord with his self-revelation to us in the incarnate economy.[118] For Epiphanius, the Gospel of salvation depended on the inner connection between the life and activity of Jesus Christ and God the Father, as the Council of Nicaea had shown.[119] Thus as with Athanasius, whose Nicene theology he upheld and developed, his outlook was governed by both soteriological and ontological concern, which was particularly apparent in his long discussions of the saving life and work of the incarnate Son, including the reality and wholeness of his humanity in rational soul as well as body. In his resolute analysis and rebuttal of heretical trends he was thrown back upon the biblical and evangelical faith of the Catholic Church, with its insistence upon the uncreated, eternal and perfect divine nature of the Son

[117]Epiphanius, *Anc.*, 6, 8; *Haer.*, 57.10; 62.7f; 63.7; 69.36, 67, 72; 73.16, etc.
[118]Epiphanius, *Anc.*, 7, 33, 57, 65, 67; *Haer.*, 62.3–7; 69.54, 56; 73.16ff; 74.4f.
[119]This is very evident in Epiphanius' longer credal statement about the incarnation: '. . . who for us men and our salvation came down and was made flesh, that is, was born perfectly of holy Mary ever Virgin through the Holy Spirit; became man, that is, assuming perfect man, soul and body and mind and all that it is to be man, without sin, not from the seed of a husband, nor in man, but took flesh into himself in one holy unity.' *Anc.*, 120.

or Word of God, and of the perfection of his earthly life and work for the redemption of mankind.[120]

With Athanasius and Basil,[121] Epiphanius held that the Nicene ὁμοούσιον implies a real distinction of Persons in God, for one Person cannot be ὁμοούσιος with himself, and insisted that each of the three Persons has true, objective and perfect subsistence in the one being of God, and indeed that the whole being of the Son and the whole being of the Spirit is the same as the whole being of Father. Each is whole and perfect God. 'We call the Father God, the Son God, and the Holy Spirit God ... When you pronounce the ὁμοούσιον, you declare that the Son is God of God and that the Holy Spirit is God of the same Godhead.'[122] It was in this light that he readily accepted the formula μία οὐσία, τρεῖς ὑποστάσεις, although he clearly understood οὐσία, not in the Basilian way as a generic term, but in the earlier Nicene way as expressing the being of God in his internal relations and as having a concrete personal meaning.[123] It is understandable, therefore, that he did not restrict the name 'Father' merely to the ὑπόστασις of the Father, and was critical of the suggestion that 'Father' does not signify οὐσία.[124]

Unlike Basil, Gregory Nyssen and Amphilochius, he did not speak of the divine Persons as 'modes of existence' but as 'enhypostatic' in God, that is, as having real, objective personal being in God and as coinhering consubstantially and hypostatically in him.[125] Moreover, his understanding of the ὁμοούσιον as applying to the inner relations of the Trinity as a whole,[126] deepened his notion of the coinherence of the Father, Son and Holy Spirit in their subsistent, enhypostatic relations, in

[120]Epiphanius, especially *Haer.*, 69, 77–79.

[121]See Basil, *Ep.*, 258, and Epiphanius, *Haer.*, 77.20–23, where it is evident that they were familiar with each other's teaching.

[122]Epiphanius, *Anc.*, 2.

[123]Epiphanius, *Anc.*, 81, *Haer.*, 73.34.

[124]Epiphanius, *Haer.*, 73.21; *Exp. fidei*, 14.

[125]Epiphanius, *Anc.*, 5–10, 67, 72, 74, 81; *Haer.*, 57.4f; 62.1ff, 6; 72.11; 74.9; 76. *Ref. Aet.*, 30; 77.22; cf. Athanasius, *De syn.*, 42; *Con. Ar.*, 4.2; *Con. Apol.*, 1.20.

[126]Epiphanius, *Anc.*, 64; *Haer.*, 36.6; 57.4; 65.8; 69.67; 72.1; 73.34; 74.1ff; 76. *Ref. Aet.*, 16; *Exp. fidei*, 21. This application of ὁμοούσιος to the Trinity as a whole had already been made by Athanasius, *Ad Ser.*, 1.27; *Con. Apol.*, 1.9.

respect of which he spoke of the Holy Spirit as 'in the midst (ἐν μέσῳ) of the Father and the Son', or as 'the bond of the Trinity (σύνδεσμος τῆς Τριάδος)'.[127] Epiphanius would have nothing to do with any form of Origenist subordinationism in God, for whatever the Father is, the Son is, and the Spirit is, in the Godhead. They are altogether coequal with the Father in honour, power, glory and dominion (βασιλεία). Their being of the Father and with the Father is beyond beginning and beyond time and beyond explanation (ἀνάρχως καὶ ἀχρόνως καὶ ἀνεκδιηγήτως) – there is no 'before' or 'after' in God, for the relations between the three divine Persons are eternally subsistent and enhypostatic in him.[128] 'There never was when the Spirit was not (οὐδὲ ἦν ποτὲ ὅτε οὐκ ἦν Πνεῦμα).'[129]

Hence Epiphanius could refer to the Son and the Spirit as the one ultimate Source, πηγὴ ἐκ πηγῆς, with the Father.[130] The Holy Spirit dwells in and flows from the inner being and life and light of the Holy Trinity, where he shares fully in the reciprocal knowing and communing of the Father and the Son. It is as such that he comes into the midst (ἐν μέσῳ) of us, proceeding from the Father, receiving from the Son, revealing God to us and making us partake in God's knowing of himself.[131] Further, like Athanasius, Epiphanius abhorred any partitive thinking of God either as he is in himself or as he is toward us. Thus he regarded God's self-giving to us in the Holy Spirit in an essentially unitary way. God is in his own eternal being what he is in his self-revelation and what he is in self-giving he is intrinsically in himself. The Gift and the Giver are one and the same. There are diverse operations of the Spirit, but they are intensely personal, for the triune God is directly and creatively at work in them all. There is only one grace (ἓν χάρισμα) and

---

[127]Epiphanius, *Anc.*, 7f, 10; *Haer.*, 62.4; 74.11; cf. Gregory Naz., *Or.*, 31.8f, and Basil, *De Sp. St.*, 38, 43, 45f.

[128]Epiphanius, *Anc.*, 46; *Haer.*, 57.4; 62.3; 69.36; 70.8; 73.16ff, 36; 74.1ff; 76. *Ref. Aet.*, 18, 21, 35f.

[129]Epiphanius, *Anc.*, 74, 120; *Haer.*, 74.10; cf. Gregory Naz., *Or.*, 29.3; 31.4.

[130]Epiphanius, *Haer.*, 69.54.

[131]Epiphanius, *Anc.*, 6ff, 11, 15, 67, 70f, 115; *Haer.*, 57.9; 62.4; 64.9; 69.18; 43; 74.4, 10; 76. *Ref. Aet.*, 7, 21, 29, 32; cf. Athanasius, *Con. Ar.*, 1.20, 33; Hilary, *De Trin.*, 2.3; and Basil, *Hom.*, 111: 'The Son includes the Spirit in his and the Father's communion.'

one Spirit (ἓν Πνεῦμα), for God himself in the fullness of his triune being is present in all his acts of creating, revealing, healing, enlightening and sanctifying.[132]

Epiphanius clearly presented his doctrine of the Son and the Holy Spirit within an understanding of the whole undivided consubstantial Trinity, and not just the Father, as the Μοναρχία.[133] He did not share the Cappadocian way of trying to ensure the unity of God by tracing it back to one underived Person. He held the whole Trinity, and not just the Father, to be the Principle of the oneness of the Godhead. Hence he laid immense emphasis upon the full equality, perfection, eternity, power and glory of Father, Son and Holy Spirit alike, and thus upon the perfection of God's Triunity. There is no hint of any detraction from the uncreated nature, dignity, or integrity of the enhypostatic reality and particularity of any one of the divine Persons in relation to the others, and thus not of the Son nor of the Spirit in relation to the Father, for each of them is fully and perfectly Lord and God, while all three have and are one and the same Godhead. No one of the divine Persons is prior to or greater than another.[134] 'In proclaiming the divine Μοναρχία we do not err, but confess the Trinity, and Trinity in Unity, one Godhead of Father, Son and Holy Spirit (τὴν Τριάδα, Μονάδα ἐν Τριάδι, καὶ Τριάδα ἐν Μονάδι, μίαν Θεότητα Πατρὸς καὶ Υἱοῦ, καὶ Ἁγίου Πνεύματος). The Son did not beget himself, neither does the Father cease to be Father in order to be Son, nor does the Holy Spirit ever name himself Christ. But he is the Spirit of Christ who is given through Christ, who proceeds from the Father and receives from the Son. The Father is enhypostatic, the Son is enhypostatic, and the Holy Spirit is enhypostatic, but there is no confounding of them, as Sabellius thought, nor is there any change in their eternity and glory, as Arius vainly declared, for the Trinity is always Trinity, without any addition, one Godhead, one Lordship, one Doxology, yet

[132]Epiphanius, *Anc.*, 7f, 67f, 70f, 119f; *Haer.*, 69.17, 52; 70.5; 72.4f; 73.16, 18; 74.5, 7, 11f; *Exp. fidei*, 14.

[133]Epiphanius, *Haer.*, 8.5; 73.16; *Exp. fidei*, 14.

[134]Epiphanius, *Anc.*, 6–8; 22, 81; *Haer.*, 66.69; 69.33; 69.37, 43; 72.1; 73.3; 74.8, 12; 76. *Ref. Aet.*, 4, 20f, 32f, 35; *Exp. fidei*, 14; *Anc.*, 6–8.

numbered a Trinity, Father, Son and Holy Spirit.'[135] 'There are not three Gods, but only one true God, since the only Begotten is one from one, and one also is the Holy Spirit who is one from one, namely, a Trinity in Unity, and one God, Father, Son and Holy Spirit (Τριὰς γὰρ ἐν Μονάδι, καὶ εἷς Θεός, Πατήρ, Υἱὸς καὶ Ἅγιον Πνεῦμα).'[136] 'There is one Trinity in Unity, and one Godhead in Trinity (μία Τριὰς ἐν Μονάδι, καὶ μία Θεότης ἐν Τριάδι).'[137] Quite clearly Epiphanius went out of his way repeatedly to drive home the truth that God is perfectly three in one and perfectly one in three.[138] Thus as he introduced the credal statement that was to be taken up by the Council of Constantinople, he wrote: 'We know the Father to be Father, the Son to be Son, the Holy Spirit to be Holy Spirit, Trinity in Unity. For one is the Unity of the Father and of the Son and of the Holy Spirit, one being, one lordship, one will.'[139]

It should be clear from these citations that for Epiphanius the central focus of belief in his doctrine of God was upon the ultimate nature and primacy of the trinitarian relations in God, for it is in them that God *is* one, and through them that we know him to be *triune*. The Scriptures acknowledge 'the same Godhead in Trinity and the same Trinity in one Godhead, and glorify the Father in the Son and the Son in the Father with the Holy Spirit, one Sanctity, one Worship, one Deity, one Glory.'[140] In fact, God *is* the Trinity, and the Trinity *is* God.[141] The Father, Son and Holy Spirit are essentially, intrinsically and coinherently One.[142] While each of the three divine Persons ever remains enhypostatically and perfectly what he is in himself (καθ᾽ ἑαυτό), they all bear upon one another mutually and coinherently in the one identical being of the Godhead, and

[135]Epiphanius, *Haer.*, 62.3; see also 62.4–7.

[136]Epiphanius, *Anc.*, 2; see also 5f, and *Haer.*, 69.77; 73.16.

[137]Epiphanius, *Haer.*, 76. *Ref. Aet.*, 33 & 35.

[138]See further, Epiphanius, *Anc.*, 22, 67; 81; *Haer.*, 69.33, 43f, 56, 59, 75, 78; 72.11; 74.4; 76.6; 76. *Ref. Aet.*, 20, 33, 35f; *Exp. fidei*, 18.

[139]Epiphanius, *Anc.*, 118.

[140]Epiphaniuis, *Anc.*, 24.

[141]Cf. Gregory Naz., 'When I say God, I mean Father, Son and Holy Spirit', *Or.*, 38.8; 45.4.

[142]Epiphanius, *Anc.*, 10.

are the Godhead.[143] 'The relation of the Father is with the Son and the relation of the Son is with the Father, and both proceed in the Holy Spirit, for the Trinity ever consists in one Unity of Godhead: three Perfections, one Godhead.'[144]

It was in the light of that doctrine of the Triunity of God, and of the conception of the Μοναρχία which it implied (that is, of a μία ἀρχή consisting of three coequal and coeternal enhypostatic Persons in whose midst the Holy Spirit is 'the bond of the Trinity'), that what Epiphanius had to say about the procession of the Holy Spirit is surely to be understood. Athanasius had taught that the Spirit is ever in the hands of the Father who sends and of the Son who gives him as his very own, and from whom the Spirit on his part receives. Since the Holy Spirit like the Son is of the being of God, and belongs to the Son, he could not but proceed from or out of the being of God inseparably from and through the Son. In the nature of the case the idea that the Spirit derives his *being* (τὸ εἶναι) from the Son just did not and could not have arisen for Athanasius.[145] In line with that teaching Epiphanius thought of the Holy Spirit, not only as having his personal subsistence 'out of the Father through the Son' (ἐκ Πατρὸς δι᾽ Υἱοῦ) but as 'out of the *same being*' (ἐκ τῆς αὐτῆς οὐσίας), 'out of the same Godhead' (ἐκ τῆς αὐτῆς Θεότητος) as the Father and the Son, for the Holy Spirit *is* God, inseparable from the Father and the Son, and as the Spirit of the Father and the Spirit of the Son he is 'in the midst of the Father and the Son', and is 'the Bond of the Trinity'. Thus it may be said that the Holy Spirit proceeds as Light from Light *from both* the Father and the Son.[146]

It was, then, in these terms that Epiphanius interpreted and filled out the succinct Athanasian statement that 'the Holy Spirit proceeds from the Father and receives from the Son', yet in such a way that the enhypostatic realities and distinct properties of

[143]Epiphanius, *Haer.*, 63.6; 65.1f; 72.1f, 10; 73.16ff, 34f; 74.11f; 76.2, 12, 20, 35; *Anc.*, 6ff, 10.

[144]Epiphanius, *Con. Haer.*, 69.54; cf. Gregory Naz., *Or.*, 23.8.

[145]Athanasius, *De sent. Dion.*, 1.17; *Exp. fidei*, 4; *Con. Ar.*, 1.16, 20, 46ff, 50; 2.18, 28; 3.1ff, 15, 24ff, 44ff; *Ad Ser.*, 1.2, 15f, 20ff; 3.2ff; 4.3f.

[146]Epiphanius, *Haer.*, 62.4; 69.54; 73.12, 16; 74.7, 10ff; 76.11; *Anc.*, 7f, 67, 71f; *Haer.*, 74.7f.

the Father, Son and Holy Spirit always remain the same in the perfect equality and consubstantiality of the Holy Trinity.[147] And it was in these terms that he put forward the credal statement, including the crucial clauses about the Holy Spirit, which was taken up by the Council of Constantinople in 381. 'We believe in one Holy Spirit, the Lord and Giver of Life, who proceeds from the Father, who with the Father and the Son is worshipped and glorified, who spoke through the prophets.'[148]

Unfortunately the original document promulgating the Constantinopolitan Creed, and the Tome sent out in support of it, are no longer extant. However, we do have the text as officially confirmed by the Council of Chalcedon. And we also have the interchange of Synodical Letters between the Eastern and Western bishops following upon the Council in 382 A.D. which, together with the confession of the catholic faith promulgated by Damasus of Rome against Macedonian and Apollinarian heresies, enable us to get some idea of what was contained in the lost Tome.[149] Moreover, a rather illuminating glimpse of what was being considered at the Council is given in the Oration delivered by Gregory Nazianzen when he resigned his office as Archbishop of Constantinople and as President of the Council.[150] He clearly regretted that the Council had not been more forthright in some of its clauses, presumably about the Deity and consubstantiality of the Holy Spirit. In its clear intention to ratify 'the evangelical faith by the three hundred and eighteen fathers at Nicaea',[151] the Council made as little change as possible in the Creed, and took an uncontroversial line in keeping close to Biblical statements in the additional clauses on the Holy Spirit. It is noteworthy, however, that it was mainly the Athanasian development of Nicene theology through Epiphanius which proved decisive.

[147]Epiphanius, *Anc.*, 72ff; *Haer.*, 74.9ff, 12.

[148]Epiphanius, *Anc.*, 119. In the following chapter a fuller statement is found which was evidently designed for the instruction of the faithful.

[149]Theodoret, *Hist. eccl.*, 5.9–11.

[150]Gregory Naz., *Or.*, 42, especially 15 & 16.

[151]Theodoret, *Hist. eccl.*, 5.9. According to Athanasius, the bishops at the Council of Nicaea had agreed that 'the decisions of one Council should be examined in another' – *De fuga*, 2.21.

The trinitarian structure of the Creed remained the same as in the form given to it by the Nicene fathers, governed by 'the faith of baptism that teaches us to believe in the name of the Father, of the Son and of the Holy Spirit'. 'According to this faith', the Encyclical commented, 'there is one Godhead, power and being (Θεότητος καὶ δυνάμεως καὶ οὐσίας μιᾶς) of the Father and of the Son and of the Holy Spirit, equal in honour and dignity and coeternal sovereignty in three most perfect hypostases, that is in three perfect Persons (ὁμοτίμου τε ἀξίας καὶ συναϊδίου τῆς βασιλείας, ἐν τρισὶ τελειοτάταις ὑποστάσεσιν, ἤγουν τρισὶ τελείοις προσώποις).' It went on to add that there was thus 'no room for the Sabellian disease in confounding the hypostases or doing away with their proprieties, and no force left to the blasphemy of the Eunomians and Arians, and of the Pneumatomachians, which divides the being, nature or Godhead, and imposes on the uncreated, consubstantial, coeternal Trinity (τῇ ἀκτίστῳ καὶ ὁμοουσίῳ καὶ συναϊδίῳ Τριάδι) some nature subsequently generated, created and of a different substance. And we preserve inviolate the doctrine of the incarnation of the Lord, keeping to the tradition that the economy of the flesh was neither without soul or mind nor imperfect, for we are fully aware that God's Word was perfect before the ages, and became perfect man in the last days for our salvation.'

It is evident that the language used in this short summary of the doctrine of the Ecumenical Council reflects reiterated forms of thought and expression found in the teaching of Epiphanius, although there are also similarities to the thought and language of Gregory Nazianzen. There is no suggestion here of a doctrine of the Unity of God as grounded in the Person of the Father, for there is a return to the more Athanasian conception of the divine Triunity.[152] Moreover, it seems clear that, while the Council of Constantinople accepted the distinction between one Being (μία οὐσία) and three Persons (ὑποστάσεις, πρόσωπα), it did not take the one being in the generic sense of the Cappadocian

---

[152]Gregory Nazianzen's thought was also clearly moving back to this unified conception of the one divine ἀρχή with which the Son and the Spirit are consociated in the one being of the Godhead – *Or.*, 42.15; cf. also his *Oration on Athanasius, Or.*, 21.13 & 34; 31.14; 34.8; 40.41.

theologians, three of whom were present at the Council, but in the Athanasian and Epiphanian concrete personal sense of *being in se*. The terms οὐσία and ὑπόστασις carried alike a concrete meaning. The divine οὐσία is indivisibly one, and while internally differentiated in three ὑποστάσεις or πρόσωπα[153] is identically the same in them all; the three Persons, πρόσωπα or ὑποστάσεις, while always what they are as Father, Son and Holy Spirit, manifest one divine activity and will, coeternal and coequal in the one being, perfection, sovereignty, worship and glory of the Holy Trinity. The Encyclical of the Western Synod sent out by Damasus of Rome, which reflects the lost Tome issued from Constantinople, contained the same doctrine about the one Godhead and sovereignty of the Holy Trinity without any detraction in respect of the Son and the Spirit, for they are wholly equal with the Father and have the same identical being.[154]

What we learn from Damasus is particularly helpful in an interpretation of the doctrine of the Holy Spirit. The clauses added to the Nicene Creed at Constantinople were meant to express belief in the Holy Spirit in a way corresponding to those about belief in the generation of the Son 'from the Father' and his indivisible oneness with the Father. However, in its formal statement about the Son, the Council omitted the clause 'from the being of the Father (ἐκ τῆς οὐσίας τοῦ Πατρός)' which had been inserted by the Council of Nicaea to make the meaning of 'from the Father (ἐκ τοῦ Πατρός)' quite precise, and in order to cut out any excuse for equivocation on the part of Arians or Eusebians. In that case it might have been judged inappropriate at Constantinople to say of the Holy Spirit that 'he proceeds from the *being* of the Father' which it had not said of the Son. In view of the fact that the Council did not speak of the Holy Spirit as ὁμοούσιος either, it might even be thought that it was 'economising the truth' at this point. However, the confession

---

[153]It is not the terms that matter, as Gregory Nazianzen pointed out at the Council, but the realities they signify – *Or.*, 42.16.

[154]Theodoret, *Hist. eccl.*, 5.11. The fact that in his Latin text Damasus used the word '*usia*' (sic!) instead of *substantia* several times seems to indicate that he had the Greek text of the Tome in front of him. For his Latin text see Denzinger-Schoenmetzer, *Enc. Symb.*, 144f.

of belief in the Holy Spirit as 'Lord and Giver of Life, who proceeds from the Father, who with the Father and the Son together is worshipped and glorified', was meant to rank the Holy Spirit fully with the Father in the lordship and glory of the Godhead. And there can be no denial of the fact that in the statements about the Holy Trinity found in the synodical correspondence of the Council the Holy Spirit is affirmed to be *of the same Godhead, power and being* as the Father and coequal with him and the Son in honour, dignity and sovereignty. Thus the Constantinopolitan Creed must be understood to confess firm belief in the Deity of the Holy Spirit, although it did not speak of him expressly as ὁμοούσιος or Θεός.

It is here that the document of Damasus is very relevant, for in Theodoret's Greek text of it the Holy Spirit is said to be 'μιᾶς καὶ τῆς αὐτῆς οὐσίας (of one and the same being) as the Father and the Son'.[155] On the one hand, Damasus declared 'If anyone denies that the Son is begotten from the Father, that is, from his divine substance (*id est de substantia divina ipsius*), he is a heretic.' And on the other hand, he declared 'If anyone denies that the Holy Spirit is truly and properly from the Father, as the Son is from the divine substance and is true God (*sicut Filium, de divina substantia et Deum verum*), he is a heretic.' Damasus then went on to assert that, far from being a creature, the Spirit is Creator along with the Father and the Son, and so to insist on 'the one and equal Godhead of the Father and of the Son and of the Holy Spirit'.[156] Finally, echoing the Encyclical from Constantinople he wrote: 'This is the salvation of Christians, that believing in the Trinity, that is in the Father and the Son and the Holy Spirit, and being baptised into it, we may indubitably believe the Trinity to have the same one true Godhead and power, majesty and substance.'[157]

The credal pronouncements about the Holy Spirit in the three-fold belief of the Church in the Father, the Son and the Holy Spirit,[158] had the effect of establishing the doctrine of the

[155]Theodoret, *Hist. eccl.*, 5.11. This was one of the regular expressions of Epiphanius, e.g. *Haer*, 74.11–12.
[156]Denz. Schoen., *op. cit.*, 169–177.
[157]*Ibid.*, 178.
[158]See Epiphanius' stress upon the triple πιστεύομεν in the Creed, *Haer.*,

Holy Spirit as perfectly coequal with the Father and the Son in the Holy Trinity but it also had the effect of bringing the doctrine of the Trinity to its full fruition in the mind of the Church. Thus at the Council of Constantinople the doctrine of the *Triunity* of God, 'one Being, three Persons', was totally accepted and became an ecumenical dogma recognised by the Eastern and Western Church alike. In all this the determination of the Constantinopolitan fathers to homologate the Creed of Nicaea, and to make the necessary additions regarding the Holy Spirit in non-technical terms (without any qualification along Cappadocian lines about the Person of the Father as the Source and Cause of the Deity and being of the Son and the Spirit) was very wise. It is worth pointing out again that the redefinition of οὐσία as an abstract generic concept, with the loss of its realistic sense as being considered in its intrinsic relations, made it difficult for people to endorse the Athanasian doctrine of the Holy Trinity: **'as it always was, so it now is; as it now is, so it always was'.**[159] If the Word (Λόγος) and activity (ἐνέργεια) of God manifest in the Gospel are not inherent (ἐνούσιοι) in his eternal being, as Athanasius had insisted, then we cannot relate what God is toward us in his economic self-revelation and self-giving to what he ever is in himself or *vice versa*. That was the danger that lurked in the Basilian distinction between the divine being and the divine energies, which had the effect of restricting knowledge of God to his divine energies, and ruling out any real access to knowledge of God in the intrinsic relations of his eternal triune being.[160]

Through grounding the unity of the Godhead in the Father as the unique and exclusive Principle of Deity and thus as the one Cause of the being and existence of the Son and the Spirit, the Cappadocian way of steering between unipersonalism and tritheism, philosophically effective as it might have been with

---

73.25; 74.13; cf. Basil, *Ep.*, 236.6.

[159]Athanasius, *Ad Ser.*, 3.7; cf. 2.7.

[160]This dangerous trend became very clear in the claim of Pseudo-Dionysius that mystical theology must reach beyond the revealed concept of *Fatherhood* in its thought of God as a superessential undifferentiated οὐσία not nameable or knowable at all in its internal relations – *De div. nom.*, 1.5ff; 2.1ff; *Theol. myst.*, 1f.

Sabellians and Eunomians, led to a serious difference between East and West. In view of the idea that the Spirit proceeds from the *Person* of the Father, i.e., by implication, from the Father *only*, Western theologians found themselves constrained to maintain that the Holy Spirit proceeds 'from the Son also', if they were really to believe in the Holy Spirit as 'true God of true God' like the incarnate Son. Eastern theologians, however, felt themselves constrained in reaction to insist that the Holy Spirit proceeds 'from the Father only' in order to preserve the unity of the divine 'Monarchy' which they considered to be undermined by the doctrine of a 'double procession' of the Spirit. As we look back it is difficult to see how that situation could have arisen if the Nicene and Athanasian understanding of the procession of the Son from the **being of God the Father** had been allowed consistently to govern the doctrine of the procession of the Spirit from the Father through the Son, as in fact it did govern the teaching of Epiphanius of Constantia and Cyril of Alexandria.

The Cappadocian theologians under the leadership of Basil made an immense contribution to the Church in spiritual understanding of the Nicene Faith, and after the death of Athanasius secured its triumph in the Church. The Council of Constantinople could hardly have taken place apart from what they had done. In taking a middle path between Sabellian and Arian deviations they helped to bring about a theological consensus on the doctrine of the Holy Trinity as it arose out of the Dominical institution of baptism and the worship of the Church. In the doctrine of the Trinity, they concentrated thought upon the concept of 'one οὐσία and three ὑποστάσεις' in such a way as to bring out the objective particularities and personal characteristics of the Father, the Son and the Holy Spirit in their dynamic unity and community with one another. Their centralisation of the concept of divine unity in the Person of the Father also had the effect of intensifying the personal relations with God in faith and worship. While that spiritual outlook continued to bear fruit in the life and devotion of the Church, the philosophical notions introduced by the Cappadocians in their arguments for the doctrine of the Trinity tended to fall away after the Council of Constantinople, although some of them were later picked up by Maximus and John of Damascus. The teaching of Gregory Nazianzen in particular, however, about Fatherhood, Sonship and Procession as dynamic and objective relations continuously subsisting in the one being of the Godhead, was taken up and developed along with the Athanasian doctrine of the mutual indwelling of the three divine Persons in a rich doctrine of coinherence which deepened theological understanding of the Triunity of God.[161]

That is very evident in the teaching of Cyril of Alexandria who would have nothing to do with the generic concept of the divine οὐσία,[162] or with the idea of causal relations within the Holy Trinity,[163] even though he could sometimes speak of the Father as 'Source (πηγή)' or 'Root (ῥίζα)' in trinitarian relations.[164] On the other hand, he carried further both Gregory Nazianzen's concept of a Trinity of hypostatic relations continuously subsisting in the Godhead,[165] and Athanasius' doctrine of the reciprocal indwelling or coinherence of the three divine Persons within the one being of the Holy and Consubstantial Trinity.[166] In accordance with the principle, so often adduced by Athanasius, that the Son has by nature all that the Father has, except being called 'Father', Cyril held that the Father is said to be greater than the Son only 'economically (οἰκονομικῶς)', and thus left no room for subordinationism in the Holy Trinity.[167]

It was this doctrine of coinherence in the one identical being of God, according to which the Father, Son and Holy Spirit mutually indwell and contain one another, while remaining what they are, that governed Cyril's understanding of the procession of the Spirit from the Father through the Son. 'The Holy Spirit proceeds from the Father and the Son (ἐκ Πατρὸς

---

[161]See again E. L. Mascall's brilliant analytical argument for the recovery of the concept of 'subsistent relations' and its ecumenical significance for Western and Eastern Churches, *op. cit.*

[162]Cyril, *De Trin. dial.*, MPG, 75.733.

[163]Cyril, *De Trin. dial.*, MPG, 75.721, 744, 769; *Thes.*, MPG, 75.128.

[164]Cyril, *De Trin. dial.*, MPG, 75.721, 769, 872.

[165]Cyril, *Thes.*, MPG, 75.553.

[166]Cyril, *In Jn.*, MPG, 74.28ff, 213ff, 552ff; *Thes.*, MPG, 75.177ff, 528f, 568ff, etc.

[167]Cyril, *Thes.*, MPG, 75.144f, 177f, 380f; *In Jn.*, 10.29f.

καὶ Υἱοῦ) for he belongs to the divine being and inheres in it and issues from it substantially (οὐσιωδῶς).'[168] As Cyril understood it, everything here depends upon the truth that the three divine Persons inhere inseparably in one another and are of one and the same being and nature. Since the Holy Spirit cannot be disjoined from the divine nature and being he proceeds *from the Father* naturally and essentially (φυσικῶς τε καὶ οὐσιωδῶς). In the same way the Holy Spirit proceeds *through his Son* for he is naturally his and is consubstantial with him (δι᾽ αὐτοῦ τοῦ Υἱοῦ, φυσικῶς ὂν αὐτοῦ, καὶ ὁμοούσιον αὐτῷ).[169] 'As the Spirit is of God, of the Father and of the Son, he derives substantially from both, proceeding from the Father through the Son (οὐσιωδῶς ἐξ ἀμφοῖν, ἤγουν ἐκ Πατρὸς δι᾽ Υἱοῦ).'[170] Moreover, Cyril thought of the historical mission of the Spirit from the incarnate Son and the eternal procession of the Spirit from the one being of God as linked essentially together, for in sending the Spirit out of his own fullness (ἐξ ἰδίου πληρώματος) he sent him as he who is eternally his own and is consubstantially and naturally one with him in the Godhead of the Holy Trinity.[171] That is to say, what God is toward us in Christ and in the Spirit he is inherently and eternally in himself in the one being of the consubstantial Trinity, and what he is intrinsically and indivisibly in his eternal Triunity he is toward us in the incarnation of his Son and in the mission of his Spirit.[172]

What was at stake here was undoubtedly the Athanasian and Epiphanian doctrine of the divine Μοναρχία as Unity in Trinity and Trinity in Unity.[173] Cyril of course rejected any notion of a

---

[168]Cyril, *Thes.*, MPG, 75.577, 580f & 585. See the whole discussion of these issues from 575 to 617, and *In Jn.*, MPG 73.209f, 604f; 74.213f, 256f, 333ff, 417, 448f, 710f, etc.

[169]Cyril, *Con. Nest.*, 4.3. Chapters 1–3, MPG, 76.168–189, were largely devoted to this theme.

[170]Cyril, *De ador.*, MPG, 68. 148.

[171]Cyril, *Con. Nest.*, 4.1, MPG, 76.172f.

[172]For the bearing of Cyril's dynamic understanding of the Incarnation upon the development of Christological and Trinitarian theology in Severus of Antioch, see I. R. Torrance, *Christology After Chalcedon*, Canterbury Press 1988.

[173]Consult the remarkable account of this doctrine in the anonymous *De Sacrosancta Trinitate*, once attributed to Cyril, MPG, 77.1120–1272, much of which was incorporated by John of Damascus in *De fide orthodoxa*, 1.8.

plurality of divine Principles or ἀρχαί. He gave no support to the Cappadocian way of resolving the issues of tritheist division or Sabellian confusion between the divine ὑποστάσεις, through the introduction of a unique consecutive causal structure in the order of trinitarian relations in the Godhead. Thus his conception of the procession of the Spirit *from the Father and the Son* cannot be interpreted in terms of the Western concept of the *filioque*, nor can his conception of the procession of the Spirit *from the Father through the Son*, as he regularly expressed it, be interpreted in agreement with the idea of Basil and his brother Gregory that the Spirit derives his being from the being of the Son, and through him from the being of the Father. Cyril's conception of the interrelation of the three perfect, coequal, coeternal, enhypostatic Persons through their wholly reciprocal indwelling and containing of one another, in which they are inconfusedly united and inseparably distinguished, was very different, for it carried within it the combined notion of μία οὐσία and μία ἀρχή. Thus the basic concept governing his understanding of the procession and mission of the Holy Spirit, and of all the distinctive operations of the Father, the Son and the Holy Spirit in creation, revelation and salvation alike, was the oneness and identity in being and nature, will and activity, power and sovereignty, of the Consubstantial Trinity, perfectly expressed in each divine Person. This was the Athanasian, Epiphanian and Constantinopolitan doctrine of the *One Being of Godhead in Trinity and the Consubstantial Trinity in Unity*, brought to succinct theological expression in the identification of the **Monarchia** with the **Triunity** of God.

The Collect for Trinity

Almighty and everlasting God, who hast revealed thyself as Father, Son, and Holy Spirit, and dost ever live and reign in the perfect unity of love: Grant that we may always hold firmly and joyfully to this faith, and, living in the praise of thy divine majesty, may finally be one in thee; who art three Persons in one God, world without end.

Index

341